A Tercentenary Publication

of the

First Church of Christ in New Haven

A. W. Elson & Co., Boston

John Davenporte

Letters of
JOHN DAVENPORT
Puritan Divine

EDITED BY

ISABEL MACBEATH CALDER

Associate Professor of History in Wells College

NEW HAVEN: PUBLISHED FOR THE
FIRST CHURCH OF CHRIST IN NEW HAVEN
BY
YALE UNIVERSITY PRESS
LONDON: HUMPHREY MILFORD · OXFORD UNIVERSITY PRESS
1937

Copyright, 1937, *by* YALE UNIVERSITY PRESS

PRINTED IN THE UNITED STATES OF AMERICA

PREFACE

THE original manuscripts or contemporary copies of more than a hundred of the letters of John Davenport, Puritan divine, have found their way into widely scattered archives and libraries. During the eighteenth, nineteenth, and twentieth centuries many of these letters have been printed in equally diverse publications. A fellowship of the American Council of Learned Societies, granted in the year 1932–1933 to complete a study of *The New Haven Colony* (New Haven, 1934), made possible a synthesis of these letters. Brought together they disclose not only the evolution of the mind of an outstanding seventeenth-century New England Puritan, but the conditions under which life in the smallest of the New England Puritan colonies was lived. For these reasons it is hoped that the publication of the letters will add to the knowledge of New England Puritanism.

Except when the manuscript of a previously printed letter could not be located, the correspondence has been prepared for publication from photostats of the original letters. Contractions and signs have been expanded. Superior letters, denoting the omission of one or more letters of a word, have been lowered, and the omitted letters, supplied in brackets. With these exceptions, the spelling, capitalization, and punctuation of the writer have been retained.

Coöperation and assistance have been rendered by many. The Public Record Office and the British Museum in London, the Massachusetts Historical Society and the Boston Public Library in Boston, Massachusetts, the American Antiquarian Society at Worcester, Massachusetts, the office of the clerk of the town of New Haven, the Hopkins Grammar School, Yale University Library, and the New Haven Colony Historical Society in New Haven, Connecticut, the Connecticut State Library at Hartford, Connecticut, and the New York Public Library have permitted the reproduction of documents in their possession, in a few instances for the first time. Mr. George Tyler of the Department of Classics in Wells College has read all Latin and Greek passages and made helpful suggestions. The Colonial Society of Massachusetts has permitted its engraving of a portrait of John Davenport to be used as a frontispiece. The First Church of Christ in New Haven has made possible the publication of the volume. To all, the editor of the letters wishes to express her gratitude.

I. M. C.

Wells College, October 9, 1937.

Contents

ILLUSTRATION

A BIOGRAPHICAL SKETCH

As the reign of Queen Elizabeth drew toward its close, Winifred (Barneby), the wife of Henry Davenport of Coventry, Warwickshire, England, gave birth to her fifth and youngest son. On Saturday, April 9, 1597, Richard Eaton, vicar of Holy Trinity Church, Coventry, baptized the infant, "John."

Of John Davenport's early life, little is known. By 1619 his mother and a brother Henry were dead and his father had married Elizabeth (Bennett), by whom he had a sixth son, also named Henry. Although the charter granted to Coventry in 1621 named Henry Davenport alderman of Smithford-street Ward for life, he was not a wealthy man, and his sons soon learned to make the most of limited means. After preparation at the Free Grammar School in Coventry, doubtless at the hands of Jeremiah Arnold, appointed master of the school in 1602, James Crauford, who succeeded Arnold in 1611, and Philemon Holland, who served as usher under both Arnold and Crauford, John Davenport journeyed to Oxford, where his brother Edward had preceded him. Although the brothers were sent to the university at great expense to their uncle, Christopher Davenport, John Davenport seems to have enrolled as a batteler at Merton College. He studied under Samuel Lane, fellow of the college, until Sir Henry Savile, warden, dismissed him because he could not afford to become a commoner. After migrating to Magdalen Hall, the young student withdrew from the university entirely because of lack of means.

At the early age of eighteen Davenport began his career as chaplain at Hilton Castle in the parish of Monk Wearmouth, palatinate of Durham. Thither he went, probably at the invitation of Mary, Lady Hilton, wife of the eccentric Henry, Lord Hilton, Baron of Hilton, to preach in the chapel dedicated to St. Katherine attached to the castle. His stay at Hilton Castle was of brief duration, however, and about 1616 he migrated from Monk Wearmouth to London. Sometime before the herald's visitation to Warwickshire in 1619 he married Elizabeth Wooley. His father and infant half-brother, living at the time of the visitation, were dead in 1627.

From the obscurity of the metropolis, Davenport was rescued by his election as lecturer and curate of the church of St. Lawrence, Jewry, June 4, 1619. This church stands close to the entrance of the Guildhall, in the heart of London, and its young curate rose rapidly to prominence. This very prominence threatened his further advancement.

From Queen Elizabeth the parishioners of the neighboring church of St. Stephen, Coleman Street, had received the privilege of electing their vicar. Upon the death of Samuel German or Jermaine in 1624, they considered one Wilson, the protégé of George Abbot, Archbishop of Canterbury, and John Davenport, curate of St. Lawrence's, Jewry. Although Wilson was a university graduate and had the favor of Archbishop Abbot, and Davenport had not yet acquired a university degree, such was the popularity of the latter in the neighborhood that, without effort on his part, he was almost unanimously elected to the vacant office, October 5, 1624, and his name was sent to George Montaigne, Bishop of London, for confirmation. But perhaps because of Davenport's following of "common and mean people" at St. Lawrence's, perhaps because he had aroused the enmity of Edward Sydenham, page of the bedchamber, James I had already instructed Bishop Montaigne to inquire into his preaching. When his name came before Montaigne for confirmation as vicar of St. Stephen's, Coleman Street, the bishop hesitated. At this point Davenport was befriended by Sir Edward Conway, secretary of state, and Mary, Lady Vere, wife of Sir Horace Vere, who represented him to both Bishop Montaigne and Archbishop Abbot as the acme of conformity. So successful were their efforts that on November 3, 1624, Davenport was inducted into the office of vicar of St. Stephen's, Coleman Street, London.

Busy years ensued. In addition to preaching and other parochial duties, Davenport was sometimes called upon to preach beyond the limits of the parish. He supported a movement for church unity, and sponsored a collection for the exiled Protestants of the Palatinate. Most important of all, he served as one of the "feoffees for the purchase of impropriations," thus taking part in a movement which, had it run its course, would have resulted in a purified church of England. In his parochial duties he was assisted by various curates, with not all of whom he remained in full sympathy.

At this time his literary activities began. He wrote an introduction to Henry Scudder's *The Christians Daily Walke in holy Securitie and Peace* in 1627; published *A Royall Edict for Military Exercises*, a sermon which he had preached before the Artillery Company of London, in 1629; and with Richard Sibbes edited the sermons which John Preston had preached at Lincoln's Inn and published them as *The New Covenant, or the Saint's Portion; The Breast-Plate of Faith and Love; The Saints Daily Exercise;* and *The Saints Qualification;* four volumes which passed through many editions.

More his own master than he had ever been before, in the spring of

1625 Davenport returned to Oxford, and, after debating with George Palmer of Lincoln College before John Prideaux, rector of Exeter College, and a great host of juniors and seniors, was awarded the degree of bachelor of divinity.

Residence within a stone's throw of the Guildhall aroused his interest in the great trading companies of the day, and he became a member of both the Virginia Company of London and the Massachusetts Bay Company.

During these years, church and state in England were undergoing a change. William Laud became Bishop of London in 1628 and Archbishop of Canterbury in 1633, and advocated greater emphasis upon the discipline and ceremonies of the Church of England. The dissolution of the parliament of 1628 and 1629 was followed by eleven years of government by king and privy council. In 1624 Davenport had proclaimed himself a supporter of the Church of England and the government of the Stuarts, but as he watched these changes, his opinions gradually altered. His reading, conferences with John Cotton and Thomas Hooker, and Laud's attack upon the "feoffees for the purchase of impropriations" combined to make him a non-conformist. Upon Laud's elevation to the archbishopric of Canterbury in 1633, Davenport withdrew from St. Stephen's, Coleman Street. While living in concealment near London he wrote an "Essay on What the Visible Church is; and The Government of it," disclosing his conversion from Anglicanism to Congregationalism. Sometime before December 3, 1633, he resigned his vicarship.

As a member of the Massachusetts Bay Company, Davenport might have been expected to turn toward New England, but, apparently, in 1633, the wilderness beyond the Atlantic was without allurement for him. The years of comparative peace in London were followed by a brief but stormy interval in the Netherlands.

Since 1607 John Paget had been minister of an English congregation at Amsterdam. An extremely jealous man, during the past twenty years he had prevented the installation of Robert Parker, John Forbes, William Ames, Hugh Peter, and Thomas Hooker, one after another, as co-pastor of the English church at Amsterdam. But at this time Paget was ill and the church was in danger of being closed, and some of the congregation sent to London and invited Davenport to come to them. Of the difficulties between Paget and the numerous candidates for the office of co-pastor, Davenport could not have been completely ignorant, for some of them were his personal friends. Looking upon Amsterdam only as a sanctuary for three or four months, until the enmity which he seemed to have aroused in Archbishop Laud had died, he accepted the invitation, however, and in the fall of 1633 betook himself to the Dutch metropolis.

Throughout the duration of Paget's illness, Davenport preached twice every Sunday to the Amsterdam congregation, and, upon Paget's recovery, continued to assist with one of the Sabbath services. At the end of five months the consistory invited him to settle permanently at Amsterdam and, without other plans, he was inclined to accept the call. Meanwhile, Stephen Goffe, emissary of Archbishop Laud in the Netherlands, had been reporting Davenport's movements to his patron and doing his best to create friction between Davenport and Paget. Egged on by Goffe, Paget soon discovered that he and Davenport differed on the questions of church government and baptism. To Davenport's call to the co-pastorship, Paget was able to have such conditions attached by the Classis at Amsterdam that Davenport could not accept it.

After all connection with the English church at Amsterdam had ceased, Davenport undertook to catechize the family of one Wytacker, with whom he lived, at five o'clock in the evening every Lord's day, after the sermons were ended. In a period of four months, the attendance at these meetings gradually mounted to about eighty, and many received much edification. At this point Davenport rented a house, and apparently planned to settle permanently at Amsterdam. To prevent the rise of a rival congregation, Paget charged Davenport and his adherents with schism, and the Classis at Amsterdam requested Wytacker to bring the meetings to an end. Abandoning the house in which he had not yet lived, Davenport withdrew to The Hague. There John Davenport, Jr., was born and baptized, April 15, 1635, and there Davenport himself lay seriously ill. Later in the same year Hugh Peter, pastor of an English church at Rotterdam, migrated to New England, and Davenport removed to Rotterdam to fill his place.

During his stay in Rotterdam Davenport was dragged into a pamphlet war. Irritated by Davenport's forced withdrawal from Amsterdam, William Best, an elder of the English church at Amsterdam and one of Davenport's adherents, sponsored the publication of five hundred copies of *A Ivst Complaint Against An Vnivst Doer* (Amsterdam, 1634). In an effort to quiet the controversy, Davenport bought up four hundred and fifty copies of this pamphlet, suppressed further publication, and issued *A Protestation made and published upon occasion of a pamphlett intitled A just complaint, etc.* (Rotterdam, 1635). To these publications, Paget replied in *An Answer to the Unjust Com-*

plaints of William Best, . . . Also, An Answer to Mr. John Davenport: touching . . . his Allegations of Scripture against the Baptizing of some kind of Infants; . . . (Amsterdam, 1635). In response to the book by Paget, William Best published *The Chvrches Plea for her Right* (Amsterdam, 1635), and John Davenport, *An Apologeticall Reply To a booke Called An Answer to the unjust complaint of W. B. Also an Answer to Mr. I. D. Touching His report of some passages. His allegation of Scriptures against the baptising of some kind of infants. His protestation about the publishing of his Wrightings* (Rotterdam, 1636). To end this pamphlet warfare, Sir William Boswell, English agent at The Hague, summoned Davenport to appear before him in April, 1636. Instead of complying, Davenport returned to England.

The England of 1636 was dominated by Charles I and William Laud. High-church Anglicanism flourished. Parliament remained uncalled, and taxes were arbitrarily levied and collected. Without hope of change in England, many were turning toward the new world. Although in 1633 Davenport had rejected New England, at this time it seemed a welcome refuge. With Theophilus Eaton, the son of Richard Eaton, who long years before had baptized him at Holy Trinity Church in Coventry, an associate in the Massachusetts Bay Company, and since 1630 a parishioner of St. Stephen's, Coleman Street, London, Davenport gathered a company from the parish of St. Stephen, Coleman Street, and its vicinity, to settle a plantation in New England. Estates were sold. The ship *Hector* of London, an almost new vessel of about two hundred and fifty tons burden, was chartered and provisions for the voyage were laid aboard. At this point the vessel was impressed for the service of Charles I, but after a delay of several months, it was released. Sometime before May 10, 1637, it set sail. On June 26, 1637, John Winthrop recorded the arrival of the group at Boston in Massachusetts Bay. There John Davenport was received into the home of his friend, John Cotton, and other members of the company probably met with similar hospitality.

By 1637 some eighteen plantations had been settled in Massachusetts Bay, and local governments established. Upon the migration of the Massachusetts Bay Company to New England in 1630, the government of John Endecott and his council had given way to the government of the Massachusetts Bay Company, and the charter issued by Charles I to the Governor and Company of the Massachusetts Bay in New England had become the constitution of a colony. Most important of all, Congregationalism had replaced the Anglican hierarchy, and the right to participate in affairs of state, to vote for officers and to hold office, was limited to members of the Congregational churches. Finally, in "Moses his judicials," John Cotton had reduced this scheme of government for church and state to writing.

After observing and studying his new environment, John Davenport found conditions in Massachusetts Bay more to his liking than either conditions in England or the situation in the Netherlands, but not yet perfect. Although the churches of Massachusetts Bay were Congregational in their government, at this moment they were rent by the Antinomian controversy. Since theocracy had been introduced only gradually, the affairs of state were less completely in the hands of the elect than seemed desirable to the new convert to the system. Finally, after the establishment of some eighteen towns around Massachusetts Bay, adequate harbors in this vicinity were no longer available. The millennium still lay beyond the horizon.

At this moment the Pequot War had just made the southern coast of New England known and available for settlement. Soldiers participating in the war had carried back to Massachusetts Bay reports of the good harbors of Long Island Sound and the fertility of the soil of southern New England, and Theophilus Eaton and a small group of companions set out, August 31, 1637, to investigate this promised land. So favorably impressed were the explorers with Quinnipiac, halfway along the coast of southern New England, that, according to tradition, some of the group remained there over the winter, to retain possession of the site, while Eaton returned to Massachusetts, to plan the removal of the Davenport–Eaton company to Long Island Sound in the following spring. While waiting in Massachusetts Bay, Davenport wrote *An Apologie of the Chvrches in New-England for Chvrch-Covenant . . . Sent over in Answer to Master Bernard, in the Yeare 1639*, and *An Answer of the Elders of the Severall Chvrches in New-England unto Nine Positions, Sent over to Them (By divers Reverend and godly Ministers in England) to declare their Judgements therein*, both published in London in 1643.

The group that had migrated from London in 1637 found many who were willing to join them in removal to Long Island Sound, older inhabitants of Massachusetts Bay, disillusioned by the Antinomian controversy, and more-recent arrivals who had not been able to find a satisfactory place of settlement in the Bay colony. With the recruits thus acquired, the Davenport–Eaton company sailed from Boston, March 30, 1638. About the middle of April they arrived at Quinnipiac.

The new arrivals found the territory along Long Island Sound depopulated by the recent Pequot War. Without charter from the

Crown authorizing them to take possession of the soil, they bought from the Indians ample territory for their immediate needs. As new-comers were attracted to Long Island Sound, additional territory was acquired from the natives, until the New Haven Colony took form on the southern coast of New England and on Long Island and even claimed territory as far south as Delaware Bay.

In this environment John Davenport passed the most important thirty years of his life. Of the leaders of the New Haven Colony, he alone resided within the limits of the colony throughout the period of its independence, and he more than any other shaped its ecclesiastical and civil policies.

In virgin territory, freed from all necessity of compromising with an existing order, with Massachusetts Bay as an example and John Cotton's code as a guide, churches and towns and colony gradually took form. At first at Quinnipiac or New Haven, and as the colony grew, at Milford to the west, at Guilford to the east, at Southold on Long Island, at Stamford to the far west, and at Branford between New Haven and Guilford, the elect of each settlement entered into covenant and gathered a church. The members of these churches alone possessed the privileges of partaking of the Lord's Supper and of offering their children for baptism, and the children thus baptized became potential church-members. All others lay beyond the fold, and gained admission only by satisfactory evidence of conversion.

In the early years the government of the plantation of Quinnipiac or New Haven served as a government for both town and colony and was far more important than the governments of the surrounding settlements. As the result of the formation of the New England Con-federation in 1643, however, a colony government was superimposed upon the whole, and the town of New Haven sank to the status of its neighbors. Participation in both town and colony governments, the right to vote and to hold office, was rigidly limited to church-members.

As pastor of the church at New Haven, John Davenport led a busy life. Week in and week out two sermons on the Sabbath and a mid-week lecture were required. On the first Sabbath of the month the sacrament of the Lord's Supper was celebrated at the conclusion of the morning service. As occasion arose baptism of the children of members and of those about to be received into the fellowship of the church was administered at the conclusion of the Sabbath afternoon service. In addition the presence of the pastor was probably expected at the weekly meetings of the members to manage the affairs of the church and at neighborhood meetings for mutual edification. In these labors, Davenport was assisted by William Hooke from 1644 to 1656, Richard Blinman in 1658 and 1659, and Nicholas Street from 1659 until Davenport's departure from New Haven in 1668. In addition the pastor attended general courts for the colony which met from one to six times a year, and town meetings which met even more frequently. Without holding public office, he frequently used his eloquence to sway public opinion at such meetings. Notable instances of this are his pleas with both colony and town for the establishment of a grammar school and college, and his opposition to the union of the New Haven Colony and Connecticut.

As an outstanding New England divine, Davenport was consulted in the ecclesiastical difficulties of his day. In the year of his arrival in New England he tried to convince Anne Hutchinson of her errors. A few years later he was consulted by Charles Chauncy regarding the administration of the sacrament of baptism. He attended a synod which convened at Cambridge, Massachusetts, September 1, 1646, to draft a form of government for the churches of New England. Just as the Church of England had changed under Laud, so New England Congregationalism gradually changed as the second generation in New England, without the convictions and experiences of the founders, grew to maturity. For the duration of his life, however, Davenport held fast to the vision of churches and commonwealth dominated by the elect that had come to him soon after his arrival in New England, and strenuously opposed any modification in the original rules and patterns. In 1646 he "observed with greife that the Tempter was tempting us." Again in 1656 he opposed any widening of the privileges of baptism. When a dispute arose between Samuel Stone, teacher, and William Goodwin, elder, in the church at Hartford, and eventually split both the church at Hartford and the church at Wethersfield and led to the settlement of Hadley in Massachusetts Bay, Davenport was consulted by the more orthodox seceders and sided with them. When a synod of the elders and brethren of Massachusetts met at Boston on the second Tuesday of March, 1662, to consider the questions of baptism and consociation of churches, Davenport prepared an opinion, and, visiting Boston in the summer of 1662, actually sat with the synod on the first afternoon of its third and final session, and, without success, tried to bring a majority of the members to his point of view.

During the years at New Haven Davenport's study was the scene of much writing. *The Profession Of The Faith Of That Reverend and worthy Divine Mr. J. D. sometimes Preacher of Stevens Coleman-street. London. Made publiquely before the Congregation at his Admission into one of the Churches of God in New-England* . . . was published in London in 1642 and included in John Cotton's *The Covenant of Gods free Grace,* . . . *unfolded* . . . *Whereunto is added, A Profession of Faith, made by* . . . *Mr. John Davenport, in New-England, at his admission into one of the Churches there* . . . (London, 1645). A manuscript in reply to John Paget's *A Defence of Chvrch-Government, exercised in Presbyteriall, Classicall, and Synodall Assemblies;* . . . (London, 1641) went to the bottom of the sea with the so-called "phantom ship" in 1646. After a delay of several years Davenport prepared a second reply, which, after its author's death, was given to the world as *The Power of Congregational Churches Asserted and Vindicated, In Answer to a Treatise of Mr. J. Paget, Intituled The Defence of Church-Government exercised in Classes and Synods* (London, 1672). *The Knowledge of Christ Indispensably required of all men that would be saved,* . . . appeared in London in 1653. After the death of John Cotton in 1652, John Davenport wrote a life of his friend. This remained unpublished, but the manuscript was used by John Norton in composing *Abel being Dead yet speaketh; Or, The Life and Death Of that deservedly Famous Man of God, Mr. John Cotton, Late Teacher of the Church of Christ, at Boston in New-England* (London, 1658). With William Hooke, Davenport prepared *A Catechisme Containing The Chief Heads of Christian Religion. Published, at the desire, and for the use of the Church of Christ at New-Haven,* which was published in London in 1659. *The Saints Anchor-Hold, In All Storms and Tempests* appeared in London in 1661. The dispute over baptism resulted in "An Essay for Investigation of the Truth"; an "Answer to the 21 Questions" submitted by Connecticut in 1656; and "A Reply To the 7 Propositions Concluded by the Synod, Sitting at Boston, June 10: 1662 in Answear to the first Question, vizt. Whoe are the Subject[s] of Baptisme"; all of which remained unpublished. *Another Essay For Investigation of the Truth,* . . . was published at Cambridge in 1663. "A Vindication of the Treatise entituled Another Essay for Investigation of the Truth" and "The third Essay containing a Reply to the Answer unto the other Essay" remained unpublished. Finally, a recommendatory epistle to the reader to Increase Mather's *The Mystery of Israel's Salvation* (London, 1669) is dated "From my study in N. Haven in N. E. the 18th. day of Sept. 1667." Publication of a work by Davenport on the Canticles, which probably belonged to his New Haven days, was awaiting subscribers in 1687.

John Davenport opposed and fought the absorption of the New Haven Colony by Connecticut. Although the settlers of the two colonies were neighbors and friends, and both had accepted the Congregational order in their churches, the movement to widen the privileges of baptism was stronger in Connecticut. Furthermore, the river colony did not limit political privileges to the elect. Although officers and freemen of the river colony were probably church-members, all inhabitants of the towns possessed the right to participate in the town government. For twenty-five years Davenport had striven to establish and maintain a little kingdom of God on Long Island Sound, and the letting down of the bars and the reception of the non-elect into full participation in town affairs which union with Connecticut would render inevitable to him seemed anathema. For more than two years he led the opposition of the New Haven Colony to absorption, and only when inclusion in the proprietary province of the Catholic Duke of York seemed the alternative did he finally submit. When friends and neighbors undertook the settlement of a new kingdom of God on the Passaic, beyond the limits of Connecticut, Davenport considered himself too aged to undergo again the hardships of a pioneer community, and relinquished the leadership to Abraham Pierson, but he sent John Cotton's "Discourse about Civil Government in a New Plantation" to the Bay to be published for the guidance of the group. Tarrying at New Haven, he refused to coöperate with the government of Connecticut, and when an invitation came to him to preach before the court of elections at Hartford, May 10, 1666, he declined.

The governments of church and state in Massachusetts had served as patterns for the New Haven Colony and to Davenport seemed far superior to the corresponding governments of Connecticut, where the halfway covenant was finding wide acceptance, and where non-church-members participated in town government. Upon the death of John Wilson, pastor of the First Church, Boston, the First Church of Boston invited him to fill its vacant pulpit. After the dissolution of the New Haven Colony Davenport no longer considered himself bound to the church at New Haven and desired to accept the call. The invitation had not been unanimous, however, for a minority in the church in Boston opposed Davenport because of his age and because of his long-standing opposition to any widening of the privileges of baptism. Probably to spare the tender spirit of the old man, his congregation at New Haven refused to release him, and so informed the church in Boston, October 28, 1667. In the following spring Davenport visited Boston, and the call was renewed. A second refusal of the church at New Haven to release its pastor, August 25, 1668, was concealed from the members of the First Church, Boston, and read to only a small group of adherents. A demand from Davenport to the church at New Haven brought a conditional release, October 12, 1668. If the call to Davenport from the Boston church had been unanimous, this letter of dismissal would probably have been considered sufficient. But the minority in the church at Boston was strenuous in its opposition, and, supported by a council of elders and messengers from the neighboring churches, which had met at Boston, August 6 to 8, 1668, was at this moment clamoring for dismissal from the First Church. Probably for this reason, James Penn, elder of the First Church, Boston, and James Allen, a member and candidate for the office of teacher, abstracted such portions of the unsatisfactory letter of dismissal as would pass for a dismissal. These abstracts were copied in the form of a complete letter and the name of Nicholas Street, teacher of the church at New Haven, appended by John Davenport, Jr. Davenport and his family were propounded for membership in the First Church, Boston, October 25, 1668; the revised letter of dismissal was read to the church, November 1, 1668, and Davenport and his son and their wives were admitted to membership. Davenport was called to the pastorate of the First Church, Boston, November 9, 1668, and ordained at a solemn service, December 9, 1668.

Meanwhile the minority of the First Church, Boston, continued to clamor for dismissal. The situation was not unlike that in the church at Hartford in 1658, and at that time Davenport had supported the right of the minority to secede. At this time, however, he stood with the majority of the church, and refused to permit the minority to separate. When the demand of the dissatisfied brethren for dismissal was ignored, a second council of elders and messengers from the neighboring churches, April 13 to 16, 1669, advised them to secede. With the approval of a majority of the magistrates of Massachusetts, the seceders gathered the Third or Old South Church of Boston at Charlestown, May 12, 1669. In the midst of the hard feeling which ensued, Nicholas Street visited Boston, June 16 to 18, 1669, and it became known that Davenport himself had not had a *bona fide* letter of dismissal from the church at New Haven, that the unsatisfactory letter of dismissal had been concealed from even his supporters in the First Church, Boston, and that an abstract prepared by James Penn and James Allen had been read to the church.

Although the dispute between the First Church, Boston, and the secessionists split both ecclesiastical and civil governments in Massachusetts Bay and occupied much of Davenport's time, he preached to the court of elections at Boston, May 19, 1669, and his efforts were subsequently published as *A Sermon Preach'd at The Election of the Governour, At Boston in New-England, May 19th 1669* (n.p., 1670). *Gods Call To His People To Turn unto Him; Together with His Promise to Turn unto them. Opened and Applied in II. Sermons At two Publick Fasting-dayes appointed by Authority* was published at Cambridge in 1669 and in London in 1670. *A Catechism Printed for the Use of the First Church in Boston* also appeared in Cambridge in 1669.

With charges of deception and forgery flying back and forth, John Davenport was stricken with the dead palsy on Sunday, March 13, 1669/70, and died on March 15, 1669/70. His body was placed in the tomb of his friend, John Cotton, today included in the burial ground attached to King's Chapel in Boston.

For voicing his opposition to Puritanism in 1624 and acknowledging himself to be a non-conformist in 1633, for lying about the presence of the regicides in the town of New Haven in 1661, for conniving at the deception practiced upon the First Church, Boston, in connection with his letter of dismissal from the church at New Haven, and for joining with the First Church, Boston, in its refusal to dismiss its dissatisfied minority, John Davenport has been charged with inconsistency, falsehood, and deception, and severely criticized by contemporaries and posterity. Yet before condemning him, one should remember that a gradual change of opinion over a nine-year interval, especially at a time when the Anglican Church itself was changing, can hardly be called inconsistency. Surrender of Edward Whalley and William Goffe in 1661 would have rendered Davenport suspect of betrayal of the relatives of a friend and former colleague to a government with which he was not in sympathy. Finally, in the period from 1668 until his death, an old man was fighting for a system of government for church and state which was crumbling on all sides. To bolster this system, longer residence at New Haven, already under the jurisdiction of Connecticut, was of no avail. The secession of the minority from the First Church, Boston, and the formation of the Third Church seemed another wedge driven in by those who favored a wider baptism than Davenport believed to be in harmony with the will of God. With baptism went the right to participate in civil affairs, and soon Massachusetts would be no better than Connecticut. However foolish the controversy may seem in the twentieth century, Davenport was fighting to perpetuate a system of government for church and state to further which he had devoted his life. The zeal of an old man for a losing cause led him to connive at deception.

John Davenport *to* Sir Edward Conway[1]

May it please your Honor/

Iᴛ hath bene the will of God (against my naturall desire of priuacy, and retirednes) to make my ministry, for the space of this sixe yeares, in London, publick, and eminent, which hath Caused some to looke vpon me with a squint eye, and hearken to my sermons with the leaft eare, and, by all meanes, to endeauor my discouragment, and disgrace; insomuch that I am traduced (as I heare, and feare) to his Ma[jesty] for a puritan, or one that is puritannically affected.

1. If by a puritan is meant one opposite to the præsent gouernment; I profes (as my subscription also testifyeth) the Contrary. My practise hath bene answerable to that profession. I haue bene a Curat, in St. Laurence parish, in the old Jury,[2] aboue fiue yeares, during which tyme, and in that place (as also the minister[3] doth offer to testifye) I haue baptized many, but never any without the signe of the Cross. I haue monethly administred the Sacrament of the Lords Supper, but at no tyme without the surplice, nor to any but those that kneeled, at which tymes, also, I read the booke of common prayers, in forme, and manner as is appointed by the church. Besides; I haue perswaded many to Conformity, yea myne owne Father,[4] and Vncle,[5] who are

1. Public Record Office, State Papers, Domestic, James I, CLXXIII, no. 42; printed in A. B. Davenport, *A Supplement to the History and Genealogy of the Davenport Family, in England and America, from A.D. 1086 to 1850* (Stamford, 1876), pp. 56–58. At this time Sir Edward Conway was a member of the Privy Council and one of the principal secretaries of state. Although the letter is undated, it was written on or before October 11, 1624, for on that day Conway wrote to George Montaigne, Bishop of London, in Davenport's behalf. See George Montaigne, Bishop of London, to Sir Edward Conway, October 14, 1624. State Papers, Domestic, James I, CLXXIII, no. 43. All Public Record Office documents have been reproduced with the permission of the Controller of His Britannic Majesty's Stationery Office.

2. John Davenport had been elected lecturer and curate of the church near the entrance to the Guildhall, London, June 4, 1619. Guildhall Library, St. Laurence Iewry London Vestry Book 1556 to 1669, p. 234.

3. Francis Boswell, a fellow of Balliol College, Oxford, served as vicar of St. Lawrence, Jewry, from January 24, 1616/7, until his death in 1631/2. He was also rector of Horton, Colebrook, Buckinghamshire. G. Hennessy, *Novum Repertorium Ecclesiasticum Parochiale Londinense* (London, 1898), pp. cxix, 267.

4. Henry Davenport. In 1621 James I appointed him alderman of Smithford-street Ward, Coventry, for life. "The Visitation of the County of Warwick in the Year 1619," Harleian Society *Publications*, XII (London, 1877), 373; *The Charter Granted by King James I. to the Mayor, Bailiffs, and Commonalty of the City of Coventry, in 1621* (Coventry, 1816).

5. Christopher Davenport. In 1621 James I appointed him alderman of Bishop-street Ward, Coventry, for life. In 1622 he was maintaining a schoolmaster for the education

Aldermen of the Citty of Couentry, and were otherwise inclined. Yea; my desire of this pastorall chardge sheweth my resolucion for con- formity.

2. If by puritannically affected, be meant one, that secretly en- courageth men in opposition to the præsent Gouernment, I profes an hearty detestacion of such hypocrisy. My publick sermons, and priuate discourses haue ever aimed at this, to perswade men to giue vnto Cæsar the things that are Cæsars, and vnto God the things that are Gods,[6] that euery soul should submitt it selfe to the higher powers, and to all manner of ordinances of man, for the Lords sake, whether it be vnto the King as vnto the cheife, or vnto gouernors (ecclesiasticall, and Ciuill) as vnto them that are sent of him.

As for other matters; my playne and open appearing in defence of the Ceremonyes hath caused vnto me some opposition from such as dissaffect them.

My Humble request, therefore, to your Hon[or] is, that it may please you to mediate with his Ma[jes]tie, on my behalfe, that such vniust imputacions may not take any impression in his Royall breast, to the iniurijng of the innocent: and to perswade with the Bishop of London[7] that nothing may Cause him to discountenance my person, or proceedings, but that I may stand vpright in his fauorable and good opinion, which his lordsh[ip] may please to testifye by admitting me into the place wherevnto I am lawfully, and freely chosen,[8] or (in

of poor children of the city, and by a will dated June 4, 1627, and proved August 5, 1629, he asked that the work be continued. By his will he left £100 to be loaned to ten young men of the Company of Weavers and Clothiers; £6 to be loaned in 40 s. amounts for a period of one year to the master and wardens of the Company of Smiths; and the rents of two tenements and two gardens, situated without Grey Friars Gate, to be used for the maintenance of annual sermons at Holy Trinity Church, Coventry, on St. Luke's Day, St. Simon's and St. Jude's Day, and St. Andrew's Day, and for the poor of Grey Friars Hospital, or, if there should be any alteration in religion, the money left for sermons was to be distributed among the poor of Bishop-street Ward. Without children of his own, Christopher Davenport was the benefactor of his brother Henry's children, sending his nephews Edward and John to the University, and in his will making pro- vision for his nephews Barneby and Christopher. "The Visitation of the County of War- wick in the Year 1619," Harleian Society *Publications*, XII (London, 1877), 373; *The Charter Granted by King James I. to the Mayor, Bailiffs, and Commonalty of the City of Coventry, in 1621* (Coventry, 1816); *An Account of the Many and Great Loans, Benefac- tions and Charities, belonging to the City of Coventry* (Coventry, 1802), pp. 15–16, 58–59; Somerset House, P. C. C., Ridley, 77.

6. S. Matthew 22. 21; S. Mark 12. 17; S. Luke 20. 25.

7. At this time George Montaigne was Bishop of London.

8. Davenport had been elected vicar of St. Stephen's, Coleman Street, London, October 5, 1624. See below, p. 21.

Case that Cannot be granted) by assuring my Continuance in the places where I am with his fauor, and loue, till it shall please God to remoue me elsewhither.

For which Noble fauor (if my præsumption be pardoned) I shall acknowledge my selfe euer bound to be

Your Hon[o]rs poore remembrancer at the Throne of Grace

JOHN DAUENPORTE

[Endorsed] October 1624. Mr. Dauenport his Lettre ffor admittance to a Benefice in London wherevnto hee is chosen.

JOHN DAVENPORT *to* Sir EDWARD CONWAY[1]

To the Right Honorable Knight, Sir Edward Conoway, Secretary to his Mai[es]ty at Royston[2] these be d[elivere]d with speed.

May it please your Honor;

M Y Lord of London is returned to London, and, wherein I thinck my selfe very vnhappy, I feare your Hono[u]r hath missed of him. I am Confident, that two words, vnder your Noble hand, of assurance, that, by your effectuall mediacion, his Ma[jes]tie is, or shall be satisfyed together with an intimacion of your Noble fauour, and wellwishing towards me, will prevayle with his lordsh[i]pp for my speedy settling, both in his good opinion, and in the place, wherevnto I am chosen. My humble peticion, therefore, to your Hon[o]r is that you would seriously, (as your manner is) take into your consideracion that the success of this buisenes is of the greatest consequence to me, (which together with the great haste it requireth maketh me thus importunate) and that, accordingly it might please your Hon[o]r to wright effectually, and speedily to the Bishop, that it may come to his hands as soone as is possible, (oh that it might be with the Bish[o]p by to morrow, at Dinner!) but I may not præscribe tymes to so free an Agent. My desire is, that your life, happines, and Honor, may be prolonged continued, and increased, whilest I remayne

Lond[on]   Your Hon[o]rs faithfull, and much obliged servant

From my house in milk street   JOHN DAUENPORTE.

neare cheapside.

october. 14th. 1624.

1. Public Record Office, State Papers, Domestic, James I, CLXXIII, no. 44; printed in part in A. B. Davenport, *Supplement* (Stamford, 1876), pp. 59–60.

2. Both James I and Charles I maintained a residence at Royston, Hertfordshire.

postscript.

The things I presume to begg, as principall fauours, at your Honors hands are these.

1. that the King (by your effectuall mediacion) be satisfyed concerning me, and that his Ma[jes]ty Would be pleased to cause so much to be signifyed to the Bishop.

2. that if the Bishop be pleased to conferr this place vpon the other,[3] that I may not suffer any disparadgment, thereby, in my reputacion, or any dammage in the places which I hold.

3. In this request I beseech your Honor to take no denyall, that howeuer this place succeed, his lordsh[i]p would intertayne a good Conceit of me, and whereas my Aduersary obiecteth that the man, whom he doeth, iniuriously, present to the place is more worthy then my selfe, because he hath taken more degrees in the Vniuersity then I haue That this may not lessen the Bishops esteeme of me, nor be divulged to my disgrace, since, I am a licensed, and Conformable minister, and that my want of degrees, proceeded not from any want of tyme, or of willingnes, or of sufficiency (as was well knowne in Oxford), but from want of meanes (my freinds being vnwilling) to keepe me longer at the Vniuersity; my hope is, after I am settled in a certayne competencye of meanes, to recouer the degrees, which some thinck I haue lost, for want of taking the first opportunity.[4] I beseech your Honor, to be earnest, and effectuall with the Bishop, that, for your sake, and at your earnest intreaty, he would spare me, in this, and so farr tender my reputacion, as that, in the close of this buisenes, those that wish me hurte may not insult; and that, for hereafter he would giue audience to none that shall traduce me to his lordsh[i]p.

Noble Sir) The ssatisfying of my humble request, in these particulars, though it be somewhat too troublesom to your Honor, yet is of the greatest consequence that can befall me, and will æternally oblige me to pray, and giue thancks to God for your prosperity.

[Endorsed] Mr. Damports Lettre. 1624

---

3. One Wilson, see below, p. 21.

4. In quest of a degree, Davenport returned to Oxford in the following spring. There he took part in disputations in the Divinity School, May 18, 1625, and received the degree of Bachelor of Divinity, June 28, 1625. Yale University Library, John Davenport, Note-Book; State Papers, Domestic, Charles I, XXVII, no. 46; Anthony à Wood, *The History and Antiquities of the University of Oxford* (2 vols., Oxford, 1792–96), II, Part I, 354; Joseph Foster, *Alumni Oxonienses, 1600–1714*, I (Oxford, 1891), 376.

JOHN DAVENPORT *to* SIR EDWARD CONWAY[1]

To the Right Honor[a]ble Knight Sir Edward Conway Secretary to his Ma[jes]tie at Royston these be d[elivere]d with speed.

May it please your Honor)

To accept the best tender of that most vnfeigned thanckfulnes, which my vnworthines Can expres for that high fauor you were so graciously pleased to vouchsafe me, in vndertaking the satisfaction of his Ma[jes]tie on my behalfe, and in mediating with the Bish[o]p so fully, and effectually, that faithfulnes, and eloquence (the one implyed in the matter, the other expressed in the manner, and phraze) seemed to contest, which should best disclose your worth in every passage. I will not descant which had the preheminence, but that, which I most admired, and accounted as the Altar that sanctifyed the gift, was the Noblenes of your spiritt manifested by being pleased, first, to cast an eye of fauor vpon one so vnworthy (as the sun casts its beames vpon the lowest shrubbs) next, to take my Case into your Noble thaughts, with such a sympathy; afterwards to wright so largly and effectually, with such Copye of words, pr[eci]ss[e]nes[s] of stile, and variety of præoccupacions, and insinuacions (able to overcom the strongest resolucion) that more could not haue bene added, or desired had the Case bene your owne; this shall oblige me in all places to acknowledge and divulge your meritts, and to bless the fountayne of all good for ioyning such an head with such an heart, and honouring such a person with such a place, and blessing his Ma[jes]tie with such a Secretary the state with such a Counsailor, and both Church and Commonwealth with such a freind so furnished with sufficiency and trueheartednes. My continuall prayers shall be for the continuance of your prosperity, and that you may be succesfull, and prosperous in all things you vndertake, as I hope you haue bene, in this. For, since the receite of your letter, the Bishop hath giuen good words to the parish, of me, they find him inclinable, but the finishing of the buisenes is respited for fourteene days, in the compas of which tyme his lordship expecteth to vnderstand the p[e]rformance of your Noble resolucion for the satisfaction of his Ma[jes]tie till which thing be assured him, he professeth that vpon perill of loss of what he inioyeth he dare not accept me. I heare that Mr. Sidnam,[2] the Kings page, hath in-

---

1. Public Record Office, State Papers, Domestic, James I, CLXXIII, no. 51; printed in part in A. B. Davenport, *Supplement* (Stamford, 1876), pp. 62–64.
2. Edward Sydenham, page of the bedchamber.

censed his Ma[jes]tie against me, because aboue a yeare since, I reproued him for swearing, at my Lady Veres,[3] which I marvayle at, since, at that tyme he pretended not onely a fauorable acceptance, but also thanckfulnes, with a free promise of future reformacion; what other particulars may be obiected I know not. My humble suite to your Honor is, that you would be pleased to deale so effectually for discouery of any præiudice wherewith his Ma[jes]tie, by misinformacion, may be possessed against mee, that I may, at the least, make advantage of this opportunity to be sett right in the good opinion of my Soueraign. And, when you shall haue satisfyed his Ma[jes]tie an easy way will be mayd for the pursuite of your Noble intendm[en]ts for my good, with the Bishop, especially, if, at your Honor[a]ble request, his Ma[jes]tie will Command two lines to be written to the Bishop, to assure him of his satisfaction, and royall pleasure that this place, (which to another will be but small)[4] should be conferred vpon me. In all which your Honor shall receiue no præiudice, but much renoune from all that shall heare of it, and, which is worth all, much peace in conscience vpon the remembrance of such an acte of mercy, with the supply of a strong Argument, whereby to expect a gracious answer from God in the tyme of need, when you shall be able to say, as Nehemiah did, Remember mee o my God Concerning this![5] My selfe shall ever be bound and found to be

Your Honors Humble, and thanckfull servant

Dat. 17. of october. 1624   JOHN DAUENPORTE

[Endorsed] Mr. Dauemport 1624

3. Mary, Lady Vere, was the youngest child of Sir John Tracy of Toddington, Gloucestershire; the widow of William Hoby of Hale, Gloucestershire; the wife of Sir Horace Vere, subsequently created Baron Vere of Tilbury; and the sister-in-law of Sir Edward Conway. Widowed for the second time in 1635, she spent the last thirty years of her life chiefly at Kirby Hall, near Castle Hedingham, Essex, where she died, December 25, 1671, in the ninetieth year of her age. "The Visitation of the County of Gloucester Taken in the Year 1623," Harleian Society *Publications*, XXI (London, 1885), 167; C. R. Markham, *A Life of the Great Lord Fairfax* (London, 1870); *The Fighting Veres* (Boston, 1888), pp. 454–455, where an erroneous date for her death is given; William Gurnall, *The Christians Labour and Reward; Or, A Sermon, Part of which was Preached at the Funeral of the Right Honourable the Lady Mary Vere,* . . . (London, 1672), p. 155.

4. The salary of the vicar of St. Stephen's, Coleman Street, was only £11 *per annum*. This was supplemented by a gratuity of £39 *per annum* to a satisfactory incumbent.

5. Nehemiah 13. 14.

JOHN DAVENPORT *to* MARY, LADY VERE[1]

My La[d]y

THE Countess of Bedford[2] wrote me word this day that my Lord of Canterbury doeth interpose for a chaplayne of his owne one Wilson, and pr[e]tendeth that the sayd Willson hath many freinds in the parish as well as I, and that those who stood for me are but a puritanicall faction.

but the Trueth is thus.

That Mr. Wilson was nominated by the Vestry to be chosen with me, but when it came to voyces, all the vestry spake for me, and onely two for Mr. Wilson.

Nor was this generallity a puritannicall faction, but 2. of the Feoffees, (there being but 3 in all) and all the cheife of the parish yea, the Arch B[isho]ps owne Brother,[3] being a Feoffee, stood for me, and so many as disliked the ceremonyes (which are but few about 5. or 6) stood for another.

I purpose to giue the Arch Bishop notice hereof but, because I am a meane man and vnknowne to him: if it will please my Lady Vere to acquaint Secretary Conoway with these occurrences which happned since my last speach with his Hon[or] God may incline his heart to vndertake the satisfying of the Arch Bishop, which he may the more easily doe, if the Arch Bishop doe vnderstand that the parish will maintayne there right, and that the meanes will be but £11 *per annum* to any other besids my selfe.

[Endorsed] Mr. Dauenport

1. Public Record Office, State Papers, Domestic, Charles I, XIII, no. 15. Although undated, this letter was probably written on or before October 18, 1624, for on that date Sir Edward Conway wrote to George Abbot, Archbishop of Canterbury, in Davenport's behalf. State Papers, Domestic, James I, CLXXIII, no. 58.

2. Lucy, the daughter of John Harington, first Lord Harington of Exton, Rutland, and wife of Edward Russell, third Earl of Bedford.

3. Maurice Abbot, a brother of George Abbot, Archbishop of Canterbury, and an inhabitant of the parish of St. Stephen, Coleman Street, London.

JOHN DAVENPORT *to* SIR EDWARD CONWAY[1]

To the Right Hon[o]r[a]ble Knight Sir Edward Conwey Secretary to his Ma[jes]tie at Royston.

May it please your Hono[u]r/

To pardon my frequency, and importunity in wrighting to your Honor, who are daily Conversant in higher employments, but such boldnes I haue conceiued, from the full vew of your Noble humillity, and fidellity, that I still presume to become sollicitour in my former suit; and now the rather, because, by a message from the Bishop, I perceiue, that his Lordship hath so well digested your last golden lines, that any assurance of the Kings satisfaction, by your happy, and succesfull mediacion will bring my troublesom buisenes to a comfortable period; wherevnto, (though it will produce much renoune to your Hono[u]r, and be a great lustre to your worth, in the eyes, hearts, and tongues of all good men, yet) I assure my selfe that your owne Noblenes, and goodnes of disposition to improue your respect with his Ma[jes]tie in doing good, by clearing, and helping those that suffer wrongfully will most forcibly perswade you. My humble and earnest peticion therefore to your Honor is, that you will be pleased to perfect the worke so happily begun, and (at the last) to draw him to the hauen, whom you haue so mercifully supported in the waues, which will easily be effected, if his Ma[jes]tie, at your intreaty will be graciously pleased to rest satisfyed with that informacion, which your Honor Can truely giue him, and, beleiue, that particular suggestions are rather fumes of spleene, then effects of Zeale to his Ma[jes]ties service, and vouchsafe to lett his loyall subiect, whose whole care shall be to doe his Ma[jes]tie faythfull service in my station, stand vpright in his good opinion, and to signifye by word or letter, that his royall pleasure is, that, if the place wherevnto I am chosen be myne by right, no præiudice at any time suggested to him or vttered by himselfe shall be any obstacle in my way; All which my humble request is that your Honor would effect with all Convenient expedicion. For your more cleare proceeding wherein I am bold to trouble your Honor with the names of those that were in the vestry whereby it may appeare, that by an vnanimous consent, not of some factious people as some haue suggested, but by the cheifest, and most,

---

1. Public Record Office, State Papers, Domestic, James I, CLXXIII, no. 64; printed in part in A. B. Davenport, *Supplement* (Stamford, 1876), pp. 64–65.

I was freely chosen.[2] The other named is my competitor. Your iudi-

2. Davenport enclosed the record of a general vestry at St. Stephen's, Coleman Street, London, October 5, 1624. Public Record Office, State Papers, Domestic, James I, CLXXIII, no. 64, i.

At a generall vestrey houlden in the Parish of St. Steeuen Colman streete ffor the election of our viccar the 5th of October 1624.

Sir Richard Smith
Morrice Abbotte
Christopher Ayer
Mr. Briggmdme
Mr. Garland
Mr. Aldersey
Mr. Lawrance
Mr. Jonson
Mr. Spurstowe
10 Mr. Keies
Mr. Jno. Hill
Mr. Simson
Mr. Barley
Mr. Throughgoode
Mr. Woln[er]ston
Mr. Smith
Mr. Evans
Mr. Tildesley
Mr. Witte
20 Mr. Watson
Mr. Hildesley
Mr. Warner
Mr. Dawkes
Mr. Barnes
Mr. Atkins
Mr. Cotton
Mr. Blackeby
Mr. ffarrowe
Mr. Gurney
30 Mr. Perkins
Mr. Taylor
Mr. Eldred
William Hill
Mr. Wells
Mr. Gwilliams
Mr. Cadwallader
Mr. Lucus
Mr. Williams
Mr. Eastwood
40 Mr. Plumner
Mr. Daniell
Mr. Graves
Mr. Sutherne
Mr. Battersby
[Endorsed] 1624

Mr. Clarke
Mr. Davis
Mr. Venge
Mr. Woodruf
Mr. Richbell
Mr. Newton
50 Mr. Starkey
Mr. Wright
Mr. Barrowe
Michaell Smith
Mr. Thackery
Mr. Chamberlin
Mr. Janson
Mr. Ellis
Mr. Lether
Mr. Shackle
60 Mr. Clarke
Mr. Grover
Mr. Wilson
Mr. Jackson
Mr. Tomson
Mr. Pewes
Mr. More
Mr. Wyer
Mr. Jones
Mr. Kisse
70 Mr. Tillet
Mr. ffox
Mr. Holmes ⎫
Mr. Whittrance ⎬ Churchwardens

Put in Election ffor the sayd viccaridge at this vestrey
Mr. Damperd
Mr. Wilson

We the Churchwardens of the Parish aforesayd doe affirme That of all the Parishioners aforesaid Ther was not aboue three or ffoure hande at the most ffor Mr. Wilson and all the rest hould ffor Mr. Damperd

Robert Holmes
Edward Whitterance

cious eye will soone decerne the difference. I desire nothing but right, else I were vnworthy to vse and enioy, the countenance of so Noble a freind. I beseech your Honor that your last motion towards the Center may be most violent and effectuall. Now lett your Humble servant feele the fruit of your interest in the Court, and the effect of your Gracious aspect for dispersing these mystes. So shall I with a free heart pray for your happines, and prayse your Noblenes, and ever rest

Your Honors faythfull and thanckfull servant

19th d. of October. 1624.   JOHN DAUENPORTE

I shall haue no good success in this suite, nor safety in the things I hold but shall lye obvious to euery mans mallice (being now suspected) vnles his Ma[jes]tie be satisfyed, and be pleased to signifye so much. Your Honor hath so good interest in the King vpon his observacion of your fidellity, and so great power with the D. of Buckingam,[3] that I doubt not the success, if you please to vndertake the buisenes, which your free promise emboldneth me to expect. Lett it be pardoned, that I press for a speedy dispatch, because delay breeds danger.

[Endorsed] 1624

JOHN DAVENPORT *to* Sir EDWARD CONWAY[1]

To the Right Honor[a]ble Knight Sir Edward Conwey, Secretary to his Ma[jes]tie at Royston.

May it please your Honor)

To pervse and accepte in few lines, and a rude draught the repræsentacion of your owne goodnes, and my thanckfulnes. And first of all I doe humbly, and heartily acknowledge, to the prayse of his Grace, Gods infinite goodnes in blessing your Hon[o]r with the Kings fauor, and me with yours whereby the malicious purposes of ill affected men haue bene, at once, both detected, and dissappointed. I dare not acknowledge my selfe guilty of that imputacion, in your last, of excess in attributs, and interpretacions, being (as I am) conscious of too much defect in eyther. My desire is to find out that *viam regiam*, betweene flattery, and ingratitude, and to walke in it, as the best and safest way. By your happy mediacion the King was satisfyed, by your

---

3. George Villiers, first Duke of Buckingham.
1. Public Record Office, State Papers, Domestic, James I, CLXXIV, no. 14.

effectuall letters the Bishop was pacifyed, and by your Hon[ora]ble fauor my selfe am, this day, to be inducted into St. Steuens in Coleman street,[2] where, whatsoeuer encouragm[en]ts I receiue, I shall acknowledge them to be the fruits of your fauor, next vnder God. My humble suite, at this tyme is that you will vouchsafe to take notice of the Bishops courteous vsage, and speedy dispatch of me, in this buisenes, for your sake, and of this bearer (the Bisho[p]s chaplayne) Dr. Worralls[3] diligence in solliciting his lord, on my behalfe, and to rest assured of the vntrueth of all those reports whereby the King was incensed against mee. The Bishop hath examined, approued, and doth purpose to certify his Ma[jes]tie of my Conformity. I hope you shall never haue Cause to repent of your goodnes formerly shewed to me, nor to be discouraged in any your intendments of future good. My continuall prayers shall be for your prosperity, and my vtmost indeauour to express my selfe, in all faithfulnes, and chearfulnes

3d of November 1624   Your Honors humble and thanckfull servant

JOHN DAUENPORTE

[Endorsed] 3. Novemb. 1624 Mr. Davemport Giues notice of his admittance into the Benefice His thanks.

JOHN DAVENPORT *to* ALEXANDER LEIGHTON[1]

Sir,

WHEN we duely Consider the distresses of the Reformed Churches in these days, we shall soone conclude with him that sayd, *Non sunt litigandi ista sed orandi tempora:*[2] neyther was it in my purpose to enter into the lists of dispute at any tyme, much less now, about such quæstions as these. For is it not worke enough to preach vnles we dispute also? or, if we must dispute, were it not better to vnite our forces against those who oppose vs in Fundam[en]talls then to be

2. Davenport's induction is recorded under date of November 4, 1624. Prob. and Admon. Act Book, Archdeac. of London, 1611–1626, fol. 190; H. F. Waters, *Genealogical Gleanings in England* (2 vols., Boston, 1901), I, 205.

3. Thomas Worrall, at this time rector of St. Botolph's, Bishopsgate.

1. Yale University Library, John Davenport, Note-Book; printed in A. B. Davenport, *Supplement* (Stamford, 1876), pp. 74–78. Alexander Leighton was a Scotch physician and divine, sometimes a resident of London. Although the copy of this letter is undated, it was probably written soon after Davenport became vicar of St. Stephen's, Coleman Street, London.

2. These are not times for disputing but for praying.

diuided amongst our selves about Ceremonialls? Who can, without sorrowe, and feare observe how Atheisme, Libertinisme, papisme, and Arminianisme, both at home, and abroad haue stolne in, and taken possession of the house, whilest we are at strife about the hangings and paintings of it? and the enimye strikes at the hearte whilest we buisy our selves in washing the face of this body. How much better would it beseeme vs to combine together in an holy league against the common Adversary, according to Joabs agreem[en]t with Abishai, if the Aramits be stronger then I thou shalt helpe me, and if the children of Ammon be too strong for thee Ile come and succor thee,[3] then thus to resemble those serv[an]ts of Saul and David, vnder the command of Abner and Joab, each of which caught his fellowe by the head, and thrust his sword into his fellowes side, so they fell downe together? For Mr. Smiths[4] private satisfaction (whose scruples about this, and some other particulars hindred his publick ministrye) I offred to com-municate with him, in a freindly Conference those grounds which moved mee to conformity herein, being perswaded that the same would also pr[e]vayle with him. He, beyond my thaught, at that tyme, acquainted you with the motion; you have broughte the matter to this issue, that I must answer, or else my ministry will suffer by my silence, whilest it is vndoubtedly received by some, that eyther out of igno-rance in these particulars, we take things as they are imposed without examining them, or, out of a corrupt mind, we dispense with our selves in these things against our knowledge, for worldly expectacions. Make good eyther of these, and then, who will beleive our reporte? who will regard our ministry? Wherefore that I may, in tyme, quench this sparke, and so pr[e]vente a greater fire, being thus Called, I accept your chalendge, and proceed to answer your quæstions.

1. Qu. Whether Kn[eeling] at Sacr[amen]t be the ordinance of God or man, or whether it had not its first institucion from Antichrist?

Ans. This quæstion seemeth to be somewhat confusedly propounded, which, that I may answer to it distinctly, must be divided into 2. quæres.

1. quæ. Whether Kn[eeling] at Sacr[amen]t be of God, or man?

Ans. 1. If it were an ordinance of man, yet it must be obeyed. 1. pet. 2. 13. so long as, neyther expr[es]sly, nor by necessary consequence, it crosseth any commandm[en]t of God. But

2. Sam. 10. 11.

2. Sam. 2. 16.

3. The seventeenth-century Puritans used both the Genevan and the authorized ver-sions of the Bible. Although he often quotes the authorized version, at this point Daven-port follows the Genevan Bible.

4. Unidentified.

2dly. I take Kn[eeling] in the generall to be an ordinance of God, a gesture appoynted of God, and sanctifyed by his word for externall Adoracion, to testifye the inward Adoracion of the minde, which a Christian may vse in any lawfull worsh[i]p of God, as in prayer, Thanksg[iving], hearing of the word, receiving of Bapt[ism] and the Lords Supper, etc. for I take it, that what the Ho[ly] Gh[ost] sayth by David. psal. 95. 6. doth sanctifye this gesture to mee to be vsed in any lawfull worsh[i]p of God; and so, by Consequence, in receiving the L[ord's] supper.

Lett vs Worsh[i]p and fall downe, and kneele, before the L[or]d.

2. quæ. Whether Kn[eeling] at Sacr[amen]t had not his first institucion from Antichrist?

Ans. 1. If it had it matters not so long as it is agreable to the rule, but 2dly. I denye it. For all the hand that the popes had in the first institucion hereof, for aughte I can finde, was for worsh[i]p of the elevated hoaste. *Honorius decrevit vt cum elevatur hostia salutaris quisque se reverenter inclinet.*[5] This Invention is ascribed by some to *Innocentius*,[6] by others to *Honorius*.[7] Whosoever invented it we disclayme it, in respect to the vse whereunto they intended it.

Zepper. polit. l. 1. c. 12. p. 137.

2. Qu. Whether Kn[eeling] at the Sacr[amen]t be a thing indifferent or no?

Ans. In it[s] owne nature it is, but being Commanded by Authoritye, and allowed by the word, I thinck it is better done then omitted.

3. Qu. Whether Kn[eeling]—be religious Worsh[i]p or no?

Ans. To speake properly, Kn[eeling] is not *ipse Cultus* but *quiddam annexum Cultui.* it is but an adiunct, and appurtenance of Worsh[i]p, not the Worsh[i]p of God nor any essentiall part of Worsh[i]p, but an accessory Complem[en]t ordained for the more Convenient dischardge of the necessary worsh[i]p of God.

4. Qu. Whether the Elem[en]ts in the Sacram[en]t be not obiectiue *a quo*, the motiue of this worsh[i]p?

Ans. The elem[en]ts are *obiectum a quo scil.* significatiue the signes

---

5. Honorius decreed that when the host was raised, everyone should bow reverently. Davenport is quoting, not very exactly, Wilhelm Zepper, *Politia, Ecclesiastica;* . . . (Herborn, 1607), pp. 136–137. *Quod postea Honorius III, qui circa annum 1226 excessit, repetivit, hoc addito, ut sacerdos frequenter doceat plebem suam, ut, cùm in celebratione Missarum elevatur hostia salutaris, se reverenter inclinet, quemadmodum lib. 3 decretal. de celebratione Missarum videre est.* Which later Honorius III, who died about the year 1226, repeated, with this addition, that the priest frequently should teach his people that, when the host was raised in celebration of the Mass, they should reverently bow, as may be seen in Book 3 of the decretals concerning the celebration of Mass.

6. Innocent III, pope from 1198 to 1216.

7. Honorius III, pope from 1216 to 1227.

moving vs to lifte vp our minds from the earthly obiect of sense bread and wine to the spirituall obiect of fayth the body and blood of Christ, which is farr from Idolatry, as shall appeare if you obiect.

5. Qu. Whether God or Christ be not the obiect of that worsh[i]p?

Ans. These 2 quæstions seeme coincident, and for that cause the answer to the former shall serve for this also till you demand another.

6. Qu. Whether Christ and his Ap[ost]les after him did not sitt at the Sacr[amen]t as they did at theyre ordinary meales?

Ans. 1. We find what gesture they vsed at Supper, but what gesture they vsed at the sacr[amen]t doth not appeare, for aught I know, in any of the 4 Evangelists, which, it may be, was concealed to pr[e]vent this obiection.

2. if the gesture did appeare, yet, I thinck, Christs example doth not binde vs without an express rule, especially, in Ceremonialls.

Thus you haue my opinion, which, I pray, Consider in loue, and accepte as the ingenuous expression of a plaine hearte desirous to be rectifyed, in case of error, or to benifitt others, if the trueth guide mee. Now, if you please, lett vs proceed to Argum[en]ts, wherein I expect, as I found in this, that you giue the first Onsett. When we haue compared *rem cum re* and *racionem cum racione*, I hope, the Trueth will breake foorth as the lighte, which, in humility, and simplicity I wish, beseeching you that nothing be done thorough Contention or vain glory: but lett vs receive the Trueth in the loue of It. Thus, expecting your answer, I cease

JOHN DAVENPORTE

A Circular Letter of THOMAS TAYLOR, RICHARD SIBBES, JOHN DAVENPORT, and WILLIAM GOUGE[1]

WHEREAS a late informacion is given to his Ma[jes]tie of the Lamentable distresse of two hundred and forty godly preachers with their wifes and families of aboute foure score desolate widdowes and sundrie thousands of godly private persons with them cast out of their houses and home out of their callings and Countryes by the furie

---

1. Public Record Office, State Papers, Domestic, Charles I, LVI, nos. 15, 16; printed in Richard Sibbes, *Complete Works*, A. B. Grosart, ed. (7 vols., Edinburgh, 1862–64), I, lviii. At this time Thomas Taylor was minister of the church of St. Mary, Aldermanbury, London; Richard Sibbes was preacher at Gray's Inn, London, and master of St. Catharine's Hall, Cambridge; and William Gouge was rector of St. Anne's, Blackfriars.

of the merciles papists in the vpper Palatinate[2] whose heavie condicion is such as they are forced to steale vp their exercises of relligion in woods and solitarie places not without continuall feare and dainger of their Liues and whose greivous want is such as they would be very thankfull for course bread and drink if they could gett it: Wee tendringe the miserie and want of deare brethren and sisters desire all godly Christians to whom these pr[e]sents may come, as fellowe feelinge members of the same body of Jesus Christ to comiserate their pr[e]sent want and enlarge their harts and hands for some present and private supply for them till some publique meanes (which hereafter may be hoped) may be raised for their releife, assuringe themselues that whatsoeuer is cast into heaven and falleth into the lapp of Christ in his members shall returne with abundant increase in the harvest: Neither lett any be discouraged least their bounty should miscarrie: for wee knowe a sure and safe way, whereby whatsoeuer is giuen, shall vndoubtedly come to their hands to whom it is intended.

2. Martij: 1626.

THO: TAYLER
RICHARD SIBBS
JOHN DAVENPORTE
WILLIAM GOUGE.

[Endorsed] The Copye of a Leter for a Gatheringe for the Ministers in the Palatinat subscribed bye Mr. Tayler. Sibbes. Damport. Gouge. [and the second copy,] note from the 4 Ministers of London: 2 Mtij 1626.

JOHN DAVENPORT to MARY, Lady VERE[1]
To the truely Noble and Worthy Lady the Lady Vere these be d[elivere]d in Hague

Madam)

A LINE or two from your Hon[o]r would haue bene to mee good newes from a farr Countrye. Mr. More[2] was a welcom messenger when he gaue mee assurance of your safe arriuall after so dangerous and

2. In the course of the Thirty Years War in Germany, Maximilian of Bavaria had taken possession of the Upper Palatinate.
1. British Museum, Additional MSS., 4275, fols. 158–159; printed in A. B. Davenport, *A History and Genealogy of the Davenport Family, in England and America, from A.D. 1086 to 1850* (New York, 1851), pp. 312–313; Massachusetts Historical Society *Proceedings*, XLII (Boston, 1909), 207–209.
2. Unidentified.

troublesom a voyadge. He that deliuered you on the sea will preserve you also on the land. How safe are you (Madam) that are hid vnder his wings, and held in his hands who is lord of sea and land? In nothing be carefull but in all things lett your requests bee mayd knowne vnto God with prayers, and supplicacions and giving of thancks. Keepe a record of speciall mercyes, they will much strengthen you against future feares. I hope to wayte vpon your Honor in England agayne ere long, if that be true which I wrote to my lord.[3] If not, yet, whilest I liue, I hope to meete you daily, in presenting our offrings and sac-rifices at the dore of the sanctuary. Be confident of this that I am ever mindfull of your Honor making mention of you in my secrett prayers night and day. I beseech your La[dyshi]p that I may still enioy the benefitt and assistance of your prayers, which, I am sure, haue bene accepted, and will still prevayle with our Alsufficient God thorough the mediacion of our Lord and Sauiour. Good Madam, lett mee pre-vayle with you to take the encouragm[en]ts which God giues you. Sett an higher price vpon your prayers. Vse and inioy that intrest which you haue in Gods fauour thorough Christ. If earthly men can giue good things to theyre children what good thing can your heavenly father denye you? Onely beleiue stedfastly. Aske in fayth and wauer not. You haue an vniust iudge granting the request of a strange wid-dow, a sleepy man satisfying the importunate desire of his neighbour though he came vnseasonably, and will not the righteous God, who is faythfull in his promises, grant the petitions of his children, whose prayers are alwayes in season to him who commandeth them to pray alwayes? Hagar was a bondwoaman cast out of the church, shee prayed not, but wept, shee looked not vp to God but vpon her Ismaell that scoffing Ismaell. Yet God heared, and helped her.[4] Will he not much more regard Sarah who leaues her owne country and fathers house to goe with Abraham in obedience to God, when shee seeketh his face by prayer for herselfe and family wherein Gods name is called vpon?[5] Doubtles he will heare when shee prayeth, and before shee speaketh he will answer. Here stay your heart (good Madam) and reioyce in the Lord: many prayers must be denyed, and refused if you want any thing that is good. But, that I may not tyre you with too much scribling, for conclusion of these rude lines written in too much hast, lett me intreat your La[dyshi]p to pr[e]sent my service to my

3. Horace, Lord Vere, Baron of Tilbury, was at this time serving under Prince Fred-eric Henry, stadtholder of the Netherlands, against the Spaniards.
4. Genesis 16. and 21. 1–21.
5. Genesis 12.

Lord Horton and his good Lady[6] excusing my not wrighting to them at this tyme by the hast of this bearer Mr. Robbert Hyrick[7] whom I presume to commend to your Noblenes beseeching you to remember my lord of his promise to hasten his præferm[en]t, with whom also I ioyne Mr. Humfrey[8] who still wayteth in the citty expecting resolucion from your Hon[or] how to dispose of himselfe. If I had but a litle more tyme I would haue written to Mr. Balmford,[9] and Mr. Sedgwick,[10] to whom I desire to be affectionatly remembred. I rest

Coleman street Your Honor[a]ble Ladysh[i]ps much obliged
Jan. 18. 1627

JOHN DAVENPORTE.

JOHN DAVENPORT *to* MARY, Lady VERE[1]
To the Right Honor[a]ble and Noble Lady the Lady Vere
these be d[elivere]d at the Hague

Lond[on]. June 30. 1628

Madam)

SINCE my recouery out of a dangerous sicknes which held me from a weeke or fourtnight before Shrouetide[2] to as long after Easter (for which I returne most humble and hearty thancks to the God of my life the father of mercyes) I haue had diuerse purposes of wrighting to your Honor, onely I delayed, in hope, to wrighte somewhat concerning the event and success of our High Commission troubles,[3] but I haue hoped in vayne, for, to this day, we are in the same condicion as

6. John Holles, second Earl of Clare, known as Lord Haughton from 1624 to 1637, had married Elizabeth, the eldest daughter of Lord and Lady Vere, September 24, 1626.

7. Robert Herrick, the poet, at this time chaplain to the Duke of Buckingham. F. W. Moorman, *Robert Herrick* (London, 1910), pp. 57–58.

8. One Humphrey was later to aid Davenport in escaping from England.

9. Samuel Balmford was minister of the English congregation at The Hague from 1630 to 1650. W. Steven, *The History of the Scottish Church, Rotterdam* (Edinburgh, 1832), p. 311.

10. Obadiah Sedgwick was chaplain to Baron Vere. An undated letter from Sedgwick to Lady Vere can be found in British Museum, Additional MSS., 4276, fol. 137.

1. British Museum, Additional MSS., 4275, fols. 160–161; printed in A. B. Davenport, *A History and Genealogy of the Davenport Family* (New York, 1851), pp. 314–316; Massachusetts Historical Society *Proceedings*, XLII (Boston, 1909), 209–210.

2. Quinquagesima Sunday and the two following days; i.e., the Sunday, Monday, and Tuesday before Lent.

3. The circular letter of March 2, 1626/7, seems to have brought its authors before the Court of High Commission.

before, delayed till the finishing of this sessions in parliam[en]t which now is vnhappily concluded without any satisfying contentm[en]t to the King, or commonwealth.[4] Threatnings were speedily reviued against vs by the new Bishop of London Dr. Laud,[5] even the next day after the conclusion of this session; wee expect a fierce storme from the inraged spiritts of the 2 Bishops; ours, as I am informed, hath a particular ayme at mee vpon a former quarrail, so that I expect ere long to be deprived of my pastorall chardge in Coleman street. But I am in Gods hands, not in theyres, to whose good pleasure I doe contentedly, and chearfully submitt myselfe. If it be his will to haue me layed aside as a broken vessell of no vse, his will be done, and blessed be his name that he hath served himselfe of me hitherto; if otherwise he be graciously pleased to continue me in my station and ministry he is able to keepe that which I haue committed to him, and I will wayte vpon his goodnes. However things succeed on earth, if he will not deliuer me out of the mouths of the lyons, yet he will deliuer me from every evill worke, and will preserve me to his heauenly kingdom. In the middest of these troubles the Lord hath not left me without many comforts, amongst which the remembrance of your former fauours, and the assurance of the present helpe of your prayers (which, I know, prevayle much with God, thorough Jesus christ our Lord) doth exceedingly comfort mee. I reioyced greatly when I heard of your health, Madam, by your Noble and worthy sonne in Law[6] (in whom I account your Honor, and his Lady your vertuous daughter very happy, as in one who, I am persuaded, doth farr exceed the most of our Nobility in the truest worth) but much more did I reioyce in vnderstanding, by some passadges in his discourse, the continuance of your resolucion to doe God all the service you can in that place, wherevnto the good hand of God, I am confident, hath brought you for some speciall end. The whole countrye lookes vpon your personall

4. After formulating the Petition of Right, the first session of the third parliament of the reign of Charles I was prorogued, June 26, 1628.

5. Charles I promised William Laud the bishopric of London, June 17, 1627. The king ordered the dean and chapter of St. Paul, London, to elect Laud to the bishopric, July 2, 1628. The new incumbent was translated to the see July 15, 1628. William Laud, *Works*, III (Oxford, 1853), 205, 208; *Calendar of State Papers, Domestic Series, 1628–1629* (London, 1859), p. 189.

6. Either John Holles, at this time known as Lord Haughton, and later as the second Earl of Clare, the husband of Elizabeth Vere, or Sir Roger Townshend, Baronet of Rainham, Norfolk, who had married Mary Vere, second daughter of Lord and Lady Vere, May 17, 1627. At this time Catherine, Anne, and Dorothy Vere were unmarried, and Susan Vere, baptized at the church of St. Bartholomew the Great, March 20, 1619, had been buried May 24, 1623. C. R. Markham, *The Fighting Veres* (Boston, 1888), *passim*.

carriadge, and vpon the ordering of your family, wherein, as Solomon shewed his wisdom to the admiracion of the Queene of Sheba,[7] so I hope, your Hono[u]r will so gloryfye God, and adorne the gospell, that we shall all haue iust cause to say, Many daughters haue done ver- tuously but thou excellest them all.[8] If this way, even by well doing you seeke glory and honor, you shall haue it on earth, and afterwards æternal life. Concerning your remoue from the Hague Dr. Sibbs and I haue had some conference (who desireth to be remembred in the best expressions of sincere loue and service to your Honor.) We both agree in this conclusion that, except absolute necessity inforce, you should not remoue your dwelling, both in respect of the benefitt your family may haue by being members of a congregacion[9] (besides theyre helpes at home) and in respect of the helpe and encouragm[en]t the ministry and course of Religion in the Hague may haue by your countenance and example. The glory that may redound to God, and the good that may accrew to your family by your continuance there will recompence the loss which you sustayne in your outward estate. But if this be not sufficient, we desire that you would propose the quæstion with your owne opinion and reasons more fully, and we will indeauour to satisfye your La[dyshi]p by a more full answer. Mr. Sedgwick wrote to me for a pr[e]acher for Sir Edw. Vere,[10] I haue one in readines for him if I may heare an answer of what I wrote to Mr. Sedgwick, to whom and to Mr. Balmford I desire heartily to be remembred. I confes my selfe indebted to Mr. Balmford for answer of his letter which I hope to satisfye ere long. I wrote letters to my Lord and your La[dyshi]p by Mr. Hyrick but never heard what became of them or him. I find a great miss of you, Madam, in the middest of my troubles, but I was not, nor am worthy to enioy such a freind. Sometimes, I thinck, I placed too much content in the inioym[en]t of your presence. Yet agayne I check my selfe fearing least I did not prize you enough. I was not thanckfull enough to you, nor to God for you. The Lord inable me now to pay my debts to my Noble Lord and your good La[dyshi]p by fervent and frequent prayers for you both. I hope ere long to be in Norfolke with my Lord Horton. My wife doth often

7. 1 Kings 10. 1–13.

8. Proverbs 31. 29. Davenport is here quoting the authorized version.

9. For an account of the English church at The Hague, see W. Steven, *The History of the Scottish Church, Rotterdam* (Edinburgh, 1832), pp. 307–311.

10. Sir Edward Vere, a distant kinsman of Horace, Lord Vere, was mortally wounded at the siege of Bois-le-Duc in the Netherlands (today s'Hertogenbosch, Brabant, Hol- land), August 18, 1629.

make mention of your La[dyshi]p with most hearty expressions of an high esteem of your worth. I rest

Your Honor[a]ble La[dyshi]ps . . .

. . . DAVENP . . .

JOHN DAVENPORT *to* MARY, Lady VERE[1]

To the Right Honor[a]ble and truely Noble Lady, the Lady Vere these be d[elivere]d at the Hague.

Madam)

THE importunity of this bearer to carry, at the least, an acknowl-edgm[en]t of the receite of the token, which it pleased your Hon[or] to send to my wife, together with my owne desire of expressing our thanckfulnes for that, and many other favours receiued from you, emboldeneth mee to this rude, and breife expression of my selfe, in so few lines, being by present vrgencye of buisenes, and some streights of tyme, this Saturday night, denyed liberty of enlarging my selfe. That ancient candor and noblenes of disposition, which you haue alwayes excercised towards me, in making a good construction of my errours, as it hath formerly imprinted in mee an high esteeme of your worth, and good opinion of me, so, at this tyme, it giues me assurance that this rudenes will be pardoned, and my desire of presenting most humble and hearty thancks to your Hon[or] will be accepted. I hoped, ere this tyme, to haue obtayned my long desire of seeing my Lord, and your La[dyshi]p with yours in England.[2] The Lord præserve you in the way and make your returne prosperous! This day I receiued a letter from your Noble sonne, my Lord Haughton, which should haue bene here, I thinck, a moneth sooner, to whom I desire to be excused that I wrighte not an answer, for want of tyme. I hope shortly to giue an answer to himselfe not in wrighting, but in speach, at your returne to England, which I wish may be hastened with all convenient speed. In the meane space, I present my humble service to his Lordsh[i]p, and to his worthy Lady. By Mr. Sedgwick, I receiued a letter from

1. British Museum, Additional MSS., 4275, fols. 164–165; printed in A. B. Davenport, *Supplement* (Stamford, 1876), pp. 360–361; Massachusetts Historical Society *Proceedings*, XLII (Boston, 1909), 212–213.

2. After the surrender of Bois-le-Duc, September 17, 1629, Lord Vere divided his time between London and the Netherlands until the attack on Maastricht in the spring and summer of 1632.

Mr. Balmford, whom I loue vnfeignedly, for the graces that shine in him. If he resolue to settle at the Hague, I beseech the father of spirits to encourage his spirit to that greate worke, and to furnish him with wisdom, and vtterance, and zeale in abundance, and to goe foorth with him, in his ministeriall labours, in much power and efficacye! I cannot wrighte to him now, but I acknowledge my selfe his debtour. Now the good Lord shew mercy to my Noble Lord, your Honor[a]ble La[dyshi]p and to your whole family, in ordering your consultacions, and resolucions to his owne glory in your wellfare, and in filling your hearts with all needfull graces, and comforts, and in protecting your persons, and preserving you in health and safety, there, and in your voyage, and in fulfilling all your necessityes! I rest, in much hast, craving pardon for this blurred scribling.

> Your Honor[a]ble Ladish[i]ps much obliged in the Lord

December. 26. 1629.   JOHN DAVENPORTE

I will not fayle to sollicite Sir Maurice Abbott in your buisenes concerning Hales.[3]

[Endorsed] Mr. Davenports letters

JOHN DAVENPORT *to* WILLIAM LAUD[1]

ANSWERS mayd by John Davenporte Bachelar in Divinity, and Vicar of St. Stephans in Colman street to certayne obiections divised agaynst him by Timothy Hood,[2] sometymes, his Curat.

1. To the first. He doeth not remember that he was angry with his Curat Tim: Hood for the cause, in the Article expressed, nor that he questioned him for the same, as is expressed in the Article. And he doeth not beleiue this Article to be true.

2. To the 2d. What this obiector meaneth by his being blamed for sitting in the surpless till such tyme as the psalme was but song, is very doubtfull, yet, for answer to this obiection, he sayth, that he doeth not beleiue that he hath at any tyme blamed the sayd Curatt for

---

3. Unidentified.

1. Public Record Office, State Papers, Domestic, Charles I, CLXXXII, no. 60. An abstract of this reply is printed in A. B. Davenport, *Supplement* (Stamford, 1876), pp. 85–88.

2. Timothy Hood was a graduate of the University of Cambridge in 1626/7 and later a preacher at St. Clement Danes. J. and J. A. Venn, *Alumni Cantabrigienses*, Part I, II (Cambridge, 1922), 402.

wearing the surpless at any such tymes as by the canons he is inioyned.[3]

3. To the 3d. he beleiueth this Article not to be true, and holdeth
himselfe vnæqually dealt withall by this obiector in that he is charged
by him with matters of privat discourse, especially seing the constant
practise of his church is to haue the surpless worne, not onely constantly once every moneth, but oftener also.

4. To the 4th. He vnderstandeth not the matters therein contayned,
neyther doeth he beleiue them to be true, as they are therein expressed.

5. To the 5th. He doeth not beleiue the matters therein contayned
to be true.

6. To the 6th. He doeth not beleiue that he forbad him to read the
letany on Sundayes, but that he told him that it was not vsually read
on that day there, nor in other churches, and he affirmeth that it is
read in his church, on Wednesdayes, and Fridayes ordinarily, and
that it hath bene read also, on the Sundayes, in his church some
tymes, since he was placed there.[4]

7. He doeth not beleiue this Article to be true.

8. To the 8th. Theyre short Cutt (as he vntruely Calleth it) is commonly an howre long, and yet onely one psalme is sung before sermon.
And he doeth not beleiue the things contayned in this Article to be
true.

9. He doeth not remember the things therein contayned as they are
therein expressed.

10. To the tenth. He hath and doeth weare the surpless according
as the Canon doeth præscribe.

11. To the 11th. The tyme when the sayd Tim: Hood was his Curatt
was the sommer season, in which tyme, diverse churches in the Citty
were not vsed, because workemen were then imployed about repayring
them. Vpon which occasion, the parishioners were constrayned to
seeke to other parishes for those helpes, which they wanted in theyre
owne. He sayth also that he the sayd John Davenporte hath often in
the pulpitt very earnestly forbidden strangers to resort to the communion in his church, and hath, both publickly, and privatly charged
the churchwardens to take Care that strangers be not admitted to the
sacram[en]t (according to the 27 Canon.)[5] And to be sure, that it

---

3. Canon 58. Ministers reading Diuine Seruice, and Administring the Sacraments, to
weare Surplisses, and Graduats therewithall, Hoods. *Constitutions and Canons Ecclesiastical 1604 With an Introduction and Notes by H. A. Wilson* (London, 1923).

4. Canon 15. The Letanie to bee read on Wednesdayes and Fridayes.

5. Canon 27. Schismaticks not to bee admitted to the Communion.

should be effected accordingly, he tooke such order that tokens[6] were provided, and he strictly inioyned every parishioner to giue in his name to the clarke, and to fetch his token. And the sayd John Davenporte doeth sitt in the vestry, after sermon, every communion day, whilest the churchwardens are going about the church to receiue theyre tokens, that so he may prevent the resort of strangers. He sayeth also, that, if he should not administer the sacram[en]t to many whom hee knoweth not, he must denye it to many of his owne parish, ffor he neyther doeth, nor ever shall be able to knowe many of them, they are so many, and (because it is not a place convenient for shop-keepers to dwell in) they so often change theyre dwellings.

12. To the 12th. His parish contayneth in it about 1400 Communicants, and by reason of the smallnes of the chancell, so many as vsually resort to the sacram[en]t cannot receiue at the communion table for which cause, he is constrayned to administer it to them from pew to pew, throughout the body of the church, as well as in the chancell. Many of these pewes are so filled, that it is impossible that many should receiue it kneeling, whereby he is constrayned to administer it to them in such gestures as they can receiue it in; neyther can he take notice of every ones gesture. But when he hath observed some to sitt that might conveniently kneele, he hath advised them to kneele, and they haue obeyed, and then he hath administred it to them. He affirmeth also that he is sure, and is able to proue by sufficient witnes, that before any complaynt was mayd, or intended by this obiectour, for aught he knoweth, that he the sayd John Davenporte, in case of refusall to kneele, hath refused to administer the sacram[en]t to the party so refusing. Concerning his wife, he sayth, that, vpon his owne knowledge, shee hath receiued the sacram[en]t at his hands kneeling, many tymes. Noyther hath the sayd Tim: Hood acquainted him the sayd John Davenporte that he observed any such thing concerning his wife, as is charged in this Article. To what is added concerning Not-Conforming ministers, he sayth, that all Not-Conforming ministers doe not hold it vnlawfull to receiue the sacram[en]t Kneeling, as he is able to declare in some with whom he hath had discourse about that matter. Neyther hath the sayd Curatt informed the sayd John Davenporte, at any tyme whilest he was with him of the contrary practise in any of them. *Et sic de cæteris.*

6. "A stamped piece of lead or other metal given (originally after confession) as a voucher of fitness to be admitted to the communion: in recent times used in Scotland in connexion with the Presbyterian Communion service, but now generally represented by a 'communion card.'" *A New English Dictionary.*

13. To the 13th. He told the s[ai]d Curat what some sayd touching that matter, and, having so done, he leaft him free to doe therein according to his owne discretion.

14. To the 14th. He answereth, and professeth that he was not present at that discourse betweene the sayd Curatt, and his man, and that he doeth not remember the particulars contayned in this Article, nor beleiue them to be true according as they are therein expressed.

15. To the 15th. The sayd John Davenporte, having observed, how for the space of a quarter of an yeare the sayd Curat had estranged himselfe from him, at last, when he came for his quarteridge, the s[ai]d John Davenporte, in a freindly, and familiar manner, as his custom was, sayd to him, Mr. Hood, Why are you, and I such strangers, that I cannot see you at home of late? His answer was, Why should I come to see you? doe you thinck I haue nothing else to doe but to see you? The cause of this estrangm[en]t of himselfe, as the s[ai]d John Davenporte verily beleiueth, was not that which is pretended in the Articles, but as it seemed to him by some speaches which fell from the s[ai]d Curatt, it was a discontent, which he had conceiued agaynst the sayd John Davenporte for that he had not imployed him in preaching for him in his absence. Neyther were any of the particulars comprised in these Articles the cause of theyre parting, but the true cause was this. The s[ai]d John Davenporte told the s[ai]d Tim: Hood at his first coming to him, that his Curatt must necessarily haue a chamber in his parish, because there is daily vse of him in so large a parish. But he, the s[ai]d Tim: Hood tooke a chamber in Dukes place,[7] which is about halfe a mile from the parish, though he might haue had one in the parish. Wherevpon greate inconveniences followed, viz. that some, who brought theyre children to be baptized, and theyre dead to be buryed had returned home with loss of theyre labour, and expectacion, if the sayd John Davenporte had not bene ready at hand to doe those offices, which when he told the sayd Curatt of, and advised him to take a chamber in the parish if he purposed to continue in that place, he refused to doe it, saying, Doe you thinck that I will take a chamber in your parish to kill my selfe? This he spake, because, at that tyme, one or 2 houses were infected in the parish. The sayd John Davenporte answered him, No, Mr. Hood, I will not bind you to it if you be vnwilling, but this I will say, he that is Curatt in this place must dwell

7. At one time or another in the course of the seventeenth century, the present Duke Street, Aldgate, St. James's Place, Aldgate, and Mitre Square, all lying in the vicinity of Aldgate, were called Duke's Place. H. A. Harben, *A Dictionary of London* (London, 1918).

in the parish. If you will not, I must of necessity haue one that will. The sayd Curatt replyed, Giue mee fayre warning, and I will be gone. So they agreed that the sayd Curatt should haue that quarter which was then begun, that, within the compass thereof he might dispose of himselfe in some other place. This agreem[en]t being mayd, and concluded betweene, the sayd John Davenport renued his former question about the cause of his so great strangenes. The s[ai]d Curatt answered him with very many bitter, taunting, iniurious, reproachfull, and false speaches. The particulars he the sayd John Davenporte hath in wrighting to shew when need shall require it. Vnto all which the sayd John Davenport returned him this answer, Well, Mr. Hood is this your requitall of the many kindnesses I haue done for you? And then he reckoned vp some particulars to the sayd Curatt, but gaue him not that harsh language as is expressed in the Article. At last, the sayd John Davenporte told him the sayd Tim: Hood what he heard of him, how he held that the signing of the child with the signe of the cross was parte of the sacram[en]t of Baptisme; contrary to the doctrine of the church of England as it is expressed in the 30th Canon.[8] Herevpon, and not vpon the words wherewith he ioyneth this speach, the s[ai]d John Davenporte sayd vnto him, if you broach such things, you will spoyle my parish, for none will suffer you to vse the cross to theyre children, if they conceiue that you make it parte of the sacram[en]t. When they were vpon parting, after he had receiued his wages, the sayd Curatt told the s[ai]d John Davenporte that he should haue occasions to be often foorth, that quarter, to seeke for his preferm[en]t. This the sayd John Davenporte thaught on, after he was gone, and of his vncivill vsage of him in his owne house, and the next evening tooke that freind who had commended the s[ai]d Tim: Hood to him, along with him, and, in his hearing, told the s[ai]d Curatt, how inconvenient it would be for them both, if they should continue together vpon such tearmes, and, in conclusion, told him that he would giue him the allowance for the whole quarter to come, as if he had stayed out the tyme, and would be at double charges to entertayne another, who should constantly attend the worke of that place, and so he should haue full liberty to follow his opportunityes, for his future settling without interruption. When the Curatt heard this he was very well content and seemed very thanckfull, and signed an acquittance, wherein he released the sayd John Davenport from all promises, and engagem[en]ts to him, and prayed God to blesse

8. Canon 30. The lawfull vse of the Crosse in Baptisme explaned.

him, affirming that he had much cause to speake nothing but good of him in every place, or to that purpose. So they mayd a finall conclusion before witnes. Since which tyme, during that whole quarter, the sayd Curatt never complayned to the s[ai]d John Davenport of any iniury, and now, as himselfe sayth, is stirred vp by others to trouble him thus iniuriously.

16. To the 16th. In this last Article the sayd John Davenporte conceiueth himselfe, not to be charged and that onely the incivility of such a guest is thereby discovered.

[Endorsed] Janua: 15. 1630: Mr. Damports answeare to the ob[jections] made bye his Curat Mr. Hood.

JOHN DAVENPORT *to* MARY, Lady VERE[1]
To the Right Honorable the Lady Vere these be d[elivere]d

Most Noble, and my much Honoured Lady)

IN the middest of my disquietments and tossings to and fro, it is some comfort, that I haue assurance of the continuance of your fauo[u]r towards mee, and of your remembrance of mee in prayer. I know, that loue which you haue bene pleased so freely to cast vpon mee will quicken you to all diligence and industry in any way and course that may conduce to the procuring of my liberty, but hitherto it hath pleased God to leaue mee in much darkenes, and many difficulties, to vnbottom mee wholly of the creature, and to reueale himselfe more clearely and fully in all issues, and euents that befall mee. Be not troubled, much less discouraged (Good Madam) at any rumors you meet with concerning my present way. The persecucion of the Tongue

1. British Museum, Additional MSS., 4275, fol. 166; printed in A. B. Davenport, *A History and Genealogy of the Davenport Family* (New York, 1851), pp. 318–320; *Supplement* (Stamford, 1876), pp. 96–100; Massachusetts Historical Society *Proceedings*, XLII (Boston, 1909), 213–215. Upon the death of George Abbot, Archbishop of Canterbury, and the appointment of William Laud as his successor, Davenport left London, August 5, 1633. Following reports that he had fled, and that a pursuivant had been sent after him, he remained in concealment. At this time he probably wrote an "Essay on What the Visible Church is; and The Government of it." (American Antiquarian Society. In L. Shattuck, *A History of the Town of Concord*, Boston, 1835, pp. 159–160, this work is credited to Peter Bulkeley, teacher of the church at Concord, Massachusetts. In F. B. Dexter, "Sketch of the Life and Writings of John Davenport," New Haven Colony Historical Society *Papers*, II, New Haven, 1877, 221–222, the work is correctly attributed to Davenport.) This letter also belongs to that period. About the middle of November he departed from England for Amsterdam in the Netherlands.

is more fierce and terrible then that of the hand. At this time, I haue
sense of both. But I can say, it is for thy names sake o Lord, that I
beare this reproach. But the iniurious surmises of those, by whom I
should be comforted and supported, many that profess religion in an
higher strayne then some others, doeth most afflict mee. I pray God it
be not layed to theyre charge! The trueth is, I haue not forsaken my
ministry, nor resigned vp my place, much less seperated from the
church, but am onely absent a while to wayte vpon God, vpon the
settling and quieting of things, for light to discerne my way, being
willing to lye and dye in prison, if the cause may be aduantaged by it,
but choosing rather to preserue the liberty of my person and ministry
for the seruice of the church elsewhere if all dores are shutt against mee
here. What I now doe and suffer is not caused by any guilt of any
practise or action done or intended by me, which may expose mee to
any iust censure of Authority, much less by a desire of ease (as some
giue out) hauing gotten a greate estate; least of all by reseruing to my
owne priuate benefitt any thing committed to my trust for the publick
good. My estate, though I am not in any present want, is not able to
maintaine mee without a calling. In the buisenes of the feoffees[2] I
haue giuen vp my account vpon oath, and the lord God who searcheth
the hearts knoweth that I am so farr from gaining by that buisenes in
my outward estate, that I am out of purse, in myne owne particular,
for the aduancem[en]t of it. The onely cause of all my present sufferings is the alteracion of my iudgm[en]t in matters of conformity to the
ceremonies established whereby I cannot practise them as formerly I
haue done. Wherein I doe not censure those that doe conforme (nay
I account many of them faithfull, and worthy instrum[en]ts of Gods
glory, and, I know that I did conforme with as much inward peace, as
now I doe forbeare, in both my vprightnes was the same, but my light
different). In this action I walke by that light which shineth vnto mee.
Lett no man say, the matters are small and what need I be scrupulous
in these things? That which the Ap[ost]le speaketh of Rom. 14 was
but a small matter, yet you see how heauy a doome he passeth vpon
him that doeth it doubting of the lawfullnes of it, v. 14. 22. 23. I haue
bene taught by my Lord and Sauio[u]r to account no com[mandmen]t
of God small, and to despise a mans way, that is, to thinck this is too
despicable and slight a thing to be stood vpon, you know what an euill
it is, pro. 19. 16. But these things are not small, neither in themselues,
nor in the consequences of them. But I haue not time to be large, onely

2. Davenport refers to his work as one of the feoffees for the purchase of impropriations. I. M. Calder, *The New Haven Colony* (New Haven, 1934), pp. 9–12, 17–19.

thus much I thaught good to present to your Hono[u]r in way of
account for the present, hoping that God will giue mee an opportunity
to make a more large and full Apollogy, for the satisfaction of all men.
They that know mee, might haue suspended theyre opinions, and
censures till they had heard from my selfe, the reason of my actions.
With much aduise of many ministers of eminent noate, and worth I
haue done all which I haue done hitherto, and with desire of pitching
vpon that way wherein God might be most glorifyed. In his due time,
he will manifest it. Mr. Harris[3] I know fully and I doe heartily loue.
He is a very worthy man of a very gracious hearte, humble, mild, of
gentle spirit, a man not at all taken notice of by the Bishops. He is
weake and sickly, but you need not be discouraged by that: for it is a
lingring weakenes wherein he may hold out long, but his spirit is very
actiue in good, he is very fitt for your occasions in all respectes. You
shall be very happy in him if you can haue him. He is one of a thousand. It is not in the Bishops power to take from you what is settled
vpon the Nobility and others by magna charta,[4] the right and power
of intertaining chaplaines. Feare it not. The good Lord strengthen
your inward man with the ioys of his spirit!

Your Honorable Ladiships much obliged
JOHN DAUENPORTE

Madam

I pray send by this bearer 2 or 3 sheetes of gilded paper. I am now
about to wright to my Lord Keeper.[5]

JOHN DAVENPORT *to* Sir WILLIAM BOSWELL[1]

*To the Right Worshipfull Sir William Boswell Knight Agent for
his Ma[jes]tie of Great Brittaine*

Honorable Sir)

WHEN I first Came into these parts, my purpose was to stay here
but 3 or 4 moneths, and, that time being expired, to returne for
England my native countrey, had not the sinister and slanderous in-

3. Unidentified.

4. Although King John conceded "That the Church of England shall be free, . . ."
(Magna Charta, Article 1), and again ". . . , that the Church of England be free, . . ."
(Article 63), Davenport read more into those clauses than they contain.

5. Thomas, Lord Coventry, was keeper of the great seal from 1625 to 1640.

1. British Museum, Additional MSS., 6394, fols. 196–197; printed in Massachusetts
Historical Society *Proceedings*, XLII (Boston, 1909), 228–230; C. Burrage, *The Early
English Dissenters in the Light of Recent Research* (2 vols., Cambridge, 1912), II, 282–284.
Sir William Boswell was English agent at The Hague from 1633 until his death in 1649.

formacion, whereof I complained in my last,[2] exasperated the Arch
B[isho]p of Cant[erbury][3] to reproachfull inuectiues, and bitter men-
aces against me in the High Commission, whereby my returne is made
much more difficult, and hazardous then I could suspect. When, in
that letter, I sayd, I am willing to excercise those gifts which God hath
giuen me etc. I vsed that expression not in affectation, but as fittest to
represent my present state, and to intimate that I am not engaged by
any relation of office for continuance here. Which, being added to
what I then wrote, and the vnseasonablenes of two or three moneths
(after my arriuall) for trauayle, and that I was but once at the Hague,
in transitû, before the last time, when I trauayled thither purposely
to present my selfe and seruice to your Ho[nor], will make a full
apollogy for my seeming neglect in that particular. The particulars,
wherein I haue changed, are no other then the same, for which many
worthy ministers, and lights eminent for godlines and learning haue
suffered the loss of theyre ministry and liberty; some whereof are now
in perfect peace, and rest, others are dispersed in seuerall countreyes,
and some yet liue in England as priuate persons, who were and are
loyall and faythfull subiects to theyre soueraigne, and haue witnessed
against hæresyes, and schysme and against all sectaryes, as Familists,
Anabaptists and Brownists, against all which I also witnes, in this
place, wherevnto I had not come, if I could haue bene secure of a safe
and quiett abode in my deare natiue country.

If that way of questioning should pass vpon all men, which your
wisdom iudgeth meete in this case (as will appeare vpon your revew
of the second question) I thinck, they that iudge me will be found, in
some particulars, to haue spoken against the gouernm[en]t of England.
All that I spake was concerning the gesture of sitting, vsed in this
countrey, in receiuing the sacrament of the Lords Supper, which I
approued, and præferred before Kneeling, grounding what I sayd
vpon Luke 22. 27 to 31, wherein I named not England nor the gouernment thereof, and so carryed the discourse, that it might be applyed as
well to the popish or Lutheran custom here as to any other, and
passed it ouer so breifly, that all I sayd may be written in a very few
lines: nor did I euer heare that any man tooke offence thereat, but
this informer, who was discontented the weeke before at a sermon
wherein some Arminian errours were touched vpon by me, which
quickened him to watch for some aduantage, wherevpon he might
ground an accusation.

2. This letter has not been found.
3. William Laud.

Whereas it pleased you to question vpon oath whether I haue not bene cause, or conscious of any English bookes,[4] or treaties printed or published in these parts since my coming ouer, or now in press, wherein the present orders and gouernm[en]t of Engl[and] in church affayres are traduced, and vndermined? My answer (but without oath till I shall be lawfully called therevnto) is negatiue. Dr. Ames his last booke intitled a fresh suit against ceremonies[5] is the onely booke, that I know of, which hath bene published since my coming into these parts, that booke with the præface was printed before I came from England, yea before the authors death, who was buried before my arriuall here. Nor haue I dispersed any of them in England, or in these countryes. My profession of being still his Ma[jes]ties loyall and faythfull subiect is in simplicity and trueth, neyther shall they disproue it, who traduce me, and if they proceed according to these beginnings, I shall be constrained to declare myne innocencie in an Apollogy printed to the vew of the world,[6] and therein to communicate the grounds, wherevpon my iudgm[en]t and practise was altered, and the reason of my departure thence hither; with such obseruations as I haue made in both places. But it is not my purpose so to doe, vnles the continuance of iniurious aspersions make it necessary, in which case the law of God and of nature bindeth men to such a Vindicacion of theyre innocency as the case requireth. Oh that the good hand of God would bring it to pass that those vgly vizzards of disloyalty and schysme being pulled off, the persons that are besmeared and deformed with these obloquies might be represented to his Ma[jes]tie in theyre owne shape and colours, viz. in the tendernes of theyre conscience, in the peaceablenes of theyre disposition; and in the simplicity of theyre intentions for the good of church and commonw[ealth] vnder his Royall Gouernm[en]t, for the continuance of whose life, and raigne in peace and prosperity I doe and shall (as I am bound) daily prostrate

4. At this time Davenport was suspected of having written "the Crowne of a Christian Martyr" or "The Crowne of Christian martyrdome," a peevish pamphlet denouncing the constitution of the Church of England supposed to have been published at Delft early in 1634. Additional MSS., 6394, fols. 178, 179; State Papers, Holland, CXLVIII, fols. 45–46; C. Burrage, *The Early English Dissenters in the Light of Recent Research* (2 vols., Cambridge, 1912), II, 285. No copy of this pamphlet has been found.

5. William Ames was professor of theology and rector of the University of Franeker and pastor of the English congregation at Rotterdam, where he died in 1633. He was the author of *A Fresh Svit Against Human Ceremonies in God's Worship* (Rotterdam, 1633).

6. Davenport published *A Protestation made and published upon occasion of a pamphlett intitled A just complaint, etc.* at Rotterdam in 1635, and *An Apologeticall Reply To a booke Called An Answer to the unjust complaint of W. B.* at Rotterdam in 1636.

my selfe with my poore prayers before the throne of grace. What account of my wayes I tender to your Ho[nor] I doe it as to his sacred Ma[jes]tie, whose worthy Agent and instrument you are in these parts, in hope that you will make such vse of it as may conduce to the satisfaction of Authority and my peace. For which Noble fauour I shall alwayes pray that you may be imployed in Honorable seruices, and blessed with Happy success in them all your dayes, and shall rest

Amsterdam   Your Hono[u]rs to be Commanded in the Lord

March 18. 1634 *stilo locj*   JOHN DAUENPORTE

[Endorsed] Dauenport. 18. Mar. 1634. Amdam.

JOHN DAVENPORT *to* the CLASSIS of Amsterdam[1]

IT doth greive me not without cause, Excellent and learned men, reverend brethren, that our first meeting happeneth to be in a way of dispute, which that it might have ben pleasing and peaceable by the full agreement of our opinions, was my cheife desire: yet my full perswasion of your (not humanitie only but allso) brotherly affection towards me, doth somwhat mittigate that sorrowing, in confidence whereof I will briefly relate to your prudence (reverend brethren) with all due reverence, the cause of the slow proceeding of my confirmation in the ministry, wherunto I seemed to be called.

The calling it selfe I professe my selfe to accept willingly, though not without trembling, and am very readie to discharge that office as I am able: but some thinges have happened betweene the call, and my confirmation, beyond my Expectation. for

1. First I vnderstand that both the worthy brethren, Pastors of the dutch Church, and the reverend Mr. Pagett,[2] did propound, and appoynt, as a condition of my admittance, that I should conforme to the orders, and customs, of the dutch Church, whereas I doe not yet vnderstand, what those orders and customs are, for which cause, I propounded to the consistory of the English Church, that some convenient time might be given me, rightly to informe my selfe concern-

---

1. The original of this letter, in Latin, was delivered to an ordinary classis which met at Amsterdam March 24/April 3, 1633/4. Nieuwezijds Kapel, Amsterdam, Acta Classis Amstelodamensis, IV, 1631–1645, fol. 36. Later it was translated by John Davenport and published in W. Best, *A Iust Complaint Against An Vniust Doer* (Amsterdam, 1634), pp. 1–8.

2. John Paget was pastor of the English congregation at Amsterdam from 1607 to 1637.

ing those canons and customs of the dutch Church, and concerning the state of this English Church, before I should; by taking upon me this Pastorall office, binde my selfe to either of them, this the consistory not only judged equall: but allso with one consent concluded that it should be so, Mr. Pagett only excepted, who would not agree with them in that matter, without consent of the Classis: whereas nevertheles, the Power of every particular Church; is cheife in its owne particular matters, (or in things which are proper to it selfe) as a Synod hath the cheife power, in things that are common to many Churches, witnes Cham. Cont. Bell. *lib.* 2.[3] With whom agree the canons of these Churches, as appareth in the Harmony of the dutch Synods, where it is decreed that only such things, shallbe brought unto the Classis, which can not be ended in the consistory. *Chap.* 7. *Art.* 6. As that which can not conveniently, be decided by the Classis shallbe brought into the Provinciall Synod. *Chap.* 8. *Art.* 6.[4]

Secondly it was required of me that I should conforme, unto a particular custom of the dutch Church for the unlimited Baptisinge of all infants, which were presented in the Church, of what nation or Sect soever, allthough, that either of the parents were christians, was no otherwise manifest, then by their (all) answering yea, at the reading of the leiturgy of baptisme publickly, or by nodding their head, or some other gesture, they seemed to be willing to answer.

First I neither did nor doe deny, to baptize their Infants who are members of this Church, which seing it is so, I desier to understand by what right, the Pastour of any particular Church, can be bound to excercise his ministry in any act of it, towards those who are not members of his Church, seing the Apostle Paul required no more of the Pastors of Ephesus, then to take heed to themselves, and to all the flocke, whereof the holy Ghoste hath made them ouerseers. *Act.* 20. 28. The same is required of Archippus, to take heade to the ministry which he had received of the Lord, (viz. amongst the Collossians) that he fullfill it. *Col.* 4, 17. as allso Peter exhorteth the Elders, saying, feed

Obj.   the flocke that is amongst you 1. *Pet.* and 2.[5] If it be objected that all that are under the Classis of Amsterdam, ought to conforme to the An. 1.   custom of the dutch Church in Amsterdam. I answer that, even for

---

3. Daniel Chamier, *Panstratiæ Catholicæ; seu Controversiarum de religione adversus Pontificios corpus,* ... (4 vols., Geneva, 1626). Chamier considers the doctrines of R. F. R. Bellarmino, cardinal and archbishop of Capua, 1542–1621, *De Libero Arbitrio,* in III, Liber II, 17–39.

4. Festvs Hommivs, *Specimen Controversiarvm Belgicarvm;* ... *Addita est* ... *Harmonia Synodorvm Belgicarvm* (Leyden, 1618), pp. 150, 151.

5. 1 Peter 5. 2.

that reason, the English Church ought not to be bounde therunto, it beinge not nessessary to require it of them, seinge that the dutch Church: (which is in the same cittie) refuseth none, but baptiseth all that are brought, without difference, especially, 2lie. Seing that the Pastor of the English Church, can not satisfie his conscience, that it is lawfull for him so to doe, yea he greately feareth: least Christ will Iudge him guilty, if he suffer himselfe to be in bondage under such a custom, which is contrary to the canon of the Apostle, let every man be perswaded in his owne minde. *Rom.* 14. 5. and whatsoever is not of faith is sinne vers. 23.

Secondly in regard of the communion of particular Churches amongst themselves, I neither did nor doe refuse to Baptise their Infants, who are not members of this Church: so that I may be satisfied, by some precise Examination, if otherwise they be vnknowne to me, that they are Christians in deed.

When Mr. Pagett asked me, what Questions I would propound, to such as are not members of this Church: nor otherwise knowne to me? I answered, I will inquire of what religion they are of, and of what Church they are members, and concerning that fayth (which they seeme to professe, and wherin they promise to educate their Children[)]. It seemes to me that herein, Mr. Pagett dealt extremely with me, in that he rejected all my labour, for a peaceable composing, prudent accommodating, and brotherly ending of matters betweene him and me privatly, or by the counsell of the Elders of his owne Church, nor would hearken to my advise for accommodation without consent of the Classis.

At laste the matter was brought to five eminent brethren, Pastors of the dutch Church: Who being desired (as it is sayd) by some of the Elders of this Church, that they would indevour to inclyne, Mr. Pagett to some freindly agreement herein, upon Mr. Pagetts request alone did in writing declare their private Iudgment in this question, yet therein they professed, that they very much approved, of my good zeale, and care concerninge the private examination of the parents or suertyes of such infants, before the child should be baptized, and that the foresayd examination, ought to be ordayned, as farre as it might stand with the edification of the English Church: (having thus sayd, they add afterwards) but if the parents or suertyes shall refuse to be examined, or if for the shortnes of time, or for other Iust cause, it can not be done, or, if, when they doe come they shall not seeme to give satisfaction, to the Iudgment of him that examineth them, the infants whose parents or suertyes, appeare to be christians, and who doe professe the christian religion, at the reading of the Leiturgie of baptisme, publickly before the Church, shall not for that cause be sent away, without baptisme.[6]

The day following, Mr. Pagett asked me, whether I would rest in the writing of the 5. Ministers? To whome I answered, the writers themselves doe not require this of me, and for ought I can see it would give them content, if an order be made in consistory to put an ende to this controversie. But if any marvell, why I did not rest in that writing, I will tell the reasons, for by what right could it be exacted or expected that I should rest in the writing, when first the wryters themselues professed that it was but their owne privat judgment. Secondly this their private judgment was nakedly prepounded, without any proofe from the word of God, whose prerogative it is to be rested in, for its owne Authoritie. Thirdly such a subjection, is greater then may bee yeilded vnto any counsell, whether of classis, or Synods, and where it hath been granted or suffered, it hath been the cause of many mischeifs in the Church, for therby the writings and decrees of men are made infallible, and equall with the word of God, which is intolerable. Fourthly those reverend brethren, take the word christian more largely then I, for they account all christians which professe christian religion at the reading of the leiturgy of baptisme publickly, before the Church, though it be done only in one word, yea or by bowing the head or body, when they say nothing, yea some of them goe so farre, that they hould that the very offering of the child to Baptisme, giveth it a right therunto, though the parents be not christians, because (they say) it may be their grandfather or great grandfather were christians, and another adds (if my memory fayles not) that infants are holy in the roote, if they be borne where the Gospell is preached. But I take the name of christians, (in this question,) in the same sence wherein the multitude of beleevers in Antiochia, were called christians. *Act.* 11, 21, 26. So that I account them to be christians children whose parents, at least one of them, in externall profession, is within the covenant. *Gen.* 17, 10. *Faithfull. Rom.* 4, 11. *Called. Act.* 2, 39. *Ioyned to some true Church:* 1 *Cor.* 5. 12. Because the seale of the covenant belongs only to those in the covenant: nor can a man be judged to be in the covenant, without faith, nor to have faith

---

6. For a brief abstract of the writing of the five ministers, see *Calendar of State Papers, Domestic Series, 1634–1635* (London, 1864), p. 469, where the document is erroneously entered under date of January 20, 1634/5, instead of January 20, 1633/4. For an English translation, see B. Hanbury, *Historical Memorials relating to the Independents, or Congregationalists* (3 vols., London, 1839–44), I, 537–538.

unlesse he be called, nor to be called, unles he be taken off, from the world, and joyned to the congregation of the faithfull: wherunto agree the divines of the dutch Church in their confessions, and all the reformed Churches, in the harmony of confessions,[7] read allso, Spe. contr. Pelag.[8] *Act.* 28, 34.[9] Kuchl. de baptism. *Thes.* 15.[10] Dr. Ames cas. Con. cap. 27.[11] to conclude, all divines agree in this.

As for that which is objected, concerning particular cases that may happen: that which Beza writes in his Epistle to the ministers of Neocomum,[12] or Perkins,[13] or Ames, in their cases, or the Professors of Leyden, in their Theses,[14] makes nothing against my opinion, if they be taken in a good sence, and made to agree with the Patern of wholesom words.

1. Obj.
Cas. con:
An.

The consequence, which some object, for the avoyding wherof, they would have infants, thus promiscuously to be baptized, doe not trouble me, because I have learned of the Apostle that evill is not to be done that good may come therof, yet in the interim, consider brethren, whether it be lawfull to drive the Pastor from the flock, that strangers may enter into the fold, or to make the Pastors calling voyd, for their sakes, that are uncalled, or to hinder the making of a covenant betweene the Pastor and his people, because he dare not give the seale of the covenant to those that are not in the covenant, or to remove the Porter from the dore of the Lords house, that the gentiles may be suffered to enter into the Temple? yea to bringe a detainment upon the English Church, for so smalle a matter, as this seemeth to you to

2. Obj.
An.

---

7. Salnar, *Harmonia Confessionum Fidei Orthodoxarum et Reformatarum Ecclesiarum, quæ, in præcipuis quibusque Europæ regnis, nationibus, et provinciis, sacram Evangelii doctrinam purè profitentur, etc.* (Geneva, 1581).

8. This work has not been identified. Pelagius was a theologian who lived from *ca.* 360 to *ca.* 420, who opposed the doctrine of original sin. In the seventeenth century his teachings were adopted by Arminius.

9. This is an erroneous citation. Possibly The Acts 28. 24. is intended.

10. Joannes Kuchlinus, *De baptismo; resp. Dav. Arnoldo* (Leyden, 1600).

11. William Ames, *Guiljelmi Amesij De Conscientia et eivs ivre, vel Casibvs, Libri Qvinqve* (Amsterdam, 1631). *Caput XXVII. De Baptismo.*

12. Théodore de Bèze, *Epistolarum theologicarum liber unus* (Geneva, 1573 and 1575, and Hanover, 1597), *Epistolae* 9, 10.

13. William Perkins, *The whole treatise of the Cases of Conscience* (Cambridge, 1606 and 1608; London, 1611; and later editions), Book II, Chapter IX, "Of Baptisme."

14. Johannes Polyander, Andreas Rivetus, Antonius Walæus, and Antonius Thysius, *Synopsis Purioris Theologiæ, Dispvtationibvs quinquaginta duabus comprehensa, Ac conscripta Per Iohannem Polyandrvm Andream Rivetvm Antonivm Walævm Antonivm Thysivm S. S. Theologiæ Doctores et Professores in Academia Leidensi* (Leyden, 1625 and 1632). The sacrament of baptism is dealt with in *Dispvtatio XLIV*, in the second edition pp. 642–660.

be, and not to regard how much the conscience of your brother is indangered, so your customs may be established: neither is this to be sleighted, that, vnles we be thus difficult in this cause, parents that joyne themselves vnto no Church will content themselves in that estate, and live, and dy libertines, if they may have the Privileges of the Church, as if they were members, which who seeth not what an occation of error, and destruction, it may be both to parents and children, so that I can not be perswaded but that in that cause, the conscience is not at all indangered, by denying baptisme, but by baptizing such very much.

3. Obj.   Concerning the troubles, which some object may arise in the English Church, vpon this occasion, which allso one applied to me, as if I should be judged to be the author o them.

An.   I propounded to you (reverend brethren,) to the English Church, yea to the whole christian world to judge, who shalbe accompted the cause therof, whether he that peaceably and privatly and quietly, desireth to be satisfied in the things wherof he doubteth, or they that imperiously deny him convenient time for that purpose, and doe bind him to such orders and customs, as he can not thinke to be equall.

Afterwards, without the desire or consent of the consistory, the matter was brought into the Classis,[15] they confirmed the writing of the five Ministers, and decreed that conformity therunto should be required of me as a condition whervpon I should be admitted: but I desired the reverend brethren earnestly; not to binde me to that condition, seing that, first, that practise, is grounded upon no authoritie of Gods Word.

Secondly, nor upon any canon of any Synod.

Thirdly, nor is required of any one to be chosen to the Pastorall office, as a condition of their admittance, in any reformed Church.

4lie. This practise is not so absolute, or unlimited in any Churches, as it is required of me.

5lie. It is propounded: as a greivance in many Dutch Churches, from whence they would be delivered and freed if they could.

6lie. It is manifest that the noble and learned Polonian Ioannes Alasco[16] Baron and Superintendent of the Church of strangers in London, in the reigne of Edw. 6th. Did obtaine and that under the

15. This was at an extraordinary classis held at Amsterdam February 17/27 and February 18/28, 1633/4. Nieuwezijds Kapel, Amsterdam, Acta Classis Amstelodamensis, IV, 1631–1645, fol. 35.

16. John Laski or À Lasco, 1499–1560, was superintendent of the church of foreign Protestants in London from 1550 to 1553.

broade seale of England, liberty not to baptize any such (as) against whom I except, which libertie your Dutch Church doe now injoy vnder our most mighty Kinge Charles, and is not in any thing bound unto any of the canons of the Church of England.

Nevertheles Mr. Paget propounded to me in the consistory that I should consider and conclude with my selfe, when I should give my last answer, whether I would promise to baptize all infants, that should be presented to baptisme, refusing none, unto which question, the next weeke I gave (in the same place) this answer, I dare not promise to baptise all that shall be offered therunto: Because the promise of doeing it, is a confession that the thing is lawfull to be done, which I doe not beleeve, yet, because I much prise your love, and desire your peace, I will, if you desire it, continue assisting Mr. Paget a convenient time, such as we shall agree upon, wherin I may make my selfe knowne better to the Dutch Pastors, and obtayne that, by their meanes, this question may be layd aside, and your Church may obtaine liberty therin, and I may more fully understand the other Customs of the Dutch Church and the state of this Churche. This proposition was cheerfully imbraced by the Elders, who consulted about allowing a years time for this purpose, wherunto I hope, you, reverend brethren, will assent. which if you doe, it shalbe my part to endeavour, that neither you may reprent of your benevolence, nor the magistrats of their indulgence, but that many thankes may be given both to you and them, both by Mr. Paget; and by the English Church, by him, for the continuance of an Assistant (such a one as he is) and by it for the preservation of peace amongst them, which all desire, wherunto I pray God to give his blessing, and to inrich you, reverend brethren, with the spirit of wisdom, Christian prudence, and the fear of God, that you may well order this busines. So prayeth.

> IOHN DAVENPORT Englishman, Bachelour
> of divinitie in Oxford. At present, a
> Stranger in Amsterdam.

Certeine Instrvctions delivered to the ELDERS of the English Church deputed, which are to be propounded to the PASTORS of the Dutch Church in Amsterdam.[1]

FIRST, the reverend brethren, Pastors of the Dutch Church under the Classis of Amsterdam, are to be intreated not to accuse Mr. Davenport, as the cause of this trouble, that that particular question concerning baptisme, between Mr. Paget is brought unto them, which by his will, should have been privatly ended between themselves, and the brethren should not have been troubled, more then was necessary with such questions, who have matters of greater moment to take care for in their classicall meeting.

Secondly let them be certified that, for many weightie reasons, Mr. Davenport can not rest in that writing of the five brethren, whose judgment nevertheles, he doth very much esteeme, concerning which matter (though he hath much to say, yet passing by other things) this alone he professeth at present, that his judgment is, that Dr. Ames, his opinion herein is most agreeable vnto the word of God, who in the 4th. booke of his cases of conscience. Chap. 27. Concerning baptisme, (having affirmed that it is nescessary that the Infants to be baptised be in the covenant, in externall profession, and estimation, in their parents, and that their is hope, that they shallbe instructed, and educated in that covenant afterwards, and that at least one of the parents is within the Church, not out of it, doth conclude, that their negligence can by no meanes bee excused, who doe promiscuously admit to baptisme whosoever is offered and by whomsoever.

Thirdly, let them understand, that Mr. Pagets former delayes in this busines of Mr. Davenports call, and his stifnes in that question concerning baptisme, without yealding any brotherly moderation to Mr. Davenport, so much as to beare with him in so small a matter, (as this seemed both to them and him to be) and to take vpon himselfe that which he can doe, (if occasion require, with full perswasion,) but Mr. Davenport can not doe with inward peace, and his rejecting all Mr. Davenports endeavours for a peaceable composing and ending of this difference privatly between themselves, or with the counsell of the Elders of his Church, and certeine sharpe and biting Sermons preached by him, of late, and his privat conferences with certeine

---

1. These instructions were read and delivered to an ordinary classis held at Amsterdam April 22/May 2, 1634. Nieuwezijds Kapel, Amsterdam, Acta Classis Amstelodamensis, IV, 1631–1645, fol. 38. They were subsequently published in W. Best, *A Ivst Complaint Against An Vnivst Doer* (Amsterdam, 1634), pp. 10–12.

persons doe abundantly demonstrate, that Mr. Paget hath no desire that Mr. Davenport should be his Colleague, but doth indevour the hinderance, rather then the furtherance therof.

Lastly. Seing peace and agreement between the Pastors doth much conduce to the edification of the Church, and seing that (for the reasons aforesayd) ther is no hope of peace and christian concord between them, Mr. Davenport being studious of the peace of the Church, his mind is wholy turned from taking upon him the office of Pastor in the English Church, in this cittie, and doth voluntarily desist from his publicke ministry in this place, and doth commend vnto God the brethren in every good worke, and committ himselfe wholy to the only wise father, to be disposed elsewhere, as it shall please his infinit wisdom, to his owne glory. April. 28. An. 1634.

That these instrvctions were written by himselfe, and by himselfe delivered to the Elders deputed, he witnesseth, by subscribing his name,

IOHN DAVENPORT.

JOHN DAVENPORT's Justification of His Conduct in Amsterdam[1]

THE same reason, which constrayned me to write in latin to the Classis, doth now compell me to translate what I then wrote for the satisfaction of the members of the English Church, as then I did not write to them till Mr. Pagets misreport of my opinion (touching the promiscuous baptising of all Infants that are presented therunto) both to the dutch Preachers and others made it necessary: So I have forborne to translate the same, 3. months together, till by injurious speaches of Mr. Pagette concerning that writing, both in the Consistory, and to severall persons, I have been often provoked therunto, for peace sake I have desisted, and purposed to sit still, but I may not let the truth suffer, by my silence, for any mans sake, neither am I so weake to be affrighted with great words, or to forsake a truth, because some men say it is an errour: I have sayd litle in comparison of what I have to say, when I am constrayned to say more, I shall shewe the reason, why I haue hitherto sayd so litle. Be assured that this English Coppie, is a true translation out of the latin, and whatsoever I wrote

1. W. Best, *A Ivst Complaint Against An Vnivst Doer* (Amsterdam, 1634), preface and pp. 9, 12–15.

in latin, is a true report of things as they passed, time will shew that I have ben more favourable in the reporte then I had cause to be.

. . .[2]

Let the reader judge, what I could say less, or more mildly, beinge to give an account of the passages in such a busines? or what passage herein might justly be thought offencive, considering the premises? And who would not have thought, that the Classis wold have approved of the desire of the Consistory, that a years time should be granted me, for the ends aforesayd? yet on the contrary, they seemed to be offended at the writing, threatened to complayn to the Magistrats and after much debate, concluded, that I shall have but a monthes time, in which if I doe not answere, categorically that I will conforme to the orders and customs of the dutch Church, and to this, particularly in question, restinge in the judgment and resolution of the 5. dutch Preachers. and joyne with the Classis, or voluntarily desist, they will complayne to the Magistrats, etc. what remained now to be done, but either voluntary desistance on my part, or violent rejection, on theirs? in this month allso Mr. Paget, both in publick and in privat, shewed his aversenes from my joyning with him more then formerly, wherfore to prevent disturbance in the Church, and further disquietment of my self upon serious consideration and good advise, I voluntarily desisted, and left the ensuing Coppie therof in Lattin and English, with the elders, with this liberty, either to shew or conceale the same, as they shold judge it most expedient, intreating them in these words or in words tending to this purpose, to express my resolution to the Classis.

. . .[3]

Though I have deserved better usage at Mr. Pagets hands for allmost 6. Months assistance of him, and have done and suffered so much to preserve his peace, and the Churches, which if I had not exercised much patience and industry, would certeinly have fallen from him, being over burdened with the losse of so many men, so much desired by the congregation, and other passages, which I will for the present spare to mention, Mr. Paget not content with former Injuries addeth these following.

First he sayth and reporteth, that he hath often desired to dispute or confer with me about this poynt, but that I refused it: wheras he knoweth we were in continuall discourse about it diverse weekes,

2. At this point Davenport gives an English translation of his letter delivered to the classis, March 24/April 3, 1633/4. See above, p. 43.

3. See above, p. 50.

before others knew of the difference, neither should it ever have ben knowne, if any brotherly love had wrought in him, or my advise and desire might have prevayled. In this time there passed 2. or 3. serious conferences between us, wherein this poynt was disputed, which I have in writing by me, nor did I ceasse till he gave over, and sayd, that seeing his judgment could not prevayle with me, he wold leave it now to the dutch Preachers, to see if they could prevayle with me; from which I disswad. earnestly, but in vayne, at last he tould me that he would speake with me alone no more about those matters, from that time I have ceased to come to his house.

Secondly, he reported that I am gone from my promise, for I sayd, I would rest in the writing of the five Ministers, but now I will not, whereas he knoweth that from the first to the last, himselfe never heard me speake any such word, and the night before they went to the Magistrates for their consent to my call,[4] he apprehended my answer rightly, and tould the Elders that he perceived that I did not rest in that writing of the 5. Ministers, further then it made way for an order to be made in the consistory, wherat he shewed himselfe dis-contented.

But one of the Elders sayd so in the consistory.   1. Ob.

That elder denieth that he sayd so, and knoweth that I sayd other-   An. wayes to him, that which he sayd, (as I am informed) was only to quiet Mr. Paget, and therfore told him that some part of that writing with an order to be made in consistory, being ioyned together, would settle things, which is farre from an intimation of any purpose in me to conforme therunto.   2. Obj.

But Mr. Paget would not have gone else to the Magistrate, if he had   An. not understood it to be so? It hath been often cleared, that he misun-derstood that Elder, if he so vnderstood him, and if he wold not upon other termes have gone to the Magistrate, the whole congregation and I am the lesse beholden to him.   3. Obj.

But he did goe to the Magistrat, and at a time when he was not very stronge, and when he came home tould his wife rejoycing, that now the busines is ended, which he would not have done, if he had not so understood it, and if he had not desired to have Mr. Davenport for his colleague.   An.

Vpon his going to the Magistrate, the busines was not ended, for the Magistrate shewed himselfe unsatisfied, concerning the cause of

4. The burgomasters of Amsterdam approved the call of Davenport to the ministry of the English church in Amsterdam January 21/31, 1633/4. Burgomasters' Resolutie-boek, Amsterdam, 1603–1649, p. 102.

my comming over, wherin how litle he spake to give satisfaction is evident, yea, what he answered, might serve rather to increase the suspition, that beinge ended, and the Magistrats satisfied by other meanes, it was so brought about by one of the Dutch Preachers interposing, that the Magistrats gave but a conditionall consent to my call, and made my conformity to this custom of promiscuous baptisinge, the condition therof, so that now matters were in a worse state then before. It is apparent that if Mr. Paget was at that time content to have me joyne with him, it was but conditionally, that I would doe whatsoever he, or the Classis would have me, upon which termes he is content to have others, whom he hath no cause to desire for colleagues with him.

4. Obj.   But Mr. Davenport did purpose to yeald, when he came from England else why would he come over having seene the questions that were put to Mr. Hooker?[5]

An.   He saw the questions in London, above a yeare before his comming over, when he was farre from any thoughtes of comming to Amsterdam, or to any place out of his owne land, and when he did come over he professed, both in England, and here, that he came but for 3. or 4. months, for which time, what need was there of his knowing, much lesse practising or conforming to the customs of the Dutch Church, and when he did consider of that question as it was put to Mr. Hooker, ther was not either in the question or answer, sufficient light to informe him of that, which time hath discovered herein, neither can any man from thence, know what in this custom is to be disliked.

5. Obj.   But Mr. Pa., did so much in that busines, that he sayth, if that were to doe agayne he would not doe it, which sheweth that at that time he desired to have you.

An.   If ever he did desire me, I have given him no cause to repent of it, but to desire it more, vnles he takes offence at this, that I dare not venture vpon doeing that which I account unlawfull, or at this, that I report the truth of things as they passed when I am provoked thervnto.

But it seemes to me that he never did desire it, for these reasons. 1. bec. before I came hither, when he heard I was to come over, he preached publickly against my resigning up my place, which afterward he justified, when I related to him the cause therof, the carriage ther-

5. "Mr. Pagetts 20 Proposicions to Mr. Hooker with his answere thereto:" have been preserved among Additional MSS., 6394, fols. 67–72. After failing to find a niche for himself in the Netherlands, Thomas Hooker returned to England, whence he sailed for New England in 1633.

in, and the consent of many worthy devines, and of the congregation it selfe therunto.

Secondly because severall times he shewed his dislike of my comming hither, without his desire or consent in sending for me, though it is apparent that God sent me hither at a needfull time, when without me they would have been destitute, he being unable to preach, or to come to the Church.

Thirdly, because he delayed the calling of me so long, that the Elders began to be impatient of his delayes, for what reasons he best knoweth.

4lie. because as soone as he found my Iudgm. differing in this poynt from his practise, he discouered how litle he desired me, by refusing all meanes of accomodation, though by them the difference might have been hid, and peremptorily resolving to have it brought into the Classis, though I tould him it would make matters worse, he pretended he might not doe otherwise, though some of the Dutch Preachers, sayd it might be best ended in the Consistory, and wished it might be so, and approved of what I had sayd to Mr. Paget, that matters would be worse else: For it is unlikly that the Classis would make an order in favour of me, to condemn their owne customs.

5lie. He pressed earnestly to have Mr. Balmford of the Hage, though he gave him the same answer to the question which I had done before I came into these parts: and since hath nominated Mr. Roe of Flushing:[6] though he in answer to a letter which Mr. Paget sent to him concerning this matter professed himselfe to be of my judgment.

6lie. Because he hath allwayes so much urged to have one that hath lived some years in this country, and hath hitherto opposed diverse worthy men that have come immediatly from England, my hope is at an end, and I must ceasse.

IOHN DAVENPORT.

---

6. John Row was minister of the English churches at Zwolle sometime between 1620 and 1628, and at Flushing from 1628 to 1645 or 1646. W. Steven, *The History of the Scottish Church, Rotterdam* (Edinburgh, 1832), pp. 306, 344.

JOHN DAVENPORT *to* MARY, Lady VERE[1]

To the Right Honor[a]ble Lady the Lady Vere
present these in Hackney.[2]

Madam)

How much it hath bene against my mind that this letter hath bene so long delayed I need not report to your Honor, who have in your owne hearte, experience of those lively stirrings of affections, towards absent freinds in theyre afflictions, and how unfeigned love, in such cases, causeth a vehement, and restles desire in freinds to be usefull and helpfull to them; as in an oven, where the fire is kept in, the heate is doubled, or as in a streame, where the course of it is stopped, the swellings of it are increased. Shortly after the sad tidings, of the greate breach which God had made in your family[3] was brought on this side the sea, by a flying report, and confirmed by diverse letters, I fell into a relapse, and was the 2d time lett blood for a feavour, and catarrh, and so remayned weake, for a season. Vpon my recovery, I wayted for a convenient messenger, accounting it unsafe to wright

1. British Museum, Additional MSS., 4275, fols. 167–168. An abstract of this letter is printed in A. B. Davenport, *A History and Genealogy of the Davenport Family* (New York, 1851), p. 321. The letter is printed in full in A. B. Davenport, *Supplement* (Stamford, 1876), pp. 361–366. Although Davenport does not state the place from which he wrote, his son was baptized at The Hague, April 15, 1635. (W. Steven, *The History of the Scottish Church, Rotterdam*, Edinburgh, 1832, p. 310.) Furthermore, this letter indicates that he was preaching before Elizabeth, Queen of Bohemia, who at this time resided at The Hague. On the other hand, a letter of Edward Misselden to Sir Francis Windebank, secretary of state, June 26, 1635, indicates that at that date Davenport was associated with Hugh Peter in the ministry of an English church at Rotterdam (*Calendar of State Papers, Domestic Series, 1635*, London, 1865, p. 151), and when Peter departed for New England, Davenport filled his place at Rotterdam, and was settled there by December 15/25, 1635. Possibly Davenport lived at The Hague after leaving Amsterdam and before settling at Rotterdam.

2. Sometime after the baptism of Susan Vere, March 20, 1619, and before the marriage of Elizabeth Vere, September 24, 1626, Lord and Lady Vere moved from their house or lodgings in the parish of St. Bartholomew the Great, London, to a house at Clapton, in the parish of Hackney, Middlesex, now a borough of Greater London. C. R. Markham, *The Fighting Veres* (Boston, 1888), p. 433.

3. Horace, Lord Vere, Baron of Tilbury, died May 2, 1635. "My Lord of *Tilbury* was buried this Week with much military Pomp here in *Westminster*, he dropp'd down suddenly at Sir *Henry Vane's* Table, and died a little after of an Apoplexy." James Howell to Thomas Wentworth, subsequently created Earl of Strafford, Westminster, May 14, 1635. *The Earl of Strafforde's Letters and Dispatches* (2 vols., London, 1739), I, 423. "While dining with Sir Harry Vane, The Hague envoy and his diplomatic friend, at Whitehall on 2 May 1635, he was seized with an apoplectic fit and died within two hours." T. Seccombe in *Dictionary of National Biography*.

by the post, least my letters should be opened by others, as some formerly have bene. And now having a conveyance that answereth my desire, oh that I were able to satisfy my desire also, in wrighting fully, and effectually to the settling, and comforting of your hearte! But that worke is above mans power. It is a glory incommunicably proper to God to be the giver of consolacion, and to his spirit to be the author of comfort: yet, seing there are breasts of consolation, thorough which spirituall refreshm[en]ts are supplyed to the hearts of beleivers, which are called the comforts of the scriptures, and that this duety lyeth upon all christians, with these words, to comfort one another, and as any members are nearer in the body joyned together, then others, so to be more speedy, and industrious in this worke, I am bold to attempt, at least so farr as may serve to express my sympathy with your La[dyshi]p, in this affliction: which is not a private cause of sorrow to your Honor alone, and to your Noble family, but a publick cause, wherein many are interested; my selfe especially, and above many, to whom his heart was enlarged and his mouth opened. With what assurance of good acceptance was I wont to speake, wright, resort to him? How strongly did that plainnes of heart tempered with much wisdom, that softnes and pliablenes of his spirit in respect of God, and his word accompanied with a magnanimous undantednes in fight with an adversary, that serious dislike of apparent evills in others, testifyed by a studious avoyding them in himselfe, knitt myne heart unto him? Yea the workings of his affections, were not weake, but strong. 1. towards God, whose favour he præferred above all things, as appeared in the many questions and cases he hath putt, for clearing to his owne heart, the assurance of his acceptance with God, and in the complacency and content wherewith he received discourses tending that way, 2, towards the word of God, which was sweet to him being dispensed publickly in the ministry, or privatly, in christian conference. 3. towards the people of God, ministers, and others, whom the more they excelled in the fruits of holynes, and righteousnes, the more he delighted in, countenanced, and incouraged, 4, towards the waies of God, whereunto he applyed himselfe carefully (so farr as he was inlightned and convinced) both in his publick command, and governm[en]t in the field, and in his private comportm[en]t in his family, resolving with Joshua that he and his houshold would serve the Lord.[4] Hence sprang his care to sanctifye the Lords day with his family, at home, as well as in the assembly: hence the daily sacrifice of

4. Joshua 24. 15.

invocation of the name of God continued morning and evening without interruption, or omission in his family: hence, his procuring that the soules committed to his trust, servants as well as children, might be taught to know, and feare God, by some able and faythfull man weekely, who was maintained for that service in his family: yea, hence arose that ardency of spirituall affections towards the salvacion of his children desiring nothing more then that they might serve God aright, and be instruments of his glory, in theyre severall places. In all which, and in other particulars, God made your La[dyshi]p an helper meet for him, yea a quickner, and encourager of him in that way, wherein you walked together as heyres of the Grace of life. So that, you cannot but have comfort in his death, when you call to mind his life: and the testimony of your conscience concerning your carriage towards him, and conversation with him (which was such as became a daughter of Sarah) whilest he lived with you, may now be your rejoycing, when he is taken from you. Vpon both which consideracions you may say to your owne heart as David, I shall returne to him, though he shall not returne to me,[5] and with that assurance quiett, and releive your spirit, as he did. Yea, looke higher (Madam) from the dead to the living. The relation which once you had to this earthly husband is ended, and ceaseth in his death, but the relation you have to our heavenly husband remayneth inviolable; with whom you communicate in all his Honours with all saints (with whom you are sett together in heavenly places in christ) and in his acceptance with the father, to whom he prayed, that the love wherewith he loved him may be on vs, and we in him. ffrom him you may expect protection, and supply of all good; for all is yours, and you christs, and christ Gods. So that it is but a conduit pipe that is broken; the fountaine being still open to you. Nor is he taken away, before you had warning of it, in a sensible decay, which a litle while hence might have come to such a pass as might have bene burthensom to himselfe, and uncomfortable to your La[dyshi]p. Ah, but he died out of his owne house, of a vomitt, which he could never beare? And doeth not God order time, place, and meanes, by his providence, to his owne prayse? An hayre of our head perisheth not without his providence, much lesse are our lives taken away without it. I will say of him as it is sayd of David, When he had served his time by the appointm[en]t of God, then he slept with his fathers.[6] But there was some other circumstance that made it greivous, it may be, that you thinck not fitt to utter. Be it

5. 2 Samuel 12. 23.
6. 1 Kings 2. 10.

what it may be. Even that is ordered by Gods hand, for some speciall end. It may be it would not have bene so heavy, in your sense, vnles that grayne had bene added, and then the tryall would not have bene so full. God so ordereth the tryalls of his servants that patience may have its perfect worke: which if it be effected in your Ladiship, by this tryall, you shall be intire, lacking nothing. Therefore when sense pleadeth to increase your sorrow, if this circumstance had not bene his death had not bene so greivous to be borne; lett fayth answer, if this circumstance had not made it so greivous, my patience had not bene so tryed, nor my submission to Gods good pleasure so fully manifested. I know, there is much difference betweene the proposall of a duety and the practise, and that, after the judgment is gayned to acknowledge the trueth and æquity of it; the will and affections are not instantly inclined to it as the best way for me, in this case: and after the will is thus wraught to the approving of it, a christian is not presently able perfectly to doe it, but he goeth about it somewhat un-skillfully, and is weake and defective in practise of it. Wherefore it will be meete to add one word or two, for your helpe therein, that you may indure chastning, which is made a noate to difference betweene punishments wherewith bastards are afflicted, and chastisements wherewith children are excercised. If you indure chastisements (sayth the Apostle Heb. 12. 5. 6.) God offereth himselfe to you as a father to his children. As if he should say, the same outward judgment may be fall a sonne and a bastard, a sonne in way of chastisment, and a bastard in way of punishment. And you shall know in which of these conditions you are, by your induring it. A sonne indureth chastisment, a bastard cannot. But, you will say, what is required to a right indur-ing of it? I answer, to a right induring of affliction it is required, first, that the understanding doe rightly apprehend and conceive of the affliction in all the causes of it. 1. that it is our heavenly father that doeth it. This made christ say, shall not I drinck of the cup that my father will have me drinck of.[7] 2. that in love he doeth it; As a father correcteth the child which he loveth; so doeth the Lord every sonne that he receiveth. 3. that he doth it for your good. He corrects us for our good, sayth the Apostle, that we may be partakers of his holynes.[8] 2dly, it is required that the will submitt to Gods hand, not onely without murmuring and repining, so David sayd, I was as dumbe, and opened not my mouth:[9] because it was thy doing; but also with con-

7. S. John 18. 11.
8. Hebrews 12. 10.
9. Psalms 38. 13.

tented quieting your selfe in Gods good pleasure, as old Eli sayd, It is the Lord, lett him doe what seemeth good in his owne eyes;[10] yea, blessing and praysing him, in giving to him the glory of his wisdom, and faythfullnes and fatherly goodnes: as Job concluded, in the losse of all, Blessed be the name of the Lord:[11] which that you may doe, you must resolve that such a condition, at such a time, and in such and such circumstances is ordered by his wisdom and counsails for the best to you, and your La[dyshi]p shall find it so in the end, after you have bene excercised thereby. 3dly, it is required that the affections be rightly ordered to a right induring of chastisment, as to love him, and feare him, and greive for having displeased him, and rejoyce in tribulation, under the assurance of his love now shed abroad in your heart, and under the hope of glory to come, which these light afflictions, which are but for a moment, cause unto beleivers or fitt, and prepare them for, whilest they looke not upon things which are seene, but upon things which are not seene: ffor the things which are seene are temporall, but the things that are not seene are æternall. All this you shall be the more fitt to doe, if in all the changes of this pilgrimage, you looke up to God as reconciled to you in Christ, and upon your afflictions as sweetened, and sanctifyed to you in the sufferings of christ, by whom you have received the attonement, the justice of God being satisfyed, and his wrath pacifyed and appeased by him, for your sake. The Lord seale the assurance hereof to your Ladiship (to whom, I am persuaded, it certainly appertaineth) by his holy spirit, of promise which is the earnest of our inheritance for the redemption purchased by christ! And by the same spirit, the Lord open the eyes of your understanding that you may comprehend with all saints the hight, and depth, and breadth, and length of his love to you in christ, which passeth knowledge! And I pray God to strengthen you by his spirit in the inward man that you may doe his will in all things with childlike obedience, and in all things suffer his will with childlike patience! Amen. So praying I rest

July. 21. 1635   Your Honorable Ladiships much obliged
                                    in the Lord Jesus

                                    JOHN DAVENPORTE

Good, Madam, pardon the blotts, and ill wrighting which were caused by much hast, wherein I was constrayned to wright, at this time, my selfe also being in some distractions by the vnquiett spirit of

10. 1 Samuel 3. 18.
11. Job 1. 21.

the old man, who to all his former injuryes addeth this, that he hath now published a tedious booke[12] in English full of reproaches and slanders against me, wherein also he doeth injury to Mr. Parker,[13] Doctor Ames, and Mr. Forbes,[14] who are at rest, and Mr. Hooker, who is farr absent, and to the best members of his owne church, whom he brandeth severall wayes, which will give the prælats too much advantage, and open the mouths of enimyes against the trueth. This I am now constrayned to answer for the trueths sake, notwithstanding all my former weakenes.[15] But our God is strong, in whom I trust that he will strengthen me to wright with such a spirit as I aught. Helpe me with your prayers. And, if any speake of Mr. Pagets booke, lett them know that I am about to answer it, and shall discover many untruthes in it, and a misreporting of the question betweene him, and me.

It may be of good use to prevent præjudice in the Queene,[16] if your Honor, when you are pleased to wright to her, and my Lady Leveston,[17] take notice of theyre favour to me, and pray them not to be præjudiced by any suggestions against me, from that booke or otherwise till they may peruse my answer. This I desire not for any use I have of the Queenes favour but that shee may not be hindred from receiving good by my ministry, which yet she well esteemeth.

12. John Paget published *An Answer to the Unjust Complaints of William Best,* . . . *Also, An Answer to Mr. John Davenport: touching . . . his Allegations of Scripture against the Baptizing of some kind of Infants;* . . . at Amsterdam in 1635. For a summary, see B. Hanbury, *Historical Memorials relating to the Independents, or Congregationalists* (3 vols., London, 1839–44), I, 527–546.

13. Robert Parker was a Puritan divine who fled to the Netherlands in 1607. For a time he served the English congregation at Amsterdam as elder and as scribe of the consistory but he apparently was kept out of the pastorate. He removed to Doesburg, Gelderland, where he died in 1614.

14. John Forbes was pastor of English congregations at Middelburg from 1611 to 1621 and at Delft from 1621 until his removal sometime before his death in 1634.

15. See above, p. 42n.

16. Elizabeth, the daughter of James I, sister of Charles I, and widow of Frederick, Elector Palatine and King of Bohemia.

17. On September 6, 1653, an annuity of £60 that had been granted by Charles I to Margaret, Lady Livingstone, wife of James Livingstone, created Lord Livingstone of Almond in 1633, and first Earl of Callander in 1641, for services rendered to the Queen of Bohemia, was more than eight years in arrears. *Calendar of State Papers, Domestic Series, 1653–1654* (London, 1880), p. 135.

JOHN DAVENPORT *to* MARY, LADY VERE[1]
*To the Right Honorable Lady the Lady Vere
pr[e]sent these in Hackney. Per a freind*

Madam)

HAVING so good an opportunity as this, by the favour this bearer
your ancient servant hath done me to acquaint me with his
purpose of returning for England, I cannot neglect to present your
Hono[u]r with a few lines in expression of my thanckfullnes for my
wives intertainm[en]t to wayte upon your La[dyshi]p in your house,
where she was much refreshed shortly after her arrivall in England,
and for the Continuance of your noble favour and affection expressed
in those wellcome lines which I received by Mr. Balmford, whose
Coming to me was a matter of much joy, both for his returne, as it
were, from prison,[2] and for the good newes of your La[dyshi]ps health,
and the hope which he gave me of your recovering that inward Comfort which outward afflictions had much abated. I Confess; I often
wished my selfe neare your La[dyshi]p, not that I thaught my selfe
able to strengthen your spirit with more healing and comforting words
then were ministred by diverse, but that I might shew the sincerity of
my desires to be in my measure serviceable for the helpe of your fayth
and joy. Which seing I cannot doe in presence as I desired and hoped;
my desire is to performe, as I may, in this papery intercourse. I know,
Madam, upon much experience of your way, that you have right in
Christ to those treasures of spirituall good things which are layed up
in him for the vessels of mercy, take your fill of them and be satisfyed
out of the wells of consolation. Are those treasures hidden? They are
in christ for you. Christ himselfe is yours and whatsoever is his for
your good. His father is your father by Adoption; his God is your God
by the Covenant of Grace, by vertue whereof all the promises are
your evidences for better hopes then the world can give. Your present
afflictions are amongst your priviledges which are sweetned by your
fathers love and sanctifyed by his spirit to the drawing of you from

1. British Museum, Additional MSS., 4275, fols. 169–170. An extract from this letter
occurs in A. B. Davenport, *A History and Genealogy of the Davenport Family* (New York,
1851), pp. 321–322. The letter is printed in full in A. B. Davenport, *Supplement* (Stamford, 1876), pp. 366–368.

2. On October 8, 1635, Samuel Balmeford, clerk, appeared before the Court of High
Commission and was judicially admonished to appear again personally within forty
days after intimation left at the house of one of his sureties, and with this admonition
he was licensed to depart to his charge in the Low Countries. *Calendar of State Papers,
Domestic Series, 1635–1636* (London, 1866), p. 82; *1637* (London, 1868), pp. 258–259.

insnaring vanities to a sweet communion with himselfe. He hath many wayes of doing you good which you know not of, and delighteth to doe above our thaughts that his wayes may appeare to be not as our wayes, but as farr above them as heaven is above earth. Whilest your spirit is troubled about the sad thaught of your losses, wants, sorrowes, give me leave to remind it of your gaines, supplyes, comforts. Have you obtained more acquaintance with God, more to be wayned from the creature, more fervency in prayer, more fitnes of spirit to resigne up your will, and wayes to the appointment and dispose of your heavenly father? The gayne doth abundantly recomppence and weigh downe your loss. Is a spirit of fayth supplyed inabling you to depend upon God reconciled to you in christ, a spirit of love, to compose your spirit to quiett itselfe in the good pleasure of a wise and loving father, a spirit of wisdom to guide your mind by a right discerning betweene things that differ, to chuse that which is most excelent, both in respect of the end and of the meanes? Whatsoever your spirituall or outward wants are; in your apprehension; such a supply is made by the good hand of a gracious God as may turne your complaints into thanksgiving. Can you rejoyce in tribulation under the hope of Glory, in Casting off the burthen of your cares upon him that careth for you, in that liberty which christ hath purchased for you of access to the throne of Grace, in that interest you have in his mediation who is your husband, surety, advocate at the right hand of God? Be your sorrowes what they Can; your joyes are greater, and as your tribulations abound, your consolations abound much more. Lay these things together, and compare your losses with your gaines, your wants with your supplyes, your sorrowes with your comforts and you will say, that you are not abased but exalted, filled not emptied, not cast off, though cast downe, but accepted, beloved, blessed. The hast of the bearer calleth me off. The good Lord perswade your heart effectually of his love, whereof you have much cause to be fully assured in christ! Ah that I Could be of any use for the service of your fayth! many ingagements bind me to it. No one shall be more ready to doe it then my selfe, who am more obliged then many. But what can a poore pilgrim, a banished man doe? That which I may performe in this condition shall not be wanting in prayers to God, or in letters to your selfe, as the knowledge of your condition or necessity shall minister occasion. I must cease wrighting, for the present, but ever remayne in vnfeigned thanckfullnes and faythfullnes

Your honourable Ladiships much obliged
in the Lord Jesus

Rotterd. $\frac{15}{25}$ December. 1635

JOHN DAVENPORT

JOHN DAVENPORT *to* MARY, Lady VERE[1]

To the Right Honor[a]ble the Lady Mary Vere present these

Madam)

THE report of that greate breach which it hath pleased the Divine providence to make in that family,[2] wherein you are so much interested, did at first somewhat astonish me, but after some recollection of my thaughts it affected me with sorrow and pitty: with sorrow for the publick loss, wherein the wholl land suffereth by the fall of such a pillar, whose wisdom and publick spirit made him of singular use, not to Norfolke onely, in his prudent managing of the governm[en]t committed to him for the good of many, but to the wholl realme, in his strong complyance with the best affected patriots in parliam[en]ts, for the promoving of any proffitable proposalls and motions for the good of the wholl nation: with pitty and compassion to his good Lady, and the tender branches, whose loss I would rather vayle then expresse, knowing how sensible love maketh us of the want of that comfort which is more deare to us then our eyes, and more usefull to us then our hands, and which we would chuse rather to injoy, in the want of all outward things, then to want in the injoym[en]t of all things. Nor can I looke aside from your La[dyshi]p (Madam) whose former wound[3] not fully cured, I feare, this occasion causeth to bleed afresh, wherewith I am the more affected, when I remember how fearfull you were, because of the infection in these parts, least by your coming thither any infection or sicknes by any of yours might be brought into the family; in which respect, the Lord hath dealt mercifully for the helpe of your spirit that this sad accident befell not at your first coming thither, nor till halfe a yeare was past, that your heart might be perfectly freed from that cause of sorrow. Nor lett

1. British Museum, Additional MSS., 4275, fols. 162–163. An extract from this letter is printed in A. B. Davenport, *A History and Genealogy of the Davenport Family* (New York, 1851), pp. 317–318. The letter is printed in full in Massachusetts Historical Society *Proceedings*, XLII (Boston, 1909), 211–212. Although no place of writing and date are given, this letter was probably written in or near London early in the year 1637, while the Davenport–Eaton company awaited the release of the ship *Hector*, which was to carry them to New England.

2. Sir Roger Townshend of Rainham, Norfolk, the husband of Mary Vere, second daughter of Lord and Lady Vere, died January 1, 1636/7. He left two sons, Roger, who died as a minor in 1648, and Horace, first Viscount Townshend, and four daughters. His widow married Mildmay Fane, Earl of Westmoreland, at Hackney, June 21, 1638. By this second marriage she had two sons, Vere, Earl of Westmoreland, and Horace Fane, and four daughters.

3. The death of Horace, Lord Vere, May 2, 1635.

your tender apprehension of your owne demerits Cause in you a suspicion that in wrath to your selfe this sorrow and loss is fallen upon your daughter and that Noble family, knowing that our daies are appointed by an æternall decree, and the number of the houres of mans life is to be found onely in that booke where all things were written before they were fashioned. I rather account it a mercy to your Noble daughter that this greate affliction fell at such time when your presence might be a comfort and support to her dejected spirit, which also is some helpe to your selfe, who, I feare, would have bene swallowed up of greife, if the affection of motherly care for your daughter did not somewhat prevayle against your sorrow and mittigate it, by turning the streame of your love (at least in a great measure) into another channell. And indeed, Madam, excess of sorrow will be at this time unseasonable in your La[dyshi]p, whom God hath sent thither and stayed there by a speciall hand of providence for another use, whereunto immoderate greife will dissable you, viz., for the comfort of your daughter, and for the helpe of those litle ones who are your owne, in a great part, as Ruths child was Naomies, give me leave to add that the Lord hath more plentifully provided for your comfort, Madam, after the death of your husband and sonne in law then for Naomi: For her owne sonne died and her daughter in law lived, but your owne daughter is spared, though your sonne in law be taken away. And for Ruths one sonne you have 2 sonnes and 4 daughters added to your Honorable family, and the life of your daughter spared both for theyre good and your comfort. Which mercy I will express in the words of the Israelitish woemen to Noomi (onely altering the number) Blessed be the Lord which hath not left thee this day without kinsmen, and theyre name shall be continued in Israel, And this shall bring thy life agayne, and cherish thine old age: for thine owne daughter, which loveth thee, hath borne unto him and she is better to thee then seven sonnes.[4] I must now crave pardon that I putt an end to this wrighting sooner then I purposed being hurryed away by unexpected buisenes which forbidds my stay any longer. The good Lord seale up the discovery of his love in your heart by the Holy Ghost, to the sanctifying and sweetning of this bitter pill! Amen.

Your Honorable La[dyshi]ps in the Lord

JOHN DAVENPORTE

[Endorsed] Mr. Davenport's letters to my Lady Vere.

4. Ruth 4. 14–15.

JOHN DAVENPORT and THEOPHILUS EATON *to* the GOVERNOR, DEPUTY GOVERNOR, ASSISTANTS, and COURT OF MASSACHUSETTS BAY[1]

To the much Honored the Governour Deputy and Assistents etc.

IT may please the worthy and much Honored Governo[u]r, Deputy, and Assistants, and, with them, the present Courte, to take knowledge that our Desire of staying within this patent was Reall and Strong, if the eye of Gods providence (to whom we have committed our Waies especially in so important an enterprise as this, which, we confess, is farr above our Capacityes) had guided us to a place Convenient for our familyes, and for our freinds. Which as our words have often expressed, so, we hope, the trueth thereof is sufficiently declared by our almost nine moneths patient wayting in expectacion of some opportunity to be offered us, for that end, to our great charge and hindrance, many waies. In all which time we have, in many prayers commended the guidance of our apprehensions, judgm[en]ts, spirits, resolucions and wayes into the good hand of the onely wise God, whose prærogative it is to determine the bounds of our habitacions according to the ends for which he hath brought us into these Countryes, and we have considered, as we were able, by his helpe, whatsoever place hath bene propounded to us, being ready to have, with Contentm[en]t, accepted (if by our stay any publick good might be promoved) smaller Accomodacions, and upon dearer termes (if they might be moderatly commodious) then, we beleive, most men, in the same Case with us, in all respects, would have done. And, whereas a place for an Inland plantacion, beyond Watertowne, was propounded

---

1. New York Public Library, Winthrop–Davenport Papers; printed in John Winthrop, *The History of New England from 1630 to 1649* (2 vols., Boston, 1825–26), I, 404–405; (2 vols., Boston, 1853), I, 484–486; Massachusetts Historical Society *Collections*, 3d series, III (Cambridge, 1833), 165–167; A. B. Davenport, *A History and Genealogy of the Davenport Family* (New York, 1851), pp. 323–325; "Winthrop–Davenport Papers," New York Public Library, *Bulletin*, III (New York, 1899), pp. 393–394. Theophilus Eaton was an inhabitant of the parish of St. Stephen, Coleman Street, London, a member of both the Eastland Company and the Massachusetts Bay Company, and joint leader with Davenport of the company of colonists that arrived at Boston from England, June 26, 1637. After vainly searching for a suitable place of settlement within the limits of the colony of Massachusetts Bay, the group turned toward the northern shore of Long Island Sound. At the time this letter was written, John Winthrop was governor, Thomas Dudley, deputy governor, and Richard Bellingham, John Humphrey, John Endecott, John Winthrop, Jr., Roger Harlakenden, Increase Nowell, Simon Bradstreet, Israel Stoughton, and Richard Saltonstall, magistrates of Massachusetts Bay.

to us, and pressed with much importunity by some, whose words have the power of a law with us, in any way of God, we did speedily, and seriously deliberate thereupon, it being the subject of the greatest part of a Dayes discourse: The conclusion was, that, if the upland should answer the meddow ground in goodnes and desirablenes (whereof yet there is some ground of doubting) yet, considering that a Boate cannot pass from the Bay thither, nearer then 8 or 10 miles distance, and that it is so remote from the Bay, and from any towne, we could not see how our dwelling there would be advantagious to these plantacions, or Compatible with our Conditions, or Commodious for our familyes, or for our freinds: Nor can we satisfye our selves that it is expedient for our selves, or for our freinds, that we chuse such a condition, wherein we must be compelled to have our dwelling houses so farr distant from our Farmes, as Boston, or Charles towne is from that place, few of our freinds being able to beare the charge thereof (whose Cases nevertheles we are bound to consider) and some of them that are able not being persuaded that it is lawfull for them to live continually from the greatest part of theyre familyes, as, in this Case, they would be necessitated to doe. The season of the yeare, and other weighty Consideracions, compelled us to hasten to a full and finall Conclusion which we are, at last, Come unto, by Gods appointm[en]t and direction, we hope, in mercy, and have sent letters to Connectacutt for a speedy transacting the purchass of the parts about Quillypieck[2] from the Natives which may pretend title thereunto. By which Act we are Absolutely, and irrevocably ingaged that way, and we are persuaded that God will order it for good unto these plantacions, whose love so abundantly, above our desarts, or expectacions, expressed, in your desire of our abode in these parts, as we shall ever retaine in thanckfull memory, so we shall account our selves thereby obliged to be any way instrumentall, and serviceable for the Common good of these plantacions as well as of those: which the Divine providence hath Combined together in as strong a bond of Brotherly affection, by the samenes of theyre condition, as Joab and Abishai were, whose severall armyes did mutually strengthen them boath against severall enimyes. 2. Sam. 10. 9. 10. 11. or rather they are joyned together, as Hippocrates[3] his Twinnes, to stand, and fall, to growe, and

2. Quinnipiac, on September 1, 1640, named Newhaven, the present New Haven, Connecticut. The first purchase of land at Quinnipiac from the Indians was not made until November 24, 1638. *New Haven Colonial Records, 1638–1649* (Hartford, 1857), pp. 1–5.

3. A Greek philosopher and physician living in the fifth and fourth centuries, B.C.

decay, to flourish, and wither, to live and dye together. In witnes of the premises, we subscribe our names

The 12th day   JOHN DAVENPORTE.
of the first moneth   THEOPH: EATON.
Anno 1638.

[Endorsed] Th[eo]p[hilus] Eaton Leter to the Court[, in a seventeenth-century hand; and] Theophilus Eaton and John Davenport. March 12th. *1638.* [in a modern hand.]

JOHN DAVENPORT's Profession of Faith[1]

I beleeve with all my heart, and confesse with my mouth.

1. Concerning the Scriptures.

THAT all Scripture is by divine inspiration, or inbreathing of God (by Scripture I mean the books of the old Testament as *Moses* and the Prophets, and of the new Testament) and is profitable for doctrine, for reproofe, for correction, for instruction in righteousnesse, that the man of God may be perfect, throughly furnished unto all good works. 1 *Tim.* 3. 16, 17. and that in all things which concern faith, and obedience, whether in Gods worship, or in the whole conversation of men, it holdeth forth a most perfect rule, whereunto nothing may be added, nor from it may ought be diminished. *Deut.* 4. 2. *Revel.* 22. 18, 19. Which also is so clear in all truths necessary to salvation, that the entrance into it giveth light, yea, understanding to the simple. *Psal.* 19 7.

2. *Concerning the Godhead in the* $\begin{cases} Vnity\ of\ Essence,\ and \\ Trinity\ of\ Persons. \end{cases}$

That God is a Spirit most holy, immutable, eternall, every way infinite, in greatnesse, goodnesse, power, wisedome, justice, truth, and in all divine perfections, 1 *Tim.* 6. 15, 16. *Joh.* 4. 24. *Isa.* 6. 6. *Exod.* 34. 6, 7. And that in this Godhead are three distinct Persons, coeternall, coequall, and coessentiall, being every one of them one and the same God, not three Gods, and therefore not divided in essence,

---

1. *The Profession Of The Faith Of That Reverend and worthy Divine Mr. J. D. sometimes Preacher of Stevens Coleman-street. London. Made publiquely before the Congregation at his Admission into one of the Churches of God in New-England* (London, 1642). A church was gathered at Quinnipiac or New Haven August 21 or 22, 1639, and Davenport's profession was probably made at that time.

nature, or being, *Deut.* 4. 3. but distinguished one from another by their severall, and peculiar relative property, the Father is of none but of himself, the Son is begotten of the Father before all worlds; the holy Ghost proceedeth from the Father and the Son, from all eternity, all together are to be worshipped and glorified.

3. *Concerning the Decrees of God.*

That God hath unchangeably decreed in himself from everlasting, touching all things, great and small, necessary, contingent, and voluntary, with all the circumstances of them, to work, and dispose them according to the counsell of his own will (yet without being Author of, or having fellowship with the sins of any) to the praise and glory of his great Name. And touching the eternall estate of men that God hath according to his most wise, free, and unchangeable purpose in himself, before the foundation of the world chosen some in Jesus Christ to eternall life, to the praise and glory of his grace, and rejected or reprobated others to the praise of his justice.

4. *Concerning Creation, and Providence.*

That in the beginning God made by his Word all things of nothing very good, and made man male and female after his own Image righteous; and as a faithfull Creator doth still uphold, dispose, and govern all things to the ends for which they were created, having care especially for man, and amongst men chiefly for the righteous and beleevers; so that neither good nor evil befalls any man without Gods providence.

5. *Concerning the fall of man and originall sin.*

That inasmuch as *Adam* was the root of all mankinde, the law and covenant of works was given to him, as to a publike person, and to an head from whence all good or evil was to be derived to his posteritie: seeing therefore that by the subtilty of the Serpent, which Satan used as his instrument, first *Eve*, then *Adam* being seduced, did wittingly and willingly fall into the disobedience of the Commandment of God; Death came upon all justly, and reigned over all, yea, over Infants also which have not sinned after the like manner of the transgression of *Adam:* hence also it is, that all since the fall of *Adam* are begotten in his own likenesse, after his Image, being conceived and born in iniquitie, and so by nature children of wrath, dead in trespasses and sins, altogether filthie and polluted throughout in soul and body; utterly averse from any spirituall good, strongly bent to all evill, and subject to all calamities due to sin in this world, and forever.

6. *Concerning mans Restitution.*

That all Mankind being thus fallen, yet the elect, and only they, are redeemed, reconciled to God, and saved not of themselves, neither by their own works, but onely by the mighty power of God, of his unsearchable, rich, free grace and mercy through faith, in Jesus Christ, who of God is made unto us wisedom, righteousnesse, sanctification, and redemption; in the relation both of a surety to satisfie Gods justice for us, and of an head to restore the Image of God that was lost, and repaire the nature that was corrupted in us.

7. *Concerning the Person and natures in Christ.*

That the Lord Jesus of whom *Moses* and the Prophets wrote, and whom the Apostles preached, is, as touching his Person, the everlasting Son of God the Father by eternall generation, coessentiall, coequall, and coeternall, God with him, and with the holy Ghost: by whom he made the world, and by whom he upholdeth and governs all the works he hath made: who also when the fulnesse of time was come, was made of a woman, of the Tribe of *Judah*, of the seed of *David* and *Abraham*, *viz.* of *Mary* that blessed Virgin, by the holy Ghost coming upon her, and the power of the most high over-shadowing her; and was in all things like unto us, sin onely excepted: so that in the person of Christ the two natures, the divine, and humane, are truly, perfectly, indivisibly, and distinctly united.

8. *Concerning the Offices of Christ.*

That Jesus Christ is the onely Mediatour of the new Testament, even of the Covenant of grace between God and man; the Prophet, Priest, and King of the Church of God for evermore; and this office is so proper to Christ, as, neither in the whole, nor any part thereof, it can be transferred from him to any other. And to this office he was from everlasting, and in respect of his Manhood, from the wombe, called, separated, and anointed most fully with all necessary gifts, as it is written, God hath not measured out of the Spirit unto him.

9. *Concerning Christs propheticall Office.*

That Christ hath perfectly revealed the whole will of God, so far as it is needfull for his people either joyntly, or severally to know, beleeve, or obey, and that he hath spoken, and doth speak to his Church, in his own ordinances by those instruments whom he sendeth, and by his Spirit.

10. *Concerning the Priesthood of Christ.*

That Christ being consecrated hath appeared once to put away sin, by the offering and sacrificing of himself, and hath fully performed and suffered all those things, by which, God through the blood of his crosse, in a sacrifice of a sweet smelling savour, might be reconciled to his elect; and having broken down the partition wall, and finished and removed those ceremoniall rites, and shadows, is now entred into the most holy place, (not made with hands) to the very heavens and presence of God, where he forever liveth, and sitteth at the right hand of Majestie, to make intercession for such as come unto the throne of grace by that new and living way: and he maketh his people a spirituall house, and an holy Priesthood to offer up spirituall sacrifices acceptable to God through him.

11. *Concerning Christs Kingly Office.* 1. *In generall.*

That Christ being risen from the dead ascended up to heaven, set at the right hand of God the Father, hath all power in heaven and earth given to him, and doth exercise his power in his government of this world over all Angels and men, good, and bad, to the preservation and salvation of his elect, and to the ruling and destruction of the reprobate: communicating and applying to his elect, the benefits, vertue, and fruit of his prophecie, and priesthood to their regeneration, justification, sanctification, preservation, and strengthening in all their spirituall conflicts against Satan, the world, and the flesh, continually dwelling in them by his holy Spirit, begetting and nourishing in them faith, hope, love, repentance, obedience, with peace and joy unto immortalitie: but on the contrary, limiting, using, restraining the reprobates his enemies by his mighty power, as seemeth good in his divine wisdome and justice, to their seduction, hardning, and condemnation, till his appearing in glory with his mighty Angels to judge both quick and dead; where he will be and separate all his elect from them for ever, punishing the wicked with everlasting perdition from his presence; and joyning together the godly with himself in endlesse glory.

12. *Concerning his Kingdom.* 2. *In speciall.*

That in the mean time besides his absolute rule in the world, Christ hath here on earth a spirituall Kingdom in his Church, which he hath purchased and redeemed to himself as a peculiar inheritance; into the body whereof he doth by the power of his Word and Spirit, gather his people, calling them through the ministery of the Gospel out of the world, and from idolatrie, superstition, and from all the works of darknesse to fellowship with Jesus Christ, and by him with the Father, and the holy Ghost, and with his people, making them a royall Priest-hood, an holy nation, a people set at libertie to shew forth the vertues of him that hath called them out of darknesse into his marvellous light, and uniteth them together as members of one body in his faith, love, and holy order unto all generall and mutuall duties: and instructs and governs them by those instruments and ordinances which he him-self hath prescribed in his Word for the edification of his bodie the Church.

13. *Concerning the Application of Redemption.*

That the holy Ghost is sent by the Father and the Son to make ap-plication of Redemption onely to those whom the Father hath by his eternall Decree given to Christ, and for whom Christ maketh inter-cession to his Father, and whom the Father accepts in Christ unto fellowship of the everlasting covenant of his free grace, having called them out of the world to fellowship with Jesus Christ by the Gospel made effectuall to that end, by the mightie power and operation of the holy Ghost. Which grace of effectuall calling is thus dispensed to a poore lost sinner awakened and humbled by the Law through the effectuall working of the spirit of bondage, judging himself worthy to be destroyed for his sins, and seeing himself utterly destitute of all help or hope of himself; The Lord in the preaching of the Gospel by the powerfull work of the holy Ghost, revealeth the fulnesse and all-suf-ficiencie of that grace, and salvation which is laid up in Jesus Christ, as the onely sutable good to him, that he also enableth him spiritually and savingly to apprehend Jesus Christ as given him of the Father. And the same Spirit having thus inlightned him, doth leav a super-naturall vertue, and impression of Gods love upon the soul, whereby the soul is drawn to close with Christ, and with that grace of God in him, so entirely that there is now nothing between Christ and the soul, but it willingly parts with all things that hinder his injoying of Christ; and by this effectuall calling all that are brought to Christ, are, 1. justi-fied, that is, absolved from sin and death, and accounted righteous unto life, for, and through Christ apprehended, received, and relied upon by faith. 2. They are adopted, that is, accepted for Christs sake to the dignitie of Gods children; they are also, 3. sanctified, that is, really changed by degrees from the impurity of sin, to the puritie of Gods Image; and lastly, they are glorified, that is, changed from the miserie or punishment of sin, unto everlasting happinesse, which begins in the inward sense of Gods love to them in Christ, whence they have hope of glory, boldnesse in accesse to God, certainty of salvation, peace, joy unspeakable; and it endeth in their full perfection in soul and body.

14. *Concerning a particular instituted Church, and the Priviledges thereof.*

That it is a company of faithfull and holy people, or persons, called out of the world to fellowship with Jesus Christ, and united in one congregation to him as members to their head, and one with another, by a holy covenant for mutuall fellowship in all such wayes of holy worship of God, and of edification one towards another, as God himself hath required in his Word of everie Church of Christ, and the members thereof.

15. *Concerning the manner of gathering a Church.*

That it is the dutie of all Christians, having renounced all false wayes of idolatrous, Antichristian, and superstitious worship, and of sin, and the world (as to instruct and govern their own families according to God, so) to joyn willingly together in Christian communion and orderly covenant, and by free confession of the faith, and profession of their subjection to the Gospel of Christ, to unite themselves unto peculiar and visible Congregations, wherin as members of one body, whereof Christ is the head, they are to worship God according to his Word: To this Church he hath given royall priviledges, as the holy Oracles, the Promises, the seals of the Covenant, his presence, love, protection, and blessing in a speciall manner, here all that acknowledge him to be their Prophet, Priest, and King, are to be inrolled amongst his houshold servants, and to present their bodies, and souls, and gifts, and solemne services for a spirituall sacrifice acceptable to God by Jesus Christ. Being thus united, they to whom God hath given gifts to interpret the Scriptures, being approved by the Church, and appointed thereunto, may, and ought to teach publikely the Word of God, by prophecying according to the proportion of faith for edification, exhortation and comfort of the Church, till such time as men may be had fit to such office or offices as Christ hath appointed to the publike Ministery of his Church; and then they are upon due triall to proceed to the choice, and ordination of those officers according to God: and then the officers are to dispense the seals of the covenant, *viz.* Baptisme of the seed of the faithfull in their infancy, and to others not yet baptized, when by profession of their faith they are added to the Church: And all of the Church that are of yeers, and are able to examine themselves, must communicate also in the Lords Supper in both kinds, *viz.* bread and wine.

16. *Concerning the Sacraments.*

That they are in the ordinance of God signs and seals of Gods everlasting covenant with us, representing and offering to all receivers, but exhibiting onely to true beleevers the Lord Jesus Christ and all his benefits unto righteousnesse, sanctification, and eternall life, through faith in his name to the glory and praise of God.

17. *Concerning the power of every Church.*

That Christ hath given the power of chusing Officers, and of receiving in, or calling of any member, to the whole body together of every Church, and not to any one member apart, or to more members sequestred from the whole, or to any other Congregation to do it for them: yet so as every Church ought to use the best help they can hereunto, and the most meet member they have to pronounce the same in their publike Assemblie, if they want Officers. And to this censure and judgement of Christ, duely and orderly dispensed, every member of the Congregation, yea, and officer also how excellent or learned soever he be, is subject. Yet ought not the Church without great care and advice to proceed against such publike persons.

18. *Concerning the Communion of Churches.*

That although particular Churches be distinct and severall independant bodies, every one as a city compact within its self, without subordination under or dependance upon any other but Jesus Christ, yet are all Churches to walk by one and the same rule, and by all means convenient to have the counsell and help one of another when need requireth, as members of one body in the common faith under Christ their onely head.

19. *Concerning Church Officers.*

That Christ when he ascended up on high gave gifts unto men, and disposed of them in severall functions, and for publike ordinary ministery, he gave Pastors, Teachers, Elders, Deacons, helpers, for the instruction, government, and service of his Church to the worlds end; and that none may usurpe or execute a Ministery in the Church, but such as are rightly called by the Church, wherof they stand Ministers, and being so called they ought to give all diligence to fulfill their ministery, and to be found faithfull, and unblameable in all things: And that this ministery is alike given to every Church of Christ, with like and equall power, and commission to have and enjoy the same as God offereth fit men, and means, and the same rules are given to all for the election and execution thereof in all places: which rules and laws it is not lawfull for those Ministers, or for the Church, wittingly to neglect, or transgresse in any part. And those Ministers thus chosen, and executing their office faithfully; every Church is bound to have them in singular love for their works sake, to reverence them according to the dignity of their office which they execute, and to provide for them that they be not entangled with the cares of this life, according to the law of Christ: And this to do not as in way of courtesie or mercie, but out of duty to them in the Lord; and having hope in God that the resurrection shall be of the just and of the unjust; of the just, to the resurrection of life, and of the unjust to the resurrection of condemnation.

20. *Concerning giving every man his due.*

That unto all men is to be given whatsoever is due to them, in regard of their office, place, gifts, wages, estate, and condition; endeavouring our selves to have alwayes a conscience void offence towards God, and towards men.

F I N I S.

JOHN DAVENPORT *to* MARY, Lady VERE[1]
To the Right Honor[a]ble Lady the Lady Mary Vere present these in Hackney

Madam)

BY the good hand of our God upon us, my deare child[2] is safely arrived, with sundry desirable freinds, as Mr. Fenwick,[3] and his

1. British Museum, Additional MSS., 4275, fols. 171–172; printed in *New England Historical and Genealogical Register*, IX (Boston, 1855), 149–150; A. B. Davenport, *Supplement* (Stamford, 1876), pp. 369–370.

2. John, the son of John and Elizabeth Davenport, was born in the Netherlands and baptized at the English church at The Hague, April 15, 1635. (W. Steven, *The History of the Scottish Church, Rotterdam*, Edinburgh, 1832, p. 310.) Upon the departure of his father and mother from England for New England in 1637, he was left in the care of Mary, Lady Vere. Apparently he was educated by his father, for he is not listed among the graduates of Harvard College. He seems to have followed a mercantile career. His son, John Davenport III, graduated from Harvard College in 1687.

3. George Fenwick was one of the group of lords and gentlemen to whom Robert Rich, Earl of Warwick, granted forty leagues of territory to the west of Narragansett River in 1632. At this time he was on his way to take up his residence at Saybrook at the mouth of the Connecticut River.

Lady,[4] Mr. Whitfield,[5] etc. to our great comfort. Theyre passage was
so ordered as it appeared that prayers were accepted, ffor, they had no
sicknes in the ship, except a litle sea sicknes, not one died, but they
brought to shore one more then was knowne to be in the vessel at
theyre coming forth: for a woaman was safely delivered of a child, and
boath are alive and well. They attained to the haven where they would
be, in 7 weekes. Theyre provisions at sea held good to the last. About
the time, when we gessed they might approach neare us, we sett a day
apart for publick extraordinary humiliacion by fasting and prayer, in
which we commended them into the hands of our God, whom windes
and seas obey, and shortly after sent out a pinnis to pilott them to our
harbour: for it was the first ship that ever cast anchor in this place.
But our pilott, having wayted for them a fourtnight, grew weary, and
returned home, and the very next night after, the ship came in, guided
by gods owne hand to our towne. The sight of the harbour did so
please the Captaine of the ship and all the passengers that he called it
The Fayre Haven. Since that, another ship hath brought sundry passengers, and a third is expected, daily. And, which is more, the Lord
our God hath here bestowed upon us the greatest outward priviledge
under the sun, to have and injoy all his ordinances purely dispensed in
a church gathered and constituted, according to his owne minde, in all
things, and hath promised that in every place where he shall so sett his
name, he will come unto his people and blesse them. And now, Madam,
my desire is that your La[dyshi]p may be assured that what ever interest I have in Jesus christ, and by him, in fellowship with his people,
at the throne of Grace, it is wholly for your advantage, if in any thing,
I may express the reality of my thanckfullnes to your Hono[u]r for
many favours formerly received, and for your helpefullnes to my litle
one in carrying him in your coach to Sir Theodore Maherne[6] for advise
about his neck, and for your cost upon him in a coate, of which bounty
and labour of your love my servant Ann[7] hath made full report to us:
The Lord recompence the same to your La[dyshi]p and to your Noble
family an 100 fold. I hope, before this time, he hath rebuked the Fea-

4. Alice, daughter of Sir Edward Apsley, widow of Sir John Boteler, and wife of
George Fenwick.

5. Henry Whitfield, rector of Ockley, Surrey, led a company drawn from Ockley,
Surrey, and Cranbrook, Kent, to New England in the summer of 1639. The group settled
at Menunkatuck or Guilford, about sixteen miles to the east of New Haven.

6. Sir Theodore Turquet de Mayerne was appointed first physician to James I in 1611
and later chief physician to Charles I and Henrietta Maria. He lived in St. Martin's
Lane, and is buried at St. Martin's-in-the-Fields. *Dictionary of National Biography.*

7. Unidentified.

vers, and small poxe in your family, and will make the losse of Mr. St. Jo[hn][8] a mercy to your daughter, whom I love and honor in the Lord. The Lord, the Holy one of Israel, our Redeemer hath undertaken to teach his people to proffitt, as well by his providences, as by his ordinances, even by all his dispensacions; accordingly I beleive he will, and pray that he may be pleased graciously to make this losse her gaine, and these tryalls evidences of his Fatherly love both to your La[dyshi]p and her, that the mortality of earthly comforts, and the dissolublenes of the marriage bond with the creature may quicken us to secure our interest in the everliving God, and our marriage with the Lord Jesus christ by an everlasting Covenant of his free Grace, which nothing can dissolve! My wife presenteth her humble service with much thanck-fullnes to your La[dyshi]p. We boath desire in like manner to salute my Lady Wake,[9] and all your Noble daughters. Had I time, I would wright to Mrs. Watson[10] your scribe. At present, I have no more lib-erty then to salute her, and to lett her know, that if her affections stand hitherward I shall gladly be usefull to her in what I may, and doe thinck that it would be comfortable to her many waies. But it is God who setts the bounds of our habitacions, to whose everlasting armes I commend your Ladiship, with all yours, in Jesus christ, in whom I rest

Your Honor[a]ble La[dyshi]ps much obliged in the Lord

Quinnipiack the 28 d of the 7th moneth JOHN DAVENPORTE
1639

8. Oliver St. John, son of Sir John St. John of Lydiard Tregoz, Wiltshire, married Catherine, third daughter of Lord and Lady Vere, January 30, 1634. After his death, his widow married John, Lord Paulet.

9. Anna, the daughter of Edmund Bray of Barrington, in Gloucestershire and Berk-shire, the stepdaughter of Sir Edward Conway, and the widow of Sir Isaac Wake.

10. Mrs. Watson was apparently still with Lady Vere in 1647. See below, p. 83. Ed-ward Watson, possibly a relative, took the oath of fidelity at New Haven in 1644, and joined the church at New Haven in 1653. *New Haven Colonial Records, 1638-1649* (Hartford, 1857), p. 138.

John Davenport *to* Charles Chauncy[1]

Reuerend and deare Brother.

THE argum[en]ts which you alledge . . . .
absolute necessity of immersion or dipping all that are baptized . . .
deliuered by the messenger of your Church . . . . to the Ch[urch]
heere, and, according to your desire I : . . . . force of your
reasons, as I . . . . the quotations of writers
further confir . . . . the issue of that daies worke w . . .
The brethren . . . the . . . . (sprinckling) did not hold forth . . .
way of . . . . ring on water and applying . . .
. . . . committed to myselfe and two of . . .
. . . . the argum[en]ts, and preparing an answer to the . . .
against the . . [m]eeting, (which is euery 3d day of the weeke, when the
members . . . . . . together)[2] commending the guidance of our spirits
to the grace . . . . . Accordingly wee haue weighed (as the Lord hath
helped vs) your . . . m[en]ts and, tho wee must approue your zeale for
the ordinance of . . . and your faithfullnesse to your light, in freely
holding it forth (as becometh the truth to bee professed) and your
greate labo[u]r in searching dilligently writers of sundry sorts, and of
eminent note and worth in the Churches of Christ, yet, I must in-
geniously professe that I am so farre from beeing convinced therby of
any vnlawfullnesse in our practice as I am more confirmed therin by
al that hath beene argued to the contrary . . . .
. . . . . and differ the writing will shew, which if any thinck meete to
reade to the church, I pray let the many quotations of Ecclesiasticall writers be . . . to them (which also you desired of mee, and I . . .
formed on . . . halfe, heere) by the necessity of the occasion that both
what you have with much Labo[u]r collected out of approued authors
might bee duely . . . , and what approbation our way hath received from
those that pleaded . . . immersion, and upon what grounds, may appeare. Accept I pray the lab[or of] our loue louingly, and bee intreated
to revise your own thoughts and . . . . ons.

1. Boston Public Library, Cotton Papers, Part II, no. 21. This letter was written in
reply to a letter of Charles Chauncy to John Davenport, "16th day of the . . .d month,
Anno 1640." *Ibid.*, no. 20. At this time Charles Chauncy was assistant to John Reyner,
teacher of the church at Plymouth. In the following year he became pastor of the church
at Scituate, and in 1654, the second president of Harvard College. See S. E. Morison,
Harvard College in the Seventeenth Century (Cambridge, 1936), pp. 320–339.

2. On every third day or Tuesday the brethren of the church at New Haven assembled
to manage the affairs of the church and to elect officers, the male members voting by
upraised hands.

Deliberandum diu etc. is safe councell in matt . . . .
of this nat . . . . publishing your iudgm[en]t in this matter, . . .
in ann . . . . . . priuate letter to mee you graunt that washing is . . .
end of bapt . . . according to Acts. 22. 16. 1 Pet. 3. 21. Eph: 5. 25. and the
. . . . Yet I see not that in the . . .
allto . . . . Heb. 10 22.) . . .
rather expla . . . . is a twofold Spri . . .
which is opposed to w . . . . which accompanieth washing . . .
to it, as to it's end . . . . latter sense it is a pouring on . . .
water, and applying it . . . . in a washing way: As it is euident . . .
ordinary experience, which . . . . washed as . . . . .
themselus, when voluntarily . . . . by the
hands of others applying water to their bodies . . . not . . . ordinan . . .
especially if it may bee so applyed, by holding them sometime under
the . . . as may expresse their buriall, and their comming from under
the . . . resurrection, and both their fellowship with Christ in his
death, buriall, and resurrection, so as may best suite with their tender-
nesse, according to Rom 6 3–6. I thincke therfore that sprinckling is
not so fitt a word to expresse the practice of these Churches, as washing by pouring on of water and therfore wish that it only might bee
vsed in this dispute. You adde an obiection which some do make, if
sprinckling bee not washing; rebaptization will certainly follow: you
answer by denying that consequence (abhorring that endlesse laba-
rynth of anabaptisme) and say that sprinckling may goe for washing
in a large sense, as having the vse of water in it. I reply. 1. Had the   Reply
object . . . instead of rebaptizing, that, if sprinckling bee not washing,
they who are baptized by sprinckling are not baptized, they might
easily haue proued it thus . . . . . . 2. for they were only sprinckled, but
according to . . . sprinckling and washing are constantly distinguished
and opposed . . . you . . . both from leuiticall ceremonies, and from
Heb. 10. 22 . . . . the force of this argum[en]t but by saying
as you doe; . . . . washing in a large sense, ...   Reply
the vse of water in it . . . hauing of the . . . of water in it that will giue
allowance to . . . . washing.
Vnlesse it haue the vse of w . . . . hich, in . . . acheth to th . . .
end, for drincking hath the . . . . in it, yet it . . . . properly called
washing, no, not in a large . . . sprinckling also . . . . hath an
vse of water in it, but . . . bee called washing, . . . in a large sense
2dly. You answer: the firme . . . (*id est*, the essence therof) may bee   2 Ans.
entire without dipping. I . . . . you define baptisme by *immersio in*   Reply
aquam, where will you find . . . . . *constituentem* (which is compounded

of the elem[en]t and of the sacra . . . action) of baptisme, in sprinckling
. . . And where there is defectes . . . . how can the essence be . . .
entire? I am heartily sorry that such an advantage is giuen by such
a . . . to the Anabaptists of such . . . . say you, I desire the . . .
rite and manner of washing appointed by the Lord, which sprinck . . .
(as I believe) . . . would . . . upon conjectures or probabilities to . . .

Reply   any worship of god upon us . . . in this point, etc. I reply, ...
your desire of the particular . . . . of washing appointed by [the]
Lord I fully joyne with you, ... that the pouring on of water
(which is commonly called . . . or sprinckling) beeing applyed to . . .
in a washing way, and so . . . . . . may bee apparently held under the
water, for a time, is the . . . . of baptizing infants appointed
by the Lord. For so much . . . . and, in the
doing, they are washed with . . . word, and . . . . the analogy
with the th . . . . measure as the . . .
tend . . . . depart from the patterns
in Scriptu . . . . examples of John[3] and of the
Eunuch,[4] y . . . . your light too much. For, those two
instances w . . . . who were washed in Rivers, into which they
descended . . . . But the Scripture affoords other instances also
that . . . light to this cause, wherin probably infants might also bee
baptized, . . . such a way, at least, as might suite infants also in all
places, and at all seasons such as the 3000 Acts. 2. and the Iailo[u]r
Acts 16 Your selfe graunt that such as were baptized in priuate houses,
and in such multitudes as Acts. 2. can hardly bee thought to bee
dipped all ouer, if not; what necessity is there that wee should conclude that they were dipped at all? but only washed by water poured
on them, and applyed in a washing way. But, if you will say, they
were dipped in some part: I desire your proof why may wee not rather
say, they were washed by pouring on of water? the vsuall manner of
washing those that goe not into the riuer to wash all ouer is by pouring
water upon them that they may bee washed therby. You see how
wee haue hastned your answer. Consider what hath . . . said . . . the
Lord giue you to hold that which is good, and put a speedy blessed
issue . . . this dispute, which I much desire may bee by your setling
there in such a . . . as may stand with the peace and ædification of that
Church, and of all the . . . Churches, according to Christ. And in any
other way, I kn[ow] you will rat[her] chuse not to bee, then to bee
setled any where. Farew[e]ll

The 2nd . . .   Yours vnfeignedly in the Lord

                                         JOHN DAVENPORTE

3. See S. Matthew 3. 6, 13; S. Mark 1. 5, 9; S. John 1. 28; 3. 23.
4. The Acts 8. 27–39.

JOHN DAVENPORT *to* MARY, Lady VERE[1]

*To the Right Honorable and truely Noble Lady
the Lady Mary Vere these present*

Madam)

IT seemeth to me, who continually beare in my hearte a thanckfull remembrance of your many favours, a long time since I heard from your Ladyship. Which I doe impute, either to your remote abode from London, or to your want of seasonable notice of opportunities for conveighing a line or two, by some fitt hand, unto these parts. In hope that you are yet in the land of the living and in health, (which I pray the living God long to continue, with all prosperity and peace!) and in Confidence that a few lines from one so much obliged will be acceptable to your Hono[u]r, I presume to present this testimony of my thanckfullnes for your constant good affection to so worth[l]ess an one; praying the God of all grace to remember all your faithfullnes to me and myne, in goodnes and mercy to your Noble selfe and your Honor[a]ble branches, both now, and in that great day, when the light of his countenance and favour in Christ Jesus will be more worth then ten thousand worldes!

Madam) you are taught of God to judge rightly of thinges that differ, and to value them, not by the deluded apprehensions of the world, but by the weight and worth which God himselfe hath putt upon them in the scriptures. Accordingly weigh all thinges, in this ballance of the sanctuary, trye all things by this standard, and perfect rule; which was the prayse of those Noble Beræans:[2] pittying the misery and follie of those, who, being mislead by fancie, catch at shadowes, neglecting the substance, whilest they admire others, and value themselves by outward and empty titles and vanityes.

You (Madam) are begotten againe to better hopes, even to the hope of an inheritance incorruptible, and undefiled, and that fadeth not away, reserved in heaven for you, who are kept by the power of God, through faith unto salvation. Let the high dignity and excellency of that condition suitably rayse your spirit, and heighten your spirituall disposition, affections, and intentions or aimes. Leave lowe and meane things, such as are all worldly thinges, to lowe and meane spirits, such as all worldly minded people are, who, whilest they are acted by the

---

1. British Museum, Additional MSS., 4275, fols. 173–174. An extract from this letter was printed in A. B. Davenport, *A History and Genealogy of the Davenport Family* (New York, 1851), p. 322.
2. The Acts 17. 10–12.

lusts of the world, doe feed continually upon the dust of the earth, according to that Curse upon the serpent, which is mystically executed upon the serpentes brood, such persons as have theyre portion in this life. As you expect great things from God, through Christ Jesus, so strive to performe great services, to returne great prayses to him, improving your time, talents, interests, all that you are, all that you have, in all things for his honour, who hath not spared his onely sonne, but given him to the death for you, and hath, with him, given you all things. We see (Madam) that the most high shaketh heaven, earth, and seaes, and all hearts. Wherefore is this? Surely, that he may, at last, settle the Kingdom of our Lord Jesus, and bowe all nations under his scepter, according to his word. Now, the good Lord shake us out of the creature, sinne, selfe, and all false bottoms, that, the things that are shaken being removed, those things which cannot be shaken may remaine! It is an houre of Temptacion, which is come upon the world to trye the inhabitants on the earth, worldly minded ones, from which he that is holy and true, that hath the Key of David etc. hath promised that they who keepe the word of his patience shall be kept by him. Lett this be our comfort, yea, lett us make this comfort our owne, by clearing our right and title to it. For the Lords controversie with his people is not yet ended, but his hand is stretched out still, and worse things are yet to come, till the slaughter of the witnesses shall be finished, which, I suppose, is not yet past, when I seriously compare the description of that time, as it is in Rev. 11. with the providences of God which have passed upon his people, to this day. Yet I beleive, that the light which is now discovered in England, concerning church order and governm[en]t, will never be wholly put out, though, I suspect, that contrary principles will prevayle, for a time, with the generallity and sundry in reputacion for godlines, till they be more renued in the spirit of theyre mind to prove what is that good, that acceptable, and perfect will of God, whereby a full and exact conformity to heavenly rules and patternes, will be hindred and overborne by such as plead for conformity to this world. Hence there will be as much need as ever for the just to live by faith, yea, by theyre owne faith. That yours, Madam, may be increased, strengthned, and perfected, is, and shall be my hearty prayer, on your behalfe, and that your wholl spirit, soul, and body be preserved blameless to the coming of our Lord Jesus.

The bearer hereof, Mrs. Brasie,[3] who was formerly your houshold

3. Probably the wife or mother of John Bracie, who took the oath of fidelity at New Haven in 1644, and sold his land in New Haven in 1647.

servant, and hath lived in this Plantation, sundry yeares, and is a member of our church, well approved among us, is able to give an account to your Hon[o]r of all things wherein you will desire to be informed concerning me and myne, in which respect, I shall forbeare to withhold your Ladish[i]p from more weighty affayres, by adding any relation thereof. Together with my selfe, my wife presents her humblest service to your Hono[u]r, being all waies mindfull of our deepe ingagem[en]ts. The Lord Jesus overshadow you, in goodnes, and dwell with you, in peace, and loving kindnes, in whom I rest

Newhaven the 13th day of the 9th m.   Madam)

1647   Your Honor[a]ble Ladish[i]ps ever obliged
                        to serve you in the Lord

                             JOHN DAVENPORTE

We boath salute Mrs. Watson affectionatly, in the Lord.

JOHN DAVENPORT *to* JOHN COTTON[1]

To the Reverend and his worthily much honoured freind and brother Mr. John Cotton Teacher to the church in Boston these present

Reverend and worthy Sir)

YOURS dated the 22th of the 1st m. 1649 was not brought to my hand till this 2d day of the 3d month 1650, whereby I understand that Brother Pierce[2] hath delivered unto you a Copie of some sermons preached by me, in our weekely lecture, wherein my intendm[en]t was to stablish the hearers in assurance that Jesus the sonne of the Virgin Mary is the onely true Messiah. The forenamed brother dilligently wrote, as his manner was, but finding that his head and pen could not

1. New Haven Colony Historical Society; photostat in Yale University Library; printed in A. B. Davenport, *A History and Genealogy of the Davenport Family* (New York, 1851), pp. 343–346. John Cotton, vicar of St. Botolph's at Boston in Lincolnshire from 1612 to 1633, and teacher of the First Church at Boston in Massachusetts Bay from 1633 until his death in 1652, was a friend who exerted great influence upon John Davenport. Although the two men were probably frequent correspondents, in 1663 Davenport asked John Cotton the Younger to return his letters to the Boston divine (see below, p. 212), and probably destroyed the correspondence, for this is the only letter from John Davenport to John Cotton that has been found.

2. Probably Mark Pierce, who had offered to teach writing and arithmetic to the children of New Haven in 1645. *New Haven Colonial Records, 1638–1649* (Hartford, 1857), p. 156.

carry away some materiall expressions, he earnestly desired me to lett him have my notes, to perfect his owne by them, which I promised him in the winter was twelve moneths. Having other hinderances, he called not for them, when he was here, but being in the Bay, and unresolved about his stay there, or passage for England, or returne hither, he wrote for those notes, clayming my promise, which accordingly I sent to him by brother Livermore,[3] with a double charge, 1, that, when he had transcribed them, he would returne my copie againe, by a safe land-messenger, not by sea; remembring that I lost my *autographum* of all the sermons I preached out of the epistle of christ to the church of Philadelphia Rev. 3. concerning the houre of Temptacion, and sundry others about christs shaking heaven and earth to establish his kingdom, in Heb. 12. which I gave Mr. Gregson,[4] at his request, to carry with him, when he went hence for England. My 2d charge was, that when he had transcribed them, he would shew them unto you, and make no other use of them then privatly for himselfe, but by your advise. This I added, because I feared that he had a purpose for the presse, from some words that I observed now and then to fall from him. Now, I am glad that you have them with you to peruse, where I pray, keepe them, till you have sifted them thoroughly. I thanck you for your faithfull advise about the Interpretacion of Phill. 2: 6. 7. 8. which I did afterwards handle at large, unto v. 12, in sundry sermons, according to the method I had propounded, for handling the grounds of religion. In those sermons I did interpret that scripture in the largest and most comprehensive sense, and particularly, as holding forth christs personall Godh[ead] humbling himselfe to Assume our humane Nature. Nor can I tell what other or narrower Interpretacion I adhæred unto, in the notes under your hand: but, well knowing that the one way and the other will suite the scope of that discourse, I leave it wholly to your wisdom, to add, or alter, as you find expedient, and analogous with other scriptures, that allegacion with its interpretacion. I shall further pray you to cast your eye, upon that type, the rocke in the wildernes, to see, whether I have safely expressed the rockes following them, which, I conceive, was that the water flowing from the rock followed them all the way in the wildernes, meaning it of that 2d rock in Rephidim and kept by them here and there in wells digged

3. John Livermore migrated from Wethersfield on the Connecticut River to New Haven before October 29, 1640.

4. About the middle of January, 1646, Thomas Gregson, one of the early settlers at New Haven, sailed for England on board the so-called "phantom ship," and was never again heard from.

Numb. 20 18.[5] which also Tertullian (*lib. de patient.*) seemeth to intend by his *petræ aquatilem sequelam*.[6] Such have bene my thaughts, but whether I did there so wright them downe, I doe not remember. Others have other apprehensions of it. If you meet with any thing, in that, or anything else, that you doe not approve, *deleatur*. I thaught it better to lett him have myne owne noates, to rectifye his, by them, then to lett him print greate mistakes for want of that helpe.[7] I wish the wrong that is done *Reipub. literariæ* by imperfect copies may warne you to improve your present season for the perfecting of as many Tractates and Commentaryes, as you have for the publick good. One thing more give me leave to propound, and, as earnestly as my modesty will permit, to importune, that you would take into your serious thaughts the question about single testimony of severall persons, who speake fully to the things, and with concurrence therein, though not joyntly in the circumstances of time and place, and to answer that logicall querk which Mr. Prudden[8] told you of, and what other Argum[en]ts you find in that postscript of Mr. Cheivers his answer to the Church[9] or which you have elsewhere mett with. You will much oblige me, if you will hasten a copie of your labours upon that subject. If you list not to appeare in the controversie, you shall be wholly concealed by me. For the managding of my speech or silence your letter of advise shall have the force of a law with me. Onely be intreated to dispatch it unto me, by the 1st opportunity, whether by land or sea. *Bis dat qui cito dat*.[10] The reason of this my earnestnes for a speedy returne I will give, at your demand, by the next, which, I beleive, you will judge to be weighty. I had rather ease then add to your burdens, but that we

---

5. Apparently an erroneous reference. Possibly Numbers 21. 18. is meant.

6. Quintus Septimius Florens Tertullianus, *De patientia, 5 fin.*

7. John Davenport, *The Knowledge of Christ Indispensably required of all men that would be saved; . . .* (London, 1653). The preface is dated, "From my study in New-haven, this 13th of the 9th moneth, MDCLII." According to a statement in the preface, the manuscript was sent by Davenport to the printer in London.

8. Peter Prudden was the first pastor of the church at Milford in the New Haven Colony. His will, dated July 26, 1656, was presented to a court of magistrates at New Haven, May 25, 1657. *New Haven Colonial Records, 1653–1665* (Hartford, 1858), p. 201.

9. For "The Trial of Ezekiel Cheever before the Church at New Haven," including Cheever's answer and postscript, a manuscript now in Yale University Library, see Connecticut Historical Society *Collections*, I (Hartford, 1860), 22–51. Censured and cast out of the church at New Haven, May 20, 1649, Cheever removed to Ipswich, Massachusetts, in December, 1650.

10. *inopi beneficium bis dat, qui dat celeriter.*
Publilius Syrus, *Sententiae,* 235.
He gives aid to the needy twice, who gives quickly.

are, in a speciall manner, called to a serious consideracion and determinacion concerning this point. The Lord Jesus dwell with you in
peace, and preserve your life and health, and comforts, and crowne
your holy labours with a plentifull blessing! In whom I rest

Newhaven the 6th d. of the 3d m.   Your obliged freind and brother
        1650   JOHN DAVENPORTE

I am told that this vessell will speedily returne againe I hope *ergo*
that you will returne an answer by him, if no other passenger come
sooner, with speed, which I earnestly desire.

[An endorsement by John Cotton reads:] Mr. Pierce tooke from me
both his owne, and your Copy long before the Receipt of this.

The Rock is sajd, Putt for the water gushing out of the Rock, by a
metonymy. And that water followed them. It was not *omen Diei Beneficium*.[11] But not all the way to Chanaan. For He should not have
needed to have struck another Rock, Num. 20. 11. nor should the
People have murmured againe for want of water:

The wells digged Num. 21. 16, 17, 18. were not to Receive the
waters of the River that followed them, but to open a fresh spring. Had
the water of the River bene Received into those wells, the water had
Descended: but the Text calleth it to Ascend. The water of the Rock
in Rephidim might well follow them, till they spake scornfully of the
Holyland, Deut. . . . 6. 24.[12] which was done chiefly Num. 16. 13, 14.
which was noe lesse then Blasphemy ag[ains]t the H[oly] Ghost.

So that the Rock may very well still goe for a Type of Christ, that
giveth vs Drink, and followeth vs all the way of our Pilgrimage in this
world, till wee sinne ag[ains]t the H[oly] Ghost. And then we marvell,
if the water of the Rock left the Israelites, that Christ leave malicious
Apostates, when they first leave, and Reject Him.

[A second endorsement in a modern hand reads:] Rev. John Davenport, New Haven to Rev. John Cotton, Boston, 6 May, 1650.

11. an assurance of daily benefactions.
12. Probably Deuteronomy 9. 6 or 16, 24.

JOHN DAVENPORT *to* JOHN WINTHROP the Younger[1]
To his Honour[e]d freind John Winthrop Esq.
these present in Pequot

Worthily Honour[e]d Sir)

UPON frequent reports of Gods gracious blessing your labours with good success, in sundry Cures, I was desirous to have made a journey to Pequot, to confer with you about the state of my body, and desired brother Andrewes[2] to signifie the same unto you, by whom I understand that there is no conveniencie for myne and my wifes and my sonnes lodging and other Accomodacions there, and that your selfe are upon a journey shortly for the Baye. I have therefore hyred this Indian to be the bearer of these lines, and pray you to returne by him your advise, not concerning my distemper, which I cannot so fully declare, by wrighting, to your satisfaction, and myne owne, as is meete, but concerning my way. My wife inclineth to our travayling with you to Boston, if you judge that a place and time fitt for me to enter into any course of physick, but I heare the Apothecary[3] wants supplyes of things, unles Carwithy[4] be come, yet I heare that Mr. Lyng[5] etc. newly returned from the Baye saw a vessel at sea, about 200 tunne coming towards Boston, and I feare that your buisenesses there will not permit liberty for that, and that my body and the season will not suite it: yet, if you advize it, as convenient, I shall consider what you propound. If not; my desire is to know, when you purpose to returne,

1. New York Public Library, Winthrop–Davenport Papers; printed in L. Bacon, *Thirteen Historical Discourses* (New Haven, 1839), pp. 366–367; Massachusetts Historical Society *Collections*, 3d series, IX (Boston, 1846), 294–295. John Winthrop the Younger was the son of John Winthrop of Massachusetts Bay. In 1635 the patentees of the Earl of Warwick appointed him governor of their territory in New England. In 1653 he was living at Pequot, subsequently renamed New London. This letter is the beginning of a long correspondence between Davenport and the future governor of Connecticut.

2. William Andrews was one of the first settlers of New Haven.

3. "This 25th of 11th mo. 1646.... It is ordered that Wm. Davice [, Davies, or Davis], the apotecary, shall have leave to sett up a payll afor his hall window and parlor window 3 foot from his howse." "Boston Records, 1634–1660, and the Book of Possessions," Record Commissioners of the City of Boston, *Second Report* (Boston, 1877), p. 89.

4. Dickery or Digory Carwithen or Carwithy, master of the *New England Marchant*, died at Boston on the morning of September 6, 1653. "Boston Births, Baptisms, Marriages, and Deaths, 1630–1699," Record Commissioners of the City of Boston, *Ninth Report* (Boston, 1883), p. 42; *Massachusetts Colony Records*, III (Boston, 1854), 322; IV, Part I (Boston, 1854), 175–176.

5. Benjamin Ling, an early settler at New Haven, sold his land in New Haven in 1655 and returned to England. In the spring of 1662 he returned to New Haven.

if God please. I was glad when he told me that you had some purpose of coming into these parts, and shall be more glad, if I may understand from your selfe, that you continue that resolution, and will be pleased to put it into execution, at your returne from the Baye, and to accept of my house for your intertainm[en]t, during your abode in these parts, there to refresh your selfe, with assurance that you shall be most heartily wellcom to us. If you require it, for the preparing of directions suitable to my case, that I give you notice of it particularly, before hand, I shall, by the next opportunity, answer your desire, upon notice when my letter may probably finde you at home: or, if you incourage us to come to Pequot, after your returne, we shall attend you there. But, if you can affoard me some liberty of discourse with you here, before your journey to the Baye, I thincke, that would be best: and I should be very much obliged unto you for that your labour of love. However; let me receive such answer as you can, by this bearer. Present my true Respects to Mrs. Winthrop,[6] with loving salutacions to Mr. Blyndman.[7] The Lord Jesus dwell with you in peace! In whom I rest

Newhaven this 20th d.   Sir, yours assured
of the 6th m. 1653.
                                        JOHN DAVENPORTE

[Endorsed] Mr. Davenport [by John Winthrop, and] John Davenport's Lett[e]r Dated Aug[u]st 20th. *1653.* [in a modern hand.]

JOHN DAVENPORT *to* SARAH COTTON[1]

Deare Mrs. Cotton)

THE departure of our freinds being more suddaine then I expected, I wanted opportunitie of saluting you, by letter, according to my desire. Yet now, hearing of another way of transmitting these lines,

6. Elizabeth (Reade) Winthrop was the daughter of Edmund Reade of Wickford, Essex, England, and the second wife of John Winthrop the Younger.

7. Richard Blinman was preacher at Pequot from 1650 to 1658. He assisted Davenport at New Haven in 1658 and 1659, during which time he lived in the house formerly occupied by William Hooke. (Massachusetts Historical Society *Collections*, 5th series, VIII, Boston, 1882, 49.) In the fall of 1659 Blinman was on his way to England, *via* Newfoundland. See below, p. 144.

1. Boston Public Library, Mather Papers, I, no. 14; printed in Massachusetts Historical Society *Collections*, 4th series, VIII (Boston, 1868), 546–547; A. B. Davenport, *Supplement* (Stamford, 1876), pp. 371–372. Sarah (Hawkridge), the widow of William Story, married John Cotton April 25, 1632. After his death she married Richard Mather, August 26, 1656.

I am encouraged to put pen to paper, to express my sincere love to you, in the Lord, and to your familie, praying you to be assured, that I doe as heartily wish all good to you and yours, as to my selfe and myne, which I would most gladly make visible, by reall and suitable effects, if I knew how, and had power in my hand answerable to my desire. But this is your comfort, that whatever deficiency is in the creature there is Allsufficiency for you and yours in God, who is your God and father in christ Jesus, by an everlasting Covenant, whereby he hath made ouer (as it were, by a deed of gift) his Allsufficiency, in respect of the fruite and benefit of it, unto you, thorough christ. Yet seing it hath pleased the onely wise God to make men his instruments, that his goodnes may be diffused and communicated unto us, in that order, and by those outward meanes, in the communion of saints, which he vouchsafeth and suiteth to that end; it will be well pleasing in his sight that you improve that channell, and those conduit pipes, for your communion with that blessed fountaine of all good. Of this kind, I know, you have plentifull helpes, daily, at hand, which you doe well, in that you make use of them, according to the opportunities which God graciously affoardeth unto you. And, if I may be of any use to yourselfe, or to any of yours, be assured that your interest in me is such, that the intimation of your desire will have the force of a strong engagement upon me for the performance of any office, and service of love, that is or shall be within my compas. In the meane time, and ever (with my wifes most affectionate salutations) I heartily commend you and yours to the grace of our Lord Jesus, in whom I rest

Newhaven the 25th d   Your assured thanckfull friend
of the 6th m. 1653.   JOHN DAVENPORT

JOHN DAVENPORT *to* JOHN WINTHROP the Younger[1]
To his Honour[e]d freind Mr. Winthrop
these present at Pequot

Honour[e]d Sir)

YOURS by brother Lyne I received, and returne many hearty thancks for your labour of love therein, and in your travailes to me, and for me. The Lord recompence an 100 fold into your bosom, and unto your family, all your helpefullnes to his people, wherein you continually doe improve your times and talents! As for me; I am fully

1. Massachusetts Historical Society, Winthrop MSS., XII, 93.

satisfyed with the good pleasure of the most High concerning me, whether in life or death. I am willing to serve his providence in the use of all good meanes for the preservacion of life, for his service, in obedience to his will revealed in the 6th Commandm[en]t,[2] and have wayted longer therein in this place, then I should have done, if I had bene free from all other cares, besides that of my selfe and family: but my tender care of this church caused me to stay so long as I have done, in these parts. If it had pleased God to bless such meanes as this countrey affoardeth for my cure, I had continued here, at least, some yeares longer, till I had made further tryall of the issues of Gods providence towards this place, in reference to the comfortable settling of all things, for the good of posterity. But now I see my call to be cleare, to hasten, with the consent of the church, for my native land.[3] In order whereunto I am about to send a footeman to the Baye, to see what accomodacions may be had, for me and myne, in Mr. Garrets[4] vessel, with a purpose to hasten thither, if the Answer be incouraging, because the season will better suite me, then if I stay for the Fleete, which is gone to the French,[5] and, I feare, will be retarded, by that designe, till the depth of winter, which will not be a fitt season for me to be at sea in, being forewarned against it, by Mr. Hopkins[6] his sad experience, and resolution thereupon. And, if I neglect this opportunity, I feare, I shall

2. Exodus 20. 13.

3. As early as 1651 there was a rumor through New England that Davenport and Eaton were returning to England. On July 5, 1654, Eaton wrote Winthrop, urging him to help Davenport to render his return to England for medical attention unnecessary. On July 27, 1654, Winthrop replied that he would help Davenport, and the latter remained at New Haven until after the absorption of the New Haven Colony by Connecticut. In 1668 he removed to Boston in Massachusetts Bay. Massachusetts Historical Society *Collections*, 4th series, VI (Boston, 1863), 76; VII (Boston, 1865), 469; Massachusetts Historical Society, Winthrop MSS., V, 14.

4. On or shortly after June 20, 1654, James Garrett brought news of the conclusion of the first Anglo-Dutch War to New England. J. Thurloe, *State Papers* (7 vols., London, 1742), II, 426, 584.

5. On July 4, 1654, Major Robert Sedgwick, with the ships *Augustine*, *Church*, *Hope*, and a small ketch, sailed to attack the French in Acadia. *Ibid.*, pp. 425-426.

6. Edward Hopkins, the brother of Henry Hopkins, warden of the fleet, the nephew of Sir Henry Lello of Ashdon, Essex, the husband of Anne Yale, and the stepson-in-law of Theophilus Eaton, migrated to New England with John Davenport and Theophilus Eaton. He settled at Hartford and was seven times elected governor of Connecticut. Leaving his insane wife with her family in New Haven, he returned to England in the fall of 1651 and died there in 1657. By a will dated March 7, 1656/7, and proved April 30, 1657, he left his estate in New England and £500 from his estate in England after the death of his widow to John Davenport and Theophilus Eaton of New Haven and John Cullick and William Goodwin of Hartford for the furtherance of grammar school and college education in New England. Somerset House, P. C. C., Ruthen, 141; printed in

lose the advantage of the next spring also, for my helpe, whereby the cure, which is now difficult, may become impossible, by the Autumne following. I am onely carefull to avoid guilt by neglecting meanes and seasons. When I have done my duety, I can quietly leave issues and events with God, in whose hands alone they are. Yesterday, while I was preaching, the feeblenes of my spirits caused mee to stopp and breake off, in the middst of my intended worke, which admonisheth me to attend to your and Dr. Shoyses[7] advise for a cessation from study and preaching, for a time. Concerning the paper you sent; the brother, whom it concerneth, hath perused it, and acknowledgeth himselfe exceedingly obliged unto you for minding his case so farr as to consult your Authors about it. I perceive that, though he inclined to thinck that the 2d particular came neare the description of his case, yet, upon conference with Dr. Shoyse, he beginnes to be of another minde, who utterly denyes that there is any species gonorr[hæ]æ in it, and he blames that brother that he did not bring him to confer with you about it, beleiving, as he saith, that he should have demonstrated to you, and to all men that it proceedes originally from that equitation which the brother saith he told you of, and the Dr. undertakes to prove by the effects of it, in the gravell and small stones, which his eyes saw. It would be too large a discourse for me to relate what the Dr. affirmeth touching that matter. Therefore I shall leave that which concernes him, in that particular, to attend my owne course. If it shall please you (worthy and deare Sir) to command me any service, for your selfe, or any of yours, in England (if it shall please him, whom windes and seas obey, to bring me thither in safety) I shall doe it as effectually as I can, through his helpe. My purpose is to make use of Dr. Wrights[8] counsail, of whose love I have plentifull experience, and who hath, in one or two letters, seriously incouraged me to returne for England, though he knew nothing of my weakenes, and wasting condition. I perceive, there is a neare relation betweene you and his wife, whom also I have long known. If you please to wright to her, I hope to de-

New England Historical and Genealogical Register, XXXVIII (Boston, 1884), 315–316; H. F. Waters, Genealogical Gleanings in England (2 vols., Boston, 1901), I, 63–65. A copy of the will on file at Hartford is printed in Massachusetts Historical Society Collections, 5th series, IX (Boston, 1885), 17–22. Here the date is erroneously given as March 17, 1656/7.

7. Dr. Chais, Chayes, Choyse, or Shoyses was a French physician at New Haven from November, 1651, to January, 1652/3, and again in 1654.

8. Laurence Wright, a friend of John Winthrop of Massachusetts Bay and physician in ordinary to Oliver Cromwell and to the Charterhouse, was at this time governor of the Charterhouse. He died October 3, 1657. See below, p. 122.

liver it with my owne hands. For my estate here, I am in greate streights, being necessitated to committ what I leave unto others, to sell away for me, as they can, and to returne the prise to me. I have mares and horses and steeres and kowes, and some sheepe. If you have a minde to buy any of them, or of my bookes, Ancient wrighters, or schoolemen, or moderne wrighters, or hystorians or expositors, I make the first offer of any thing I have, or houshold stuffe, to your selfe, and shall accept, for paym[en]t, bills for England, or beaver here: and, if you be not provided to pay, at present, I will give you what time you will desire being assured that I deale with a just, and faithfull Gentleman, and my much Honoured freind. *In publica commoda peccem si longo sermone morer tua tempora.*[9] Therefore I shall cease to add further to your troubles, or to divert you from your pressing imploym[en]ts. My wife joynes with me in returning many thancks to you for your former greate kindnes to us. My sonne is mindfull of his promise and would have sent a few lines to you, but I stayd him, for this time. Be pleased to present our respectfull salutacions to Mr[s.] Winthrop. The Lord Jesus dwell with you in peace, and multiplye his favours upon you and yours! In him I rest

Newhaven the 24th d. of   Sir,
the 5th m. 1654
                                          Your obliged freind

                                          JOHN DAVENPORT

I am at somewhat the more rest in my spirit, in this difficult undertaking, because our Teacher[10] is willing to abide here, till the next yeare, to see the church supplyed with some fitt instrum[en]ts that may, by the blessing of Christ, carry on the ministeriall worke in this church, after our departure hence, though he thinckes to send his

---

9. . . . *in publica commoda peccem,*
   Si longo sermone morer tua tempora,
                         Horace, *Epistles*, II, 1, 3-4.

   The bard, methinks, would do a public wrong
   Who, having gained your ear, should keep it long.
               J. Conington, *The Satires, Epistles, and Art of Poetry of Horace
               Translated into English Verse* (London, 1870), p. 149.

   10. William Hooke came to New Haven from Taunton in the colony of New Plymouth in 1644. He served as teacher of the church at New Haven until he returned to England in 1656. In the mother country he became one of the teachers at Whitehall, and, in 1658, was also settled at the Savoy. Massachusetts Historical Society *Collections*, 4th series, VII (Boston, 1865), 590.

family before, for the good of his posterity, whereunto he hath strong incouragem[en]ts from England.

My wife remembers me to desire a word or two of advise from you, to make our passage by sea the more safe and comfortable. My wife is very weake, at sea, not well able to beare the smells and troubles in the vessel. My selfe doe finde weakenes increasing upon me, which makes my wife doubt, whether it will not be worse with me at sea, Dr. Shoyse thincks it will doe me no hurt. What helpes you can propound will come acceptably to us. *Iterum vale.*

I heare that a messenger is sent to you, but it is done, *me inconsulto,* nor did they desire to see or at all did know the particulars in your letter to me. I marvaile at the manner of theyre proceeding, but love covers infirmities. It is from theyre greate love to me, which sweetens and beautifyes all things, notwithstanding some mixture of imperfections. Brother Lynes talking amongst them, I heare, hath caused it.

[Endorsed] Mr. Davenport [by John Winthrop.]

JOHN DAVENPORT *to* JOHN WINTHROP the Younger[1]
To his Honoured freind John Winthrop Esq.
these present at Hartford[2]

Hon[oure]d Sir)

AFTER Brother Molthrops[3] returne, I sent another letter to you, by the way of Gillford,[4] dat[ed] the 22d of the 6th.[5] Therein I propounded my apprehension touching the months of Octob[er] and 9ber and desired your serious thoughts, whether that might not be a tolerable and hopefull season for our transportacion to Engl[and], which I still desire, and now the rather, because, probably, that will be the time for the fleet to be upon theyre voyadge thitherward: and then, in an ordinary way, the Michaelmas[6] stormes will be over, and the cold of

1. Massachusetts Historical Society, Winthrop MSS., XII, 93; printed in Massachusetts Historical Society *Collections*, 3d series, IX (Boston, 1846), 297–299.
2. Hartford, located on the Connecticut River between Windsor and Wethersfield, was the principal town of the colony of Connecticut.
3. Mathew Moulthrop was one of the first settlers of New Haven.
4. Founded in 1639, Guilford was the second town of the New Haven Colony to be settled and the third town of the colony in size.
5. No copy of this letter has been found.
6. The feast of the archangel Michael was a church festival celebrated September 29.

winter avoided. Also to your quæries, about an house[7] and convenient transportation of yours hither, from Pequot, I wrote what our Governo[u]r suggested and undertooke, with whom you will now have opportunity of satisfying your selfe by orall discourse. I concluded those lines thus. Though it pleaseth you to insist in the difficulties formerly alleadged, concerning my case, as still deterring you from giving me such encouragm[en]t as I desire, and, as, you see, my case requireth; yet, if you will, but in two or three words, say thus much to me; That I may venture to stay here this winter (neglecting the opportunity of this passage in the 8th and 9th monethes) without manifest danger of rendring my selfe incurable, by delaies, and that you will applye such meanes as you conceive to be suitable to my condition; I will willingly, upon such encouragm[en]t from you, stay, this winter, wayting upon God for his blessing. Whereunto I shall now add the reason of my desiring such incouragm[en]t from you, which is, for the satisfaction of my conscience, because of the 6th commandm[en]t, that I have not, of myne owne head, or without a justifiable ground, waved such a season as Gods providence seemeth to present unto me, by the fleete, wherein Brother Martin[8] is M[aste]r of a speciall good ship, where good accomodations may be rationally expected, if he hath seasonable notice of my purpose. Also I find this clause in your last letter. (If, upon further thaughts, you can consider any thing that may be usefull, for the stopping of my distemper, that may be had, you will wrighte further and, if you can find meanes to prepare any special *arcanum* that may probably doe me good, for the stopping the proceeding thereof, you will not neglect to indeavour.) This clause I looke at as a full expression of your love and desire of procuring my recovery, by the blessing of God, and as a strong obligacion unto me to returne many hearty thancks to you for such a favour. Nor can I omit to intreate your effectuall prosecution of that your purpose towards me, and some notice from you whether you have considered and found accordingly, to your owne satisfaction, and, whether I may expect, with relyance upon you, any helpe from you, this Autumne, the season now beginning to suite the use of meanes. Pardon (worthy Sir) this boldnes and

7. The town of New Haven offered the Malbon house, to the south of the residence of John Davenport, to John Winthrop the Younger as a gift if he would settle permanently at New Haven, or rent free if he came but for a time. To better direct the ironworks at New Haven, Winthrop at first agreed to rent the house, and on July 7, 1657, purchased it outright, paying for it in goats. *New Haven Colonial Records, 1653–1665* (Hartford, 1858), p. 120; *New Haven Town Records, 1649–1662* (New Haven, 1917), pp. 241, 313–314, 319.

8. Captain Robert Martin of the *Hope*, flyboat.

interruption of your more weighty affaires, and be pleased to returne speedily as cleare and satisfying an Answer as you can, that I may understand my way, by the will of God, upon whom I waite, desiring to be found alwaies in his way, as one wholly unbyassed to any way of my owne choosing. Farewell, Hon[oure]d Sir, in o[u]r L[or]d Jesus, in whom I rest

Newhaven the 11th d   Your very much obliged freind to serve you
of the 7th m 54   JOHN DAVENPORT

[Endorsed] Mr. Davenport [by John Winthrop, and] Sept[embe]r 11th. *1654.* [in a modern hand.]

JOHN DAVENPORT *to* JOHN WINTHROP the Younger[1]
To his Honour[e]d freind John Winthrop Esq.
these present in Pequot

Hon[oure]d Sir)

YOURS of the 13th of this instant[2] I received in the evening of the 16th by brother Lynde, and returne many hearty thancks for your labour of love therein, and for your Answers to my quæries and motion. By the former; I finde my spirit at liberty to continue here, this winter, seing you conceive it will not render my case incurable, the preventing whereof was the prevailing motive for my undertaking a voyadge for Engl[and] at this season, in obedience to the 6th commandm[en]t, which otherwise I should not have put my selfe upon; as for other weighty reasons (in relation to my person and family) so principally, in my pastoral care for this church, whom I desire to see supplyed with suitable helpe, to theyre satisfaction (if theyre owne neglect of opportunities hinder not) before my removeall hence. By the latter; I find my selfe incouraged to waite upon God for his blessing upon such meanes as you thinck may be good, and shall be pleased to prescribe: whereunto I shall willingly submit, upon your promise of all your endeavours, so farr as God inables you, and I doe wholly commit my selfe to your faithfull care, though, you say, you are in the darke about the very particular case, which yet seemes to be some-

---

1. Massachusetts Historical Society, Winthrop MSS., XII, 93.
2. No copy of this letter has been found.

what like unto that, whereof Langius[3] speakes. But, whereas you are pleased to add some cautions (viz. if distance continued doe not hinder or want of materials, or such hinderances as you cannot foresee) To the last I have nothing to answer, but that the things which God keepes in his owne hands are among the secrets, which belong to him, not to us: upon him therefore I waite, in hope that he will averte all such hinderances. For the 2d, it would have bene to my satisfaction to have received, either some intelligence from you that you have or know how to procure fitt materials, or some directions from you what I should send for unto the Baye, here being an opportunity, at present, of sending by Joseph Alsop,[4] who returnes thence shortly againe, to whom I would have committed the note of particulars, to bring them from thence, upon myne accompt, and to leave them with you, at his returne. Or, if you shall now send me a note seasonably, I may transmit a letter to Boston, by the commissioners,[5] at theyre returne home, which, it is thaught, will be in the beginning of the next weeke. For it is æquall that the materialls which are for my benefit should be paid for by me. And, if the present season be lost, I feare, we shall shortly be shut up, for this winter. To the first, seing you may be certaine of an house, and of transportacion, to your content, without any charge to your selfe, to be with us, this winter, and for as much longer as you please, with most hearty welcom, and the earnest desire of us all; will not that suite your occasions, as well, at least, as the house that is offered you at Hartford furnished to your hand? Especially, considering that your owne furniture will be transported hither, which you may employ, as you please, without any feare of hurting what belongs to another. And I assure you that you have more hearts desirous of you here, then there are hands unto that invitation, and you should soone have as many, if not more hands unto a written invitacion from hence, if the Governour[6] were returned from the commissioners. I hope, the Agues among the people with you are abated, if not wholly ceased. We also have sundry excercised with them, yet gently, by the mercy of God. Had I opportunity of conference with you, I should say more, then I thinck fitt to commit to paper. Sir, I thanck you for your intelligence: In answer whereof I have sent you some printed papers sent

3. Andreas Langius, *Resp.* Πανακειας πατρος ἐπιβοηθουντος *Subsequentes De Doloroso Intestinorum Affectu, Ileo, Positiones Medicas. Præside* . . . *C. F. Crocio,* . . . *proponit A. L.* (Marburg, 1656).

4. Joseph Alsop had settled at New Haven as early as 1644.

5. The commissioners of the United Colonies of New England met at Hartford from September 7 to 25, 1654.

6. Theophilus Eaton.

to me from London.[7] The Lord Jesus dwell with you in peace and loving kindenes! In whom I rest

Newhaven, the 19th d. of the 7th m. 1654   Sir,

Your obliged freind

JOHN DAVENPORT

My selfe and wife present most affectionate and respective salutacions, together with your selfe, to Mrs. Winthrop, and Mrs. Lake,[8] and Mr. Blindman etc. We long to injoy you and your family with us, by the will of God.

My wife prayeth me to postscribe a word or two concerning our maid servant, about whom she had some speech with you. She is 21 yeares old. She had paine in her leggs, with swelling, and paine in her back and head, with illnes in her stomack and grypings and stoppages, about a weeke before you came hither: then Dr. Choyse gave her a purge, after which she was better, but getting cold upon it, she was much as before, though somewhat lightsommer, yet her leggs swelled againe and so continue, more or less, ever since, they now pitt and will stand so, she hath not noted how long. She is troubled with wind and water in her stomake, yet she sleepes well and hath competent appetite and digestion. She hath her monethly evacuacions but not well. One moneth she had but a very litle touch of them. The note inclosed I am desired to transmit unto you.

Here is a report, I thinck, from Barbadoes,[9] that France and Spaine

7. In June, 1654, there were being published in England: *Certain Passages of every dayes Intelligence; The Faithful Scout; Mercurius Politicus; A Perfect Account of the Daily Intelligence; Perfect and Impartial Intelligence; A Perfect Diurnall, or, Occurrences of certain Military Affairs; A Perfect Diurnal of some Passages . . . in relation to the Armies; Perfect Occurrences; Severall Proceedings of State Affairs; The Weekly Intelligencer; The Weekly Post.* Catalogue of the Pamphlets, Books, Newspapers, and Manuscripts relating to the Civil War, the Commonwealth, and Restoration, Collected by George Thomason, 1640–1661 (2 vols., London, 1908), II, 427–428.

8. Margaret (Reade) Lake was the daughter of Edmund Reade of Wickford, Essex, England, the elder sister of Elizabeth (Reade) Winthrop and Thomas Reade, a colonel of the parliamentary army, and the wife of John Lake. In 1623 she was the mother of a son John and a daughter Anna. At the date of this letter, her husband was living in England, where he died before January 18, 1661/2. Massachusetts Historical Society *Collections,* 4th series, VI (Boston, 1863), 115; VII (Boston, 1865), 130, 204; 5th series, I (Boston, 1871), 99; *Proceedings,* VI (Boston, 1863), 254–258.

9. Barbados, an English colony in the West Indies, with which New England had much commerce.

joyne together,[10] and there will be warr betweene them and England. Its said, for confirmacion, that an English vessel bound for some Spanish Island, diverted its course upon intelligence hereof received *in transitu.*

[Endorsed] Mr. Davenport [by John Winthrop, and] Mr. Davenport's Lett[e]r, dated Sept[embe]r 19th. *1654.* [in a modern hand.]

JOHN DAVENPORT *to* JOHN WINTHROP the Younger[1]
To his Honoured freind John Winthrop Esq.
these pr[e]sent in Pequot

Hon[oure]d Sir)

I THANCK you for your speedy Answer of my last by the returne of your Indian. Brother Lynde advised me not to pay him, but to leave it to you to satisfye him, saying that you could better treate and agree with them then I can. I cannot well satisfye my selfe in following this counsail, unles you will put both this and all other charges that any way befall, upon occasion of my concernm[en]ts, upon myne Accompt In hope and expectation whereof I am glad that you have such a messenger at your command, by whom I may heare from you, as my Case may require. Since the change of the season, I find, that, as it

10. Actually France and Spain were at war from 1653 to 1659. Perhaps in anticipation of war between England and France, Sedgwick and the fleet sent to take New Netherland turned from plans to attack New Netherland to an attack on the French in Acadia. After taking Fort St. John, Port Royal, and Penobscot, they returned to Boston, whence they sailed for England, November 14, 1654. War between England and France did not materialize, and on November 3, 1655, a treaty of peace was signed by the two powers at Westminster. (C. Jenkinson, ed., *A Collection of All the Treaties of Peace, Alliance, and Commerce, between Great-Britain and Other Powers, . . . 1648, to . . . 1783*, 3 vols., London, 1785, I, 81–85.) Although Cromwell had offered Spain an alliance against France, an English fleet under Generals William Penn and Robert Venables sailed from Portsmouth, England, December 26, 1654, to attack the Spanish island of Hispaniola in the West Indies, and war between England and Spain followed. The attack on Hispaniola proved a failure, but the expedition succeeded in taking Jamaica. There it was reinforced by Sedgwick with a fleet of twelve ships and eight hundred men, and there the man who had planned or taken part in attacks on England's three rivals in North America died, May 24, 1656. Charles II was on not unfriendly terms with the house of Hapsburg, and after his restoration to the throne of England, war between England and Spain was ended by proclamation, September 10, 1660.

1. Massachusetts Historical Society, Winthrop MSS., III, 139; printed in Massachusetts Historical Society *Collections*, 4th series, VII (Boston, 1865), 487–489.

growes cooler, my spirits are more at liberty, and returne nearer towards former strength But the cause of my weakening still remaines,
as before. Sir, not knowing when I shall have an opportunity of sending to the Baye, and hearing that a vessel is bound from Milford[2] to
Boston, in hope, that it may touch at Pequot, I have made bold to
send the inclosed unto you unsealed that you may read it, and explaine, or add, or put out what you please seing in yours to me the
quantity of saffron, liquorish, and anniseeds is not mentioned, nor is
it declared that the rest of the particulars, besides corall and pearle,
are not to be had at Mr. Davis, if they cannot be procured at the
shipps. My purpose is to wright unto London by the 1st opportunity,
before the departure of this fleete, for the things you are pleased to
mention But I much doubt that we shall not receive them in the beginning of the spring: for shipps seldom come to Boston, till May. But
I wayte upon God, and, *eo nomine*, shall not neglect any meanes, in
using whereof I may serve his providence, with hope and expectacion
of his blessing, through Jesus Christ. Dr. Shoyse hath none of the
bookes mentioned in your note. He is now upon a voyadge for Virginia,
with Mr. Allerton.[3] Sir) I earnestly looked over your letter for some
word of incouragem[en]t to expect your wintring with us, at least. Be
pleased to declare your purpose, that a convenient house may be ready
for your reception and intertainm[en]t, as well as our hearts are. I was
sorry for a passage in your postscript, that you doe wholly decline and
resolve against transportacion without charge to yourselfe, seing it is
but æquall that what is done for our benefit, should be without charge
to you, and the contrary is not æquall. You may be pleased to choose
a vessel, to your owne content, and to agree for it, if you have any at
hand, but let it be upon us to pay for it. Or, if you still resolve against
that, let that be done which will be to your owne contentm[en]t, onely,
if you cannot accomodate your selfe with a vessel there, let not that
hinder your coming to us, but let us have notice of your mind, that we
may provide and send one for you seasonably. I am sorry for the continuance of the Agues with you. The Lord Jesus rebuke them and
restore health to the plantacions: I heare Mr. Stones[4] Ague hath left
him. Blessed be God. Present my service and my wifes to Mrs. Win-

2. Milford was the third town of the New Haven Colony to be settled and the second
town of the colony in size.

3. Isaac Allerton, Sr., was a merchant of Plymouth, New Amsterdam, and New
Haven.

4. Probably Samuel Stone, teacher of the church at Hartford.

throp and Mrs. Lake. The Lord Jesus dwell with you in peace and loving kindnes! In whom I rest

Newhaven this 27th of the 7th m.   Your obliged freind
1654   JOHN DAVENPORTE

The messenger is more slow to returne then I expected, as the date will shew. But, I thinck, he stayd for brother Lynde. If the pinnase from Milford be gone, be pleased to speed away the inclosed to Boston by the 1st opportunity, by land, or sea.

[Endorsed] 1654 Mr. Davenport to J. Winthrop [in a modern hand.]

JOHN DAVENPORT *to* JOHN WINTHROP the Younger[1]
To his Honor[e]d freind John Winthrop Esq.
these present at Pequot.

Hon[oure]d Sir)

YOUR welcome lines, dat[ed] Jan. 16,[2] I received, by this Indian, and read, with gladnes, giving thancks to God and you. To God; for your health, and the health of your family, and towne. To you; for your loving remembrance of me, and myne, and for your mindfullnes to prepare for us against the fitt season, as also for my brother Hooke, who returneth, by my pen, hearty thancks for your respects towards him, which I signifyed unto him. The winter hath bene extraordinarily long, and sharpe, and sickly among us. Sundry have bene afflicted with paine in theyre heads, and sides, and stoppings at theyre breasts; some were taken with greate cold and shyvering: others with sweating, but most with inward cold. Some are taken away, by death, viz., 4 of this church, and some of the Towne, besides children: but most are restored to health againe, though slowly. Your presence with us, this winter, might have bene, by the providence of God, a greate blessing to the wholl towne. I hope, the season will shortly be altered, and then I desire that we may proceed unto further use of meanes, for the perfecting of what remaines to be attended, in order to my health, by the blessing of God, whereby I found some good, as I apprehend, in the

1. New York Public Library, Winthrop–Davenport Papers; printed in L. Bacon, *Thirteen Historical Discourses* (New Haven, 1839), pp. 367–368; Massachusetts Historical Society *Collections*, 3d series, X (Boston, 1849), 6–8; "Winthrop–Davenport Papers," New York Public Library, *Bulletin*, III (New York, 1899), 396–397. Although the letter is undated, from the public fast held ten days before, Leonard Bacon has fixed the date as March 10, 1654/5.

2. No copy of this letter has been found.

strengthning of my spirits for performance of my ministerial worke, this winter, with some abatement of one cause of my weaknes, whereof I gave you notice, though it still abideth with me, in some degree. My familye hath bene kept from the common sicknes in this towne, by the goodnes and mercy of God, this winter, onely Edmund,[3] my man servant, hath bene excercised with it, neare unto death, but he is now, through the mercy of God, in an hopefull way of Recovery. I have received some letters from England, in Trumbolls[4] vessel, whereby I perceive that things are there in a doubtfull state,[5] and, because I should be too tædious, if I should relate particulars, I send you, by this bearer, such bookes of Intelligence,[6] as were sent me, and in the same you will find inclosed some notes of the Cases of some among us, who desire to improve this opportunity to crave your advise and helpe. It is a singular fruite of Gods favour to you that he is pleased to make you his instrum[en]t in doing good to many. Yet I would not that your family should be indammaged thereby, which cannot be without guilt of unthanckfullnes in them, who returne not according to the benefit received. The fleete is gone from Engl[and] for Hispaniola, Mr. Winslow[7] is one of the Councell, not Governo[u]r for aught I can learne. The small poxe hath bene the death of many in England, and the spotted Feaver. Capt. Astwood[8] of Millford is there dead having

3. Edmund Tooly was Davenport's servant. In the concluding years of the Protectorate, he visited England, returning to New Haven before August 11, 1660. He died in 1685.

4. Probably John Trumbull of Cambridge, Massachusetts, in 1636 and 1647, and Charlestown, Massachusetts, in 1645, captain of a trading vessel.

5. The first parliament of the Protectorate met September 3, 1654, and tension between parliament and the army was soon evident. Parliament was dissolved by Cromwell, January 22, 1654/5.

6. At the end of 1654 the following newspapers were being published in England: *Certain Passages of every dayes Intelligence; The Faithful Scout; Mercurius Politicus; A Perfect Account of the Daily Intelligence; A Perfect Diurnall of some Passages . . . in relation to the Armies; Severall Proceedings in Parliament; The Weekly Intelligencer; The Weekly Post. Catalogue of the Pamphlets, Books, Newspapers, and Manuscripts relating to the Civil War, the Commonwealth, and Restoration, Collected by George Thomason, 1640–1661* (2 vols., London, 1908), II, 430.

7. The general conduct of the expedition against Hispaniola was entrusted to five commissioners of whom Edward Winslow, several times governor of New Plymouth, was one. After the repulse at Hispaniola and before the taking of Jamaica, he died at sea, May 8, 1655. S. R. Gardiner, *History of the Commonwealth and Protectorate, 1649–1660* (3 vols., London, 1901), III, 347.

8. John Astwood of Milford was appointed agent of the New Haven Colony to England, October 12, 1653. He died in England between June 27, 1654, the date of his last will and testament, and August 31, 1654, the date of its proof. H. F. Waters, *Genealogical Gleanings in England* (2 vols., Boston, 1901), I, 81.

1st taken a great cold, after his arrival, whereupon he was smitten with a dead palsey, on one side, of which he dyed. I hope, we shall injoy your much desired company, with Mrs. Winthrop, at our house, sometime this moneth, where you may be assured of hearty welcom, as the best part of your intertainm[en]t. The Lord Jesus dwell with you in peace, and loving kindenes! to whose grace I recommend you and yours affectionately, with respective salutacions of yours[elf] and Mrs. Winthrop and Mrs. Lake, in boath our names, I rest in him

Yours obliged

JOHN DAVENPORTE

Mrs. Disborough,[9] and Goodman Jones[10] of Gillford, dyed of the small poxe in England or Scotland. Mrs. Bressey, a member of this church, hath buryed 3 children, in a moneth, of the small poxe, in England, yet, its thaught, by some, that the 3d child dyed of the plague, as Mrs. Evance[11] informeth me, but Mrs. Bressey, in her letter to me, saith, they all dyed of the small poxe. I find my selfe somewhat weaker, in my spirits, and in my backe, since our last fast, which was 10 daies agoe.

Postscript[12]

Ex D[octo]ris Shoysij Autogræpho, 22° Aug. 54 quod ostendere tibi, quum tuo me contubernio dignatus eras, negligebam, Apographum hoc accipe. Viginti Annis abhinc Rhotordami flavâ icteritiâ laboravit. Triennium abhinc, mense Junio præterito, post longam equitationem sub ar-

9. Dorothy (Whitfield) Desborough, the wife of Samuel Desborough of Guilford, returned to England with her husband in 1651 and died in 1654.

10. Probably Thomas Jones, one of the first settlers of Guilford, who left Guilford at about the same time that Samuel Desborough returned to England. B. C. Steiner, *A History of the Plantation of Menunkatuck and of the Original Town of Guilford, Connecticut* (Baltimore, 1897), p. 46.

11. John Evance of New Haven married Anna Yong at St. Stephen's, Coleman Street, London, May 2, 1624. About 1655 he returned to England. His will, dated December 13, 1660, and proved May 2, 1661, gives the name of his wife as Susanna. His widow married Henry Hatsell. Somerset House, P. C. C., May, 71.

12. From the letter of Dr. Shoys, August 22, 1654, which I neglected to show to you, when you deemed me worthy of your company, accept this transcript. Twenty years ago in Rotterdam he suffered from yellow jaundice. Three years ago, in June last, after a long ride under a burning sky, his very dear wife seated behind him, he discharged bloody puss without irritation, or at least very little, without pain, without thought of coition, which continues. Two years ago he suffered twice from nephritis.

From which it is deduced that the cause of the condition is heat of the liver and kidneys. For as Fernel said regarding the procreation of man, Chapter 2, just as the liver draws fluid from the intestines *via* the mesenteric veins: so the testicles draw matter which is located in the loins and kidneys from the vena cava *via* the seminal vessels.

denti cælo, charissimâ ejus uxore a tergo insidente, sanguinem purulen-
tum excrevit, sine titillatione, aut saltem exiguâ, sine dolore, sine coitus
cogitatione, quod continuat. Biennium abhinc Nephritide bis laboravit.

Ex quibus colligitur causam affectus esse epatis et renum Caliditatem.
Nam, ut inquit Fernelius,[13] de hom[inis] procr[eatione]. cap. 2°, Jecur ex
intestinis succum rapit per venas mesenterij: sic testes per seminis vasa
materiam sugunt a vena cava, quæ lumbis et renibus assistit. Inde in-
fertur excrementa illa purulenta ex renibus per venam cavam descendere
ad vasa spermatica præparantia, et ita non cocta a testibus excerni. Nam
quodcumque a testibus absolute coactum coctumque est, id, ut colore album,
ita et substantia crassum redditur. Hæc ille.

Decem dies abhinc publicum apud nos jejunium celebratum est, ex quo
renum, dorsique debilitatem, sensi, atque adhuc sentio.

[Endorsed] Mr. Davenport [by John Winthrop, and] John Davenports
Lett[e]r. *no Date.* [in a modern hand.]

John Davenport *to* John Winthrop the Younger[1]

To the Right Worship[fu]ll his worthily much Honour[e]d freind
John Winthrop Esq. these present in Pequod

Honour[e]d Sir)

IT troubled me, not a litle, that the want of a pillion to carry my wife,
and of horses to bring us back from brother Molethrops, and some
buisenes to be attended, by appointm[en]t, at 3 aclock, that afternoone, in the towne, compelled us to part from you, at the water side,
whom we purposed to accompany unto his farme. But I hope the Lord
brought you safe and well to your family, and there comforted you
with the effects of his good providence, towards yours, in theyre well-

From which it is inferred that those purulent excrements descend from the kidneys
through the vena cava to the awaiting spermatic vessels and without preparation are
discharged from the testicles. For that which is completely prepared and discharged
from the testicles is both white in color and thick in substance. He said these things.

Ten days ago a public fast was celebrated here, after which I felt a weakness in my
kidneys and my back and I still feel that weakness.

13. Jean Fernel or Joannes Fernelius, a French physician who lived from 1497 to 1558,
was the author of *Vniversa Medicina* (Frankfurt, 1592; Leyden, 1602 and 1645). Davenport quotes p. 158 in the 1592 edition, p. 202 in the 1602 edition, and p. 303 in the 1645
edition.

1. New York Public Library, Winthrop–Davenport Papers; printed in L. Bacon,
Thirteen Historical Discourses (New Haven, 1839), pp. 369–370; Massachusetts Historical Society *Collections*, 3d series, X (Boston, 1849), 8–10.

fare. Mr. Samuel Eaton[2] and his wife[3] returned lately from Hartford, where they were boath ill: they say, its thaught that aire is infected, at present. Sundry have bene excercised with a distemper like to that which prevailed here, the last winter, but they are in an hopefull way of recovery: and Captaine Connant[4] is better. They have putt such houshold stuffe as they shall have use of, into a vessel bound hitherward, purposing to keepe house here. The 3 weekes, during which you purposed to be absent from us, are now expired; therefore here is now a general expectation of your returne: for which cause brother Molethrop is sent, to waite upon you, or to know the precise time thereof, that horses may be seasonably sent, to meete you, at the Rivers mouth (so many as may suite your family) and that some thing may be done towards the fitting of your house, for theyre intertainm[en]t. My earnest and hearty desire is that you would be pleased to accept this Townes offer, and to settle your habitacion among us, though you should dwell here but some part of the yeare, and another part of it at Pequod, or wheresoever else your occasions may invite you to be. My wife joyneth with me in that request, and in presenting respective and affectionate salutacions to your selfe, with Mrs. Winthrope and Mrs. Lake, and she prayeth you to be assured that any thing we have shall be at your service. Sister Glover[5] newly returned from Long Island puts us in feare that you are in some thaughts about transporting your family to the Baye, or to Connectacut, but I cannot beleive either, though, I beleive, you may be invited to boath. I hope that this messenger will put a period to all such intimacions, either by your personal returne with him hither, or by some letter from you certifying the determined time, when we may expect you. For you freely promised to stay with us, at least, a moneth or 6 weekes, this spring, for the carrying on further what you have begun, in my case and Mrs. Hopkinses[6]

2. Samuel Eaton, the son of Theophilus and Anne (Lloyd) Eaton, was a graduate of Harvard College in 1649 and a fellow of the college from 1650 to 1653. He died in July, 1655.

3. Mabel (Harlakenden), the widow of John Haynes, was married to Samuel Eaton November 17, 1654. She died within two or three days of her husband in July, 1655.

4. Possibly Joshua Conant, a son of Roger Conant, and sea captain of Marblehead, Massachusetts. F. O. Conant, *A History and Genealogy of the Conant Family* (Portland, 1887), p. 136.

5. Ellen or Elinor (Russell) Glover, the wife of Henry Glover, an inhabitant of New Haven as early as 1644.

6. Anne (Yale) Hopkins, the insane wife of Edward Hopkins, was left in the care of her family at New Haven when he returned to England in 1651. She was probably taken to England by her brother, Thomas Yale, who sold his lands at New Haven February 5, 1655/6, and departed, returning in the summer of 1659. After the death of Edward Hopkins in 1657, Anne (Yale) Hopkins remained in England, where she died December 17, 1698.

etc. Then we shall have opportunity of conferring, *de futuris*. In the meane time, and ever, the good Lord recompence all your labour of love an 100d fold unto you and your family, and make your journey to us speedy and prosperous! In whom I rest

Newhaven this 14th   Your obliged and thanckfull freind and servant
day of the 2d m. 1655   in any office of love

JOHN DAVENPORTE

Mr. Pell,[7] they say, reports at Millford that the Dutch Governo[u]r[8] is slaine by Spaniards, *sed ubi, quomodo, quando, quare, nondum constat. Verte folium*

Postscript
    Upon a confident report that you was gone to the Baye, bro: Molethrop staid, and so my letter, though sealed, was not sent. Yesterday, another report said that a pinnas was sent from the Baye to fetch you, but you could not goe, being hindred by sicknes. This report excited me to speake with our Governo[u]r that one might be sent speedily, and, I hope, bro: Molethrop will be procured to be our messenger, also it occasioned my opening of my letter againe, and adding this postscript; to certifye you that I both pray and long to heare of your recovery, and have good hope, through the mercy of God in christ Jesus, that you shall live to doe him much more service in the land of the living. Onely let us know how it is with you, speedily, and when we shall expect you, and what you will have done about the house and lot, and be assured that you are in our hearts and in my prayers that your soul may be bound up in the bundle of life with the Lord our God, in Jesus christ, your Lord and ours, in whom I rest

This 19th d. of the 2d m. 1655

[Endorsed] Mr. Davenport [by John Winthrop, and] Dated (~~Feb'y 19th.~~) 1655 19th 2d mo.=19 April '55 I: B. [in a modern hand.]

---

7. Thomas Pell, a physician at New Haven as early as 1642, was at this time a resident of Fairfield.

8. On his own responsibility, Peter Stuyvesant, director general of New Netherland, sailed for the West Indies, December 14/24, 1654, to establish trade between New Netherland and the English and Spanish islands. Although he failed in his purpose, he lived to return to New Netherland in the summer of 1655. J. R. Brodhead, *History of the State of New York* (2 vols., New York, 1853), I, 596, 603; E. B. O'Callaghan, *History of New Netherland* (2 vols., New York, 1855), II, 276, 285.

JOHN DAVENPORT *to* JOHN WINTHROP the Younger[1]

To the R[igh]t Worsh[i]p[fu]ll his much Honoured freind
John Winthrop Esq. these pr[e]sent in Pequot

Sir)

JOSEPH ALSOP being now returned from the Baye, we have taken the
1st opportunity of sending him, with his vessel, to accomodate
your much desired transportacion, with your family, unto us. Be
pleased to accept this as a testimony of the reality and fervency of our
desire to injoy your much longed for, and worthily much esteemed
presence with us, and to favour us with a suitable answer, in assurance
that none can be more welcom hither, then you and yours, nor can you
and they be more welcom to any then to us. Sir) I have received from
England almost all the particulars you appointed me to wright for,
which I desire you may see and dispose of as you shall find best. Salute
Mrs. Winthrop and Mrs. Lake affectionately in boath our names. My
sonne presents his humble service to you. The good Lord recompence
all your labours of love towards me an 100 fold, and make your passage safe, speed[y], and comfortable! In whom I rest

Newhaven, the 6th   Sir
day of the 5th m. 1655   Yours to honour and serve
                                                          you in the Lord

                                                    JOHN DAVENPORT

My wife hath not bene well, but weake and feeble-spirited, this
weeke.

[Endorsed] Mr. Davenport [by John Winthrop, and] John Davenport's Letter dated July 6th. *1655*. [in a modern hand.]

---

1. New York Public Library, Winthrop–Davenport Papers; printed in L. Bacon
Thirteen Historical Discourses (New Haven, 1839), pp. 370–371; Massachusetts Historical Society *Collections*, 3d series, X (Boston, 1849), 11–12.

JOHN DAVENPORT *to* JOHN WINTHROP the Younger[1]
To his Honoured freind John Winthrop Esq.
these present in Pequot

Hon[oure]d Sir)

WE did earnestly expect your comming hither, with Mrs. Winthrop
and your familie, the last light moone, according to your purpose signifyed to us, having also intelligence that a vessel wayted upon
you, at Pequot, for that end, and were thereby encouraged to provide
your house, that it might be fitted, in some measure, for your comfortable dwelling in it, this winter. My wife was not wanting in her
endeavours to set all wheeles on going, all hands, that she could procure, on worke, that you might finde all things to your satisfaction.
Though she could not accomplish her desires, to the full; yet she proceeded as farr as she could, whereby many things are done, viz. the
house made warme; the well cleansed: the pumpe fitted for your use:
some provision of wood is layed in, and 20 loades will be ready, when-
soever you come: and sundry, who have received helpe from you,
have by my wifes instigation præpared 30 bush[els] of wheate for
the present and Sister Glover hath 12£ of candles ready for you. My
wife hath also procured a maid-servant[2] for you, who is reported to be
cleanly, and saving, her mother is of the church, and she is kept from
a place in Connectacut (where she was much desired) to serve you.
At last, Joseph Alsop arrived here, in safety, on the Lords day, and, in
the Assembly, gave thancks for his comfortable passage. By him I
received, (instead of your selfe and yours, whose presence was heartily
desired by us all) a letter from you, dated on the day before his arrivall, whereby I understood that some providences intercurring hindred and dissappointed your reall Intentions of coming, with your
family, to us, both before, and by him. The hazzard and danger suspected, you now see, was more in ungrounded imaginacions of those
who laboured to hinder your proceeding, then in the reality and trueth
of the cause prætended by them. Yet we have hope that, by another
vessel (I heare, Mr. Yongs,[3] *nî fallor*) you will be accomodated, for

1. Massachusetts Historical Society, Winthrop MSS., Autograph Letters, 1587–
1675, IA, 121; printed in Massachusetts Historical Society *Collections*, 3d series, X
(Boston, 1849), 12–14; A. B. Davenport, *A History and Genealogy of the Davenport
Family* (New York, 1851), pp. 346–348.

2. The daughter of Richard Beckley, one of the first settlers of New Haven.

3. On September 20, 1655, the commissioners of the United Colonies of New England
commissioned John Youngs, Jr., son of the pastor of the church at Southold, to ply up
and down between Pawcatuck and Pequot in a vessel with six, ten, or twelve men, to
watch the movements of Ninnegrett, the Niantic. This Youngs did through the winter
and spring of 1655–1656.

transportation of your familye, and what you purpose to bring hither, and that you incline to improve that opportunity, wherof I am glad. Many hands are daily at worke for the iron-buisenes:[4] onely your presence is wanting, to sett all things in a right course. If Mrs. Winthrop knew how wellcome she will be to us, she would, I beleive, neglect whatsoever others doe, or may be forward to suggest, for her discouragement. Salute her, with due respect, in my name and my wifes, most affectionately, together with Mrs. Lake. The Lord Jesus pave your waye, and make your journey to us speedy and prosperous! In whom I rest

Newhaven this 22 of the 9th 55   Sir)

                      Yours exceedingly obliged

                          JOHN DAVENPORT

My wife had a man in pursuite that would be very fitt to manadge your Island,[5] and the motion proceedes in an hopefull way, if a marriage, which he is about, doth not hinder. My sonne presents his humble service to your selfe and Mrs. Winthrope.

Sir William Constable[6] and Mr. Tillinghast[7] are taken away by death in England, boath buryed; the one, in London; the other in Norfolke with great honour. Also Capt. Fen[8] is dead in Barbadoes, and Mr. Nowel,[9] at Charles Towne. Mr. Leverets[10] wifes violent aversenes from his settling in the Colledge,[11] he saith, causeth him to desist from that buisenes. So, that worke must waite for a better season.

4. Due to the efforts of John Winthrop the Younger, an ironworks company was organized, February 13, 1656, to further the ironworks between New Haven and Branford. After his removal to Hartford in 1657, Winthrop leased his interest in the works to Thomas Clarke and William Paine of Boston.

5. The general court of Connecticut had granted Fisher's Island to John Winthrop the Younger, April 9, 1641. *Connecticut Colonial Records, 1636–1665* (Hartford, 1850), pp. 64–65.

6. Sir William Constable, parliamentarian, regicide, and a member of the first, second, and fourth Councils of State, died June 15, 1655. Buried in Westminster Abbey, his body was disinterred after the Restoration.

7. John Tillinghast, rector of Trunch, Norfolk, died in London early in June, 1655.

8. Possibly Robert Fenn, a London sea captain.

9. Reëlected assistant May 23, 1655, Increase Nowell of Charlestown, Massachusetts, died November 1, 1655.

10. The wife of William Leverich or Leveridge, recently settled at Oyster Bay, Long Island.

11. Davenport had long labored to establish a college at New Haven. At this time the plan seemed near fruition. *New Haven Colonial Records, 1653–1665* (Hartford, 1858), pp. 136–138.

My wife complaineth of a paine in the soles of her feete, especially in the evening, sometimes it burnes. Yet in the day, and after she hath bene a while in bed, it doth not trouble her. Sir, I thanck you for the 2 bookes you sent me to peruse which I am reading dilligently.

[Endorsed] Mr. Davenport [by John Winthrop, and] John Davenport's Lett[e]r Dated Nov[embe]r 22d. *1655.* [in a modern hand.]

John Davenport *to* John Winthrop the Younger[1]
To his Worthily much Honoured freind John Winthrope Esq.
these pr[e]sent in Pequot

Hon[oure]d Sir)

By Joseph Alsop we did expect your arrivall, with your family, here, and your abode with us, this winter. But, instead of yourselfe, I received your lines, whereby I understood that your real purpose of transporting your familie was, contrary to your expectation, utterly dissapointed. If you knew how much our hopes of injoying you with us comforted us, you would easily apprehend how much the frustration of them damped us. And, if Mrs. Winthrop knew how welcome she would be unto us, she would neglect whatsoever others may suggest to discourage her from coming to us. And, because I understood, by Joseph Alsop, how boysterously some of your plantation opposed your voyadge, with your familie, to us ward, and intimated that the vessel was rotten and your lives would be endangered by the voyage, I signifyed, in a letter, which I sent to you, by Higby,[2] that, on the Lords day, after his departure from Pequot, which was the next day after the date of your letter to me, as I remember, Joseph Alsop gave publick thancks, in the congregacion, for his safe and comfortable passage. And, that you might know what preparacion was made for your comfortable being in your house, this winter, I shewed, in the same letter, how carefull and active my wife hath bene to procure hands to prepare your house, whereby your well is cleansed, and a new pumpe set up, and the roomes are made warme, and tables with some chayres are provided. The 20 loads of wood, you mentioned, are ready, and some

1. New York Public Library, Winthrop–Davenport Papers; printed in L. Bacon, *Thirteen Historical Discourses* (New Haven, 1839), pp. 371–372; Massachusetts Historical Society *Collections*, 3d series, X (Boston, 1849), 14–15; A. B. Davenport, *A History and Genealogy of the Davenport Family* (New York, 1851), pp. 326–327.

2. Edward Higby was a Stratford boatman who, apparently, journeyed among the towns on Long Island Sound.

already laid in. The rest waite but for your coming. Also 30 bush[els] of wheate, and some candles. Which, together with other things, I signifyed, that you may see, and Mrs. Winthrop also, how earnestly your coming to us is expected and desired. You will now receive some further intelligence from Mr. Goodyeare[3] concerning the iron-worke, unto which there is a great forwardnes in the people generally, which, it seemes, is somewhat checked by your absence, at this time. Sir) I thanck you for the bookes you sent me to reade, which I am dilligently perusing. My wife tooke care of your apples, that they may be kept safe from the frost, that Mrs. Winthrop might have the benefit of them. Now the Lord pave your way to us, and make your journey safe comfortable and prosperous! In whom I rest

Newhaven the last of the 9th. 55   Yours exceedingly obliged

JOHN DAVENPORTE

Sir) I forgate to give you notice, that my wife hath provided for Mrs. Winthrop a cleanly thrifty maide-servant, sister Becklyes daughter, whom she kept from a service at Connectacute, where she was much desired; in expectation of your coming.

[Endorsed] Mr. Davenport [by John Winthrop, and] Nov[embe]r 30th. ~~1659~~ 1655 I. B. [in a modern hand.]

JOHN DAVENPORT to JOHN WINTHROP the Younger[1]

Honour[e]d Sir)

THIS Indian-bearer giving me notice of his purpose to goe unto you, I cannot prætermit such an opportunity of saluting yours[elf] with Mrs. Winthrop and Mrs. Lake. Sir) I received your letter with the præscriptions you was pleased to send me, and am in the use of them, wayting upon God for his blessing, to whom your labour of love is undoubtedly acceptable in Jesus christ, as it is also obligatory to me, in the strongest ingagements of love and thanckfullnes. It hath pleased the most High to make this part of the winter so moderate and comfortable, that we are encouraged to hope that we may injoy your presence with us ere long, which is much desired of all; and that it may be accelerated, so farr as may stand with your conveniencie, and

3. Stephen Goodyear, deputy governor of the New Haven Colony, and interested in the ironworks.
1. Massachusetts Historical Society, Winthrop MSS., Autograph Letter, 1587–1675, IA, 121.

health. I looked at the hast which Totoket² made in the iron-buisenes as an hurry of Temptation, because they did not first consult yourselfe about the termes, whereupon they should proceede, and the order wherein, that all might be carryed on, to your satisfaction, who, by right, should order the wholl buisenes to your owne content. This drew on sundry of ours also into fellowship with them, in the same dissorder. But I am persuaded that your coming will set all in a right way. I know not what conveniency presents itselfe for the transportacion of yourselfe and yours hitherward, by sea. If you choose rather to come by land, my horse at brother Molethrops, will be ready to serve you, and what other horses you require, upon notice given of the number, they shall be ready. My wife presents her humble service to yourselfe and Mrs. Winthrop, so doth my sonne John. The Lord Jesus dwell with you in mercy, and peace and loving kindenesses! In whom I rest

Newhaven the 4th day   Sir
of the 11th m. 1655

                           Yours obliged

                            JOHN DAVENPORTE

[Endorsed] Mr. Davenport [by John Winthrop, and] John Davenport's Lett[e]r. Dated Jan[ua]ry 4th *1655*. [in a modern hand.]

JOHN DAVENPORT *to* JOHN WINTHROP the Younger¹

To the Right Worship[fu]ll John Winthrope Esq. Governo[u]r of Connectacut Colonie these present in Hartford²

Honour[e]d Sir)

THOUGH my spirit is much streightned and indisposed, for wrighting letters, by that late dreadfull stroake upon us, from the hand of the most High, in the loss of our incomparable Governour,³ and my faithfull freind, under which we still bleed, and, I feare, unto the death of our politique body, unles God be pleased to shew himselfe, in the mount, above all that we can aske or thinck; yet I willingly take

2. Totoket or Branford, the smallest of the towns of the New Haven Colony.
1. Yale University Library, printed in Massachusetts Historical Society *Collections*, 4th series, VII (Boston, 1865), 489–490; A. B. Davenport, *Supplement* (Stamford, 1876), pp. 378–379.
2. Following his election as governor of Connecticut, May 21, 1657, John Winthrop the Younger took up his residence at Hartford in the colony of Connecticut.
3. Theophilus Eaton, governor of the New Haven Colony, died January 7, 1657/8.

this sad occasion to salute your selfe, and Mrs. Winthrope, respectfully, and affectionately, in the Lord, in boath our names, who long to see your face, in your best season.

The inclosed, whereunto this serveth for a cover, will shew you what the case and desire of brother and sister Herrymans[4] is. With them I also joyne my humb[l]e request, that you will be pleased to consider and advise speedily, that, if it may be, his eyesight may be preserved, and his eye healed. Being assured of your readynes hereunto, as unto every worke of mercy, I cease to diverte you from the weighty affaires under your hand, and to detaine you from this present necessary worke of mercy which craves your serious consideration and speedy helpe. The Lord guide you in boath, and prosper all your endeavours for the good of many, and of this our brother! My sonne also presents you with an Account of his negotiation about the buisenes you commended to his care. Farewell in our Lord Jesus. In whom I rest

Newhaven   Sir)
this 21 of the   Your obliged freind and serv[an]t in
11th m. 57. in the evening
                                            the Lord

                                                      JOHN DAVENPORTE

[Endorsed] Mr. Davenport about G: Herrimans Ey. [by John Winthrop.]

JOHN DAVENPORT *to* JOHN WINTHROP the Younger[1]

To the Right Worship[fu]ll John Winthrope Esq. Governo[u]r of Connectacute these present in Hartford

Honoured Sir)

THOUGH, this being the last day of the weeke, and by Mr. Blynmans staying, the Lords day, at Gillford, I am dissappointed of his expected helpe, so that the wholl worke of preaching, boath times,

4. A settler of New Haven as early as 1644, and a freeman in 1646, John Harriman, Heardman, or Herriman was keeper of the ordinary at New Haven in 1648. He bought the house of Stephen Goodyear at New Haven in 1659, and served as alternate townsman in 1660. Although F. W. Lamb, *Lamb Savory Harriman Family Records* (n.p., 1900), p. 12, says that the Harriman family is of Rowley, Yorkshire, England, origin, the name does not occur in the transcripts of the parish registers of Rowley for the years 1620–1625 and 1630–1640 preserved in the office of the Registrar of the Diocese, York. Furthermore, Davenport's letter of November 18, 1658 (see below, p. 132), would indicate that John Harriman had some knowledge of Kent, England.

1. Massachusetts Historical Society, Winthrop MSS., III, 140; printed in Massachusetts Historical Society *Collections*, 4th series, VII (Boston, 1865), 490–492.

and administring the Lord supper, lyeth upon me, whereby I am constrayned to be as breife, in these lines, as I may; yet, seing a worke of
mercy towards brother Herryman, by his wifes desire, urgeth me to
wright, at this time, this messenger, brother Molthrope, purposing to
travaile, from his farme, to youward, betimes on the 2d day; I may not
omit this opportunity, of saluting your selfe, and Mrs. Winthrope, and
yours, in boath ours, and my sonnes names, with all due respect, and
sincere love, in the Lord. For brother Herryman; they have applyed
what you sent to his eyes and finde some benefit by it. For it opened
the liddes gradually, by litle and litle and gave him ease. But, upon
the opening of his eyeliddes, they find that, in the eye, where the sight
was, is a mattery substance, which brother Peck[2] thinckes flowed out
of it, (peradventure it is the chrystaline humor). He saith it is ragged,
or like white ragges undissolved, which, yet, he thincks, may be easily
dissolved: and from the ball of the eye groweth a carnous substance,
which covereth the neather eye lid all over, and at the end of it, in the
corner of the eye, by his nose, is a tumor of a pretty bignes. Hereby,
his eye seemes to be as 2 eyes to them that looke upon it. Yet sister
Herryman saith, she can see his eye under that excrescence. The excrescence is red, and so is his eye. On the 5th day last, he tooke the
powder, which worked very well, but most upwards, which, sister
thincks, increased the swelling about his eye. Brother Peck thincks
that his eye hath no sense [in] it, nor can they yet say, whether the
sight be wholly lost, or not, till that white mattery substance be taken
away, which is before it. About which he doth not take any course till
your further advise come. He thincks also that what you sent works
too slowely, but that we leave to your wisdom, as also to advise what
you judge best for the future. He purposeth to put a litle sugar candie
into it, for the present, which, he saith, may doe some good, and no
hurt, til they may receive further directions from your selfe. My wife
presents, with her service, the remaynder of the rootes she sent you
before, as a testimony of her readynes and desire to be any way serviceable to you, to whom we boath owe much more then we are able to
performe. The Lord Jesus dwell with you in peace! In whom I rest

Newhaven the 30th d of   Sir
the 11th m. 1657
               Yours exceedingly obliged

                  JOHN DAVENPORT

2. William Peck was admitted a freeman at New Haven October 29, 1640. He was the
father of Jeremiah Peck, who at this time was schoolmaster at Guilford, and later, master of the colony grammar school.

Sister Herryman came to me, since I wrote thus farr, and saith, that her Husband could stirre his eye yesterday a litle, and this day, more, and that, that excrescence from the ball of his eye (which she likeneth to a wheate straw) and toucheth the underlid, lookes a litle paler then it did, and that the eye lid growes more plyable, and he can open it a litle himselfe. That tumor by the side of his nose, she saith is about the bignes of a litle pea. The white that covers the black and darke colour of his eye is as bigg as a penny, and in the middest of that is that ragged matter I wrote of before. Brother Herryman thincks that he pricked his eye with the bodkin and that might cause this ragged thing about his eye. Sister Herryman and he boath thinck that what you sent workes well. For he findes that he can stirr his eye which before was as a thing dead, and other good effects. He is also at good ease

[Endorsed] Mr. Davenport rec: feb: 3: [by John Winthrop.]

JOHN DAVENPORT *to* the CHURCH at Wethersfield[1]

Hono[u]red and Beloved in our Lord Jesus

THE answer of the ch[urch] of christ at Newhauen to your Lett[e]r for advise, upon the question proposed, touching your admitting the persons mentioned[2] in to ch[urch] ffellowship with you, was such as that time could pr[e]sent. Since that returne such of the Eld[e]rs of the Councell whose liberty would permitt it, haue met togeth[e]r in

1. British Museum, Lansdowne MSS., 93, fols. 213–214; printed in Connecticut Historical Society *Collections*, II (Hartford, 1870), 88–93. Although this letter is undated, its contents indicate that it was written in February, 1657/8.

2. From 1656 until their removal to Hadley, Massachusetts, in 1659, William Goodwin, ruling elder of the church at Hartford, John Cullick, and others were engaged in a bitter quarrel with Samuel Stone, teacher of the church at Hartford. In an attempt to heal the breach, a council of elders of Connecticut and Peter Prudden, pastor of the church at Milford in the New Haven Colony, met at Hartford, June 11, 1656; again, this time with John Norton and other elders and messengers of seven churches of Massachusetts Bay, at Hartford in April, 1657; and a third time at New Haven about February, 1657/8, apparently after the dissenters of the church at Hartford had applied to the church at Wethersfield for admission. "Papers relating to the Controversy in the Church in Hartford. 1656–1659." Connecticut Historical Society *Collections*, II (Hartford, 1870), 51–125; "The Diaries of John Hull," American Antiquarian Society *Transactions and Collections*, III (Boston, 1857), 180, 188; *Connecticut Colonial Records, 1636–1665* (Hartford, 1850), pp. 312, 314, 317; *Massachusetts Colony Records*, IV, Part I (Boston, 1854), 328, 368; G. L. Walker, *History of the First Church in Hartford, 1633–1883* (Hartford, 1884), pp. 166–174; S. Judd, *History of Hadley* (Springfield, 1905), pp. 3–13.

this Towne, which themselues chose as most convenient for them all
to meet in from their sev[e]rall places. At their request and with the
consent of this Ch[urch]³ I was sometimes (as my occasions would
permitt) pr[e]sent with them, not as one of them, but as a stranger
willing to receive light from them, that thereby I might with the
bett[e]r satisfaction unto my selfe, and you, signifye myne appr[e]hen-
s[ion]s touching that weighty question, both to your selues and to this
Ch[urch] in due season. I shall leaue it to those Reverend Eld[e]rs to
act in that way which is proper to them, for issuing the question betweene the Ch[urch] of Hartford and yourselues for their dismission,
from thence and admittance into your ffellowship. ffor my selfe I confesse I looke at such contentions in the Ch[urch] at Hartford, so long
continued and with such distance of sp[iri]t, and sharpe opposition,
and bitternes, as highly dishonorable to god, and Jesus chr[ist] and
ch[ri]st[ian] religion and to the way of the Congr[e]gationall Ch[urche]s,
and as of dangerous consequences to all the Church[e]s in these ends
of the earth, both by an evill example and by their tendancy to involue all the ch[urche]s in some ffellowship of their contentions, if the
most high be not pleased to avert that storme, which the cloud that is
there gathered seemeth to threaten: In the form[e]r we see how just
cause we all haue to be humbled before our holy and jealous God, for
those weights, which pr[e]sse the minds of men downe wards, and selfe
wards, and to watch and pray, and strive to mortifye dayly the sin
that so easily besets us; whence it is that a Brother (as well ecclesiasti-   Pro: 18. 19
call and Naturall) offended is hard[e]r to be won then a strong citty
and their contentions, are like the bars of a castle. As for the latt[e]r
the dang[e]r of hurt by such an ill example, wilbe removed if we attend
to those good examples, and to that perfect Rule of walking in Broth-
[e]rly loue, with all lowlines and meeknes, with long suffring forbearing
one anoth[e]r in loue, endeavo[u]ring to keep the unity of the sp[iri]t
in the bond of peace, which the script[ure] holdeth forth unto us, to
guide our feet into the wayes of peace, and to arme them as with
greaues or leg harnesse⁴ ag[ain]st scandals from the contrary practise
of others: The other dang[e]r of being involued in contentions, hath
hith[e]r to deterred me from medling in these differences, till it should
please the only wise God, to call me therunto, by whose good providence I haue bin exempted both from publique acting, as not being
called to assist in the Councell and from acting by way of private
advise to that Ch[urch]. Yet seeing your selues, Hono[u]red and Be-

3. The church at New Haven.
4. I Samuel 17. 6.

loved, haue bin pleased to write unto the ch[urch], the Communion of [churches] bindeth us to satisfye your Godly desires as we are able, least oth[e]rwise we should be found to be unto you as wat[e]rs that faile in the time of need. Therfore I shall first give you a breife account of what I haue don to informe my selfe of the truth that concerns your q[ue]st[i]on and aft[e]rw[a]rd shew unto what issue my thoughts are come. For the 1st I find that the whole ch[urch] at Hartford unanimously cons[en]ted to call a counc[e]ll of Eld[e]rs of that colony with whom they joined Mr. Prud[den][5] of this Colony, to giue their advise for the ending of differ[e]nc[e]s betw[een] them, by which act the Ch[urch] did put the whole pow[e]r of judging one anoth[e]r about the matters so referred out of their owne hands into the hands of that councell, with submission to that judgm[en]t it being according to script[ure] and held forth to them with consent am[on]g the Eld[e]rs of that Councell. 2ly that councell thus called left their finall determinacion with them, in writting subscribed by them all as the result of the debates they had with both partyes till they had produced what they would, and of the debates among themselues touch[in]g the differ[e]nc[e]s and the meanes of remou[in]g them, which was 1st that mutuall satisfaction should be given on both sides each to other, by acknowledg[in]g their faults in the particul[ar]s mentioned in that writting, 2ly that if differ[e]nces should againe breake forth or not be healed, the dissenting Brethren should craue their dismission and the ch[urch] should giue it them. 3ly I haue seen and considered as the time would permitt that Counsell defense as the time would permitt of their proceeding in that businesse ag[ains]t Mr. Stones opposition published to their reproach,[6] wherein they produce many argum[en]ts for their justification which defence was read before Mr. Stone and Mess[engers] and Eld[e]rs that came from the Bay[7] and left with them, but no answ[e]r hath bin returned to it and them to this day. 4th The Eld[e]rs of the s[ai]d Councill do further testify that the brethren form[e]rly called dissenting haue fully attended the determinacion of the Counsell in both the advices left with them 1st By giving satisfac-

5. Peter Prudden, pastor of the church at Milford in the New Haven Colony.

6. At the moment or soon after the verdict of the council which assembled at Hartford, June 11, 1656, Samuel Stone published a reply. G. L. Walker, *History of the First Church in Hartford, 1633–1883* (Hartford, 1884), p. 158; Connecticut Historical Society *Collections*, II (Hartford, 1870), 72.

7. In an effort to heal the breach in the church at Hartford, John Norton, teacher of the church at Boston, and representatives of six other churches of Massachusetts Bay journeyed to Hartford in April, 1657, to sit with the members of the first council. At this time a pacification seems to have been arranged.

tion to remove offences on their part 2d By craving their admission when all means became ineffectuall for the setling of peace with brotherly love among them; the Pacification also being frustrated which the Rev[e]r[end] Eld[e]rs and Messeng[e]rs from the Bay endeavo[u]r[e]d: the breth[ren] being out of hope of obtaining their dismission have sep[a]r[a]ted thems[elves] from that fellowship with which they cannot walk as it becometh brethren to walk togeth[e]r in ch[urch] Communion yet still they would gladly receive their dismission to ag[ai]n walke in ch[urch] estate and ord[e]r either among thems[elves] or with some other ch[urch] which the Counsell judged to be necessary as their case was and that therefore the ch[urch] should grant it them there being no oth[e]r way left for peace. The withdrawn persons have since sent a large writing to the ch[urch] at Hartford[8] wherein they prove the necessity of this their withdrawing and charge the blame of it upon that other party compelling them thereto, and have sent it to the ch[urch]: yet neith[e]r is that writing answ[e]r[e]d nor the dismission which thems[elves] and others for them have craved granted but denyed. 5[th] The Eld[e]rs of the s[ai]d Counsell doe furth[e]r testify that Mr. St[one] and the ch[urch] at Hartf[ord] have violated the determinacion of that Councill in both parts of their advice by their nev[e]r giving the satisfaccion pr[e]scribed for the healing of offences and now by their not giving the offended breth[ren] their dismission. And now what rem[ains] to be done those persons who have propounded thems[elves] to your fellowship desire to walk in the ord[e]r and acc[ording] to the rules of the Gospell they are also known to yours[elves] and to all the peo[ple] of G[o]d that have acquaintance with them to be Godly nor doth the ch[urch] at Hartf[ord] deny this to be true, but there are differences and there upon offences unremoved. True and there are so on both sides. They are for their memb[e]r[s] and qualities a party not to be despised. Where offences are mutuall, satisfacion must be mutually given and taken, but here only the dissenting breth[ren] must be urg[e]d to give satisfacion and the oth[e]r party tho[ugh] offend[e]rs in the appr[e]h[ensions] and consciences of these breth[ren] off[e]r no satisfacion to them neith[e]r for matt[e]rs past tho[ugh] the Counsell requir[e]d it nor for oth[e]r offences [gi]uen them from that time to this day. Their nearnesse of habitacion to your town and ch[urch] is such that they may with lesse inconve[nience] joyn with you than sundry farms in many plantacions can with the ch[urche]s of whom they are members. If all ch[urche]s should refuse

8. No copy of a letter from the secessionists to the church at Hartford after the council of April, 1657, has been found.

to accept them bec[ause] the ch[urch] at Hart[ford] will not dismisse them tho[ugh] their councill advise it as a th[ing] necessary and as it is reported their Hono[u]r[e]d Gov[e]rno[u]r[9] and Deputy[10] have labo[u]r[e]d to perswade them to it as conducing to their publike peace; it would follow that they should be wholly deprived of ch[urch] fellowship whom the consc[iences] of all that know them judge to be fitt for that state: And that the determinacion of a councill chosen by both parties is of no validity for the ending of strife and contention in a ch[urch] and soe the onely means which is left to the ch[urche]s within thems[elves] for the ending of diff[e]r[ences] and for the releife of the oppr[e]ss[e]d will become vain and of non effect which besides the reproach to the way of Congrega[tional] ch[urche]s suited to script[ural] rul[es] and patterns may discourage many from entring into ch[urch] fellowship. I wish from my h[ea]rt that for these and sundry other reasons Mr. Stone and the ch[urch] at Hartford would be pleased yet to grant their dismission without any Conditions or delay that there might be some provision made for the setling of peace in the ch[urche]s and plantations of that Colony but if he and they are unalt[e]rably resolved for the negative unlesse upon unequall conditions, Be ye pleas[e]d Hono[u]r[e]d and Beloved in the Lord to consid[e]r wheth[e]r upon their councill sentence and conclusion it will not be safer that you rec[eive] them then that you refuse it, espe[cially] seing there being admitted into your fellowship will not exempt them from giving just satisfaction to any whom they have offended but rather oblige them more strongly thereunto and seing if all ch[urche]s should refuse them in this case where to would this come in the issue but to say in effect to these G[o]dly persons goe out of this land or if you will stay in it you shall not serve God in the way of ch[urch] Communion but far be that from any of the ch[urche]s of ch[ris]t. Yet that ye may walke ord[e]rly in rec[eiving] them, it will be your part to act therein by advice of that Councill which the whole ch[urch] chose who I suppose either have enquired or will ab[out] the ch[urche]s attendance to their advice in this poynt and declare their conclusive consent about it, which being done in a way of approving your admittance of them unlesse mo[re] convincing light be held forth for the contrary then any that hath yet appeared I must professe and doe that I se[e] no satisfying reason for which mys[elf] or any oth[e]rs should withdraw broth[e]rly communion from yours[elves] for so rec[eiving] them into your ch[urch] fellowship or from them being so received and I beleeve that this ch[urch] will be

9. John Winthrop the Younger.
10. Thomas Welles.

of the same minde whom yett I cannot engage therein without their consent which straights of time deny me lib[e]rty of taking at pr[e]sent, but I shall if God permit send a speedy account thereof to your Rev-[eren]d Pasto[u]r[11] to be Communicated to you by the first opportunity. Now the G[o]d of peace putt a speedy and gra[cious] issue and conclusion to these disho[nora]ble and uncomfortable contentions and stablish peace with truth and holinesse in your holy fellowship and ours and in all the ch[urche]s of the s[ain]ts: which satan labo[u]rs to corrupt or disturbe. The Lord rebuke him even the Lord that hath chosen his ch[urche]s: and tread him und[e]r foot as he will shortly In whom I rest Hono[u]r[e]d and Beloved

Your servant and brother in the faith and fellowship of the Gospel

JOHN DAVENPORT.

[Endorsed] Mr. Davenports lett[er] 1658

JOHN DAVENPORT *to* JOHN WINTHROP the Younger[1]
To his Honour[e]d freind John Winthrope Esq.
these present at Hartford

Honour[e]d Sir)

THE frequent raines, and other seasons, have hindered the passage of my returne of Answers to your loving lines, which else had bene in your hands before this time. You are still pleased to multiply ob-ligem[en]ts upon me by the cordials you sent me, a 1st and 2d time, unto which is added your serious invitacion of me, my wife and sonne, unto your house, that any further meanes might be used for my good. Sir, I am exceedingly ingaged to you and Mrs. Winthrope for your

11. At this time John Russell, Jr., Harvard College 1645, was pastor of the church at Wethersfield. On March 11, 1658, the general court of Connecticut forbade the church at Wethersfield to receive the dissenters of the church at Hartford. Turning to Massachusetts Bay, Cullick and Goodwin petitioned the general court of May 19, 1658, for a grant of land within its limits. Upon condition that the dispute at Hartford be settled, the general court of Massachusetts granted the request. Led by John Russell, Jr., dissenting minorities of the churches at Hartford and Wethersfield migrated to Norwottuck or Hadley, Massachusetts, in the spring of 1659. In Connecticut a council of elders to settle the dispute failed to materialize, and on September 26, 1659, a council of Massachusetts elders met at Boston. On October 7, 1659, after the settlement of Hadley was well under way, this council arrived at a settlement in which neither faction escaped without blame.

1. Massachusetts Historical Society, Winthrop MSS., III, 141; printed in Massachusetts Historical Society *Collections*, 4th series, VII (Boston, 1865), 492–494.

greate love herein. My wife hath bene very dilligent in what you committed to her, as taking delight to be any way serviceable to you. She hath spoken twise with Mrs. Eaton.[2] Her answer is, that she would speake with yourselfe. She speakes no further to that matter, but asketh when you will come? Nor doe I see what answer she can well give. For, though she be sole executrix, yet the estate is to be divided, according to the will, and she hath but her part. Nor hath she yet given in an Inventory to the Court. For your ground; my wife speedily, even the same day she received your letter, spake with sundry about it, and received this Answer, that there is no Indian corne to be planted, in that quarter, this yeare. Brother Boykin,[3] who hath formerly used some of it, was willing to have taken it, but saith, that it is overrun with wild sorrel, and it will require time to subdue it and put it into tillage, being at present unfit to be improved. Yet, if you let it for some considerable tim[e] he is willing to be one, in conjunction with others, to take it. Goodman Finch[4] was in our harbour, when your letter came, and my wife went presently downe, and met with yong Mr. Lamberton,[5] to whom she delivered your letter, she spake to one or two to goe aboard his vessel, but he set up saile and went out, but shortly after he came in againe, then Mr. Lamberton spake with him, he offred some so bad beaver that my wife would not take it, that which he hath paide is 2£, wanting an ounce, at 7 s. per pound, my wife spake twise with him her selfe, he saith the debt is 30 s. and he will paye the rest a fourtnight hence. Thus you have an account of the particulars mentioned in your letter. We did hope to have seene your selfe and Mrs. Winthrope here, before this time, which we shall be glad of, in your best season, but rather, which we most desire, to see you with your familie settled here, in your owne house, as a fixed dweller among us. My unfitnes for so long a journey, and your multiplicity of buisenesses there, together with sundry other consideracions, plead irrefragably against my coming to Hartford, at this time yet some here, if they knew the time, when you will be pleased to remove from thence, to settle here, will gladly make a journey thither, to accomodate your remove, and to attend you therein. I shall now cease to diverte your

2. Anne (Lloyd), the widow of Thomas Yale and Theophilus Eaton, returned to England in September, 1658, and died there before August 19, 1659. Massachusetts Historical Society *Collections*, 5th series, VIII (Boston, 1882), 51; see below, p. 143.

3. Jarvis Boykin of Charlestown, Massachusetts, was among the first settlers of New Haven.

4. Possibly Daniel Finch of Fairfield.

5. George Lamberton, Jr., was the son of George Lamberton, one of the first settlers of New Haven, lost on a voyage to England in the "phantom ship" in 1646.

mind from more weighty affaires by more lines, onely, with presenting myne my wifes and sonnes humble service to your selfe and Mrs. Winthrop, with my affectionate salutacions to your daughters, I commend you, Sir, to Gods gracious guidance in the greate affayres under your hand, and to his blessing upon your selfe and family, and rest in him

Newhaven the 20th d. of the 2d m. 58   Sir,

Yours obliged

JOHN DAVENPORTE

Postscr[ipt].

Sir) I am ashamed to send this letter thus blurred and blotted, but I have not time to wright another, brother Herryman, the bearer, being to goe early in the morning, whereof I knew not til late, this evening. One thing my wife desireth to add, viz. that she received for you of Mr. Goodenhouse[6] 30 *s.* worth of Beaver, and 4 *s.* in wampum. She purposeth to send your beaver by brother Alsop to the Baye, when the best time is, to sell it for your advantage, and afterwards to give you an account what it comes to. Mr. Goodenhouse makes account that this is his wholl debte. Your letter to Sarjeant Baldwin[7] my wife purposeth to convey to him by the 1st opportunity. Sister Holbadge[8] hath paid to my wife in part of her debt to you a bushel of winter wheate. There rests, she saith, 10 *s.* more, which she will pay as soone as she can.

[Endorsed] Mr. Davenport [by John Winthrop.]

JOHN DAVENPORT *to* JOHN WINTHROP the Younger[1]

To the Right Worship[fu]l his much Honour[e]d freind
John Winthrope Esq. Deputy Governo[u]r of
Connectacut these present in Hartford

Honour[e]d Sir)

I RECEIVED 2 letters from you, and returne many thancks to you for them boath, and for the Intelligence contained in them. The death of those 3 men, and the mortality in the countreyes in England, are

6. Samuel Goodanhouse was a Dutch merchant who became an inhabitant of New Haven in 1647. *New Haven Colonial Records, 1638–1649* (Hartford, 1857), pp. 139, 355.

7. Richard Baldwin of Milford.

8. The widow of Arthur Halbich, Halbidge, or Holbridge of New Haven.

1. Massachusetts Historical Society, Winthrop MSS., III, 141; printed in Massachusetts Historical Society *Collections*, 4th series, VII (Boston, 1865), 495–497; A. B. Davenport, *Supplement* (Stamford, 1876), pp. 379–381.

sorrowful tydings. That which concernes the Lord Fairfaxe[2] answers my former opinion. I hope, we shall speedily receive our letters from London, and thereby the true state of the publick affaires there etc. Dr. Wright hath twise written to me to encourage my returne to London. However God shall be pleased to order my way, I am truely sorry for the loss of such a man, whose hearte was towards God, and his people. Concerning our Court matters here; the last election-day[3] was the saddest to me that ever I saw in Newhaven, by our want of him,[4] whose presence etc. was wont to make it a day of no less contentm[en]t, then solemnity. Being weary, after my sermon, I was absent from the Court. The 1st newes that I heard from thence added to my sorrow. For I heard that Mr. Goodyeare[5] was wholly left out in the choyse of magistrates, whereas I had bene secure, thincking they purposed to choose him Governour. But, the day following, upon enquiry into the cause of it, I received such answer as cleared unto me that it came to pass, not by any plot of men, but by the overruling providence of God. For, the proxies generally voted for Mr. Goodyeare to be Governo[u]r, and Mr. Leete,[6] Deputy, and none of them gave theyre votes for Mr. Goodyeare to be deputy governour, if the former fayled, nor to be magistrate, but put in blancks to boath, taking it for granted that he would be chosen Governour. But, before they proceeded to election, some of the Deputies of the court propounded and urged the necessity, or great expediency, in respect of our condition, at present, of having the Governour present among us. Hereunto the freemen generally consented, and hereby the election fell upon Mr. Newman,[7] to be Gover-

2. Thomas, third Lord Fairfax, married Anne, the fourth daughter of Lord and Lady Vere, at Hackney, June 20, 1637. He was a parliamentarian but out of sympathy with the Protectorate and at this time was living in retirement at Nun Appleton, Yorkshire, and York House in the Strand. Although he coöperated with Monck in bringing about the restoration of Charles II to the throne, in the years immediately following, when "the air was heavy with rumours of rebellions and insurrections," his name was associated with several plots against the crown, but, disowning the connection, he was not imprisoned. A daughter, Mary Fairfax, married George Villiers, second Duke of Buckingham, September 15, 1657. C. R. Markham, *The Life of the Great Lord Fairfax* (London, 1870); D. Ogg, *England in the Reign of Charles II* (2 vols., Oxford, 1934), I, 208–209; *Calendar of State Papers, Domestic Series, 1661–1662* (London, 1861), pp. 461, 465; *1663–1664* (London, 1862), pp. 216, 315, 337, 352.

3. May 26, 1658.

4. Theophilus Eaton had died January 7, 1657/8.

5. At this time Stephen Goodyear was absent in England.

6. William Leete was one of the first settlers of Guilford.

7. Francis Newman succeeded Theophilus Eaton as governor of the New Haven Colony in 1658. On April 23, 1660, the town of New Haven bestowed the Malbon house, recently repurchased from John Winthrop the Younger, upon him and his wife for life. He was in declining health in the following October, and died November 18, 1660. *New Haven Town Records, 1649–1662* (New Haven, 1917), pp. 449, 453. See below, p. 182.

no[u]r and Mr. Leete, Deputy Governour, for this yeare. To this latter the proxies, for the most part, concurred, and most of the present free-men. The votes of the present freemen and some few proxies carried the election for Governo[u]r to Mr. Newman by plurality of votes, which he strongly refused, but importunity of many in the Court, at last, overcame him to accept it. And some of Mr. Goodyeares freinds and relations spake earnestly, when those 2 were chosen, to hinder his being chosen to magistracy, alleadging such reasons as they had. What the minde of God is herein, time will shew. The Court sate, since the election, til this day, and have passed thorough many weighty buise-nesses,[8] by the helpe of Gods presence with them, to good satisfaction, both to themselves, and others. Give me leave to add a touch upon your buisenes about your lead mine,[9] which I make bold to suggest onely unto your selfe. I am informed that one found in a letter written to another from London, that lead is of good value, probably, above what you know. My wife telleth me that she spake with one, who told her that he found, in that letter, that they will give £8 per tun for lead in the bigger peeces, and £5 per tun, for the smaller peeces, and 20 s. per tun, for the dust of it, which, it may be, you cast away as of no use. This intimation may be of use to you, we boath thaught, to prevent some loss you might sustaine by those that will, probably, be trading with you for the lead knowing of what esteeme it is in London, and concealing it from your selfe, for theyre owne advantage. My sincere love maketh me thus bold to acquaint you with any thing which may be *e re vestrâ*,[10] to know. I hope, Mrs. Winthrope and your wholl familie is in health, because I heare nothing to the contrary. The good Lord continue it, with his favour and loving kindnes in Jesus christ to your selfe and them all. We boath, with our sonne, present our humble serv-ice to you boath, and our affectionate salutacions to them. The Lord Jesus dwell with you in peace! In whom I rest

Newhaven, the 3d   Sir/
d. of the 4th m. 58.   Yours much obliged

                                              JOHN DAVENPORT

[Endorsed] Mr. Davenport [by John Winthrop.]

8. Among the accomplishments of this session of the legislature was a law against Quakers modeled on the laws of the Massachusetts general courts of October 14, 1656, and October 14, 1657.

9. The black lead mine in which Winthrop was interested was located at Tantiusques, Massachusetts, sixty miles west of Boston, slightly west of Quinebaug River, and north of the colony line. In it Thomas Clarke and William Paine of Boston and Mathew Gris-wold of Saybrook were also interested. Massachusetts Historical Society *Collections*, 4th series, VII (Boston, 1865), 405, 409; 6th series, V (Boston, 1892), 67, 294–295, 297–299, 432.

10. to your advantage,

JOHN DAVENPORT *to* JOHN WINTHROP the Younger[1]

To the Right Worship[fu]ll John Winthrope Esq.
these present in Hartford

Honour[e]d Sir)

A REPORT, that you was gone to the Baye, put me from my purpose of sending the inclosed, til I might certainely know where my letter might finde you. I have now received intelligence, by John Thomas,[2] that you are at Hartford, and that Mrs. Winthrope hath bene very ill, and in greate danger of her life, but is now, by the mercy of God, recovered. Blessed be his name for this mercy to her, and to your selfe and yours in her recovery! But withall he saith that yourselfe are very ill, and have taken physick, this day, and that he stayed 3 houres to understand how it wraught, and is informed that it wraught well. This giveth us some ground of hope that God will graciously bless the meanes for restoring your health, whose life we account exceeding precious, and a blessing to many. He who hath given you a mercyful heart to others, in theyre sicknesses, hath promised that you also shall obteyne mercy. We are not wanting to you in our prayers, since we heard of your state, which was but this night, nor shall we cease from praying for your life and health, til we heare that our petition is answered for your good. Be pleased to let us heare from you by the 1st opportunity, how it is with you. My wife desireth to send something suitable to your present condition, but knoweth not what, til she heare further concerning you. At present she sends you a few fresh raysons, and a litle licquorish, and your owne unicornes horne which she hath kept safe for you, since you sent it for Mrs. Eaton. My wife is ashamed to send so few raysons, but she hath no more so good. Were it not that I am loath to trouble you with many lines, I should wright much more concerning other matters, and particularly to returne thancks for your mindfulnes of me for a vent for some of my horses, by Mr. Adis,[3] concerning which I hope to have an opportunity of speaking with you ere long. The Lord Jesus be with you, and blesse meanes for your recovery!

---

1. New York Public Library, Winthrop–Davenport Papers; printed in L. Bacon, *Thirteen Historical Discourses* (New Haven, 1839), pp. 372–373; Massachusetts Historical Society *Collections*, 3d series, X (Boston, 1849), 19–20; A. B. Davenport, *A History and Genealogy of the Davenport Family* (New York, 1851), pp. 327–329.

2. John Thomas was one of the early settlers of New Haven.

3. About 1658 William Addis of Gloucester, Massachusetts, removed to New London, where he bought the house of Richard Blinman in the following year.

With presenting my service and my wifes, and sons, to Mrs. Winthrope, with yourselfe, and our love to yours I rest,

Newhaven the 20th d. of the 5th m. 1658

Sir,

Yours much obliged

JOHN DAVENPORTE

[Endorsed] Mr. Davenport [by John Winthrop, and] Dated July 20th. *1658.* [in a modern hand.]

JOHN DAVENPORT *to* JOHN WINTHROP the Younger[1]
To the Right Worship[fu]ll John Winthrop Esq. *these present in Hartford*

Honoured Sir)

WE have with longing desires long expected your returne, with your familie, to your owne habitacion, at Newhaven, as accounting your dwelling among us a special favour from God, and a common good to all the people, especially in this sickly time when many are afflictively excercised, with grypings, vomitings, fluxes, agues and feavers, though more moderately in this Towne, by the mercy of God, then at Norwalke[2] and Fairefield.[3] Yong Mr. Allerton[4] who lately came from the Dutch, saith, they are much more sorely visited there, then these parts are. It is said, that at Mashpeag[5] the inhabitants are generally so ill, that they are likely to lose theyre harvest, through want of ability to reape it. Mr. Harbert[6] of South Hold, is so ill, at Manatoes,[7] that there is litle, if any, hope of his life. Brother Alsop is come from the Dutch, with a purpose to have bene gone to the Baye, before this time, but the afflicting hand of the Lord hath stayed him, by great illnes, accompanied with a giddynes in his head, and much sleepynes,

1. New York Public Library, Winthrop–Davenport Papers; printed in L. Bacon, *Thirteen Historical Discourses* (New Haven, 1839), pp. 373–375; Massachusetts Historical Society *Collections*, 3d series, X (Boston, 1849), 21–23.

2. Norwalk, a Connecticut town, was settled about 1650.

3. Uncoa or Uncoway, within the limits of Connecticut, was settled in 1639, and re-named Fairfield in 1645.

4. Isaac Allerton, Jr., the son of Isaac Allerton of New Haven, graduated from Harvard College in 1650 and thereafter engaged in the mercantile activities of his father.

5. Probably Maspeth or Mispat, part of Middelburgh or Newtown, Long Island.

6. John Herbert of Southold died before September 16, 1658. *Southold Town Records*, I (New York, 1882), 440.

7. Manhattan.

and burning. It comes by fitts, every other day. My wife giveth him, this day, a portion of your powder, whereof the supplye that you left in her hand is spent. The extremities of people have caused her to part with what she reserved for our owne family, if need should require. It hath pleased the Lord to spare us hitherto. Yet my wife hath bene, diverse times, this summer, and stil is, valetudinarious, faint thirsty, of litle appetite, and indisposed, sundry times, yet goes about and is betweene times, better, and chearful yet ordinarily, in the mornings, shee feeles a paine, in the bottom of her backe. Edmund is not wel, yet goes about. The good Lord prepare us for all changes, that under all changes of providences, we may have suitable changes of spirit, to honour, serve, and please God therein! Amen.

Sir) I will not hide from you what is here reported, though I can not easily beleive it, because I received no such Intelligence, at any time, from your selfe. Timothy Nash[8] saith, He cannot understand, from your selfe, or from Mrs. Winthrop, or from the people at Hartford, that you have any purpose of ever returning hither to dwell here. And Nath. Kimmerly[9] saith, from your owne words, that you thought to have come to Newhaven, but now you thinck, you shall not see us, this yeare. If it be so; we have cause to be sensible of a greate loss to us, who have long comforted our selves in hopes of injoying you in a way of dwelling here: not onely for the good that many may receive by Gods blessing upon your endeavours for theyre health, but for your company, which for itselfe, is precious and contentful unto us. If you would please to stock your Farme and to give order to have your land at Newhaven improved, you might live comfortably upon that which is your owne, in this place. The people here also would be ready to serve you with theyre labours, and to take hold of all good occasions of declaring theyre thanckfulnes, really, as they are bound to doe, for your large and liberal helpefulnes to them: in distributing whereof my wife is but your hand, who neither receiveth, nor expecteth any recompence for that, but desireth that all acknowledgem[en]ts and retributions may be returned to yourselfe.

Sir) It pleased you, when I was excercised with that swimming disiness, to send me a paper, Feb. 20. 57,[10] containing in it certain portions of powder, which I never opened, til this day, because it pleased God to release me from that distemper, without it. And in perusing the

8. Timothy Nash or Naish, a smith at New Haven.
9. Nathaniel Kimberly, the son of Thomas Kimberly, one of the first settlers at New Haven.
10. No copy of this letter has been found.

letter you then sent, I find it commended as also useful for my other distemper, in regard of the magisterium of corall, which is in it. Hereupon, I desire to know, whether you will advise me to make use of it for that, though the disiness, through Gods mercy, hath not troubled me, since the spring began, unto this day. Edward Preston[11] came lately from Long-Island, and saith, many Indians there are very sick, and 12 were dead before his coming thence. My wife and son joyne with me in presenting our service to your selfe and Mrs. Winthrope, and our loving salutacions to your children. The Lord Jesus dwel with you in peace and loving kindenesses! In whom I rest

Newhaven, the 4th   Sir,
d. of the 6th m. 58
                                        Your exceedingly obliged

                                            JOHN DAVENPORTE

Sir)

My wife desires a word or 2 of advise from you, what is best to be done for those grypings, and agues, and feavours; but she is loath to be too troublesom. Yet as the cases are weighty so she desires to goe upon the surest ground, and to take the safest courses, and knoweth none whose judgm[en]t she can so rest in as in yours.

[Endorsed] John Davenport's Letter Dated Aug[u]st 4th. *1658.* [in a modern hand.]

Letter of Attorney of JOHN DAVENPORT, JOHN CULLICK, and WILLIAM GOODWIN[1]

KNOW all men by theise Presents that Wee John Davenport Bachel-lo[u]r of Divinity, and Pastor of the Church of Newhaven, John Cullick, and William Goodwin of Hartford vpon the River of Connecticut in New England, Doe (by vertue of pow[e]r given vs by the last will, and testament of Edward Hopkins Esq[ui]r[e] somtyme of Hartford afores[ai]d Deceased) Make, Ordaine, and Constitute our

11. Edward Preston was the son of William Preston, one of the early settlers of New Haven.

1. New Haven, Hopkins Grammar School Records, I, 8–9; printed in "The Wyllys Papers," Connecticut Historical Society *Collections*, XXI (Hartford, 1924), 127–128, where the following statement is appended: "The aboue written is a true Copy extracted out of the Trustees Book at N: Hauen nouemb[e]r 23 1711 Per John Alling Assistant." John Alling, 1647–1717, was the son of Roger Alling, an early settler of New Haven.

trusty and beloved ffreinds Thomas Bull,[2] Nathaniell Ward,[3] and
Edward Stebbing[4] all of Hartford afores[ai]d, our true, and lawfull
Attorneyes, for vs, and in our names, according to the last will, and
testam[en]t of the afores[ai]d Edward Hopkins Esq[ui]r[e], to Act Receive, Sue for Recover, and Dispose of according to Order received or
that they shall Receive from vs, or any others intrusted by vs, of all
debts, dues, or demands, appertaining to vs, and due by bonds, Bills,
Books, Voyages, Accompts, or any other way, from any person, or
persons, whatsoever. Giving, and graunting our s[ai]d Attorneyes, All
full, and lawfull pow[e]r to Ask, demand, sue, Implead, Arrest, Imprison
Or to vse any lawfull way for procureing of the same, As alsoe out of
Prison to Release, discharge, Acquitt, to Compound, Referr and Ar-
bitrat any difference whatsoever, And to give as full, and legall
discharges to any person, or persons, as if we were personally pr[e]sent:
And further we doe Give vnto our s[ai]d Attorneyes full power to
Sell, Barter, Exchang, or any other way to transact all, and every our
occasions in our absence, according to theire best discression, and
Judgm[en]t And to Constitute any person or persons vnder them, or
either of them as theire Attorneyes for that end. And we doe by theise
pr[e]sents, Ratify, Confirme, and allow whatsoever our s[ai]d Attorneyes shall lawfully doe, or Cause to be don in, and about the
pr[e]misses, as if we our selvs Personally Acted therein. In wittness
whereof we have heervnto put our hands, and Seales this 30th of September 1658.

The Interlineing betwixt the 21th and 22th Line, we owne to be our Act.

Signed, Sealed, and delivered	JOHN DAVENPORT:	*
in the pr[e]sence of	JOHN CULLICK:	*
JOHN WEBSTER[5]	W[ILLIA]M GOODWIN.	*
NICHOLAS STREET[6]		
ANDREW BACON.[7]		

The afores[ai]d l[ett]re of Attorney is a true record of the Originall.
By me W[ILLIA]M JONES[8] No[ta]ry publiq[u]e.

2. Thomas Bull was one of the original settlers of Hartford, Connecticut.

3. Nathaniel Ward was an early settler of Hartford who later removed to Hadley,
Massachusetts.

4. Edward Stebbin, Stebbing, or Stebbins was an early settler of Hartford.

5. John Webster was an early settler of Hartford who later removed to Hadley.

6. Nicholas Street succeeded William Hooke as teacher of the church at New Haven.
Although in Connecticut State Library, New Haven, Connecticut, First Church of
Christ and Ecclesiastical Society, Records 1639–1926, I, 3, the date of Street's ordination is given as November 26, 1659, in a letter of December 6, 1659, Davenport says
that Street was ordained November 23, 1659. See below, p. 146.

7. Andrew Bacon was an early settler of Hartford who removed to Hadley.

8. On William Jones, the son-in-law of Theophilus Eaton, see below, p. 137n.

JOHN DAVENPORT *to* JOHN WINTHROP the Younger[1]

To the Right Worship[fu]ll his much Honoured freind
John Winthrope Esq. these present in Hartford

Honoured Sir)

THESE few lines are to Congratulate your returne to your familie, as I hope, in health, and to give you an account of my negotiacion with ours about the iron-worke, the issue whereof is according to your minde as the inclosed to Capt. Clarke[2] from our Governo[u]r,[3] will shew which I send inclosed, that it may more speedily be conveyed to him, by land, then we can expect it will be by sea. The Lord also bless the intended marriage of your eldest daughter to Mr. Newman,[4] for many comforts to you boath and to your familie, and to themselves! Be pleased to present myne, my wifes, my sons humble service to Mrs. Winthrope, together with your selfe with many thanckes to her for her great kindenesses to us when we were at Hartford. In great hast I must *manum de tabulâ*. The Lord Jesus dwell with you and yours in peace and loving kindnesses! In whom I rest

Newhaven the 22th of
the 8th 58.

Yours obliged

JOHN DAVENPORT

[Endorsed] Mr. Davenport [by John Winthrop, and] Dated Octob[e]r 22d. *1658*. [in a modern hand.]

1. New York Public Library, Winthrop–Davenport Papers; printed in L. Bacon, *Thirteen Historical Discourses* (New Haven, 1839), p. 375; A. B. Davenport, *A History and Genealogy of the Davenport Family* (New York, 1851), p. 329.

2. Thomas Clarke of Boston, Massachusetts.

3. Francis Newman. Under date of November 3, 1658, John Winthrop the Younger sent the letter of Governor Francis Newman of New Haven to Thomas Clarke and this letter of John Davenport to himself to John Richards at Boston, to be delivered to Clarke, requesting that a copy of Governor Newman's letter to Clarke and the letter of John Davenport to himself be returned to him. Massachusetts Historical Society *Collections*, 5th series, VIII (Boston, 1882), 53.

4. Elizabeth or Betty, the daughter of John Winthrop the Younger, was born in 1636. In 1658 she married Antipas Newman of Wenham, Massachusetts, apparently against the wishes of her brother Fitz John Winthrop. After Newman's death in 1672, she married Zerubbabel Endecott, a physician of Salem, Massachusetts, the second son of John Endecott of Massachusetts. Massachusetts Historical Society *Collections*, 5th series, VIII (Boston, 1882), 47.

JOHN DAVENPORT *to* JOHN WINTHROP the Younger[1]

To his Honoured freind John Winthrope Esq. Deputy Governo[u]r of Hartford these pr[e]sent in Hartford

Honoured Sir)

I WROTE my former letter in such haste that I forgot one particular, which, having a litle more time, I shall now add. One Mr. Blackleach[2] of Boston is come hither with commodities. He was wholly unknowne to me before. But he came to our house, and had speech with my wife, and while they were in discourse I came into the roome, and welcommed him etc. He knew not where to bestow his goodes, at present, and propounded whether he might be at your house, til he could looke about him, to provide for himselfe elsewhere. I told him, I knew not how soone yourselfe might come. He answ[ere]d, that he would be ready to leave it at a daies warning, onely he desired to be there, for the present. Hereupon I made bold to consent that he might be in your Hall, for the present. I now heare that he hath written to yourselfe for liberty to lay up his barrels of porke and corne etc. that are to be paid him for his goodes in your garret. I heare also that Brother Andrewes hath moved for the use of a roome there, this winter, without which he is likely to want the liberty of the ordinances, all this winter, being very weake, and unable to come from the Farmes to the Towne every weeke. I promised, and my wife also, to speake to your selfe about that motion, if we had mett with you at Hartford, which we should have done. But you was absent, and after my returne home, I heard no more of Brother Andrews his motion, and thereby it was out of my minde when Mr. Blackleach spake to me. Brother Andrewes doth not desire to use the garrets. But I shall leave the wholl buisenes to be issued as your selfe shall judge best. Farewel

Yours obliged

JOHN DAVENPORTE

[Endorsed] about Mr. Blackleech and G. Andrewes [by John Winthrop.]

1. Massachusetts Historical Society, Winthrop MSS., III, 142; printed in Massachusetts Historical Society *Collections*, 4th series, VII (Boston, 1865), 497–498. This letter is undated but John Blackleach wrote to John Winthrop the Younger on the same subject October 18, 1658. (*Ibid.*, pp. 149–150.) Furthermore, the contents of this letter indicate that it followed both Blackleach's letter and Davenport's letter to Winthrop of October 22, 1658.

2. John Blackleach was a Boston merchant who later removed to Hartford in the colony of Connecticut.

John Davenport *to* John Winthrop the Younger[1]
To the Worthily much Honour[e]d John Winthrope Esq.
these present at Hartford

Honour[e]d Sir)

Two letters I received from you, the 1st dat[ed] Sept. 29, the 2d Nov: 14.[2] The 1st I have already answered, I perceive, to your satisfaction, and I hope, Capt. Clarke and Mr. Paine[3] will proceed with encouragem[en]t upon our Governours letter to them,[4] though I read not the contents. For he telleth me that he wrote to the same purpose, as he did to your selfe. Before that; I received a letter from you, with a packet, that was brought to Boston, from Newfoundland, for which, and your care about transmitting it safe to my hands, I humbly returne many thancks to you. The packet was from Brother Hooke, who presents his respectful salutacions, in the Lord, to your selfe and Mrs. Winthrope, and among other things, gives me notice of the decease of your brother,[5] with whom he dined once, at his owne house, and another time at Mr. Peters[6] his house, and speakes honourably of him, but saith that he had not seene your son,[7] whence I collect that he was gone to Scotland, or some whither else. He also makes

---

1. Massachusetts Historical Society, Winthrop MSS., III, 142; printed in Massachusetts Historical Society *Collections*, 4th series, VII (Boston, 1865), 498–500.

2. No copies of these letters have been found.

3. William Paine of Boston, Massachusetts. He died October 10, 1660. See below, p. 179.

4. See above, p. 129.

5. After serving as a colonel in the parliamentary army and representing Banff and Aberdeen in the parliament of 1656, Winthrop's half-brother, Stephen Winthrop, died in London in 1658.

6. In 1641, as one of three agents of Massachusetts Bay, Hugh Peter, pastor of the church at Salem, Massachusetts, returned to England, where he became deeply involved in the affairs of the mother country. In 1659 Davenport was informed "that Mr. Hugh Peters is distracted, and under sore horrors of conscience, crying out of hims[elf] as damned, and confessing haynous actings." (See below, p. 145.) On January 9, 1659/60, he was turned out of Whitehall; on May 11 the Council of State and on June 7 the House of Commons ordered his apprehension; on June 18 he was excepted from the act of general pardon and oblivion; on September 2 he was arrested and committed to the Tower; on October 13 he was tried and condemned; and on October 16 he was executed at Charing Cross. *Commons Journals*, VIII (n.p., n.d.), 57, 68; *Dictionary of American Biography*.

7. Fitz John Winthrop apparently went to England about January, 1657/8. At this time he was a lieutenant in the regiment of infantry of his uncle, Colonel Thomas Reade. On December 21, 1659, he was commissioned captain by George Monck. Expected home from England in the spring of 1660, he was apparently detained by smallpox. In company with his father and brother, he finally returned to New England in 1663. See below, pp. 153, 173, 216.

mention of a Captaine that was hanged for robbing your brothers house, with some others, all having theyre faces covered with theyre handkerchers, but this Captaines cover fell off from one side of his face, whereby your brothers 2. servants knew him. But, at the Gallowes, he denied the fact, yet was executed, because he was looked at as a man of so large principles and conscience, that his word was not to be regarded. Sundry other things also he communicated to me, *quæ nunc transcribere longum esset*,[8] and I am put upon streights, having heard, late, this night, that the Bearer, Mr. Pinchins[9] man, is to be gone early in the morning. For the other letter; I have spoken with Mr. Crane,[10] and Brother Cooper,[11] once, and againe, about the contents of it. Here is no question made of your real intendm[en]ts for the good of the ironworke and of this place, nor suspicion of your seeking selfe-advantages thereby, to the hurt of this place. They know not your publick spirit that have any such surmises. But you are so well knowne here, that you may be secure in this that all here have such assurance of your affections to the publick good, that no such lowe and unworthy thoughts of you are in any of theyre mindes. Though you have bene pleased to signifie your willingnes to surrender your Interest, requiring nothing but what you have lent to the worke, yet I finde no willingnes in them to cloze with that motion. As for the £7 to be paid to Mr. Lake;[12] you will receive theyre Answer inclosed. Whereunto I shall add, that, upon my further urging them to pay it to Mr. Lake and to put it unto the general Account, they replyed, that they could not doe that, til they might speake with your selfe, that, upon sufficient Reasons received from you, they might satisfie those that intrust them. They are now, upon the failing of the stones sent by Mr. Goodyeare, solicitous that they[re] worke may not falle, and, understanding, by John Heardman, that there are good stones to be had at Quarry-Hill,[13] 20 miles from London, which are used in an iron-worke, 4 miles off from that place, and found to be good, they are wrighting to Capt. Clarke and Mr. Paine, to intreate them to make

8. which at present it would take too long to transcribe,

9. John Pynchon, the son of William Pynchon, who in 1636 led a group of settlers from Roxbury in Massachusetts Bay to Springfield on the Connecticut River.

10. Jasper Crane was one of the first settlers of New Haven. About 1651 he removed to Branford.

11. John Cooper was agent of the New Haven undertakers in the ironworks.

12. Thomas Lake was a Boston merchant who had married Mary Goodyear of New Haven.

13. Probably Quarry Hill in the hundred of Wachlingstone, Kent. E. Hasted, *The History and Topographical Survey of the County of Kent*, II (Canterbury, 1782), 341.

use of theyre correspondents in London, that those stones may be procured and sent by the first shipp in the spring. He saith they may be bought for 20 *s*. per tun, which is farr below what the merchant at Milford demands for bringing stones from the Isle of Wight. They also desire the helpe of your letter to Capt. Clark and Mr. Paine to further this designe. Sir, be pleased to present, with myne, my wifes and sons humble service, together with your selfe, to Mrs. Winthrope, with many thancks to her for our loving intertainment, at your house. We all wish unto you boath many blessings and comforts in the marriage of your daughter, which, we suppose, is now finished. The Lord Jesus dwell with you in mercy and peace and loving kindnesses, and multiply blessings upon your branches! In him I rest

Newhaven the 18th day
of the 9th m. 1658

Yours ever obliged
JOHN DAVENPORTE

[Endorsed] Davenport. [by John Winthrop, and] Nov[embe]r 18th. *1658.* [in a modern hand.]

JOHN DAVENPORT *to* JOHN WINTHROP the Younger[1]
To his Honoured freind John Winthrop Esq.
these present in Hartford

Honour[e]d Sir)

THOUGH I have, together with the rest intrusted by you, subscribed our common letter, yet I shall add a few lines, as myne owne letter to your selfe, to whom I am so particularly obliged, that I cannot omit to present my respectfull salutacions to yourselfe and Mrs. Winthrop, with many thancks for the Intelligences[2] I have received from you, in several letters, and for the powders you sent to my wife, and for the Almanack,[3] which I had not seene before, though, since my receite of yours, the president of the Colledge[4] sent me one. The Author of it is

1. New York Public Library, Winthrop–Davenport Papers; printed in L. Bacon, *Thirteen Historical Discourses* (New Haven, 1839), pp. 375–377; Massachusetts Historical Society *Collections*, 3d series, X (Boston, 1849), 23–25.

2. In the year 1658 *Mercurius Politicus* and *The Publick Intelligencer* were being published in England. *Catalogue of the Pamphlets, Books, Newspapers, and Manuscripts relating to the Civil War, the Commonwealth, and Restoration, Collected by George Thomason, 1640–1661* (2 vols., London, 1908), II, 435.

3. Zechariah Brigden, *An Almanack of the Coelestial Motions for This Present Year of the Christian Æra 1659* (Cambridge, 1659). See S. E. Morison, "The Harvard School of Astronomy in the Seventeenth Century," *The New England Quarterly*, VII (1934), 8–14.

4. Charles Chauncy.

wholly unknowne to me, save by his name in the title page. In the next page, speaking of 4 ecclipses, this yeare, he may seeme to some to be willing to be accounted *sapientum octavus, utpote qui terram planetarum octavum ænimo suo fingit, contra communem Astronomorum sententiam.*[5] For he saith, twice shall this planet, whereon we live, and its concomitant the moone, widdow each other of theyre sun-derived lustre. Now, the place, whereon we live, is the earth. The place, I say, not the planet. But he is not willing *solus sapere.* Therefore for his 4 proposicions he produceth, in his last page, sundry authors, who, he saith, have answered the objections from scripture ag[ains]t this opinion. I have not read theyre answers. But, if that be the breife, or summe of them, which he notes, it will not be found, upon an exact search, to be satisfying. However it be; let him injoy his opinion; and I shall rest in what I have learn[e]d, til more cogent Argum[en]ts be produced then I have hitherto met with. Sir) your motion about letting your house to N. K.[6] etc. came to me wholly beyond my expectacion. I did, indeed, expect (according to your promise, as I understood it) to heare from you, upon your returne from the Baye, the result of your thoughts and purposes, viz. your resolucion, whether to returne to inhabit it with your familye and when, or to sell it to the Towne, who bought it, that they might freely give it to your selfe, or put it into your power, as your owne, upon what termes you propounded (seing you would not accept it upon free gift, because you would preserve your liberty, to dwell in it, as your occasions would permit). But what they then did, and others stirred them up unto, I assure you, was in respect to the common good, which was hoped for and expected by us all from your selfe, dwelling among us with your familie. Nor would they have taken such pay for it from any man in the countrey, but your selfe. Which I note, that you may see theyre love to you, and desire of injoying you among us. There are few houses vacant in the Towne, that are so fit as that for entertainm[en]t of persons of publick usefullnes. Such men the Towne wants. If your selfe and yours dwell in it, it will fully satisfye all, none will desire any other, and my selfe, and myne, will most rejoyce therein. But, if your other occasions, will not permit that; this way of letting it unto such men will not be for your proffit, nor for the Townes satisfaction. Your house and lot hath suffered much hurt already, and will more, in this way, and this Towne will lose theyre end; for they would never have let it pass out of theyre

5. the eighth of the wise men inasmuch as he was one who conceived in his own mind the earth as the eighth of the planets contrary to the accepted opinion of astronomers.
6. Nathaniel Kimberly.

hands, but in hope of injoying your selfe, which if they cannot obtaine, I perceive, it will, in the next place, best satisfie them, if you please to give them leave to buy it of you. I thaught it my duety to signifie thus much to your selfe, and shall add onely this, to prevent missinterpretacions, that, as the house is your owne, so all doe grant that it is in your owne power to doe with it as you please. If you please to let it to N. K. etc. you may. Onely you may be pleased to reminde that this is not that use of that house, which will answer the townesmens ends, and the townes expectacion, and necessities. With myne, my wifes and sons respectful and affectionate salutacions and service presented to your selfe, and Mrs. Winthr[op] and your branches, I rest, Sir

Newhaven the 18   Yours obliged
d. of the 1st m. 165$\frac{8}{9}$
                                                JOHN DAVENPORT

[Endorsed] Mr. Davenport about selling the house [by John Winthrop, and] John Davenport's Lett[e]r. March 18th. *1658/9.* [in a modern hand.]

JOHN DAVENPORT *to* JOHN WINTHROP the Younger[1]
The Right Worship[fu]ll much Honoured John Winthrope Esq. these present at Hartford

Honoured Sir)

I RECEIVED yours, both of the 24th of the 1st m, Called March, and of the 8th of the 2d, called April,[2] and have communicated them, both with the Honoured Governor[3] etc. entrusted by you, and with the Townesmen.[4] All consent for returning many thancks to you for your love to us all, and to the Towne, so fully expressed therein, especially, by your declaration of your unwillingnes, yea, very unwillingnes to be seperated from us, who have much more cause, and are really, as unwilling to be deprived of your much desired residence among us, with your familie, at least sometimes, as your occasions will

1. New York Public Library, Winthrop–Davenport Papers; printed in L. Bacon, *Thirteen Historical Discourses* (New Haven, 1839), pp. 377–378.
2. No copies of these letters have been found.
3. Francis Newman.
4. On May 17, 1658, John Gibbs, Henry Lindon, John Cooper, Samuel Whitehead, Jarvis Boykin, Thomas Munson, and William Bradley were chosen townsmen for the year ensuing. *New Haven Town Records, 1649–1662* (New Haven, 1917), p. 354.

permit, according to that liberty you was pleased to reserve unto your selfe, when you bought the house. The conclusion of our last conference was, that matters should stand, in the state they are in, all resolution about disposing of the house should be suspended, til we might speake with your selfe, which, I am told, will be shortly. The sooner the better. For we long to see you and to speake with you, mouth to mouth, and some say that your house and orchard have suffred much by your so long absence. We heare that N. K.[5] doth improve some of your land already; so that there will be no inconvenience to your selfe by this delay. We shall be glad, if it may produce in your selfe and Mrs. Winthrope a resolution to possesse and injoy it your selves, that so we may injoy you. But of these things we shall speake more when we meete. In the meane time, and ever, the Lord Jesus delight over you and yours, to doe you good! In whom I rest,

Sir,

Your much obliged

JOHN DAVENPORTE

My selfe, my wife, and son, present our humble services, with most affectionate salutacions, to your selfe, Mrs. Winthrope, and your children.

Newhaven the 15th
day of the 2d m. 1659.

[Endorsed] Mr. Davenport rec: Apr: 16: [by John Winthrop, and] John Davenport's Lett[e]r. April 15th. *1659.* [in a modern hand.]

5. Nathaniel Kimberly.

JOHN DAVENPORT *to* JOHN WINTHROP the Younger[1]
*To the Honoured John Winthrop Esq. Governo[u]r of
Connectacute these present*

Honoured Sir)

MR. RUTTERFORD[2] being now arrived here from the Baye telleth us that Mr. Yale[3] is come, which also his letter to me from the Baye confirmeth. He saith Sister Hannah Eaton[4] is offred an husband,[5] a godly man who hath 2 children and £200 *per annum*. He purposeth to come with brother Alsop, who is expected here speedily. I have a letter from my brother Hooke, but no intelligence, since the change of governm[en]t,[6] from him though from other hands I have. One letter I send you to read with desire that you will returne it to me againe, at your leasure that I may answer it. I have also sundry weekely Intelligences.[7] But in them there is not much news since the change of governm[en]t. I have sent you 3 or 4 other bookes, which I have not yet

1. Massachusetts Historical Society, Winthrop MSS., III, 143; printed in Massachusetts Historical Society *Collections*, 4th series, VII (Boston, 1865), 501–502; A. B. Davenport, *Supplement* (Stamford, 1876), p. 382.

2. Henry Rutherford was an inhabitant of New Haven. He took the oath of fidelity August 5, 1644, and was admitted a freeman October 26, 1659. *New Haven Colonial Records, 1638–1649* (Hartford, 1857), p. 139; *New Haven Town Records, 1649–1662* (New Haven, 1917), p. 419.

3. After taking his sister, Anne (Yale) Hopkins to England, Thomas Yale was at this time on his way back to New Haven.

4. The daughter of Theophilus and Anne Eaton, Hannah Eaton was baptized at St. Stephen's, Coleman Street, London, in October, 1632, and was brought to New England by her father and mother in 1637. After her father's death, she returned to England with her mother in September, 1658. St. Stephen's, Coleman Street, Register.

5. Hannah Eaton married William Jones of the parish of St. Martin's-in-the-Fields, Middlesex, July 4, 1659. With the restoration of Charles II to the throne, Hannah and William Jones, William and Nathaniel, two sons of the latter by an earlier marriage, and Hannah, an infant daughter, migrated to New Haven. Massachusetts Historical Society *Collections*, 4th series, VII (Boston, 1865), 501 n.

6. Oliver Cromwell died at Whitehall September 3, 1658, and was succeeded by his son, Richard Cromwell. On November 29 the latter called a parliament, which met January 27, 1658/9, and recognized him as Lord Protector. Pressed by Lieutenant General Charles Fleetwood and Major General John Desborough, Richard Cromwell consented to the dissolution of parliament, April 22, 1659, and recalled the Rump Parliament, to meet May 7, 1659. To this latter body he submitted, May 25, 1659.

7. In April and May, 1659, there were being published in England: *The Faithful Scout; Mercurius Politicus; The Publick Intelligencer; The Moderate Informer; The Weekly Intelligencer. Catalogue of the Pamphlets, Books, Newspapers, and Manuscripts relating to the Civil War, the Commonwealth, and Restoration, Collected by George Thomason, 1640–1661* (2 vols., London, 1908), II, 435–436.

time to peruse, nor scarse my letters as I would, being filled with impedim[en]ts at this time. Were you here, I could take up your spare time with pleasing diversions by reading varietyes of occurrences in the world. All the use that I make of such things is to see how things worke towards the Accomplishm[en]t of the prophesies that concerne these times, and to know how to pray suitably to changes of providences. Present myne, my wifes and sons humble services, together with your selfe, to Mrs. Winthrope, and our loves to yours. I feare how it is with Mrs. Pierson,[8] having heard nothing from thence all this day. If she be alive; the Lord send forth his word and heale her, and many sick and weake persons among us! Farewel, in our Lord Jesus, in whom I rest

Newhaven, the 28th d   Sir
of the 5th m. 1659.

                         Yours obliged

                           JOHN DAVENPORT

The messenger sent last yeare is returned to the Baye and hath brought 30 tun of stones for the ironworke.[9] Excuse my hast.

[Endorsed] Mr. Davenport Rec: July: 28: [by John Winthrop, and] 1659 Mr. Davenport to John Winthrop [in a modern hand.]

JOHN DAVENPORT *to* JOHN WINTHROP the Younger[1]
To the Honoured John Winthrope Esq. Governour of Connectacute these present in Hartford

Honour[e]d Sir)

I SUPPOSE, Mr. J. C.[2] hath reported unto you, what he received (by word of mouth, because I wanted time and liber[ty] to wright what I would) from me, for that end, concerning the state of affaires in England, upon this unexpected change, whereby the lord protectour is reduced unto the state of a private gentleman, by his voluntary act, at

---

8. The wife of Abraham Pierson, pastor of the church at Branford.

9. On the effort to obtain stones for the ironworks, see above, p. 132. Davenport mentioned the arrival of stones in a town meeting at New Haven, August 8, 1659. *New Haven Town Records, 1649–1662* (New Haven, 1917), p. 412.

1. Massachusetts Historical Society, Winthrop MSS., III, 143; printed in Massachusetts Historical Society *Collections*, 4th series, VII (Boston, 1865), 502–504; A. B. Davenport, *Supplement* (Stamford, 1876), pp. 383–384.

2. Probably John Cullick, with Davenport one of the trustees of the Hopkins bequest.

the persuasion of the L[or]d General Fleetwood L[or]d Disborough etc. yet the Colonels and cheife leaders of the army in Scotland (among whom I find your wifes brother, Colonel Read[3] his name) have petitioned the revived long lasting parliam[en]t, now reassembled, upon the desire of the army, to allow the last lord protecto[u]r £20000 *per annum*, during his life, whereof £10000 *per annum* is to be inheritance to that house, in recompence of his fathers faithful and Honourable services for the good of the commonw[ealth].[4] It is also, by others, desired that the Lady Dowager may have £10000 *per annum* conferred upon her, during her life, as a marke of Honour and thanckfulnes in reference to her deceased Husband.[5] The people seeme to be very well pleased with this change, and to promise to themselves great good thereby. But, *quicquid id est, timeo Danaos vel dona ferentes.*[6] I suspect that Jesuites have an hand in turning the wheele,[7] to introduce the K[ing] of Scots.[8] Wherein I am the more strengthned by an offer of £40000 made by a Quaker, as it is said, for White Hall, which, together with Hampton Court and Greenewitch and other of the Kings houses, is set to saile.[9] Probably, the Jesuites purse shall pay that summe in the name and by the hand of a Quaker, to settle there, in time, a Jesuites Colledge. For, the marriage betweene France and

3. Thomas Reade, the brother-in-law of John Winthrop the Younger, was a colonel in the parliamentary army.

4. On May 12, 1659, the army petitioned the restored Rump Parliament that debts contracted by Oliver and Richard Cromwell, since December 15, 1653, be paid; that an annual income of £10,000 be settled upon Richard Cromwell and his heirs; and that an additional £10,000 be settled upon him for life. *Calendar of State Papers, Domestic Series, 1658-1659* (London, 1885), pp. 345-346.

5. The army also asked that an annuity of £8,000 be settled upon Elizabeth (Bourchier) Cromwell.

6. *quidquid id est, timeo Danaos et dona ferentes.*

Virgil, Aeneid, II, 49.

Whate'er it be, a Greek I fear,
Though presents in his hand he bear.

J. Conington, The Æneid of Virgil Translated into English Verse
(London, 1919), p. 37.

7. Although on August 15/25, 1658, Sir Edward Nicholas, secretary of state, reported to Charles II that many priests and Jesuits had gone from Zealand to England (*Calendar of State Papers, Domestic Series, 1658-1659*, London, 1885, p. 114), no connection between the Jesuits and the restoration of Charles II to the throne of England has been found.

8. Charles II.

9. In the summer and fall of 1659 the sale of Hampton Court and Whitehall was under consideration. Edmund Ludlow claims to have prevented the sale of Hampton Court. C. H. Firth, *The Memoirs of Edmund Ludlow* (2 vols., Oxford, 1894), II, 101-102.

Spaine,[10] and the foiles of the K[ing] of Sweden,[11] and the interest
which they may gaine in the K[ing] of Scots, may fill them with hopes
of reducing England *sensim, sine sensu*,[12] to become, as in former times,
the popes asse againe, which may make way for the slaying of the
witnesses,[13] which is the 1st thing to be done, before theyre rising, and
the burning of Rome, and the calling of the Jewes. But I forget that
you are upon your journey to the Baye, where you will receive full
Intelligence of all things. My brother Hookes letter[14] was written before this change. He purposed a letter, and, I beleive, hath written
one, to your selfe,[15] though it is not yet brought to my hand; because
he doth not mention your name in my letter, and because, in his
former letter, he promised to wright unto you. The Lord make your
journey safe comfortable and prosperous! We want your presence here
exceedingly. Many among us are sorely visited and distressed, and
some distracted, in the paroxisme of theyre disease, for a time, which
taketh them in theyre heades with extreme paine, as sister Beamont,[16]
brother Myles[17] and his son, his daughter also hath bene neare unto
death, but I hope that, through the mercyes of God, they are somewhat better. All John Thomas his house have bene downe, his wife is
stil very weake, and himselfe not strong, and all brother Doelitles[18]
house, excepting himselfe, *cum multis alijs*. Mrs. Pierson is in a hopeful way. Mr. Pierson hath bene touched so that he could not keepe the
fast, last 4th d[ay] but wisely tooke the physick in the beginning and
will, I hope, doe well. Many questions my wife hath about the various
excercises of people under this afflicting hand of God. Some she purposeth to send inclosed in this. To which if you have time to returne an

10. In 1658 and 1659 Cardinal Mazarin and Luis de Haro were arranging the pacification of France and Spain. The Traité des Pyrénées, November 7, 1659, provided for the
marriage of Louis XIV and the Infanta María Teresa. Henri Vast, *Les Grands Traités
du Règne de Louis XIV*, I (Paris, 1893), 79-187.

11. At this time England and Sweden were at peace.

12. gradually, without perception,

13. Possibly a reference to Revelation 11.

14. This letter has not been preserved.

15. For a letter of William Hooke to John Winthrop the Younger, March 30, 1659,
see Massachusetts Historical Society *Collections*, 4th series, VII (Boston, 1865), 590-593.

16. —— (Jackson), the widow of Eleazar Stent and the wife of Thomas Beamont.

17. Richard Miles, Sr., was an early settler at New Haven and Milford, and at different times, a member of the churches of both towns and a deacon of the church at New
Haven. In 1655 the town of New Haven requested him to establish a bakehouse for
biscuit and in 1662 he undertook the operation of the town mill. He had a son Richard
and a daughter Ann. *New Haven Town Records, 1649-1662* (New Haven, 1917), pp. 260,
521.

18. Abraham Doolittle was a settler at New Haven as early as 1644.

answer, be pleased, together with it, to returne to me my copie in your hand of Mr. Hopkins his will.[19] Myne, my wifes and sons humble respects being presented to your selfe and Mrs. Winthrope, and our love to yours, I rest

Newhaven the 5th day of the 6th m. 1659. Yours obliged

JOHN DAVENPORT

[Endorsed] Mr. Davenport [by John Winthrop, and] 1659 Mr. Davenport to Gov[erno]r Winthrop [in a modern hand.]

JOHN DAVENPORT *to* JOHN WINTHROP the Younger[1]
To the Honoured John Winthrop Esq. Governour of Connectacute Colonie these present in Hartford

Honoured Sir)

I RECEIVED, by brother Wakeman,[2] 3 letters to my selfe (besides those that my wife and son received, together with your bountiful supplies of medicines for our sick neighbours and freinds, which are many) for which your great labour and liberality of love I returne many hearty thancks, being exceedingly obliged to you for the same. I received also my copie of Mr. Hopkins his will, and Mr. Lyngs letter, and the printed papers, which last you might have retained with you. I shall onely, at present, add that, since my wrighting to you, I have received letters and bookes, and written papers from my ancient and Honoured freinds Mr. Hartlib,[3] and Mr. Durie,[4] wherein I finde sun-

19. Thomas Yale had sent Davenport a copy of Edward Hopkins' will from England. See below, p. 162.

1. Massachusetts Historical Society, Winthrop MSS., III, 144; printed in Massachusetts Historical Society *Collections*, 4th series, VII (Boston, 1865), 504–506; A. B. Davenport, *Supplement* (Stamford, 1876), pp. 384–386.

2. An early settler at New Haven, John Wakeman was at this time a deputy to the particular court at New Haven.

3. Samuel Hartlib was the son of a Polish merchant and his English wife. He himself followed a mercantile career but combined with it an interest in many other fields.

4. John Durie or Dury, 1596–1680, was a Protestant divine who devoted his life to the promotion of Christian unity. At the restoration of Charles II, he sought to continue his work with the help of Lord Chancellor Hyde and the Duke of Manchester. A letter to Charles II seeking to vindicate his conduct during the Interregnum remained unanswered and Archbishop Juxon declined to grant him an interview. In 1661/2 he proceeded to Cassell, Hesse, Germany, where he died in 1680. While vicar of St. Stephen's, Coleman Street, London, Davenport endorsed Durie's work. In 1631 Davenport was one of the signers of John Durie's *Instrumentum Theologorum Anglorum*, a document

dry Rarities of Inventions and projects for common good, of sundry kindes, which I long for an opportunitie to communicate to your selfe, might your first leasure give us an occasion of personal discourse together. They are too many to be transmitted unto you, by passengers, and yet such as, I beleive, will affoard singular contentm[en]t to your publick spirit, and probably, you will finde some particularities among them, which may be advantagious to your private proffit, in the improvem[en]t of your Fishers Island etc. I cannot conceale any thing from your selfe, such is my unfeigned love, that I can conjecture may be *e re vestra*[5] to know. Your report of Mrs. Winthropes illnes and danger would have deepely afflicted me, had it not bene allaied with the hopes of her recovery. Yet, as it is, we cannot but sympathize with her and your selfe, in this afflicting providence, yet so as acknowledging Gods mercy, to his praise, who ordered the circumstances of it so favourably, that it should befall her, while your selfe was present with her, that she might have thereby both comfort and helpe for her cure, by his blessing. The good Lord goe on in healing to heale, and in restoring to restore her unto perfect health and strength, with a sanctifyed and blessed fruite of this his Fatherly chastisem[en]t, that you may rejoyce together in his goodnes all your daies, and be satisfyed with his mercies in Jesus christ! I am sorry for the sicknes and weakenes of your 2 daughters,[6] beseeching the God of our life and health to send forth his word of blessing with the meanes to heale them, and to sanctifie them, with the rest of your branches, to himselfe, in Jesus christ! In whom I rest,

Newhaven. the 19th day   Sir)
of the 6th moneth 1659   Your much obliged freind and serv[an]t

Verte folium.   John Davenporte

Postscript
    Sir) Because I cannot, by a pencile, I must, under a vaile, represent

favoring church unity. Gunnar Westin, "Negotiations about Church Unity, 1628–1634," *Uppsala Universitets Årsskrift 1932 Teologi 3* (Uppsala, 1932). See also *Calendar of State Papers, Domestic Series, 1631–1633* (London, 1862), p. 75; John Durie, *A Summarie Account of Mr. Iohn Dury's Former and Latter Negotiation: For the procuring of true Gospell Peace, . . . amongst the Protestant Churches, and Academies* (London, 1657); J. Westby-Gibson in *Dictionary of National Biography.*

    5. to your advantage
    6. At this time Elizabeth Winthrop was married to Antipas Newman of Wenham, Massachusetts. Margaret Winthrop was living with the Newmans. Lucy, Martha, and Anne Winthrop were unmarried and presumably living at home. Massachusetts Historical Society *Collections*, 5th series, VIII (Boston, 1882), 383.

unto you my wifes deepe sense of your tender affections and greate love towards her, expressed in your letter to my son, wherein you was pleased to shew how the report of her least illnes affected you. For I want words to declare her transcendent thanckfulnes for the same.

Concerning Mr. Yale; she hath treated with him as effectually as she could, and more fully then she would, if it had bene for her selfe, for your having the linnen and pewter and cushions, urging the full consent of his mother, under her hand. But to that he replyed that his mother was now dead and so her act was void, and that he is bound to attend his order, which is to send them to England. My wife told him that she did not doubt that, if Mrs. Hannah knew it, she would consent. But he stil insisted in his want of power to doe it. The chayres and stooles, of which you spake, Mr. Yale is willing to sel. If Mrs. Winthrope please to have them, my wife would doe her indeavour to answer her desire therein, upon notice from you. My wife thincks you had better buy new linnen in England, and you will there have better pennyworths. For Mr. Newman our Govern[ou]r, hath now a suite for a Table cloath, a dozen of Diaper napkins and a towel, of Dammask fashion, for 26 shillings.

We long to heare of Mrs. Winthropes perfect recovery and of perfect health restored to your familie. *quod faxit Deus! Etiam atque etiam vale.*[7]

Tuissimus
J D.

[Endorsed] Mr. Davenport rec: Aug: 20 [by John Winthrop, and] 1659 J Davenport to Gov Winthrop [in a modern hand.]

JOHN DAVENPORT *to* JOHN WINTHROP the Younger[1]

To the Honoured John Winthrop Esq. Governo[u]r of Connectacute Colonie, these present at New London

Honoured Sir)

YOUR quick departure from Hartford, after my sons Returne home from thence, denied me an opportunity of expressing our due thancks for your loving intertainm[en]t of so bold a visitour, whereof he speaketh much, and yet is not satisfied with what he hath spoken,

7. May God grant it! Again and again farewell.
1. New York Public Library, Winthrop–Davenport Papers; printed in L. Bacon, *Thirteen Historical Discourses* (New Haven, 1839), pp. 378–379; Massachusetts Historical Society *Collections*, 3d series, X (Boston, 1849), 25–26; A. B. Davenport, *A History and Genealogy of the Davenport Family* (New York, 1851), pp. 330–331.

thincking it falles shorte of what he should speake, to express your and Mrs. Winthropes kindenes to him. Sir, you know, the affections of parents are apte to sympathize with theyre children, and to take contentment in what they finde to be justly pleasing and comfortable to them. Hence it is that I desire to take this first overture, for conveyance of these few lines, in way of thanckfulnes, from us boath, to your selfe (as I have already done to Mrs. Winthrope, by J. Latimer)[2] for the same. And to let you know that I have received a large letter from Mr. Blinman dat[ed] Aug. 22 whereby I understand that God hath braught him and his to Newfoundland, in safety and health, and maketh his ministry acceptable to all the people there, except some Quakers, and much desired and flocked unto, and he hath made choise of a ship for Barnstaple,[3] to his content, the M[aste]r being Godly. After these passages and his notifying to me the Lady Kircks[4] respectful and loving mention of me whom, she saith, she hath heard in London, he addeth to what I had heard from Engl[and] that a fine of £5 is put upon any that shall name the last protector.[5] 2. that the L[or]d Henry is sent for out of Ireland and outed of his place.[6] 3. that 4 are sent from Engl[and] and 4 from France, and 4 from the states, to see whether they can compose matters betw[een] Sweade and Dane.[7]

2. No copy of this letter to Elizabeth (Reade) Winthrop, sent *via* John Latimer, Latimore, or Lattimore of Wethersfield, Connecticut, has been found.

3. Barnstaple, Devonshire, England.

4. In 1633 Sarah, the daughter of Sir John Andrews, was married to Captain David Kirke, born in France and knighted in Scotland. By a charter dated November 13, 1637, Sir David Kirke became one of the proprietors of Newfoundland. He migrated to the colony as governor in 1638, and established his residence at Ferryland. After his death in prison in England about June, 1653, his widow continued to live at Ferryland. Harleian Society *Publications*, XVII (London, 1883), 33; D. W. Prowse, *A History of Newfoundland* (London, 1896), pp. 141-157.

5. No indication of such a law has been found.

6. On June 7, 1659, the House of Commons ordered Henry Cromwell, lieutenant and governor general of Ireland, to deliver up the government of Ireland and to return to England. On June 15 Henry Cromwell submitted to commissioners appointed by the House of Commons to relieve him. On July 4, 1659, he reported to the House of Commons at Westminster. *Commons Journals*, VII (n.p., n.d.), 674, 705.

7. War between Sweden and Denmark had broken out, June 1, 1657, and Denmark had ceded much of her territory to Sweden, February 26, 1658. At this time England, France, and the Netherlands were coöperating in an effort to induce the warring powers to make peace. On the recommendation of the Council of State, the parliament of England appointed Edward Montagu or Mountagu, Algernon Sidney or Sydney, Sir Robert Honywood, and Thomas Boone commissioners and plenipotentiaries to the kings of the two countries, June 9, 1659. By a treaty of May 27, 1660, Denmark recovered some of her ceded territory. *Commons Journals*, VII (n.p., n.d.), 677, 700; *Calendar of State Papers, Domestic Series, 1658-1659* (London, 1885), p. 368; C. Jenkinson, ed., *A Collection of All the Treaties of Peace, Alliance, and Commerce, between Great-Britain and Other Powers, . . . 1648, to . . . 1783* (3 vols., London, 1785), I, 103-110.

4. that £30000 is demanded for the old protectors funeral, which the parliam[en]t refuse to pay. Some urged that those that had the mourning cloaths should pay for them, that the commons might not be charged.[8] 5 that the last protector was like to be appr[e]hended for the Debt, but withdrew: whereupon the parliam[en]t gave him 6 moneths liberty to come to termes with Creditors.[9] 6. that Mr. Hugh Peters is distracted, and under sore horrors of conscience, crying out of hims[elf] as damned, and confessing haynous actings. He concludes, for the trueth hereof *sit fides penes Authorem*.[10] 7. that there is an Ambassador gone for Spaine.[11] Lastly, that the fleet in the West Indies have taken almost an incredible mass of Treasure in some Spanish Townes there.[12] Reported by a ship in that harbour where Mr. Blinman lyes, that met a frygot at sea going home for. I shall not add, at present, but my desires for your safe journey to the Baye and speedy returne to your Family and then to Newhaven and my wifes with our sons respectful and most affectionate salutacions and humble service.

Newhaven. the 28th d. of the   Yours exceedingly obliged
7th m. 1659   JOHN DAVENPORTE

[Endorsed] Mr. Davenport [28] of 7ber 1659 [by John Winthrop, and] Mr. John Davenport's Lett[e]r. Dated Sep[tembe]r 28th. *1659*. [in a modern hand.]

8. The expenses of the funeral of Oliver Cromwell were enormous. Mary A. E. Green says that "£150,000 can hardly be too large for the entire expenses of the funeral." On August 25, 1659, a committee appointed by the restored Rump Parliament reported that £19,303 0 *s.* 11 *d.* was still due and unpaid for mourning alone. *Calendar of State Papers, Domestic Series, 1658–1659* (London, 1885), p. xi; *1659–1660* (London, 1886), pp. 5, 146.

9. After his submission to the restored Rump Parliament, May 25, 1659, Richard Cromwell was troubled by debt. On July 4 parliament excepted him from arrest for a period of six months, and on July 16 granted him an annual income of £8,700. This annuity was not paid, and early in the summer of 1660 the former Protector fled to France. *Commons Journals*, VII (n.p., n.d.), 664–665, 704, 726; C. H. Firth in *Dictionary of National Biography*.

10. let responsibility rest with the author.

11. At this time there were rumors of impending peace between England and Spain. *Calendar of State Papers, Domestic Series, 1658–1659* (London, 1885), pp. 194, 254, 339.

12. No account of this has been found.

JOHN DAVENPORT *to* JOHN WINTHROP the Younger[1]
To the much Honoured John Winthrope Esq. Governo[u]r of
Connectacute Colonie these present in Hartford

Hon[oure]d Sir)

HAVING received 2 letters from you, since your returne from the Baye, one dat[ed] the 16th of the 9th m. which was delivered unto me, on the 23d day, after the ordinacion of brother Street to be our Teacher, whilest we were at supper: the other dat[ed] the 2d d[ay] of this 10th m.[2] brought by John Thomas, by whom I should have returned answer of the 1st, if he had given me seasonable notice of his journey to Hartford. Both these letters, I perceive, you was pleased to wright, at such houres in the night, as rather called you to refresh your body, wearyed with the labours of the day before, with rest and sleepe, then to minde such offices of love as added to your labour, and hindred that rest, which nature required. But such is the power of your love that it will not yeeld to nature, to be thereby hindred in its course and excercise. Myne owne heart would accuse and condemne me, as unthanckful, if I should not answer your love with such returne, as I may, at present, though the notice of John Palmers[3] journey towards you is given me, at a time, when I am full of buisenes, in preparing for the lecture, having bene hitherto much hindered by inevitable diversions. Sir) The hurt that befell so many, by theyre owne rashnes, at the Draw Bridge, in Boston, being on the day that the Quakers were executed,[4] was not without Gods special providence, in judgment and wrath, I feare, against the Quakers, and theyre Abettors, who will be

1. Massachusetts Historical Society, Winthrop MSS., III, 144; printed in Massachusetts Historical Society *Collections*, 4th series, VII (Boston, 1865), 507–511.
2. No copies of these letters have been found.
3. John Palmer of Fairfield, Connecticut.
4. 'William Robinson and Marmaduke [Stephenson or] Stevenson, Quakers, were executed at Boston, October 27, 1659. On the return of the people from the execution, a portion of the drawbridge fell, and several persons were injured, some of whom died in consequence. There were two bridges at this period over the "Mill Creek." The one in Hanover Street, which was the most ancient, was always known as the "Mill Bridge;" the other, in the present North Street, late Ann Street, and earliest known as "The Fore Street," was invariably designated, in the old records, as "The Drawbridge."' N. B. Shurtleff, in Massachusetts Historical Society *Collections*, 4th series, VII (Boston, 1865), 507–508 n. Shurtleff cites: George Bishope, *New England Judged* (London, 1661), p. 110; (London, 1702/3), p. 135; William Sewel, *The History of the Rise, Increase, and Progress Of the Christian People called Quakers*, ... (London, 1722), p. 233; "The Diaries of John Hull," American Antiquarian Society *Transactions and Collections*, III (Boston, 1857), 189.

much hardned thereby. But so it must be, by theyre obstinacy, who, haveing sinned out theyre light, stumble and fall at every event of his providence, whom, in the Trinity of persons, they denye, and reject in his written word, *qua tale* and his ordinances in the churches, and his magistrates in the Commonw[ealth]. I am sorry for Sir George Booth,[5] especially, if it be he, who, I thin[k] it is, a gentleman, about myne age, and who was of Waddam-Colledge[6] in Oxford, in my time, and accounted very hopeful then, and since he inherited his Fathers estate, which was greate, he was accounted Religious, at least, a freind to the Godly partie, in Cheshire, where he was of eminent note and powerful influence throughout that countie and the neighbour counties. I doubt, he was more acted by ill counsailours then by his owne spirit, in this greate enterprize, which a litle προνοια[7] would have stopped him from, as that which would be frustraneous, as to his intendm[en]t, and bring certaine ruin upon his person and familie. But it is the Lord, whose judgem[en]ts are unsearchable who hath thus left him, that we may learne, by his example, to feare alwaies and to walke continually in excercise of our dependance upon him for the guidance and governm[en]t of his holy spirit, in all our waies, and to beware of me[n] who offer themselves as freinds and guides and counsailors, that we be not drawn by them into præcipices. I am very sorry that the General Court at Boston did not accept Colonel Temples motion,[8] which had

5. A supporter of the Protectorate, in the summer of 1659 Sir George Booth took part in an uprising against the revived Rump Parliament which had displaced Richard Cromwell. After taking Chester, he was defeated by Lambert near Nantwich bridge and captured at Newport Pagnell. Released on bail, he became a member of the Convention Parliament and, on the occasion of the coronation of Charles II, he was created Baron Delamere. Foster gives no indication of his attendance at Oxford. Furthermore, he was too young for Davenport to have known at Oxford. T. F. Henderson in *Dictionary of National Biography*.

6. Wadham College, Oxford, founded in 1610.

7. πρόνοια, foresight.

8. After the conquest of Acadia or Nova Scotia by the English under Sedgwick in 1654, Colonel Thomas Temple, brother-in-law of William Fiennes, first Viscount Saye and Sele, became one of the proprietors of the colony. Oliver Cromwell appointed him to the governorship of the province, September 17, 1656, and Temple set out for New England in the following year. After the restoration of Charles II to the throne, Temple returned to England, where he was created a baronet of Nova Scotia, July 7, 1662, and recommissioned governor of the colony. By the treaty of Breda, 1667, Nova Scotia was returned to the French. Temple removed, first to Boston, and later to London, where he died in 1674. To prevent the execution of the Quakers in 1659, Temple offered to carry them away and to provide for them at his own charge. Two or three magistrates and the deputies prevented the acceptance of the offer. *Dictionary of National Biography;* George Bishope, *New England Judged* (London, 1661), p. 119; Thomas Hutchinson, *The History of the Colony of Massachusets-Bay*, I (London, 1760), 200.

bene a cleare way, and incomparably the best expedient, for freeing all
the Colonies from the Quakers, who would have feared that kinde of
banishm[en]t more then hanging, it being a real cutting them off from
all opportunities and libertie of doing hurt in the Colonies, by gaining
proselytes, which would have bene more bitter then death to them. I
blesse God for your safe returne, through such inconveniences in your
way. The Lord preserve your life and health, for the good of many!
My wife humbly thancks you for the supply you sent her by John
Tomas, and craves pardon for her boldnes in that kind so frequently.
We had good hope that we might have injoyed your much-desired
presence with us, before this time, and doe now wish that, when you
come next, you will be pleased to bring your familie and dwell in your
owne house among us, if your occasions will permit it. My wife prayeth
yourselfe and Mrs. Winthrop to accept a small token of Marmalet of
Quinces, which she hath made as good as she could, and hopes you
boath and your daughter Mrs. Ann[9] will find them to be good and comfortable for your stomachs and spirits. The booke concerning Bees,[10]
which you desired, I now send you, by John Palmer, and with it 3
others viz., 1. An office of Address.[11] 2. An Invention of Engines of
Motion.[12] 3. A Discourse for divisions and setting out of lands in the
best forme etc.[13] These 3 are small bookes in 4to. I shall add unto them
a 4th booke in 8°, called Chymical, medicinal and chirurgical addresses.[14] These are a few of many more which are sent to me. I hoped
for an opportunity of shewing them to you here, and shall reserve
them for you, til a good opportunity.

9. Anne Winthrop, at this time unmarried. She married John Richards September 1,
1692.

10. *The Reformed Common-Wealth of Bees. Presented in severall Letters and Observa-
tions (by various persons) to Sammuel Hartlib Esq. With the Reformed Virginian Silk-
Worm* (London, 1655).

11. *Considerations Tending To the Happy Accomplishment of Englands Reformation in
Church and State. Humbly presented to the Piety and Wisdome of the High and Honourable
Court of Parliament* (London, 1647). The principal title-page reads: *A Brief Discovrse
Concerning The Accomplishment of our Reformation: Tending to shew, That by an Office
of Publike Addresse in Spirituall and Temporall Matters, the Glory of God, and the Hap-
pinesse of this Nation may be highly advanced.* This publication was followed by *A further
Discoverie Of The Office of Pvblick Addresse for Accommodations* (London, 1648).

12. Cressy Dymock, *An Invention of Engines of Motion Lately Brought to perfection.
Whereby May be dispatched any work now done in England or elsewhere, (especially Works
that require strength and swiftness) either by Wind, Water, Cattel or Men* (London, 1651).

13. William Potter, *A Discoverie For Division or Setting out of Land, as to the best
Form. Published by Samuel Hartlib Esquire, . . .* (London, 1653).

14. *Chymical, Medicinal, and Chyrurgical Addresses: Made to Samuel Hartlib, Esquire*
(London, 1655).

My ancient Honorable freind Colonel Bel[15] died last sommer at Barbadoes, where he was the 1st Governo[u]r, and so continued many yeares. With much importunity he desired my settling there with him. I received a letter from him, the last winter, full of love, and a token in sugar, and returned an Answer with a Token, by Mr. Palmes,[16] which never came to his hands. He was 70 yeares old when he wrote to me.

My wife prayeth me to add a word about the marmalate, that, if you find sinamon in it, you shall not need to feare binding: for she hath put other things into it, which are opening and cooling. One that was very ill found much good by it, which she addes, to encourage you to take it. And, about the supply, you sent, she saith, that, though she desired it, for the good of the people, that needed it, yet she had rather have bene without it, then you should get hurt by sitting up too late. The Lord recompence all your labour of love, in mercyes to you and yours! My selfe, wife and son present our humble services to yourselfe and Mrs. Winthrop, with our affectionate salutacions to all your children. I rest

Newhaven the 6th d. of the 10th m   Yours much obliged
    1659   JOHN DAVENPORTE

Postscript)

Sir) I am mindful of our Debte, for our part in the vessel that transported us, with you, unto Seacunck.[17] But we neither know what it is, nor in what, we are to make paiment, nor to whom: whether, to Mr. Bryan,[18] or to his son, or to yourselfe, if you have already discharged

---

15. Philip Bell was lieutenant governor of Bermuda from March 6, 1627, to October, 1629; governor of the island of Old Providence off the Mosquito Coast from February 7, 1631, to 1636; deputy governor of Barbados in 1641; and governor of Barbados from 1645 to 1649. He was the "first governor" of Old Providence Island, off the Mosquito Coast, not of Barbados. Davenport's statement in this letter would indicate that he had considered settling at Old Providence! C. M. Andrews, "List of Commissions, Instructions, and Additional Instructions Issued to the Royal Governors and Others in America," American Historical Association, *Annual Report, 1911* (Washington, 1913), I, 407, 417, 510; *Calendar of State Papers, Colonial Series, 1574–1660* (London, 1860), *passim;* A. P. Newton, *The Colonizing Activities of the English Puritans* (New Haven, 1914), *passim.*

16. Edward Palmes of New London took over the Winthrop homestead at New London in 1660 or 1661 and subsequently married Lucy Winthrop.

17. Possibly the present Seeconck, Massachusetts, not far from Providence, Rhode Island.

18. Alexander Bryan, one of the first settlers of Milford. Richard Bryan, his son, was schoolmaster at Milford.

it. Be pleased to certifie me concerning the premises, that I may doe accordingly.

The canded Comfrye-Rootes, which my wife sendeth to you are not so white, as she desireth. The reason, she saith, is, because they were boyled with Barbadoes sugar, though clarified, yet they were canded with white sugar: but, she saith, they would have bene whiter, if they had bene canded with loafe sugar. The tast nevertheles is good. She prayeth you to excuse the colour, and to accept her love, in so small a thing.

The letter, as you see, was not sent according to the date, and the messenger is altered, from John Palmer to John Thomas: because the former stayeth in these parts longer then we expected.

The 8th d. of the 10th m. 59

[Endorsed] Mr. Davenport about the Quakers executed [by John Winthrop, and] Dec[embe]r 6th. 1659. [in a modern hand.]

JOHN DAVENPORT *to* JOHN WINTHROP the Younger[1]
To the Right Worship[fu]ll John Winthrope Esq. Governo[u]r of Connectacute these present in Hartford

Honoured Sir)

JOHN PALMER is not yet gone, whereby I have liberty to add a post-script to my former letter,[2] upon new intelligence from Nichols[3] of Boston, from Virginia, which I received after the inclosed was sealed. He saith that he came from Virginia, the 23d of Jan. that there are 70 ships from England, which raiseth the price of Tobacco to 12 *d.* per pound that a few daies, before he came thence, there arived some shipps from England, which came from thence, 6 weekes before, that is, in the beginning of 10ber. These shipps bring word that the parliament was then sitting,[4] and matters in England were in peace. There is some confirmation of the report of the Lord Lamberts going forth with

1. New York Public Library, Winthrop–Davenport Papers; printed in L. Bacon, *Thirteen Historical Discourses* (New Haven, 1839), pp. 379–380; Massachusetts Historical Society *Collections*, 3d series, X (Boston, 1849), 29–30.

2. No copy of this letter has been found.

3. Mordecai Nichols was a mariner of Boston, Massachusetts.

4. The revived Rump Parliament sat from May 7, 1659, to October 13, 1659, when the army interrupted its procedure, and from December 26, 1659, to March 16, 1660. On February 21, 1660, Monck ordered it to receive the secluded members of the Long Parliament.

20000 to meet General Monck from Scotland with 20000.[5] The storie runs thus, in Sir Henry Moodies[6] report sent in his letter from Virginia to an English man, a captaine at Manatoes. The presbyterians, in Scotland and England, flock much to General Munck, who now ingageth himselfe for them, and theire interesse, and is come forth, upon that account, with the forenoted army, as farr as Worcester,[7] whither General Lambert is gone, with his armie, to stopp his proceedings. General Mountigue,[8] it is said, is come to London, and complyeth well with the parliament. Farewel.

This afternoone the Captaine[9] hath bene with the Governo[u]r,[10] to excuse his not appearing at the Court of Magistrates, by his former illnes in body, having a loosenes, with vomiting blood; and his not sending his Atturney, by his want of one, his surgion would not,

5. After defeating Sir George Booth, Colonel John Lambert fell out with the revived Rump Parliament. With Fleetwood, he drove it from Westminster, October 13, 1659. In a vain attempt to oppose the advance of George Monck into England, he marched north, November 3, 1659.

6. Possibly the son of Deborah, Lady Moody, of Gravesend, Long Island.

7. Monck could not have been at Worcester. He did not cross the Tweed into England until January 2, 1659/60.

8. Under date of September 9, 1659, Edward Montagu or Mountagu, admiral and general and patron of Samuel Pepys, in 1660 created first Earl of Sandwich, records in his journal: "I came to London." R. C. Anderson, ed., *The Journal of Edward Mountagu, First Earl of Sandwich, Admiral and General at Sea, 1659-1665* (London, 1929), p. 46.

9. A case between Richard Raymond of Salem, Massachusetts, and John Penny, captain of the *Roebuck* of London, England, over the seizure by Penny, under the navigation act of 1651 or a Swedish or Portuguese commission, December 7, 1659, of the *Black Eagle*, a vessel of Dutch origin, and its cargo, both claimed as the property of Raymond, a league or a league and a half off Stamford Point, whence the prize was carried into New Haven harbor and, without inventory being taken, was partially disposed of, came before the court of magistrates at New Haven February 15-18, and 28, 1659/60, and, because of the ignorance of the court of the navigation act of 1651, was referred to the court of admiralty in England. In the name of the king of Portugal, servants of Captain Penny seem also to have seized a vessel of John Scott at North Sea, Long Island. The rescue of this vessel by Lyon Gardiner resulted in a similar case between Penny and Gardiner before Governor Winthrop at Hartford, March 17, 1659/60, and lawsuits between Lyon Gardiner, plaintiff, and Captain John Penny and George Lee, defendants, and John Scott, plaintiff, and John Griggs, defendant, before the particular court at Hartford, March 30, 1660. *New Haven Colonial Records, 1653-1665* (Hartford, 1858), pp. 327-347, 351, 359, 380, 387; Massachusetts Historical Society *Collections*, 5th series, I (Boston, 1871), 385-387; VIII (Boston, 1882), 56-57; "Records of the Particular Court of Connecticut," Connecticut Historical Society *Collections*, XXII (Hartford, 1928), 211.

10. Francis Newman.

Phillip Scot[11] would not, but he conceales that he who tooke the prize was in his ship who was most fit to have bene sent to the courte and forgetts to excuse his refusal to yeeld to a sequestration of Mr. Raymonds goodes til the cause were tryed, though the governo[u]r sent the Marshall to him with a warrant, for that end, and sundry other things. The governo[u]r is almost over come with his faire words. But he speakes not a word of submitting his cause to theyre tryal, yet seemes willing to leave Mr. Raymunds vessel and goodes, in the courts hands, for part of security and to binde his 12th part in the ship, for the other part of security, (which is as none, because it is not standing security.) that he will have it tryed in England, within twelve moneths, if Mr. Raymond be bound and give security to prosecute ag[ains]t him. What the issue will be, a litle time will shew. In the meane time, his spirit is somewhat lower, in shew, then it was. Againe farewel.

The 22th d. of the 12th m. 59

[Endorsed] Mr. Davenport rec feb: 24 [by John Winthrop, and] Feb-[ruar]y 22d. *1659.* [in a modern hand.]

JOHN DAVENPORT *to* JOHN WINTHROP the Younger[1]
To the Right Worship[fu]ll and worthily much Honoured John Winthrope Esq[ui]r[e] Governo[u]r of Connectacute these pr[e]sent in Hartford.

Honoured Sir)

YOURS, dat[e]d the 27th of this moneth,[2] I received, by one of Farefield, whose name I know not, and in it an Almanack[3] inclosed, for boath which I returne many thancks, and send inclosed a copie of a wrighting, which Mr. Atwater[4] brought from the Baye, which I read with joy and thancksgiving unto God, beleiving it to be a true Narration of the state of things in England, and the last that is come to our

11. Philip Scott was the son-in-law of Thomas Pell of Fairfield, Connecticut. Massachusetts Historical Society *Collections,* 5th series, VIII (Boston, 1882), 56.
    1. The manuscript copy of this letter has not been found. It is printed in Massachusetts Historical Society *Collections,* 3d series, X (Boston, 1849), 30-31; A. B. Davenport, *A History and Genealogy of the Davenport Family* (New York, 1851), pp. 349-350.
    2. No copy of this letter has been found.
    3. Samuel Cheever, *An Almanack for the Year of Our Lord 1660. By S. C. Philomathemat.* (Cambridge, 1660).
    4. Joshua Atwater of Boston, Massachusetts.

hands. So that the other reports of Naylers[5] being Governour of Bristow, and of the fight betweene General Munck and Lambert[6] etc. I looke at as misreports. I hope also that the fight reported to have bene in London will not be found true, in all particulars, at least. I am sorry for your loss of Mr. Talcot,[7] of whose decease I heard, but not how his diseases were found to be incurable, til I read your letter, whereby it is most cleare to me that no art of man could cure him. I hope now that you will either receive your son safely arrived, in the next ship, from London, at Boston, or good newes from him. By this time I am apt to thinck that a Parliament is assembled[8] for the establishment of that great Commonw[ealth] upon sure foundacions of trueth and righteousnes, by the blessing of the most High, to whose grace, in Jesus Christ, with myne, my wifes, and sons humble services presented to you boath and affectionate salutations to your daughters, I heartily commend your selfe, and all yours, resting in him

Newhaven the 29th of the 1st m. 1660.   yours ever obliged

JOHN DAVENPORTE.

[Endorsed] Mr. Davenport.

5. Probably James Nayler, 1617–1660, the Quaker, who after being released from Bridewell, September 8, 1659, returned to Bristol. He was never governor of Bristol.

6. No battle was fought between Monck and Lambert. After Monck crossed the Tweed, January 2, 1659/60, Lambert fled to the south. Monck came upon Lambert's army at Newcastle, January 5, 1660. Part he disbanded; part he enlisted in his own army.

7. John Talcott of Hartford died March 23, 1659/60.

8. After its dispersal by the army, October 13, 1659, the revived Rump Parliament reassembled, December 26, 1659, and sat until March 16, 1659/60. The secluded members were received February 21, 1660. On the call of the Long Parliament, the Convention Parliament assembled, April 25, 1660.

John Davenport *to* John Winthrop the Younger[1]

To the Right Worsh[i]p[fu]ll John Winthrope Esq. Governo[u]r of Connectacute Colonie these pr[e]sent in Hartford

Honour[e]d Sir)

YESTERDAY, Mr. Gilbert,[2] and Deacon Myles, brought unto me a letter, written by yourselfe to Sarjeant Whitehead, about your house, which, it seemes, was an answer to a letter sent, by I know not whom, nor when, to yourselfe, in the name of the Townesmen,[3] and with theyre consent, that they might purchase the house, for the use of the Towne. From brother Herrymans discourse with my wife I understand that himselfe and brother Wakeman had speech with you, to promove that motion. All this was done, and written, without my knowledge and my wifes and sonnes; they did not, nor any from, or for them, make it knowne unto me, in the least, that such a letter or message should be sent unto you. Two of the brethren, who were not Townesmen spake with me formerly about theyre feare of losing the Governo[u]r, for want of an house, and propounded yours, concluding, from your owne wordes, that you would not dwell here, though, if there had bene any ground of hope of the contrary, they would not have propounded it. This I add, that I may doe them right. My advise was that they would not send to you about it, and, to stay them from so doing, I told them that I heard you purposed to come hither shortly (For so Daniel your man had reported) and did thinck that they would waite for that. These things I thus particularly relate, that you may see that I had not the least hand in what they have done, nor consent to it, nor knowledge of it. When the forenamed shewed me your letter, and enquired what I would doe, in reference to the power and trust you was pleased to commit to me, about alienating your house, I told them, as I had said unto yourselfe before, that I must desire to be excused from acting in that buisenes, and did refuse it, and doe stil pray you to wave me in that imploym[en]t, who shall in other things denie

1. New York Public Library, Winthrop–Davenport Papers; printed in L. Bacon, *Thirteen Historical Discourses* (New Haven, 1839), pp. 381–382; Massachusetts Historical Society *Collections*, 3d series, X (Boston, 1849), 31–33; A. B. Davenport, *A History and Genealogy of the Davenport Family* (New York, 1851), pp. 331–333.

2. Mathew Gilbert was one of the first settlers of New Haven. He served as magistrate of the colony from 1658 to 1661; deputy governor from 1661 to 1664; and magistrate in the final year of the New Haven Colony's existence.

3. At this time Roger Alling, Samuel Whitehead, Nicholas Elsey, James Bishop, John Cooper, William Davis, and Abraham Doolittle were townsmen, with John Harriman as alternate.

you nothing that I am fit to doe, if I may really pleasure you thereby. My son also hath refused to act in that matter. Had a letter bene brought to us to subscribe for inviting you to bring your familie, when you shall finde a convenient time and to come and dwell in your house and the sooner the wellcommer etc. we should have signed that with boath our handes. What is done I have not yet heard, therefore cannot give you account of it. While I paused a litle, having written thus farr, I heare that the two mentioned in the first line have alienated your house.[4] If it be so; I am heartily sorry, that what we have so many yeares desired and hoped for we shall be thus deprived of, viz. your neighbourhood, which we doe highly value and therefore cannot but looke at our loss as exceeding greate. My wife received Mrs. Winthropes loving token, the sugar loafe she was pleased to send her, for which she returneth her many thanckes, yet is sorry to have it from her, to whom she accounteth herselfe obliged otherwise rather to send unto her. With myne, my wifes and sonnes humble services to you boath and Respectfull and affectionate salutations to your daughters, commending you boath and yours unto the everlasting armes, I rest, Sir,

The 5th d. of the 2d m. 1660   Yours exceedingly obliged

                                                              JOHN DAVENPORTE

We desire to receive some intelligence of your and Mrs. Winthropes etc. purpose of coming to us, whose house shall be as your owne and you will much cheare us, if you say we shall injoy you here shortly.

[Endorsed] Mr. Davenport about the sale of the house [by John Winthrop, and] Mr. John Davenport's Lett[e]r no Date 5 April 1660. I. B. [in a modern hand.]

4. On April 3, 1660, Mathew Gilbert and Richard Miles, Sr., acting for John Winthrop the Younger, alienated to John Cooper and Roger Alling, townsmen, acting for the town of New Haven, the house which Winthrop had bought July 7, 1657. *New Haven Town Records, 1649–1662* (New Haven, 1917), p. 446.

JOHN DAVENPORT *to* JOHN WINTHROP the Younger[1]

Honour[e]d Sir)

I RECEIVED yours, by brother Benham,[2] whom God preserved from being drowned, in his journey homeward. The river by Mr. Yales farme, was swolne high, his wife was fearfull of riding thorough it. God provided an helpe for her, at the instant, by a passenger,[3] who travailed from Windsor[4] to Branford, to Mr. Cranes, whose daughter he had marryed: he helped Sister Benham over a tree. But her husband adventuring to ride thorough, a foote of his horse slypped, so he fell into the water, and his horse, as he thincketh, fell upon him, or struck him with his foote; for he had a blowe on his head. But, through the mercy of God, is now well. This day, Mr. Attwater, being at our Lecture, speakes of a letter newly received from his wife, who wrightes her feares that she shall never see him againe, doubting that he was cast away, the last storme, whereby, she saith, sundry vessels about Boston have suffred much hurte, and some persons are cast away, and a ship also, if I mistake not, at Cape Cod. But God ordered things so, by his good providence, that Mr. Atwater was then at New London, in a safe harbour. Even now, Major Hawtherne,[5] and Mr. Richards,[6] are come from the Dutch. They are gone into the Towne, to dispatch some buise-

1. New York Public Library, Winthrop–Davenport Papers; printed in L. Bacon' *Thirteen Historical Discourses* (New Haven, 1839), pp. 382–383; Massachusetts Historical Society *Collections*, 3d series, X (Boston, 1849), 33–34; A. B. Davenport, *A History and Genealogy of the Davenport Family* (New York, 1851), pp. 333–335.

2. John Benham, Sr., was a settler at New Haven as early as 1640. On November 16, 1659, he took as his second wife, Margery, the widow of Thomas Alcock of Dedham, Massachusetts. Margery Benham died a few weeks after her arrival at New Haven. Benham himself died before December, 1661.

3. Thomas Huntington of Windsor, Connecticut, was the husband of Hannah, the daughter of Jasper Crane of Branford.

4. Windsor was one of the original towns of Connecticut.

5. William Hauthorne of Salem, Massachusetts.

6. John Richards of Boston, Massachusetts. He married Elizabeth (Hawkins), the widow of Adam Winthrop, the brother of John Winthrop the Younger, in 1654, and Anne Winthrop, the daughter of John Winthrop the Younger, in 1692.

The general court of Massachusetts of May, 1659, granted a group of settlers a plantation ten miles square, forty or fifty miles west of Springfield, two thirds of the way to Fort Orange. The session of the general court of October 18, 1659, sent Hauthorne and Richards to Peter Stuyvesant, director general of New Netherland, to claim territory on the Hudson River, near Fort Orange. The two men were returning from New Netherland at this time. The general court of October 16, 1660, gave the grantees permission to transport men to the new settlement and to defend themselves against Indians and others. *Massachusetts Colony Records*, IV, Part I (Boston, 1854), 374, 395, 438. See below, p. 160.

nes, but will returne to supp and lodge at my house. I doe not yet know whether they purpose to returne to Boston, by land, or sea, yet prepare these lines, *in omnem eventum*, to send by them, if they goe by land, or by some other conveyance, if I can heare of any. Sir, I thanck you for my sight of Mr. Knowles[7] his letter to Mr. Joanes.[8] That which he speakes of a parliam[en]t in Scotland,[9] I cannot receive. For, I suppose, England will not suffer it. I stil hope, that things in England are in an hopeful way. The Lord Jesus dwell with you in peace! Myne, my wifes, and sons humble services are affectionately presented to your selfe and Mrs. Winthrope, with our salutations to your daughters. Having other letters to wright, in answer to freinds in the Bay, I am compelled to take off my pen: but shall alwaies remaine

Newhaven the 13th of the   Sir
2d 1660
                                   Yours exceedingly obliged

                                   JOHN DAVENPORTE

Mr. Price of Salem and his wife,[10] present theyre services to yourselfe and Mrs. Winthrope, in a letter brought to me by Major Hawtherne. They are importunately desirous to stay Mr. Higgenson[11] with them at Salem, for continuance, and in way of office.

[Endorsed] Mr. Davenport [by John Winthrop, and] dated April 13th. *1660*. [in a modern hand.]

7. Possibly John Knowles, a non-conformist divine, who had held the office of teacher in the church at Watertown, Massachusetts, returned to England, served as lecturer at Bristol Cathedral, and after the Restoration lived in London, where he seems to have been in touch with William Hooke. A. Gordon in *Dictionary of National Biography*; Massachusetts Historical Society *Collections*, 4th series, VIII (Boston, 1868), 584.

8. Possibly John Jones, from 1637 to 1644 pastor of the church at Concord, Massachusetts, and at this time of Fairfield, Connecticut, who must have known Knowles, and who knew Winthrop.

9. Actually, at the summons of Monck, representatives of the burghs and shires assembled at Edinburgh, November 15, 1659, and were authorized to maintain order in Scotland during Monck's absence. They again met with Monck, December 13; and, after his departure from Scotland, in February, 1659/60. P. H. Brown, *History of Scotland*, II (Cambridge, 1902), 377.

10. Probably Walter and Elizabeth Price of Salem, Massachusetts.

11. Teacher and pastor of the church at Guilford in the New Haven Colony since 1643, John Higginson set out for England in 1659. Stopping at Salem, Massachusetts, where his father, Francis Higginson, had labored, he was persuaded to remain. He was ordained as pastor of the church at Salem, August 29, 1669. "The Diaries of John Hull," American Antiquarian Society *Transactions and Collections*, III (Boston, 1857), 195.

JOHN DAVENPORT *to* JOHN WINTHROP the Younger[1]

Honour[e]d Sir)

CAPTAINE CULLICK and Mr. Goodwin have bene with me, by whom I understand that some were appointed, both from the General Court and from the towne of Hartford to speake with them, to know what portion of Mr. Hopkins his estate (with the disposal whereof, for the ends specified in his will, we are entrusted) shall be allowed unto the said colonie or towne.[2] Our joynt-Answer thereunto is; that we doe judge it inconvenient for us to answer that quæstion, til the general court be pleased to declare, 1, That they accept of that copie of Mr. Hopkins his will, which is delivered unto the courte already, as Authentical and sufficient for the end whereunto it is produced. 2 That the said court acknowledge us three to be invested with power, by virtue of the said will, to dispose of the estate bequeathed unto us, according to the true mind and intent of the Testatour, to our best understanding. 3. That all sequestrations, encumbrances and disturbances whatsoever from that General Court be so taken off, that we may prosecute and settle the buisenes that concernes our Trust, without impedim[en]t, or interruption. These things being done, to our satisfaction; we shall seriously consider what answer we may give to the præmised quæstion, according to God and the Trust committed unto us.

1. Massachusetts Historical Society, Winthrop MSS., III, 145; printed in Massachusetts Historical Society *Collections*, 4th series, VII (Boston, 1865), 514.

2. Both Cullick and Goodwin were among the seceders from the church at Hartford, and had recently removed to Hadley, Massachusetts.
The session of the general court of Connecticut of August 18, 1658, had ordered an inventory of the Hopkins estate to be taken. On June 15, 1659, it sequestered the estate. On October 6, 1659, a copy of the will of Edward Hopkins was delivered to the general court of Connecticut, and the sequestration was removed. On February 23, 1659/60, the sequestration was renewed. On May 17, 1660, the general court again ordered an inventory of the estate to be taken. On October 3, 1661, Goodwin offered the colony £350 and the court appointed a committee to treat with the trustees. Finally, on March 10, 1663/4, after the trustees had agreed to grant £400 of the bequest to Hartford, the sequestration was removed. On December 3, 1664, the town of Hartford appointed a committee to receive the £400 from Edward Stebbing and Thomas Bull. The unwillingness of the general court of Connecticut to release the Hopkins estate, and the unwillingness of the trustees to bestow any part of the bequest upon Connecticut and Hartford merely reflect the bitter quarrel at the moment going on in the church at Hartford. *Connecticut Colonial Records, 1636–1665* (Hartford, 1850), pp. 322, 338, 341, 345, 350, 374–375, 418; Connecticut Historical Society *Collections*, VI (Hartford, 1897), 144. See above, p. 114n.

In witnes whereof we subscribe our Names.

At Newhaven. the 19th day of the 2d moneth. In the yeare 1660

JOHN DAVENPORTE

JOHN CULLICK

WILL: GOODWIN

[Endorsed] Mr. Davenport Capt. Cullick Mr. Goodwin answer about Mr. Hopkins legacy [by John Winthrop.]

JOHN DAVENPORT *to* JOHN WINTHROP the Younger[1]

To the Right Worship[fu]ll and Worthily Honoured
John Winthrope Esq. Governo[u]r of Connectacute
Colonie these present at Hartford

Honoured Sir)

I RECEIVED, by Mr. Goodwin, the Intelligences from England,[2] which I now returne, with many thancks, by the same hand. Here is a report brought from Virginia, by a ship lately arrived there from England, in 5 weekes, that the King of Scots is in London,[3] which I doe no more credit then that report of the Quakers, concerning General Munkes being in London,[4] and sole General, by Lamberts and Fleetewoodes laying downe theyre commissions,[5] or the establishm[en]t of

1. Massachusetts Historical Society, Winthrop MSS., III, 145; printed in Massachusetts Historical Society *Collections*, 4th series, VII (Boston, 1865), 511–513; A. B. Davenport, *Supplement* (Stamford, 1876), pp. 387–388.

2. In January and February, 1659/60, there were being published in England: *An Exact Accompt of the Daily Proceedings in Parliament; The Loyall Scout; Mercurius Politicus; The Monethly Intelligencer; Occurrences from Forraigne Parts; The Parliamentary Intelligencer; The Publick Intelligencer; A Perfect Diurnal of Every Dayes Proceedings in Parliament. Catalogue of the Pamphlets, Books, Newspapers, and Manuscripts relating to the Civil War, the Commonwealth, and Restoration, Collected by George Thomason, 1640–1661* (2 vols., London, 1908), II, 437–438.

3. This was an erroneous report. Charles II did not land at Dover until May 25, 1660.

4. With four thousand foot, and eighteen hundred horse, Monck arrived at Westminster February 3, 1659/60, and marched into the City to reduce it to submission to parliament February 9, 1659/60. C. H. Firth in *Dictionary of National Biography*.

5. On November 24, 1659, the Council of State commissioned Monck absolute commander-in-chief of all forces in England and Scotland. On December 26, 1659, the revived Rump Parliament gave command of the army to a commission of seven, thus depriving Lambert and Fleetwood of their commissions. On January 26, 1659/60, parliament confirmed Monck's commission as commander-in-chief of the forces in England and Scotland. C. H. Firth in *Dictionary of National Biography;* Sir Richard Baker, *A Chronicle of the Kings of England* (London, 1674), p. 691; *Commons Journals,* VII (n.p., n.d.), 797, 823.

the presbyterian way.[6] All which, I hope, with many other rumours, will be found not true, in sundry particulars, when we shall receive our letters from England. Besides that ship, at Cape Anne, Lievtenant Cooke[7] speakes of another also, at Cape Codd, which I thinck, is that, of which Sister Atwater[8] wrote. Major Hawtherne and your brother, Mr. Richards, went out of this Harbour, in the evening after the 6th day, towards Road Island,[9] purposing to travaile, by land, from thence to Boston. The Dutch Governour complemented with them, in liberal intertainm[en]t, but, for the principal buisenes about which they came, he denied to give them liberty of passing up the river, alleadging, that it would cost him his head, if he should permit that, and some of the Dutch traders threatened, that themselves would cut off his head, if he should grant that unto the English. Yet he offred them, to refer the wholl matter to England and Holland, with acquiescence in theyre determination, which our freindes refused, urging theyre line, against which the Dutch Governo[u]r demanded, why they had not claimed it all this while? They answ[ere]d, that they finde more need of it now, then formerly. He pleaded long possession. They replyed that the English had right to Hudsons river, before them, and proved it, more largely then I can now declare. The issue is, they parted placidely, and our freindes are to make theyre report to the general court, at Boston. In conclusion, they told them that they should returne again towards the end of summer. I perceive, if that buisenes proceedes, as Major Hawtherne thincks it will, all the colonies are likely to be ingaged in a warr with the Dutch. Concerning what you are pleased to propound, I shall take the 1st opportunitie to speake with the Townesmen,[10] that a good part of that which they are to paie, in reference to the house be paide, according to your order, to Mr. Yale. I could wish that you had expressed *quantum*. I understand, by Mr. Goodwin, that his house is hyred for you to dwell in. The courses that the general court take about Mr. Hopkins his legacie seeme to me very strange viz., that they would know what portion of it they shall have and yet hinder his Trustees from receiving what belongs to that estate, by sequestracions, one after another, whereby the estate will suffer no small loss, some being

6. On February 21, 1659/60, Monck ordered the guards to admit the secluded members of the Long Parliament, and for a time Presbyterians hoped for recognition of their religion. See below, pp. 177–178n.

7. Perhaps Lieutenant Richard Cooke, a member of the First Church, Boston, Massachusetts.

8. See above, p. 156.

9. Rhode Island.

10. See above, p. 154n.

ready to deliver up what they had purchased, because they will not have a litigious title, and one hath waved his bargaine, upon that account: others, who were ready to have paid, what they owe to the estate, now refuse to paye, pretending the courts order, whereby, when the sequestracion shall be taken off, there is danger that, through loss of the season, when they were prepared to paye, there will be a loss of the paym[en]t itselfe the Debtours pleading theyre dissabilitie now. And the pretence, whereupon the sequestracion is the 2d time laid on, is, that the Inventory is not given in, whereas some of the court, it seemes, know that it was left with our Atturneies in Hartford, by Capt. Cullick, with a trust to be by them presented to the court, which they also acknowledge and take the blame wholly upon themselves. But I doe not love contentions. We have agreed in the Answer, which I send inclosed. Myne, my wifes, and sons humble services being presented to yourselfe and Mrs. Winthrope, with our affectionate salutacions to your daughters, with my hearty desires and prayers continued for an abundant blessing from heaven upon you boath and all yours, in N. E. and old, I rest

Newhaven. the 20th d. of the 2d m. 1660   Yours ever obliged etc.

JOHN DAVENPORTE

Sir) you may please to communicate the inclosed to the General Court,[11] or theyre committee, as our joynt Answer.

[Endorsed] Mr. Davenport about Mr. Hopkins legacy [by John Winthrop.]

JOHN DAVENPORT *to* the GENERAL COURT OF THE NEW HAVEN COLONY[1]

Quod fœlix faustumque sit![2]

ON the 4th day of the 4th Moneth *1660* John Davenport Pastor to the Church of Christ, at Newhaven, pr[e]sented to the Hon[oure]d General Court at Newhaven as followeth:
Memor[an]dum,

11. Either John Winthrop the Younger failed to take up the matter with the general court or the general court disregarded his communication.
1. Connecticut State Library, Manuscript New Haven Colonial Records, 1653-1664, fols. 256-260; printed in *New Haven Colonial Records, 1653-1665* (Hartford, 1858), pp. 369-374.
2. Happy be it and prosperous!

1 That sundry yeares past, it was concluded by the said Generall Court, that a small Colledg (such as the day of small things will permitt) should be settled in Newhaven for the Education of youth in good Litterature, to fitt them for publick services, in Church and Commonwealth, as it will appeare in the publicke Records.[3]

2 Herevpon the said John Davenport wrote vnto our Hon[oure]d ffreind Edward Hopkins Esq., then liveing in London, the Result of those Consultations. In answere wherevnto the said Edward Hopkins, wrote vnto the said John Davenport a letter dated the 30th of the 2d Moneth called Aprill *1656* Begining with these words, "Most deare S[i]r, the long continued respects I have received from you, but especially the speakeings of the Lord to my heart by you, have put mee vnder deepe obligations to loue, and a returne of thankes beyond what I euer have or can expresse, etc." then after other passages (which being Secretts hinder mee from shewing his letter) he added a declaration of his purpose in reference to the Colledg about which I wrote vnto him, "That which the Lord hath given mee in those parts, I euer designed the greatest part of it, for the furtherance of the worke of Christ in those ends of the Earth, And if I vnderstand that a Colledge is begun, and like to be carried on at Newhaven for the good of Posterity, I shall give some Encouragm[en]t therevnto." These are the very words of his letter, But,

3. Before Mr. Hopkins could returne an Answere to my next lett[e]r, it pleased God to finish his dayes, in this world: Therefore by his last will, and Testament, (as the Copie thereof, transcribed and attested, by Mr. Tho[mas] Yale, doth shew) he committed the whole Trust of disposing his Estate in these countryes (after some personall legacies were paid out) vnto the publick vses mentioned, and bequeathed it, to our late Hon[oure]d Gouerno[u]r Theoph[ilus Eaton] Esq. his ffather in Law, and to the aforesaid John Davenport and ioyned with them, in the same Trust, Captaine John Cullick and Mr. William Goodwin.

4 It haveing pleased the most High to afflict this Colony greatly by takeing from it to himself, our former euer hono[u]r[e]d Gouerno[u]r Mr. Eaton: The Surviving Trustees, and legatees met together to consider, what course they should take, for the discharge of their Trust, and agreed, that each of them should have an Inventory of the afore said Testatours Estate, in New-England, in houses, and goods, and lands, (which were prized by some in Hartford intrusted by Captaine Cullick and Mr. Goodwin) and in debts, for the gathering in whereof, some Attorneys were constituted, impowered, and imployed by the

3. See above, p. 108.

three Surviving Trustees, as the writeing in the Magistrates hands will shew.[4]

5. Afterward at another meeting of the said Trustees, they considering that by the will of the dead; they are ioyned together in one Comon Trust, agreed to act with mutuall consent in performance thereof. And, considering, that by the will of the Testatour two of Newhaven were ioyned with two of Hartford, And that Mr. Hopkins had declared his purpose to further the Colledg intended at Newhaven, they agreed that one half of that Estate which should be gathered in, should be paid vnto Mr. Davenport for Newhaven, the other half to Captaine Cullick and Mr. Goodwin, to be improued for the vses, and ends forenoted where they should have power to performe their Trust which because they could not expect to have at Hartford they concluded, it would be best done by them in that New Plantation[5] vnto which sundry of Hartford were to remoue, and were now gone. Yet they agreed that out of the whole an £100 should be given to the Colledg at Cambridg in the Bay, the estate being £1000. as Captaine Cullick beleeued it would bee, which we now see cause to doubt, by reason of the Sequestrations laid vpon that estate, and still continued by the Generall Court at Hartford wherevpon some refuse to pay their debts, and others forsake the purchases they had made, to their great hinderance of performing the will of the deceased according to the Trust committed to them, and to the endamagem[en]t of the Estate.

6. The said John Davenport acquainted the other two Trustees, with his purpose, to Interest the Hono[u]red Magistrates, and Elders of this Colony, in the disposall of that part of the Estate, that was, by their agreement to be paid therevnto, for promoueing the Colledgwork, in a graduall way, for the Education of youth in good literature, so farr as he might, with pr[e]serving in himself the power comitted to him for the discharge of his Trust: they consented therevnto. Accordingly on the Ellection day, it being the 30th day of the Third Moneth, he delivered vp into the hands of the Hon[oure]d Gouerno[u]r and Magistrates the writeings that concerne this businesse, (viz. the Copie of Mr. Hopkins his last will and Testam[en]t and the Inventory of his Estate in New England and the apprizm[en]t of his goods and the writeings, signed by the Surviveing Trustees, for their Attornyes, and some letters between the other Trustees and himself) Adding also his desire of some particulers for the well performing of the Trust as followeth.

4. See above, pp. 127–128.
5. Hadley, Massachusetts.

1. He desireth of Newhaven Towne, that the rent of the oyster shell feild,[6] formerly seperated and reserved, for the vse and benifit of a Colledge, be paid from this time forward towards the makeing of some stocke for disbursments of necessary charges, towards the Colledg til it be set vp, and afterwards to continue for an yearly rent as belonging to it, vnder the Name, and Title of Colledg land.

2 That, if no place can be found more convenient; Mrs. Eldreds lott,[7] be given for the vse of the Colledg, and of the Colony Grammer Schole, if it be in this Towne, else onely for the Colledge,

3 That parents will keepe such of their sonns constantly to learning in the Schooles, whom they intend to Traine vp for publick service-ablenes, and that all their sonnes may learne at the least to write, and cast vp accounts competently, and may make some entrance into the lattine tongue.

4 That if the Colony settle £40. *per Annum* for a common schoole, and shall add an £100. to be paid towards the building or buying of a schoole house and library, in this Towne, seeing thereby this Towne will be freed from the charges which they have beene at hitherto, to maintaine a Towne schoole they would consider what part of their former Salary may be still continued, for future supplies towards a stock for necessary expences about the Colledg or schoole.[8]

2 He humbly desireth the Hon[ou]r[e]d General Court of the Colony of Newhaven, *first* that the £40. *per Annum*, formerly agreed vpon to be paid by the seuerall Plantations, for a common Grammer-schoole, Be now settled in one of the Plantations which they shall judge fittest, and that a Schoolemaster may forthwith be prouided to teach the three languages Lattine, Greeke, and Hebrew, soe far as shall be necessary to pr[e]pare them for the Colledge, and that, if it can be accomplished, that such a Schoolemaster be Settled by the end of this summer, or the begining of winter, the payments from the seuerall Planta-tions may begin from this time. *Secondly* that if the Common Schoole be settled in this Towne The Hon[ou]r[e]d Gouerno[u]r, Magistrates, Elders, and deputies, would Solemnly, and together visit the Grammer

6. The town of New Haven refused to grant the income from the oyster shell field until a college was actually under way at New Haven. *New Haven Town Records, 1649–1662* (New Haven, 1917), p. 457.

7. Mrs. Eldred's lot was located to the north of the common. The grammar school was never erected upon it.

8. New Haven's response was niggardly. On July 11, 1660, Governor Newman, the court, and townsmen of New Haven agreed to pay £10 of the schoolmaster's salary and to furnish dwelling and school houses. *New Haven Town Records, 1649–1662* (New Haven, 1917), p. 459.

Schoole once euery yeare, at the Court for Elections to examine the Schollers profficiency in learning. *Thirdly* that for the payments to Bee made by the Plantations, for the Schoole, or out of Mr. Hopkins estate, towards the Colledge, one be chosen by themselues, vnder the name, and Title of Steward, or Receiuer for the Schoole, and Colledg, to whom such paym[en]ts may be made with full power given him by the Court, to demand what is due, and to persecute, in case of Neglect, and to give acquittances in case of due paym[en]ts received, and to give his account yearely to the Court, and to dispose of what he receiveth in such provisions as cannot be well kept, in the best way for the aforesaid vses according to advice. *fourthly* that vnto that end a Committee of Church members be chosen, to meet together, and consult and advise, in emergent difficult cases, that may concerne the Schoole, or Colledge, and which cannot be well delayed til the meeting of the General Court, the Gouerno[u]r being alwayes the cheife of that Committee. *ffiftly*. the s[ai]d John Davenport desireth that, while it may please God to continue his life, and abode in this place, (to the end that he may the better performe his Trust) in reference to the Colledge, that he be alwayes consulted in difficult cases, and have the power of a Negatiue vote, to hinder anything from being acted, which he shall proue by good reason, to be pr[e]judiciall to the true intendment of the Testatour, and to the true end of this worke. *Sixtly* that certaine Orders be speedily made for the Schoole, And when the Colledge shall proceed, for it also, that the Education of youth may be carried on sutably to Christs ends, by the counsail of the Teaching Elders in this Colony. And that what they shall conclude with consent, being approued by the Hon[ou]red Magistrates, be ratified by the General Court. *Seaventhly* because it is requisite, that the writeings which concerne Mr. Hopkins his Estate be safely kept, In Order therevnto the said John Davenport desireth, that a co[n]venient chest be made with 2 locks, and 2 keies, and be placed in the house of the Gouerno[u]r or of the Steward, in some safe Roome, til a more publick place, (as a library or the like) may be pr[e]pared, and that one keye be in the hand of the Gouerno[u]r, the other in the Steward[s] hand, that in this chest all the writeings, now delivered, by him to the Magistrates may be kept, and all other Bills, Bonds, accquitances, Orders, or whatsoeuer writeings that may concerne this busines be put, and kept there, And that some place may be agreed on where the Steward, or receiver may lay vp such prouisions as may be paid in, til they may bee disposed of for the good of the Schoole or Colledge; *Eightly* because our sight is narrow, and weake, in viewing and discerning the compasse of things that are before vs, much more in foreseeing future contingencies, he further craveth liberty for himself, and other Elders of this Colony, to propound to the Hon[ou]r[e]d Gouerno[u]r, and Magistrates what hereafter may be found to be conducible to the well carrying on of this Trust according to the ends proposed, and that such proposals may Be added vnto these, vnder the name and Title of VSEFUL ADDITIONALLS: and confirmed by the General Court. *Lastly*, he hopeth he shall not need to add what he expressed by word of Mouth, that the Hon[ou]r[e]d General Court will not suffer this gift to be lost from the Colony, but, as it becometh Fathers of the Commonwealth, will vse all good endeavo[u]rs to get it into their hands, and to assert their right in it for the Comon good, that posterity may reape the good fruit of their Labours, and wisdom, and faithfullnes, and that Jesus Christ may have the service and hono[u]r of such prouision made for his people in whom I rest

JOHN DAVENPORT:

To these motions I desire that the Answere of the Court, together with this writeing may be kept among the Records for the Schoole, and Colledge.

JOHN DAVENPORT *to* JOHN WINTHROP the Younger[1]

To the Right Worship[fu]ll John Winthrope Esq. Governo[u]r of Connectacute-Colonie, these present in Hartford

Honoured Sir)

THIS is the first opportunity presented to me of returning an Answer to the 2 last letters I received from you. Brother Benham indeed (whose good, and sweete spirited, wife the Lord hath taken from him, since his returne, and a yong childe of one of his sons, is since dead, in his house, where also one of his sons wife lyeth very weake) he went to Hartford, but gave me no notice of it before, that I might prepare a letter for him. Brother Myles, at his returne from the Baye, comforted us with hopes of your recovering strength. For he told us that you looked better, when he returned, then you did, when he went to the Baye. Our desire is fervent to see you and Mrs. Winthrope here, by the will of God, as soone as may be. I hope, the change

1. New York Public Library, Winthrop–Davenport Papers; printed in L. Bacon, *Thirteen Historical Discourses* (New Haven, 1839), pp. 383–384; Massachusetts Historical Society *Collections*, 3d series, X (Boston, 1849), 34–36.

of aire would hasten your recovery, and the perfecting of your strength by the blessing of God. For we are by the seaside, and my house shall be as your owne, for your use. And to us it will be a singular refresh-m[en]t and contentment to injoy your presence and abode with us, as long as your occasions will permit. Be pleased to accept this serious and hearty invitation, and to answer it really, in coming to us, and staying with us, that you may be refreshed with the sea aire, and we with your sweete and much desired fellowship. If you feare that you shall burthen us; be assured of the contrary, that we shall looke at it as a real testimony of your love and confidence in us and in our love, which is unfeigned toward you boath, and all yours, and as a most ac-ceptable gratification of our earnest desire to injoy you with us as long as we may. My selfe, wife, and son had bene with you, before this time, if I durst have adventured upon such a journey, which yet I should have done, though with some hazzard, if my coming might have bene of any necessary beneficial use to you. One day, in the spring, I rode forth with our Governo[u]r,[2] to stirr my body and take the aire, but when I returned home, though we had bene out but an houre or two, my urine grew so high coloured, that my wife thaught it was bloody, and hath ever since continued very high coloured, and many times she observes a black settlem[en]t in it. I have bene, for above a fourtnight, costive, though not wholly without stooles but once in 2 daies, at least, and, of late, once every day I doe some what at the stoole. *Dejectio quidem pauca est, et cum difficultate, quandoque etiam cum inani conatu egerendi, quam tenesmum noncupant Medici.*[3] I am daily, at least, every morning, til I have breakasted, troubled with a paine at the bottom of my belly, most usually on the left side and, at other times also, after walking. Yet my appetite and digestion are good, considering the season. For hot weather weakens, and almost prostrates my spirits, when it is extreme. My wife also hath bene weake in her spirits, and weake stomached. Yesterday, about an houre before sunset, she tooke 6 grains of the rubila,[4] and had 3 vomits and one stoole, and both is better and lookes better, this day, by Gods blessing

2. Francis Newman.

3. Ejection indeed is little, and with difficulty, and sometimes with a vain attempt of discharge, which physicians call a straining at stool.

4. On rubila, a remedy frequently prescribed by John Winthrop the Younger, see O. W. Holmes, "The Medical Profession in Massachusetts," *Medical Essays 1842–1882* (Boston, 1883 and 1891), p. 335; W. R. Steiner, "Governor John Winthrop, Jr., of Con-necticut, as a physician . . . ," Johns Hopkins Hospital *Bulletin*, XIV, No. 152 (Novem-ber, 1903), 294–302; *ibid.*, XVII, No. 188 (November, 1906), 357–360; Massachusetts Historical Society *Collections*, 6th series, V (Boston, 1892), 6 n., 342, 380–381.

upon the meanes. Yet she spitteth, all this day, more then formerly, white frothy matter, and is weakish in her spirits and not well in her head and hath bene very thirsty the most parte of this day. She had an earnest desire to have made a journey to visit you, but could not effect it. Sir) I humbly thanck you for the Intelligences[5] I received in your letters, and for the 2 weekely Intelligences, which brother Myles brought me, I thinck, from your selfe, and which I returne inclosed, by this bearer, with many thancks. I did hope that we might have received our letters by Capt. Pierse,[6] before this time. But we have no newes lately from the Bay. Brother Rutterford and Brother Alsup are boath there, so also is our Teacher Mr. Streete. The 2 former, I hope, will returne, some time the next weeke. Then probably we shall have some further newes. The Lord fitt us to receive it, as we aught, what ever it may be! Sir) I long to heare of your perfect recovery of health and strength, and to understand from you, that your purpose is to be with us shortly, and when we may expect your coming to us, with Mrs. Winthrope etc. In the meane time, and ever, the Lord Jesus dwell with you, in mercy, and peace, and loving kindnesses! In whom I rest

Newhaven. the 20th   Sir/
of the 5th 1660
                Yours exceedingly obliged

                     John Davenport

[Endorsed] Mr. Davenport July 20 *1660.* [by John Winthrop.]

5. In April, 1660, there were being published in England: *An Exact Accompt of the Daily Proceedings in Parliament; Mercurius Politicus; Mercurius Publicus; The Parliamentary Intelligencer; The Publick Intelligencer. Catalogue of the Pamphlets, Books, Newspapers, and Manuscripts relating to the Civil War, the Commonwealth, and Restoration, Collected by George Thomason, 1640–1661* (2 vols., London, 1908), II, 438.

6. Captain John Pierce arrived at Boston July 27, 1660. John Hull gives the name of the ship Pierce commanded in 1663 as the *Society,* but as he gives the same name for another ship which arrived at about the same time, this may be an error. Pierce commanded the *Royal Exchange* in 1668. "The Diaries of John Hull," American Antiquarian Society *Transactions and Collections,* III (Boston, 1857), 208, 209, 210; *Calendar of State Papers, Colonial Series, 1661–1668* (London, 1880), no. 1797; F. W. Gookin, *Daniel Gookin, 1612–1687* (Chicago, 1912), pp. 104, 106, 110.

JOHN DAVENPORT *to* JOHN WINTHROP the Younger[1]

Honoured Sir)

HAVING so sure a conveyance, I returne the inclosed, with acknowl-edgm[en]t of my very greate obligem[en]t unto you, for your labour of love, in putting such a taske upon yourselfe, at such a time, as the transcribing of the weekely intelligence, from the 3d to the 10th of the 3d m.[2] and in gratifying mee, so unworthy, with the perusal of it. Whereby I understand the state of the publick, in our deare native countrie, and doe wish that sundrie of our relations and freinds were well settled in these ends of the earth. I heare nothing yet concerning Capt. Pierse his arrival, which I much wonder at. For I perceive that he hath bene about a quarter of an yeare, in his voyadge. I wish that he be safe. I am in expectacion of our Teachers returne, with bro: Rutterford, every houre. In the letter, which Mr. Richards conveyed to me, from him (for which I returne hearty thancks to him, and for his kinde acceptance of such intertainm[en]t as we could make, on the suddaine, with my resalutations to them boath) brother Streete re-porteth a strange passage which he heard at Boston, which, it may be, will minister some matter of laughter unto you, as it doth of indigna-tion unto me. It is this. A company being mett some where in England (he thincks they were 5th monarchy men)[3] and Sir Henry Vane[4] with

1. Massachusetts Historical Society, Winthrop MSS., III, 146; printed in Massa-chusetts Historical Society *Collections*, 4th series, VII (Boston, 1865), 515–517; A. B. Davenport, *Supplement* (Stamford, 1876), pp. 389–390.

2. An issue of *Mercurius Publicus*, which for the moment had supplanted *Mercurius Politicus*, covered the week of Thursday, May 3, 1660, to Thursday, May 10, 1660. With other news, it contains accounts of rioting throughout England, and a declaration of the General Convention of Ireland denouncing the proceedings against the late king in a pretended High Court of Justice in England.

3. During the Interregnum some of the extreme sectaries interpreted passages of the book of Daniel to mean that the Assyrian, Persian, Greek, and Roman kingdoms were soon to be succeeded by a fifth monarchy, or the reign of Christ for a thousand years. See J. K. Hosmer, *The Life of Young Sir Henry Vane* (Boston, 1888), pp. 428–433; L. F. Brown, *The Political Activities of the Baptists and Fifth Monarchy Men in Eng-land during the Interregnum* (Washington, 1912), *passim*.

4. Henry Vane the Younger, governor of Massachusetts from 1636 to 1637, sailed for England August 3, 1637, where he was knighted in 1640. A parliamentarian, he sup-ported the Commonwealth and the army under Lambert, but opposed the Protectorate and the activities of George Monck. Although not originally a Fifth Monarchy man, while imprisoned in Carisbrooke Castle he seems to have fallen under the influence of John Rogers, and in 1659 and 1660 he was coöperating with that faction. Following the Restoration, he was excluded from the act of general pardon and oblivion, June 11,

them; it was propounded, that, seing christ was not yet come, they should thinck of some one that should be cheife among them, til he shall come, and, that being consented to, it was considered, whom they should choose, and it was concluded, with common consent, Sir Hen[ry] Vaine, thereupon one rose up with a viol of oile, which he poured on Sir Hen[ry] Vaines head, and called him King of Jerusalem. *sit fides penes Authorem.*[5] Men, it seemes are serious about setting up Kings. Our comfort is, that the Lord raigneth and his counsels shall stand. In rightly obeying this King we shall become faithful to whatsoever powers he settes over us. We have much sicknes among us, both in the Farmes and towne by the afflicting hand of the most High renued upon us, righteously. Some wholl families and sundry particular persons. Some have greate paine in theyre heades and stomacks some, violent evacuacions upward and downeward some burning etc. My wife also, having wholly spent your supply, is destitute of Rubila, which some have desired, but returned empty. My wife tooke the pilles you formerly commended to her, in the evening after the last Lords day, about an houre before supper, and found good effects of the operation of them the next morning (onely it was sooner then formerly, about one aclock in the morning, and with much more gryping then before; which my wife imputeth to her costivenes about a weeke together, after she had taken the Rubila,) though she was weakened thereby, all the day after, and is so stil (if it should continue, as she is distemperd, she desires to know whether she should take the rubila, or the pilles) yet, I beleive, the blessing of God hath done her good thereby, for which, as for many favours, be pleased to accept our joynt thancks, who cease not to pray for your continuance in health, and for the blessing of God upon all your indeavours for the good of many, with returne of an 100dfold, in mercies and loving kindnesses, to you boath and to all your branches.

Be pleased to present myne, my wifes and sons humble services, together with yourselfe, to Mrs. Winthrope, and our respectful affec-

1660, and imprisoned in the Tower. He was ordered to be transferred to the Scilly Isles, October 25, 1661, but was brought back to the Tower in the following April. Arraigned on June 2, 1662, he was tried and found guilty on June 6; sentenced to death, June 11; and executed on Tower Hill, June 14, 1662. C. H. Firth in *Dictionary of National Biography*; J. K. Hosmer, *The Life of Young Sir Henry Vane* (Boston, 1888); L. F. Brown, *The Political Activities of the Baptists and Fifth Monarchy Men in England during the Interregnum* (Washington, 1912); *Lords Journals*, XI (n.p., n.d.), 163; *Commons Journals*, VII (n.p., n.d.), 806, 841; VIII (n.p., n.d.), 143, 152, 287, 317, 342, 368.

5. Let responsibility rest with the author.

tionate salutations and thancks to Mr. and Mrs. Richards. The Lord Jesus dwell with you in peace! In whom I rest

Newhaven. the 1st d. of   Sir,
the 6th m. 1660.

                Yours exceedingly obliged

                  JOHN DAVENPORTE

Auctarium)

Honoured Sir) The unexpected opportunity of transmitting these lines, which I gladly embrace, did both streighten me in wrighting the premises, and thereby occasion my forgetfulnes, being in hast, of that which I should have added, in answer to your former very loving lines, which I received the last weeke, in answer to myne, concerning my wifes weakenes, and my bodily distemper. We boath returne many hearty thancks to you for your good directions, which we keepe, as precious, to follow them, as occasion may require. I hope that, by the mercy of God, my body is about to returne to its former state, the paine being much abated, and that difficulty and frequent *irritus conatus egerendi*[6] ceasing, in a good degree. I am now content to let nature acte, of itselfe, in hope that, by Gods blessing upon suitable diet, I shall be well againe, in due time. Though we are sorrie that we shall want your precious company so long, as til the commissioners come,[7] yet we are comforted with hope of injoying it then, and Mrs. Winthropes etc. with you, at our house, which, we pray you, to accept for your and her lodging and intertainm[en]t, with assurance of our rejoycing in that hope.

[Endorsed] Aug[u]st 1st. 1660. Mr. John Davenport to 1st Gov[erno]r Winthrop of Connecticut [in a modern hand.]

6. ineffectual effort of discharging
7. On September 6, 1660, Simon Bradstreet, Daniel Dennison, Josias Winslow, Thomas Southworth, John Winthrop the Younger, Mathew Allyn, Francis Newman, and William Leete, commissioners of the United Colonies of New England, met at New Haven.

JOHN DAVENPORT *to* JOHN WINTHROP the Younger[1]

To the Right Worship[fu]ll John Winthrope Esq. Governo[u]r of Connectacute these present at Hartford

Honoured Sir)

I RECEIVED a former letter from you, by Mr. Bishop,[2] who, in his returne from your parts hitherward, tooke a wrong path twise and was so bewildred that he lost his way, from Wethersfield, and lay in the woods, in a very cold night, and came not to us, til the last day of the weeke towards noone. But, I hope, he hath no hurte, but is returned in safety and health, by the mercy of God to his family. I will not now trouble you with the reasons of my returning those papers[3] unto you, but accept thanckfully your freindly admonition, for the future, not to erre againe, on that hand. We boath pray you to accept our hearty thancks for your supplies of Rubila, both then, and now againe, by this bearer. The report is true which you have heard of much sicknes in this towne and the Farmes about it. The Lord be mercyful to his people and rebuke our distempers, and sanctifie his afflicting hand to them and us all! It is true also that Mr. Pierse is come. Brother Rutterford also and Brother Alsop are come to us, and have brought with them our Teacher, whose deare wife,[4] and our much beloved Sister the most High hath taken to himselfe, both from him and us. She was buried the day before his arrival. They have also brought Mr. Joanes, and his wife, Mrs. Hannah Eaton, and her infant, with 2 sons of his, by a former wife, and 2 servants, etc. They have declared themselves to be unsatisfyed with brother Yale selling away sundry things in the house, and with his Agreem[en]t with Mr. Hill[5] about the division made of Mr. Eatons estate. Some discouragem[en]t

---

1. Massachusetts Historical Society, Winthrop MSS., XII, 94; printed in Massachusetts Historical Society *Collections*, 3d series, X (Boston, 1849), 37–39; A. B. Davenport, *A History and Genealogy of the Davenport Family* (New York, 1851), pp. 350–353.

2. James Bishop of New Haven.

3. According to the endorsement on this letter, papers about the church at Wethersfield.

4. Possibly Alice, the sister of Elizabeth Poole, an ancient maid, the founder of Taunton, Massachusetts. See S. H. Emery, *The Ministry of Taunton* (2 vols., Boston, 1853), p. 157; *History of Taunton, Mass.* (Syracuse, 1903), p. 175. Before August 1, 1661, Nicholas Street took as his second wife, Mary, the widow of Francis Newman. *New Haven Town Records, 1649–1662* (New Haven, 1917), pp. 485, 489, 512.

5. Valentine Hill of Boston, Massachusetts, the husband of Mary Eaton, the daughter of Theophilus Eaton and his first wife.

seemes to be upon theyre spirits concerning theyre settling here[6] yet they are buisyed about disposing the goods they have brought with them and accomodating theyre dwelling in the house. Time will shew what theyre future resolution will be. Edmond is come, who presenteth his humble service to your selfe, and to Mrs. Winthrope. He found out your son, who is captaine of a troupe of horse in Colonel Reades Regiment, whom he also saw upon the Exchange.[7] You son is well recovered, by the mercy of God, from the small poxe. He was with him againe, the day before his coming away, by his bed side, and brought letters from him to your selfe, etc. which he gave to Mr. Amos Richardson,[8] at his desire, purposing, as he said, a journey to New London where he was to meete with you. But, when Edmond saw that he went not, but stayed above a weeke, Edmond, being to come for N[ew] Haven, desired him to lett him have the letters againe, that he might bring them unto you more speedily then, he suspected, they would be handed to you, by Mr. A. R. But he utterly refused to let Edm[ond] have them so they remaine stil in his hands. Concerning Mr. Peters I heare litle, onely from bro[ther] Hooke, that the Lord Craven[9] waytes hopefully for the restitucion of his lands, wherein, he saith, Mr. Peters hath a share, he is of kinne to Monck, and sometimes dineth with him. Your son told Edmond that he purposeth to returne for N[ew] E[ngland], the next yeare. My brother Hooke is valetudinarious, having bene afflicted with a very greate fluxe of Rheume, accompanied with an erisipilus unto danger of death; he hath still an ill stomach, and spleenish distempers. His wife[10] also hath her bodily infirmities. He hath prevailed with a kinsman of yours to wrighte unto you the story of these late yeares in Engl[and],[11] whom he commends

6. William Jones remained at New Haven. He served as magistrate of the New Haven Colony in 1662 and 1663; deputy governor of the New Haven Colony in 1664; an assistant of the colony of Connecticut in 1665 and annually thereafter; and deputy governor of Connecticut from 1692 to 1698. He died in 1706.

7. The Royal Exchange, London, erected in Queen Elizabeth's time.

8. Amos Richardson, a merchant of Boston, Massachusetts. On September 5, 1660, Winthrop acknowledged receipt of a letter from Fitz John Winthrop. Massachusetts Historical Society *Collections*, 5th series, VIII (Boston, 1882), 62.

9. William, Lord Craven, subsequently created Earl of Craven, a royalist, followed Charles II to England, where he recovered his estates.

10. Jane (Whalley) Hooke, the sister of Edward Whalley and the cousin of Oliver Cromwell. In her youth Roger Williams had vainly besought her aunt, Joan, Lady Barrington, for her hand.

11. For the letter of John Maidston to John Winthrop the Younger, March 24, 1659/60, see J. Thurloe, *State Papers* (7 vols., London, 1742), I, 763–768; Massachusetts Historical Society *Collections*, 3d series, I (Boston, 1825), 185–198.

for a greate wit, parts, and copious language, and choise for Intelligence etc. His letter I send inclosed, with some others, and one from Mr. Hartlib, who thinckes you live in this plantacion, and hath sent a large wrighting unsealed, that I might peruse it, which, though I want time to read over, I choose rather to send it to you, then to detaine it. He hath sent also sundry wrightings and bookes, some to your selfe, some to me. But I cannot heare of them, in these pinnasses, which makes me doubt, they are stayed in the Bay, at Mr. Ushers,[12] which I the rather suspect, because Mr. Hartlib, and bro[ther] Hooke certifie me that Mr. Dury[13] also hath sent some papers and bookes to the 2 Teaching Elders at Boston,[14] and to me. If it shall please you to imploy Mr. A. R. therein, he will inquire of Mr. Usher, and procure them to be conveyed to your selfe, and myne, by your helpe, to me. Many things I might add, which it would be too tædious to wright, and would be more fittly communicated to you, if we might injoy your much desired presence here. The 2 Gentlemen of greate qualitie arrived in the Baye, are Colonel Whaley,[15] and his son in law, Lievtenant Colonel Goffe.[16] I hope to see them here, after the Commissioners are gone, if not before. I might hope to see them before, upon my letter, but I deferr that, on purpose, that your chamber may be free for your reception and Mrs. Winthropes, when the Commissioners meete. I must now breake off, rather then conclude, with myne, my wifes, and sons, humble services presented to your selfe and Mrs. Winthrope, and our prayers for all good to you boath and and yours, remayning

Newhaven, the 11th   Sir,
d. of the 6th m. 1660   Yours exceedingly obliged
                              JOHN DAVENPORTE

Sir)
    I mistooke, in my letter, when I said, Colonel Whalye was one of the Gentlemen etc. It is Commissary General Whaley, Sister Hookes brother, and his son in law, who is with him, is Colonel Goffe; boath Godly men, and escaped pursute in Engl[and] narrowly.
    Etiam atque etiam vale.

[Endorsed] Mr. Davenport Aug: 11th. *1660*. Papers from Mr. Hartlib etc. and the papers about Wethersfeild church [by John Winthrop.]

12. Hezekiah Usher, merchant and bookseller of Boston, Massachusetts.
13. On John Durie or Dury, see above, pp. 141–142n.
14. John Wilson and John Norton, pastor and teacher of the First Church, Boston, Massachusetts.
15. Edward Whalley, the regicide.
16. William Goffe, the regicide.

Excerpts from a Letter of JOHN DAVENPORT and the MINISTERS of the NEW HAVEN COLONY *to* JOHN DURIE[1]

FLAGRANTE Schismatis *Incendio, Ecclesias, quas oportebat Arctissimo Pacis et Unitatis Vinculo Colligari, misera in sectas* Invisa Deo Lacerabat Erinuys; *Usque adeo ut qui mutuam contra communes Hostes opem conferrent, proh dolor! Concertationes* Midianiticas *invicem agunt; Sicut Enim Juvenes quos ad Dimicandum Abnerus Provocabat, se mutuis Vulneribus Confecerunt; Sic, quorundam Vitio, qui partes potius agunt*

1. Cotton Mather, *Magnalia Christi Americana* (London, 1702), Book III, Part I, Chapter IV, pp. 54–55; A. B. Davenport, *Supplement* (Stamford, 1876), pp. 393–395. In 1738 the original copy of this letter was in the possession of Samuel Mather, pastor of the Second Church, Boston, Massachusetts, and a son of Cotton Mather. Samuel Mather, *An Apology For the Liberties of the Churches in New England* (Boston, 1738), p. 166. Although the excerpts are undated, Davenport's letter may have been written in response to the books and papers sent to him by Durie in the summer of 1660. (See above, p. 174.) If so, it was dated after August 11, 1660.

Cotton Mather's translation of the passages reads:

While the Fire of *Schism* has been raging, the *Hateful Fury* has miserably torn to Pieces, the Churches that should have been held together in the strictest Bonds of Love and Unity; insomuch that they who should have united, for mutual Help against the common Enemy, alas, have even fallen upon one another, *as in the Day of Midian.** As the young Men, upon the Provocation of *Abner*, wounded one another to Death;† thus, by the Fault of some, who do the part rather of *Bad Wranglers*, than of *Good Preachers*, there do arise in the Reformed Churches, those *Broils* and *Strifes*, and Animosities, and *Schisms* and Scandals, which offend the *Weak*, and afflict the *Good*, and are no little Satisfaction to the Enemies of *Gospel-Truth*.

But now that the *Keeper of Israel*, the *God of Peace*, hath put it into the Hearts of many Churches and Rulers, to apprehend it necessary, that a Cure should be sought for these Wounds, Behold! The Minds of all Good Men, do with a raised Hope expect an Happy Close of these Mischiefs; and with most hearty Prayers, do beseech the *Father of Mercies*, that he would, by the Grace of his Spirit, according to his Word, please to direct the Counsels and Actions of his Servants, for the Glory of his own Holy Name.

You have done Right Well, Reverend *Brother*, in that you have, after a Brotherly manner, unto the Promoting of this Affair, in the *Communion of Saints* invited us, who belong to the same Mystical Body, with your selves, under One Head, our Lord Jesus Christ.

Nevertheless, 'tis not to be made an Article of Complaint against the *Orthodox*, as if they would hinder or delay the *Peace* desired so much among the *Reformed Churches*, because they do, as Necessity shall call for it, use that *Liberty* of *Refuting Errors*, which *Peace* ought to be no Bar unto; and by their Example, would rescue the future *Peace* from the Extremes wherewith it would be rendred Faulty.—For we reckon that as well to *Judge* what things are *Errors*, as to *bear* with such Errors in Weaker Brethren, are *both* of them agreeable to what we have been taught by the Apostles. The *Toleration* of our Erroneous Brethren, should not be without *Rebuking*, but it should be without *Rejecting* of those Brethren.

*Possibly a reference to Judges 7. 22.
†2 Samuel 2. 14–16.

male Disputantium, *quam bene* Evangelizantium, *Jurgia, Lites, Animorum Divortia, Schismata et Scandala, in Ecclesiis Evangelicis Suboriuntur, non sine gravi Infirmorum Offendiculo, nec sine Summo Bonorum Omnium Mærore, ac Inimicorum Evangelicæ Veritatis Oblectamento.*—

Nunc Vero, Postquam Custos Israelis, Deus Pacis, *dedit in Corda tot Ecclesiarum et Magistratum, ut Vulneribus istis Medicinam faciendam esse, Necessarium Judicarint, En! Bonorum omnium Animi, in Spem erecti, Malorum istorum Salutarem Clausulum Expectant, et Votis intimis, Patrem Misericordiarum Vobiscum invocant, ut Spiritus sui Gratia, Secundum Verbum Suum, Consilia et actiones Servorum Suorum dirigere, ad Sancti Nominis Sui Gloriam dignetur.*—

Recte quidem fecisti, Reverende Frater Duræe, *quod nos etiam in eodem Vobiscum Corpore, Sub eodem Capite Jesu Christo, Constitutos, ad Negotium hoc, in Sanctorum Communione, Promovendum, fraterne invitasti.*—

Dica Vero non est Orthodoxis *impingenda, quasi Optatissimæ illi* Paci, *quæ inter Scissas* Evangelicas Ecclesias *quæritur, Offendiculum posuerint, et Remoram qui Necessitate Postulante, ea utuntur Libertate Refutandi Errores, quam Pax non debet impedire: adeoque suo Exemplo futuram pacem præmuniant, à Vitiis in Excessu positis.—Quippe quod sincere de Erroribus Judicare, et Errores tamen in Fratribus Infirmis Tolerare, Utrumque Judicamus esse Apostolicæ Doctrinæ Consonum* Toleratio *Vero Fratrum Infirmorum, non debet esse absque* Redargutione, *Sed tantum absque* Rejectione.

JOHN DAVENPORT *to* JOHN WINTHROP the Younger[1]

To the Right Worship[fu]ll John Winthrope Esq. Governo[u]r of Connectacute Colonie, these present at Hartford

Honour[e]d Sir)

THOUGH I am, at present, in præparacion for the lecture, to morrow, yet having newly received a letter from Capt. Clarke, and hearing that one at the ordinary purposeth a journey towards the Baye, in the morning, who, I suppose, will goe by Hartford, I make bold to send you the Intelligence which I receive from England, by

1. Massachusetts Historical Society, Winthrop MSS., XII, 94; printed in Massachusetts Historical Society *Collections*, 3d series, X (Boston, 1849), 42–44; A. B. Davenport, *A History and Genealogy of the Davenport Family* (New York, 1851), pp. 353–355.

way of Newfoundland, to the middle of July,[2] which informes, that those who were of the High court of justice and condemned the former King, theyre estates are confiscate, 20 of them imprisoned, three of them like to die, viz. Jones, Harrison, and Say (if I doe not misreade) and that Dr. Goodwin, Mr. Nie, and Mr. Peters are in prison, and likely to lose theyre lives,[3] and that there is a consultacion to settle church discipline,[4] in a way of joyning Episcopacy and presbytery, by

2. In July, 1660, there were being published in England: *An Exact Accompt of the Daily Proceedings in Parliament; Mercurius Publicus; The Parliamentary Intelligencer; Mercurius Politicus; The Publick Intelligencer.* Catalogue of the Pamphlets, Books, Newspapers, and Manuscripts relating to the Civil War, the Commonwealth, and Restoration, Collected by George Thomason, 1640–1661 (2 vols., London, 1908), II, 438–439; *A Transcript of the Registers of the Worshipful Company of Stationers, from 1640–1708 A. D.* (3 vols., London, 1913–14), II, 272, 280.

3. Introduced into the House of Commons, May 9, 1660, An Act of Free and Generall Pardon Indempnity and Oblivion became law, August 29, 1660. (12 Charles II, c. 11.) From the benefits of this act were excluded: thirty-two living persons including Hugh Peter and two unknown executioners; nineteen living regicides with the proviso that, if they were attainted, their fate would rest with the king and parliament; six surviving regicides and Sir Arthur Hesilrige for punishment other than capital; John Lambert and Sir Henry Vane the Younger. Twenty others were excluded from holding any ecclesiastical, civil, or military office. In addition, twenty-four deceased regicides were attainted as to their estates. Of those excluded from the benefits of the act, thirteen regicides and Sir Henry Vane the Younger were executed; and twenty-five regicides, Lambert, and Hesilrige were imprisoned for life. Of those mentioned by Davenport, John Jones was arrested June 2, 1660, and committed to the Tower. He was excepted from the act of general pardon and oblivion, June 6, 1660; tried October 12, 1660; and executed October 17, 1660. Thomas Harrison was arrested early in May, 1660, and committed to the Tower; excepted from the act of general pardon and oblivion, June 5, 1660; brought to trial October 11, 1660; and executed at Charing Cross October 13, 1660. William Say was excepted from the act of general pardon and oblivion June 6, 1660. Escaping to the Continent, he died there about 1665. Doctor Thomas Goodwin, independent divine, was deprived of his office as president of Magdalen College, Oxford, May 18, 1660, but seems otherwise to have gone unmolested. John Goodwin, republican divine, who had succeeded Davenport as vicar of St. Stephen's, Coleman Street, London, was ordered into custody, June 16, 1660; excepted from the act of general pardon and oblivion, June 18, 1660; omitted from the exception, August 13, 1660; and incapacitated from holding any public trust by the act as it was finally passed. But Davenport's reference cannot be to John Goodwin, for he does not seem to have been entitled to the prefix of "Doctor." Philip Nye, independent divine, was excepted from the act of general pardon and oblivion, June 18, 1660; omitted from the exception, August 13, 1660; and incapacitated from holding any public trust in the act as it finally passed parliament. *The Statutes of the Realm* (9 vols., London, 1810–22), V, 226–234; D. Ogg, *England in the Reign of Charles II* (2 vols., Oxford, 1934), I, 154–155.

4. A passage in the declaration of Breda, April 4/14, 1660, promised liberty of opinion in matters of religion; a royal declaration of October 25, 1660, promised a review of the Book of Common Prayer, and aroused further hope on the part of non-conformists. On March 21, 1660/61, letters patent authorized a group of Anglicans and Presbyterians

agreem[en]t that Each Bishop in his Diocese shall have a select number of presbyters joyned with him, the commonn prayer to be established, but with some alteracions: some Ceremonies to be left indifferent; as bowing at the Name of Jesus, the Surpliss, cross in Baptisme etc. That good men are under some sufferings, many being turned out of theyre places: but greater things feared: Spaine like to make peace: France like to differ. The good Lord prepare his people in old Engl[and] and New, for what they and we may expect, and, in the meane time, give us hearts to sympathize with afflicted Joseph![5] We, at Newhaven, are stil under Gods afflicting hand. The good Lord sanctifie it to us all! Our Governo[u]r[6] stil continues very weake, eates litle, and ill digests what he eates, is ill after it, yet, til he takes something, findes a gnawing at his stomach, is commonly coldish. Once he tooke the Rubila, but finding himselfe sundrie times ready to faint away, hath not bene willing to take it againe nor his wife that he should, though we persuaded and encouraged him thereunto. I feare what the issue may be, if some better course be not taken for his recovery then Mr. Auger[7] præscribed. Also our Teacher is very sick. The last lecture day, he purposed to preach, though he found an aguish distemper, the day before, and continued in that purpose til the 2d drumme, but then was compelled to take his bed. So there was no sermon. Afterward he hoped that it would be a quotidian, and leave him at the 4th fitt, as it did, here, in the spring, and once before, at Milford. But it is plainly the disease, and he hath, after his cold a burning without sweate, and was very ill with it, this day. He is also troubled with detention of his urine, and when he voided it, it was sharpe and hot. I much feare what the issue will be. I persuaded him, what I could, to take the Rubila, but doe not finde him inclinable, though he is burthened in his stomach. He slept not, the last night, and had a burning fit, this afternoone, he takes very litle of any thing, and desires litle or nothing. My wife made

to meet from time to time during the ensuing four months in the master's lodging at the Savoy in the Strand or elsewhere to review the Book of Common Prayer. Although Richard Baxter drew up a reformed liturgy, the conference came to an end without arriving at any conclusions. A revised Book of Common Prayer was arranged by the convocation of 1661. All hopes of the non-conformists were shattered when the acceptance of this revision was made compulsory by the act of uniformity, May 19, 1662, to go into effect on St. Bartholomew's Day, August 24, 1662. 14 Charles II, c. 4; H. Gee and W. J. Hardy, *Documents Illustrative of English Church History* (London, 1896), pp. 588–594; R. Baxter, *Reliquiæ Baxterianæ* (London, 1696), pp. 303–372.

5. A reference to Genesis 37.
6. Francis Newman.
7. Nicholas Auger or Augur, physician and trader at New Haven.

some things for him, he tooke a litle of it. Upon drincking some beere from the ordinary which was harsh and sowre, he fell into a vomiting, which brought up much yellow stuffe, yesterday. The good Lord direct to the meanes, which he will bless for his recovery! Mr. Jones tooke the Rubila 4 times and followed your other directions, and is, by the blessing of God, in an hopefull way. His fittes, he thincks, have left him, though some grudgings he findes hanging about him. He doth not know of my wrighting, at this time. I beleive, Mr. Jones himselfe will wright to you, when he findes himselfe able. And I am persuaded that your advise will prevaile with our Governour to take what course you may please to præscribe. He knoweth not of my wrighting, at this time, because my letter is now to be sent away, the messenger being to be gone, betimes, in the morning. The Lord Jesus dwell with you and yours in mercy and peace and loving kindnesses! With our humble service to yourselfe and Mrs. Winthrope, and our loving salutations to all your branches, my wife, and son joyning with me therein, I rest

Newhaven the 17th d of the 8th m. 1660   Yours exceedingly obliged

JOHN DAVENPORTE

We heare that Mr. Paine and Mr. Web[8] are boath dead.

[Endorsed] Mr. Davenport Oct: 17: 1660 [by John Winthrop.]

JOHN DAVENPORT *to* JOHN WINTHROP the Younger[1]

To the Right Worship[fu]ll John Winthrop Esq. Governo[u]r of Connectacute these present at Hartford

Honoured Sir)

SERO *sapiunt Phryges.*[2] If I had as wel used my πρovoία[3] in preparing a letter, as I was dilligent in hearkening after opportunities for transmitting it; I had not bene thus surprized, before I had begun my letter. Brother Benham, just now, telles me that his companie is gone before, and he is going to Hartford. I blame him for not letting me know, last night, but in vaine. Yet I urge his stay, a very litle, that I may write these few lines, whiles he is buisied about mak-

---

8. Henry Webb, a Boston merchant, died September 7, 1660.

1. Massachusetts Historical Society, Winthrop MSS., III, 146; printed in Massachusetts Historical Society *Collections*, 4th series, VII (Boston, 1865), 517–519.

2. *Sexti Pompei Festi De verborum significatione*, C. O. Mueller, ed. (Leipzig, 1839), p. 343. The Trojans are wise when it is too late.

3. πρóvoια, foresight.

ing up your curtaines, which had bene with you, before now, if my wife could have procured him, or John Thomas to have carryed them. I hope, you will now receive them, by him. Concerning the matter of the Indians;[4] I hope, Mr. Gilbert hath or will give you a cleare account. If the Indians, you are pleased to mention, should revenge themselves upon ours; they will greately wrong the Innocent. For our Indians had no hand in that buisenes, nor have spoken the least word, for aught I can learne, to animate our men to what is done. And that which, it seemes, bro[ther] Yale and bro[ther] Cooper have spoken to your Indians, I never knew, nor heard of, but by your letter: Nor will there be any thing done by any of ours to hinder your Indians in theyre hunting. But for the purchase; it was made above 20 yeares past, without any seeking, on our part, upon an offer made to our then Governo[u]r[5] etc. It was of Mantoweeze that the land was bought, whereby N[ew] H[aven] bounds extended neare unto the Cold Spring,[6] beyond pilgrims harbour.[7] But of these things if you desire it, our Governo[u]r[8] will give you full Intelligence, when he shall be able, which, I hope, will be shortly. For the wrightings of that transaction are in his hands. The other buisenes, which concernes the paim[en]t of Mr. Jones, is so farr ended as that you may cast off all care about it.

4. This reference is to a dispute between the New Haven Colony and Connecticut regarding the boundary between the two colonies. On April 23, 1660, a town meeting at New Haven authorized Thomas Yale, William Andrews, John Cooper, John Brockett, and Nathaniel Merriman, with the help of Montowese, the late proprietor, to set out the bounds of a parcel of land toward Connecticut to prevent future differences. When this committee marked trees to the north of Pilgrims Harbor, Daniel Clarke, secretary of the colony of Connecticut, protested both against the acts of the committee and against the chapter entitled "Indians" in the New Haven Colony code of laws of 1656, which seemed to claim all land between the Connecticut and Hudson rivers and all of Long Island for the New Haven Colony. On May 29, 1661, a general court of the New Haven Colony appointed William Leete, governor, Mathew Gilbert, deputy governor, Benjamin Fenn, Robert Treat, and Jasper Crane, magistrates, John Davenport, Sr., George Hubbard of Guilford, and John Nash of New Haven a committee to treat with Connecticut. *New Haven Town Records, 1649–1662* (New Haven, 1917), p. 448; *New Haven Colonial Records, 1653–1665* (Hartford, 1858), pp. 409–410, 593; Connecticut State Library, Connecticut Archives, Foreign Correspondence, II, no. 4.

5. Articles of agreement between Theophilus Eaton, John Davenport, and other English planters at Quinnipiac, on the one part, and Montowese, son of an Indian sachem living at Mattabezeck, on the other part, were signed December 11, 1638. *New Haven Colonial Records, 1638–1649* (Hartford, 1857), pp. 5–7.

6. Cold Spring lay on the west side of the ridge known as Lamentation Mountain. *Connecticut Colonial Records, 1689–1706* (Hartford, 1868), p. 450.

7. Pilgrims Harbor, the present West Meriden, lay to the north of Wallingford. *Connecticut Colonial Records, 1665–1677* (Hartford, 1852), pp. 53, 127.

8. Francis Newman.

For Mr. Jones tould me, speaking with him about it it, that he accepts the Townesmen for his pay M[aste]rs, and doth not looke to you for it. By a letter from Capt. Gookin[9] I understand that the 1st worke the King did, after his settlement, was the solemne funeral of his Father,[10] and the next, was the pardoning of all, but 7,[11] and the 3d was, a serious urging the parliam[en]t to be speedy, in paying the souldiers and Navie theyre arreares.[12] There is a truce with Spaine,[13] in order to a peace. We heare, from Manatoes, that the Hollanders are likely to fall off from Spaine.[14] *Hæc raptim!*[15] My selfe wife and son present our humble services to yourselfe and Mrs. Winthrop, with our affectionate salutacions to yours. I rest

Newhaven. the 30th day   Yours exceedingly obliged
of the 8th m. 1660
                                          JOHN DAVENPORTE

    Bro[ther] Streete came to see me yesterday.

[Endorsed] Mr. Davenport about the Indian purchas of N: H. bounds [by John Winthrop, and] 1660 J Davenport to Gov Winthrop [in a modern hand.]

9. Daniel Gookin of Cambridge, Massachusetts, visited England in 1650 and 1655. In the latter year he was employed by Cromwell to return to New England to push the settlement of Jamaica in the West Indies, recently conquered by the English. Failing in his mission, he returned to England in 1658. The restoration of Charles II to the throne of England caused him to seek refuge again in New England, and he crossed the Atlantic in the vessel of Captain John Pierce, which arrived at Boston July 27, 1660. F. W. Gookin, *Daniel Gookin, 1612–1687* (Chicago, 1912).

10. Charles I was buried in the Royal Chapel of St. George, Windsor, February 9, 1648/9. After the Restoration, Charles II intended that his father's body should be deposited in King Henry the Seventh's Chapel, but St. George's Chapel had been so changed since 1649 that the body of Charles I remained unlocated until 1813. C. W. Coit, *The Royal Martyr* (London, 1924), pp. 368–374.

11. See above, p. 177n.

12. An Act for the speedy disbanding of the Army and Garrisons of this Kingdome (12 Charles II, c. 15) was passed by the session of parliament that met April 25, 1660.

13. A royal proclamation of September 10, 1660, declared the cessation of hostilities with Spain from May 25, 1660, the day of the king's landing in England. *Calendar of State Papers, Domestic Series, 1660–1661* (London, 1860), p. 262.

14. Spain had recognized the independence of the Protestant Netherlands in the treaty of Westphalia, 1648, but relations between the two countries remained bad.

15. [I have written] This in a hurry!

JOHN DAVENPORT *to* JOHN WINTHROP the Younger[1]

To the Right Worship[fu]ll John Winthrop Esq. Governo[u]r of Connectacute Colonie, these present in . . .

Honour[e]d Sir)

I PERCEIVE, you have received from others the sad intelligence of the decease of our Honour[e]d Governo[u]r,[2] my very deare and precious freind. We hoped that he was in a good way of recovery from his former sicknes, and were comforted with his presence in the publick Assembly, 2 Lords daies and at one meeting of the church one a weeke day, without any sensible inconvenience. And, on the morning of the day of publick Thanksgiving,[3] he found himselfe encouraged to come to the publick Assembly. But, after the morning sermon, he told me that he found himselfe exceeding cold from head to toe, yet, having dined, he was refreshed, and came to the meeting againe, in the afternoone, the day continuing very cold. That night, he was very ill, yet he did not complaine of any relapse into his former disease, but of inward cold, which he and we hoped might be removed by his keeping warme and using other suitable meanes. I beleive, he did not thinck that the time of his departure was so neare, or that he should die of this distemper, though he was alwaies prepared for his greate change. The last day of the weeke, he desired my son to come to him the next morning, to wright a bill for him to be praied for, according to his direction. My son went to him, after the beating of the 1st drum, but, finding himselfe not fit to speake much, he praied him to wright for him what he thaught fit. When the 2d drum beate, I was sent for to him. But, before I came, though I made hast, his precious immortal soul was departed, from its house of clay, unto the soules of just men made perfect. We were not worthy of him, a true Nathaniel,[4] an Israelite indeed, who served God, in christ, in sincerity and trueth. He honoured God in his personal conversacion, and in his Administracion of cheife magistracie in this Colonie And God hath given him honour

---

1. New York Public Library, Winthrop–Davenport Papers; printed in L. Bacon, *Thirteen Historical Discourses* (New Haven, 1839), pp. 385–386; Massachusetts Historical Society *Collections*, 3d series, X (Boston, 1849), 44–46; A. B. Davenport, *A History and Genealogy of the Davenport Family* (New York, 1851), pp. 335–338.

2. Francis Newman died Sunday, November 18, 1660.

3. Because of illness in the colony, a court of magistrates at New Haven, October 17, 1660, was unable to select a date for a day of public thanksgiving to be celebrated throughout the colony, and left the choice of a date to the elders at New Haven. They seem to have chosen Wednesday, November 14, 1660.

4. S. John 1.47.

in the hearts of his people. My losse and my sons, who tooke greate contentm[en]t in his company, as he also did in his, is very greate, and our greife answerable. But the publick loss is farr greater, and answerably it is generally bewailed, God recompencing his faithfulnes with his living desired and dying lamented. It becomes us to lay our hands upon our mouthes, yea, to put our mouthes in the dust,[5] remembring whose doing this is. Yet, in respect of meanes, I could wish 2 things. 1. that, in his former sicknes, he had wholly and onely followed your directions. 2 that, he had forborne coming forth, that cold day. But Gods counsailes shall stand, whose will is the 1st and best cause of all things, and the very errours of men shall serve to accomplish his purposes, who is holy in all his waies, and righteous in all his workes. Sir) what I wrote, in my former, concerning Mrs. Coghen,[6] I had from Anth. Elcock,[7] who received it in the Baye, viz. that she was discontented that she had no suitours, and that she had encouraged her Farmer, a meane man, to make a motion to her for marriage, which accordingly he propounded, prosecuted and proceeded in it so farr that, afterwards, when she reflected upon what she had done, and what a change of her outw[ard] condicion she was bringing herselfe into, she grew discontented, despaired, and tooke a greate quantity of ratts bane, and so died. *Fides sit penes Authorem.*[8] Sir) I humbly thanck you for the Intelligence you was pleased to give me of an opportunity of transmitting a letter for London, which is a thing that I earnestly desire, and doe make bold to commit it to your owne care, seing you are pleased to give me that liberty, and hearing that the vessel is yet at Hartford. The letter is of greate importance: the safe and speedy handing of it to Mr. Robb. Newman[9] will be a reall advantage to me and the miscarrying of it, no small dissadvantage. In which respect, if you conceive, it will be more speedily and certainly conveyed to him, by this way then by the ship at Boston; I desire it may be sent ac-

5. Lamentations 3. 27–31.
6. Martha, the sister of Increase Nowell of Charlestown, Massachusetts; the widow of Thomas Coytemore or Coytmore of Charlestown, Massachusetts, of John Winthrop of Boston, Massachusetts, and of John Cogan, Coggan, or Coggin of Boston, Massachusetts, died October 24, 1660. ("The Diaries of John Hull," American Antiquarian Society *Transactions and Collections*, III [Boston, 1857], 195–196.) No earlier letter of Davenport to John Winthrop the Younger concerning her has been found.
7. Anthony Elcock of New Haven.
8. Let responsibility rest with the author.
9. Robert Newman was one of the first settlers at New Haven. About 1650 he returned to London, where he is described as a citizen and vintner in 1654. H. F. Waters, *Genealogical Gleanings in England* (2 vols., Boston, 1901), II, 1080.

cordingly with the more strong ingagem[en]t for committing it to a
sure hand, at Barbadoes, to be delivered to Mr. Newman, in London,
as the matter is of more consequence; that an answer may be returned
from him by the 1st ship from London to Boston, in the spring. Having
thus opened the case, I crave leave to commit it wholly to your selfe
to take that course with it, which you shall judge most suitable. I shall
not add, but myne, my wifes and sons humble services to your selfe
and Mrs. Winthrope, with our respectful and affectionate salutacion
to your son and daughters, praying the Lord to continue your life
unto them, and theyres unto you, and to multiplye his favours and
blessings upon you and them, through Jesus christ! In whom I rest

Newhaven. the 27th d. of the 9th m.   Sir,
1660.
                                        Yours ever obliged

                                        JOHN DAVENPORTE

   The miscarriage of a letter, which I formerly sent to London, by
way of Barbadoes makes me so desirous that this may not miscarry.
   My wife heares by one, in this Towne, that a Dr. of physick in England saith that conserve of Rue will hinder propagacion of children.
She desires to understand your judgem[en]t concerning it.

[Endorsed] about Mr. Nevmans death. rec. Nov: 28 1660 [by John
Winthrop.]

JOHN DAVENPORT *to* JOHN WINTHROP the Younger[1]

*To the Right Worship[fu]ll John Winthrope Esq. Governo[u]r of
Connectacute-Colonie these present at Hartford*

Honour[e]d Sir)

I MAKE bold, at my wifes request, to send my man with these lines,
whereby you may understand that it hath pleased the most High
to visite this plantacion againe with a renewed stroke of his mighty
hand, by vehement coughs and coldes, from which but few persons, no
families, are free, in one degree or other. Some are very ill and in greate
danger. My son also whom God hath preserved long in health, (whether
by leaving off his coate, one day, which was very cold, or how else, my
wife knowes not to be sure) by the hand of our God, is much weakened
and distempered with a cold, which began, as he thinckes, on the 3d

---

1. Massachusetts Historical Society, Winthrop MSS., XII, 95.

day last, being the 11th d[ay] of this moneth, and on the 5th day he had a good stomack at noone, but none at night and he coughed much that night, and was ill; and the next day he was very ill, all day, dull, and listles, and stomachles, and complained of weakenes, was much troubled with coughing and rheaume in his eies and nose. Both that night, and the last day, he coughed much and was exceedingly troubled with winde both in his belly and stomach. While we were at duetyes, for the beginning of the Sabbath, he was troubled with a greate paine in his eare, which made him groane much, whereof God gave him ease about 10 a clock that night by blessing some meanes that my wife used but his rest and sleepe was much hindred by his frequent coughing, that night. Yesterday, being the Lords day, my wife gave him 8 graines of Rubila, about 9 a clock in the morning. It was long before it wraught, he was costive the day before. It wraught 1st by stoole, which was not loose, a good while after, he had a pretty large vomit: after that, a small stoole not very loose: after that another litle one very loose. In the working of the physick, he was very sick and so faint and feeble, that he could not helpe himselfe in the least things, but Edmond was faine to lift him up in his armes to his bed. He was also troubled, one while, with paine in his belly, another while, was very sick in his stomach: he profferd and desired to vomit all the afternoone but could not, but that one time: at last, toward candle lighting, he had another large loose stoole. Since, his stomach is very flat and weake, is against any sweete thing, he was drie, in the night, and sometimes called for beare and tooke litle else, but a litle gruel towards morning. He groaned in his sleepe, and tooke his wind short, hath a paine in his head and is, at present, somewhat dull of hearing, which we impute to winde in his head. He complaines of paine in his head, with coughing, and of winde in his belly and side. Coughing and winde are his greatest troubles, at present. He is stil very weake in his stomach, and spittes abundantly. He complained, at 1st, most of his head, but now, though he is stil ill in his head, yet it it is most in his stomach. My wife observed twise that his urine, when it was cold, was thickish and yellowish. He telles my wife that he findes himselfe so weake, after the physick, that he cannot take it againe. We earnestly desire your advice touching the præmises. Mrs. Joanes also, hearing of our purpose, desires that a letter from her may be conveyed unto you.[2] The Lord Jesus recompense all your helpfullnes to his people with plentiful blessings upon your selfe and yours. Boath our services and our sons to yourselfe and Mrs. Win-

---

2. No copy of this letter has been found.

thrope with affectionate salutacions to all your children, being presented, I rest,

Newhaven. the 17th day   Sir,
of the 10th m. 1660

          Yours deepely engaged

           JOHN DAVENPORTE

Be pleased to pardon these blotts and marginal addicions, which are to satisfie my directour, and . . .[3]

[Endorsed] about . . . sickness. Dec. 17 1660 [by John Winthrop.]

JOHN DAVENPORT *to* JOHN WINTHROP the Younger[1]
To the Right Worship[fu]ll John Winthrop Esq. Governo[u]r of Connectacute Colonie, these present in Hartford

Honoured Sir)

MANY hearty thancks for your last greate labour of love in so many precious directions, and in the things you sent for my deare son, being premised, in boath our Names, and our sonnes also, who findes himselfe deepely ingaged unto you, for the same. Upon a new Accident my wife desireth me to wright againe to you for further advise with giving an account of what hath passed, since my mans returne, which was on the 4th day toward evening. The day before, pretty late in the afternoone of the 3d day, my wife made him a glyster with annis seedes, fennel seedes and a good handfull of Mallowes, and an handful of wheate bran, and sweetened it well with sugar. That gave him 3 stooles, of different degrees, but the last was least. On the 4th day, he was much troubled with winde, and a greate cough, and much paine, which also continued on the 5th day. Nor had he any stoole since the glyster, on the 3d day. He was also very weake, and said to my wife that the rubila would kill him, if he tooke it againe, he found himselfe so weake whereby we were in very great streights what to doe. Yet considering seriously what you wrote by way of encouragem[en]t to take the rubila, and not to suffer him to be costive, which, at his desire, I read to him also, and considering the difficulty of seing our way, to our satisfaction, we called upon God for his guidance herein, and we agreed, he also consenting to it, after prayer, to give him a dose of rubila, one graine more then before, because that wraught so litle.

3. The last two words are illegible.
1. Massachusetts Historical Society, Winthrop MSS., XII, 95.

Himselfe also consented to have 9 graines. Accordingly it was given him about 2 aclock after noone, on the 5th day. After his taking it, he was but litle sick but he was exceeding dull and heavy, and complained of a paine under his short ribbes, that when his Mother asked him, how he found himselfe, he answered, Mother I cannot tell how I am, I am like a logg, he said, he found an heavynes in his stomach. I thaught he slept, but my wife thaught rather it was an extreme dullnes in his head rather then sleepe. He had grypings in his belly several times. It did not worke by vomit, but by stoole, and gave him onely one large loose stoole. We tryed suppositors but the butter could not be put up into his body, nor the raysons well, it was very troublesom to his weake body etc. and in the end came to nothing they are so limber. In the time of the physicks working, my wife could get him to take but one porringer and an halfe of posset drinck and water grewel, but most of it was posset drinck. After the working of it was over, toward night, he grew a litle more lightsom, and finding an ill tast in his mouth after the physick, he said to my wife, Mother, you know sick folke will long, or desire, and was very desirous to have an apple roasted or baked, that he might eate some of the pap of it. My wife was fearful, because of the physick, yet, at his earnest desire, yeelded, and gave him some of it, he was exceedingly pleased with the tast of it and did eate it with much delight. After that he desired some beare, not so warme as he had usually before in his sicknes taken it, which he had, and, after that had some litle rest. But shortly after he had a most tormenting paine of winde in his body, which forced him to skreame out and to sweate much. On the 6th day, as soone, as possibly they could prepare it, my wife gave him the glyster, which you prescribed, and put your powder into it. But some of it being spilt by the badnes of the bladder, my wife doubtes, it wanted a pretty deale of a pinte, that was given him. It was in his body about 2 houres before it wraught, in which time, he had much paine. He had, at last, one stoole about the quantity of a pinte, as it was thought, and voided much winde. Yet his paine continued, with shifting, under his short ribbes, on the leaft side, and in his back back and an heavynes in his head (where also he had greate paine, the day before) he complained also of a paine in his belly and in his stomach, and of roughnes in his tong and of drynes in his mouth. For which he had a mouth water, since the taking whereof he did not complaine of that, last night. And for his paine he had a cataplasme of a pinte of new milke, an handfull of flaxe seed beaten, a litle hand full of mallowes, a litle wormewood, and a litle saffron, with fat of an hen, applyed to his leaft side, where his paine was most, whence my wife began to feare a pleurisie, but because it shiftes she is now out of that feare. All that have bene with him doe wonder hearing winde so to breake from him, and most downeward, and yet his paine to continue. In the time, while the rubila was working, his coughing was nothing so much as at other times. His coughes have bene of different sorts. His 1st cough, though it was greate, brought up much flegme. Since that he had another of a different sound, hard, and one would thinck it came from the top of his throate. Now, he hath a short cough, in fits, which so pierceth his side, where the paine lies, that he said to his mother that he was girt with paine all the day. He is so weake that he cannot turne him selfe and scarse stirr himselfe in his bed, but needes the helpe of others: and by reason of his paine, he is held, in his side, and where the paine is, with a man and a woaman, or with two woemen, one the one side and the other, his paine is so various and shifting, yet most under his short ribbes, or in his back. His water continues high, and when it is cold, it is thickish and like the colour of paler coloured oranges. This day, his voice is very hoarse and he is much spent, which my wife thincks, may come from his coughings and frequent groanings. He would sleepe, yet is hindred by his cough. This night he had an houres quiet sleepe, and 3 other sleepes, though not so quiet, but with moaning and groaning. I must conclude with leaving the pr[e]mises to your serious consideracion with Gods direction. But if the Lord would encourage your heart and it might stand with your health, which we highly prize, to come your selfe, we should account it a singular mercy in you and favour from God, and some were in expectacion of it, at my mans returne the last time. But I shall not urge any thing to your hurt or danger. With our services to Mrs. Winthrop, and love to your children, I rest

Yours exceedingly obliged

JOHN DAVENPORTE

Edmund saith (now I have done my letter) that the rubila was 3 houres before it wraught, and that the stoole was not very large and that was all and that as he laies his hand upon my sons side he feeles the winde stirr up and downe, like a quick thing.

I know not how the weather may prove or my mans strength. Sir you see our need of a speedy answer, if it were possible, by some winged messenger, if an Indian could bring it sooner than Samuel[2] can, I will pay him for his paines whatever you please to promise.

He is very weake stomachd and my wife is fearful what to doe.

2. Unidentified.

My wife saith that this morning she saw 2 f . .³ like dropps of blood from his nose in his cloath and that Mrs. Goodyeare⁴ saith, her children having the could and cough bled before they mended.

[Endorsed] Mr. Davenport about his sons sickness Dec: 23 1660 [by John Winthrop.]

JOHN DAVENPORT *to* JOHN WINTHROP the Younger¹

To the Right Worshipfull John Winthrope, Esq[ui]r[e], Governour of Connectacut, these present in Hartford.

HONOURED Sir,—It was in my purpose to have written more largely to you then the hast of this unexpected sad occasion will permit. Therefore, respiting that to a fitter season, I shall limit this to the present case, which you will find reported, as it was told my son,² by the sickmans wife,³ who is Joseph and Timothy Nashes owne sister, a member of our church, and now in danger to be left a yong widow, with sundry small children, if God take away her husband, a member also of our church, called Talmage.⁴ Be pleased to take his case into your serious consideration. And the Lord guide you to præscribe what he will bless, for the helpe and recovery of him, upon whom a wholl familie dependes for daily bread, as the onely instrument in Gods hand for theyre outward subsistence; and who is approved in the church, as a man fearing God and faithful in all his dealings with men! My wife and son joyne with me in presenting our humble services to your selfe and Mrs. Winthrope, with our affectionate salutations to yours; with our desire that you would desist from your purposed voiage for England,⁵ at least, for this yeare; for sundrie reasons, which to me seeme

3. Two letters are illegible.

4. Margaret (Lewen), the widow of both George Lamberton and Stephen Goodyear.

1. The manuscript copy of this letter has not been found. It is printed in Massachusetts Historical Society *Collections*, 4th series, VII (Boston, 1865), 519–520. A. B. Davenport, *Supplement* (Stamford, 1876), pp. 390–391.

2. "A Description of the sad and afflicted state of Bro: Rob: Talmage:" dated "The 16th. of June. 1661." by John Davenport, Jr., occurs in Massachusetts Historical Society, Winthrop MSS., XII, 98.

3. Sarah (Naish or Nash) was the wife of Robert Tallmadge, Talmadge, or Talmage of New Haven.

4. Robert Talmadge died before October 3, 1662.

5. On his way to England to secure a charter for the colony of Connecticut, John Winthrop the Younger, accompanied by his youngest son, Wait Still Winthrop, embarked on the *Trou* or *Trowe* at New Amsterdam about July 8/18, 1661. *Documents relating to the Colonial History of the State of New York*, hereafter cited as *New York Colonial Documents*, II (Albany, 1858), 460.

weighty, but I want time, at present, to offer them to your consideracion. The Lord guide you in such resolucion and acting in this matter
as may be safest for your selfe, and best for your familie, etc! In whom
I rest

Newhaven, the 16th of the 4th m. 1661. Sir,

Yours obliged,

JOHN DAVENPORT.

[Endorsed] Mr. Davenport, about Goodman Talmage sickness. [by
John Winthrop.]

JOHN DAVENPORT *to* THOMAS TEMPLE[1]

Noble S[i]r/

WHOM Though Vnknowne to me by fface, as allso I am to your
Selfe, I Honnour for your Noble Disposistion, and for your neare
Relation, to my, Euer Honoured, Lord, Viscount, Say And Sele,[2] unto
whom I haue bene Continually, Neare 40 yeares Past, Excedingly
Obliged, for Sundery Testimoneyes of his Speciall ffauo[u]rs towardes
me when I liued in London, and when I was in Holland; and after my
Retturne thence to London And Since my abode in this Wildernesse,
which hath bine aboue 24 Yeares. If the most high hath taken him
ffrom us, by Death, as I am Informed he hath, The King hath lost the
Best of his Peeres and Counsaleirs, for Godley Wisdome and ffaith-
fullnesse, The Church and People of god an Assured Pattron, The
Commons and Parliament a most Emminent Patriott, the Nobility a
Singular Patteren and ornament, And my Poore Worthlesse Selfe a
most Hono[u]r[a]ble and ffaithfull frend And that in a time when I
haue most need of his helpe, which, I am assured Would not haue

---

1. Public Record Office, C. O. 1: 15, no. 81; printed in Massachusetts Historical Society *Collections*, 3d series, VIII (Boston, 1843), 327–330; A. B. Davenport, *A History
and Genealogy of the Davenport Family* (New York, 1851), pp. 356–360. For Thomas
Temple, see *ante*, p. 147n. Although the copy of this letter enclosed by Temple in a letter
to Sir William Morrice, secretary of state, August 20, 1661, is dated August 19, 1661, the
original was probably dated August 9 or 10, 1661, for a letter could not have been sent
from New Haven to Boston and been copied by Temple in less than nine or ten days.

2. William Fiennes, first Viscount Saye and Sele, was at this time Lord Privy Seal and
a member of the Privy Council. On July 10, 1661, he wrote to John Endecott, governor
of Massachusetts Bay, that he had not long to live, but that letter could hardly have
been received in New England and its contents reported to New Haven at the time
Davenport wrote this letter. Fiennes died April 14, 1662.

ffailed my Confident Expectation, if any Complaint against me had bene Presented to his Hono[u]r with the rest of his Maj[es]ties Most Hono[ura]ble Councell. *Multis ille Bonis fflebilis Occiditt, Nulli fflebilior quam mihi,*[3] Yett as long as his right hono[u]r[a]ble Son; my Lord Fines[4] liueth he Cannot Die, ffor in him and I hope in his Posterity, that Noble ffamiley, will be like that Golden tree the Boughes and Branches Whereof fflourished in a Continewall Succession.

> *Vno Avulso non defficit alter*
> *Aureus Et Simili ffrondescens Virga Mettallo*[5]

S[i]r being Encouraged by some Expressions of your good affection toward mee, Brought to my Knowldge by one who came lateley from Boston, heither; I take the Boldnesse to desire this ffauor, that you would be pleased to Cast your Eyes uppon the Enclosed, Appoligie Which I fformerly Transmitted to the Deputy Goven[ou]r of Massachusets to be by him Communicated to the Generall Courte,[6] In it you will ffind myne Innocyency, in Referance to the 2 Collenells,[7] to be shuch as might Secure mee ffrom all feare of Danger and ffuther Molestation from his Ma[jes]tie, in that Respecte, yet because I am senseble of of Possible Misrepresentations of mine acctions, and Intentions, I humbley Craue leaue to Intreate you to lay up in the Repositorie of your minde, your memorie, The true state of my Case that you may speake a good an Seasonable word of truth in the Cause of the Dumbe and deafe, when God shall haue Brought you in Saftey to London, as occasion may be offered in the Kings Courte, would my age which is past the great Climactercall yeare, and the weaknesse of

3. *multis ille [Quintilius] bonis flebilis occidit,*
   nulli flebilior, quam tibi, Vergili.
   > Horace, *Carminum*, I, 24, 9–10.

By many a good man wept, Quintilius dies;
   By none than you, my Virgil, trulier wept:
   > J. Conington, *The Odes of Horace*.

4. James Fiennes, second Viscount Saye and Sele.
5. . . . . *primo avulso non deficit alter*
   aureus, et simili frondescit virga metallo.
   > Virgil, *Aeneid*, VI, 143–144.

One plucked, another fills its room,
And burgeons with like precious bloom.
   > J. Conington, *The Æneid of Virgil Translated into English Verse*
   > (London, 1919), p. 179.

6. At this time Richard Bellingham was deputy governor of Massachusetts. No communication from Davenport to Bellingham has been found.
7. Edward Whalley and William Goffe.

my Boddy, which is Vnder sensible decaies as well Shute with so long a
Voyage as my minde is Propense to it, I should not ffear to answer,
any thing that can be suggested or objected against mee, in his Ma-
[jes]tie[s] presence; being Confident in the Kings Justice and æqunimi-
tie, that uppon a faire hearing I should be accquitted, and some in
Boston who raile against mee, should haue their Injurious Mouthes
Stopped, what Libbirty is Denyed Vnto me, if God Inclyne and Encourage your hearte theirunto, a word ffrom your Noble selfe Spoken
in Season may be blessed of god to make up, with aduantage, and to
Worke ffauorable and Right apprehensions and persuations of mee in
his Ma[jes]tie, and shuch of his most Hono[ura]ble Councell, as you
may haue occasion of Discourse with aboute these matters. This is my
great Intendment in this lines, humbly to Craue your mindfullnesse of
me and helpeffullnesse Toward mee in this Excigent, And not for my
Selfe alone doe I make this humble Request, But allso on the Behalfe
of this Poore Colloney,[8] and of our Goueno[u]r and majestrates,[9] who
wanted neither will nor Industery to haue serued his Ma[jes]tie, in apprehending the 2 Collenells, but were Preuented and Hindered by gods
ouerruilling Prouidence,[10] which with held them that they Could not
Exciqute their true Purpose theirin; And the same Prouidence Could
haue done the same, in the same Curcumstances; if they had bine in
London, or in the Tower, The Case was thus, The Collenls hearing
that some who had Entertained them, at their Houses, were in Ex-
treeme danger, uppon that Accoumpt to Preuent the same, Came from
another Colloney where they were, and had bine Somtime, to N[ew]
H[aven] Proffessing, that their true Intentions, in their Coming att
that time was to yeld themselues to be apprehended, for the afforesaid
Purpose and accordingly they staied 2 dayes, This was knowne in the
Towne, The D[eputy] G[overnour] waited for the Comming of the
Gouen[ou]r and other Majestrats to this towne on the 2d day which
they allso did according to fformer Aggrement, Imediately Vppon their
Coming together; they fell into a Consultation, being out of any ffeare

8. The New Haven Colony.

9. At this time William Leete was governor, Mathew Gilbert was deputy governor,
and Benjamin Fenn, Robert Treat, and Jasper Crane were magistrates of the New
Haven Colony.

10. After appearing in the town of New Haven on Monday, June 24, 1661, Whalley
and Goffe took up their residence with Micah Tomkins in Milford, August 19, 1661.
Thomas Hutchinson, *The History of the Colony of Massachusets-Bay*, I (Boston, 1764),
213–219; Ezra Stiles, *A History of Three of the Judges of King Charles I.* (Hartford,
1794), pp. 25–26; L. A. Welles, *History of the Regicides in New England* (New York,
1927), pp. 33–72; *The Regicides in Connecticut* (New Haven, 1935), p. 17.

of that which ffollowed, Before they had Issued their Consulltation which was not long, the Collenels were gon away, no man knowing how nor whether, Thereuppon a Diligent search was Renewed, and many were sent fforth on ffoote and horse backe, to recouer them in to their hands, But all in Vaine. I beliue if his ma[jes]tie Rightly Vnderstood the Curcumstances of this Euent he would not be displeased with our majestrates, but to accquiesce in the Prouidence of the most high well Knowing that the way of man is not in him selfe, but god worketh all things according to the Counsaile of his owne will, It is now high time that I begge pardon for putting so much trouble uppon you, and that I Conclude with my Prayers to him, whom windes and seas obey, to ffill your sailes with ffauorable windes and to Carrie your Person as uppon Eagles winges[11] ffar aboue the reach of all hurtfull Dangers, till he shall haue landed you safe at your desiered Port, and then to make you a Blessed Instrument of some good unto this Poore Colloney and to my selfe, For which I shall Remaine

N[ew] H[aven] the 19th day of the 6 mounth   Noble S[i]r
Called Aug[u]st 1661   Your Humble Serv[an]t and obliged ffaith-
                                   ffull ffrend

JOHN DAUENPORT

S[i]r If my lord Saye be yet *in vivis*, be pleased to Communicate the inclosed to him, with the reason of my not writing to his hono[u]r, at Present, and my Earnest desier of his ffauorable helpe, that the King may be rightly Informed, Concerning me in this matter; if you shall find he is not in the land of the liuing my humble request is the same to my lord Fines, But if his hono[u]r haue not Sufficient Intrist in those about his ma[jes]tie for shuch a purpose my Intreaty to your selfe is the same afore mentioned. Allso if the Deputy Goven[ou]r Mr. Bellingham hath not Rec[eiv]ed that Letter and the Appoligie to the Generall Courte which I sent aboue 5 weekes since be pleased to let him peruse this and gett a Coppie of it (I meane the appoligie) transcribed and Retturne yours againe to your Noble selfe, to be Improved as you find opertunity to the best aduantage on my behalfe, lastley lett it please you to accept a booke newly Come forth[12] which I make bold to Present vnto you for a *Vade mecum*, in your voyage at sea, and for an helpe to to ffix your Ancho[u]r a right when you come to land

11. Exodus 19. 4.

12. John Davenport, *The Saints Anchor-Hold, In All Storms and Tempests* (London, 1661).

and for Euer, the lord Jesus be with you both at sea and land and to Etternity as a mighty Saviour Amen Farewell, *int[e]rim*.

[Endorsed] New Haven 19 Aug[u]st 1661. Letter [and] Concerning Goff and Whaley.

JOHN DAVENPORT *to* ELIZABETH WINTHROP[1]

To his Honoured freind Mrs. Winthrop these present in Boston or leave this letter with the packet at Mr. Amos Richardsons merchant in Boston to be delivered to her hands with safety and speed

Honoured Mrs. Winthrope)

THIS is onely to salute you, with due respect and sincere affection, as one to whom I confess my selfe to be exceedingly obliged, and to cover the inclosed, from your precious husband, that it may come safe to your hands, by this our approved freind, Capt. Clarke, who, I know, will speedily deliver it to yourselfe. From one passage in your worthy husbands letter I perceive that he longed, in winter, for the returne of the spring, that he might take the first opportunitie of returning unto you[2] which confirmes my beleife of what Capt. Seely[3] reportes, that we may expect his returne, by the will and blessing of God, some time the next moneth. The good Lord, whom windes and sea obey, fill his sailes with favourable windes, and carrie him and his companie, as upon Eagles wings,[4] farr above the reach of all hurtfull dangers, and make his returne full of comforts and blessings to you and your family, and to many others, for whose good he hath allwaies bene ready to improve his precious talents and time! If Capt. Clarke returne, by the way of Hartford, to Boston; he will bring you another letter, of later date, inclosed to Mr. Willis.[5] You will also receive from

1. Massachusetts Historical Society, Winthrop MSS., III, 147; printed in Massachusetts Historical Society *Collections*, 4th series, VII (Boston, 1865), 520–521; A. B. Davenport, *Supplement* (Stamford, 1876), pp. 391–392.

2. Delayed by the claims of John Clarke, agent of Rhode Island and Providence Plantations, Winthrop did not return to New England until June, 1663.

3. Robert Seely of New Haven had returned to England in 1659 but sought refuge again in New England soon after October 12, 1661. Massachusetts Historical Society *Collections*, 4th series, VIII (Boston, 1868), 177.

4. Exodus 19. 4.

5. Samuel Wyllys of Hartford was at this time one of the magistrates of Connecticut.

me, by this bearer, bookes of newes,[6] which, when you have perused, he desires they may be sent to Mr. Stone or Mr. Willis for freindes there to see. Be pleased to present my respectful salutacions to Honoured Mr. Symons[7] and his wife, to your son and daughter Newman, and to your daughter, Mrs. Lucie,[8] and to all yours. The Lord Jesus dwell with you and them in mercy and peace and loving kindnesses! In whom I rest

Yours exceedingly obliged

JOHN DAVENPORT

My wife and son present theyre humble service to yourselfe, with salutacions to all yours, affectionately.

N[ew] H[aven] the 14th day of the 2d moneth, called April. 1662

[Endorsed] Mr. Davenport 1662 [by John Winthrop.]

From Mr. DAVENPORT Jun: 2[1]

A BREIFE Relation of some newes ffrom England: 1: That many of the people of god are imprissoned,[2] very sad times feared to be approaching: (2) Corne is very deare,[3] noe sect soe much favored as

6. At this time there were being published in England: *Mercurius Publicus; The Kingdomes Intelligencer. Catalogue of Pamphlets, Books, Newspapers, and Manuscripts relating to the Civil War, the Commonwealth, and Restoration, Collected by George Thomason, 1640–1661* (2 vols., London, 1908), II, 440.

7. Samuel Symonds of Ipswich, Massachusetts, at this time an assistant of the colony of Massachusetts Bay, whose second wife, Martha, the widow of Daniel Epps, was a daughter of Edmund Reade and a sister of Elizabeth (Reade) Winthrop.

8. Lucy Winthrop, who subsequently married Edward Palmes of New London.

1. Boston Public Library, Mather Papers, I, no. 23, p. 4 *verso;* printed in Massachusetts Historical Society *Collections,* 4th series, VIII (Boston, 1868), 172; A. B. Davenport, *Supplement* (Stamford, 1876), pp. 374–375.

2. For the hostile attitude toward non-conformists in England at this time, see *Calendar of State Papers, Domestic Series, 1661–1662* (London, 1861), p. 155.

3. Under date of October 12, 1661, William Hooke wrote Davenport, "Corne fayling very much." On October 28, 1661, Benjamin Ling wrote, "Corne is now at 10 s. B[ushe]ll and expected to be dearer." On February 13, 1661/2, one Brooks, possibly Robert Brooke, a New England merchant of "Croocked Friers," wrote, "a famine of bread is sorely threatned." On February 14, 1661/2, Robert Newman wrote, "for a loafe of bread which was wont to be sould for 5 *ds.* is now sould at 2 *s.* 6 *d.*" Finally, on March 31, 1662, William Hooke wrote, "corne is very dear." Massachusetts Historical Society *Collections,* 4th series, VIII (Boston, 1868), 173, 178, 181, 184, 196.

the quakers,[4] none soe much troden vnder foote as the Presbiters:[5] 3 gr[ea]t Grumbling in E: I: S[6] but P. B[7] sayes theye will still all, The 30th of the pr[e]sent mo[nth] December feared to be a bloody day if the L[or]d pr[e]vent not;[8] S[i]r H[enry] Vane Coll. Lambert, with some others Committed to Gernsey Castle sent for to come to Tryall:[9] The 1.° day the Parl[iamen]t sate they gave the K[ing] £20000 as some Affirme.[10]

Mr. Wharton[11] brought this newes ffrom the Bay inclosed in a letter which came by the way of Barbadoes: One thing more I have heard by the way of Virginia viz. *Animi populi in Scotia Contra Episcopos amarescuntur et nonnulli interficiuntur: Sed vix quicquam quod fertur Credendum est:*[12] Concerning the 2 Collonells[13] (who were formerly here) theres noe speech lately:

4. With this statement neither Samuel Pepys nor Richard Baxter agrees.

5. By An Act for the Uniformity of Publique Prayers (14 Charles II, c. 4), which became law May 19, 1662, and went into effect August 24, 1662, all non-conforming ministers were deprived of their places.

6. England, Ireland, Scotland.

7. Unidentified.

8. No reason for this statement has been found.

9. See above, p. 177n.

10. On November 21, 1661, the second day of the autumn sitting of the Restoration Parliament, it was "*Resolved*, upon the Question, *Nemine contradicente*, That the Sum of Twelve hundred thousand Pounds shall be speedily raised for Supply of the King's Majesty's present Occasions." *Commons Journals*, VIII (n.p., n.d.), 317.

11. Richard Wharton of Boston, Massachusetts.

12. namely the minds of the people in Scotland are inflamed against bishops and several are killed: but hardly anything that is reported can be believed.

13. Edward Whalley and William Goffe. On February 17, 1661/2, John Winthrop the Younger had written to Davenport, "I doe not heere of any trouble like to be to yourselfe or any other about those matters. There is noe more speech of those things that I can heere of." Massachusetts Historical Society *Collections*, 4th series, VIII (Boston, 1868), 183.

A Letter from Mr. DAVENPORT Jun: 2[1]

I SPAKE with one that came from England in July last[2] he tould me that—Brother to—[3] came into Eng[land] with the Queene Mother[4] and there speaking of his Br[other] s[ai]d he was a Traytor and that he could not be saved being noe Catholick one pr[e]sent answered that the K[ing] was noe Catholick *ergo*—he replyed 2 or 3 yeeres would shew whatt he was. The occasion of this discourse was one (a disaffected person) s[ai]d that C: G.[5] was a moderate man: C[aptain] Seely saith R. P.[6] is gon towards Germany, that the K[ing] is favourably enclined to him etc. Hen[ry] Cromwell[7] liveth about the Court and enjoyes all his estate: Coll. Hewson[8] is s[ai]d to be deade beyound sea: By the way of Virginia I heere (but they say its Treason to say soe) that things are as bad as in Queene Maries dayes:[9] this came by a shipp which (Mr. Hudson[10] saith) came from Eng[land] 12 weekes agoe: I have heerewith sent you some printed Acts.[11]

Memorandum the Acts last mentioned were passed 30th July *1661* the substance of most of them were sent by Mr. W: W:[12] as in No. 1:

[Marginal note] Sect. 3: 2 of 4 mo[nth] *1662*

1. Boston Public Library, Mather Papers, I, no. 23, p. 6 *recto;* printed in Massachusetts Historical Society *Collections,* 4th series, VIII (Boston, 1868), 181; A. B. Davenport, *Supplement* (Stamford, 1876), p. 375.

2. Unidentified.

3. After serving as chaplain to the forces of Sir Horace Vere in the Low Countries, chaplain to Charles I, and supervisor to Sir William Boswell, English agent at The Hague, Stephen Goffe, the brother of William Goffe, the regicide, turned Catholic and entered the congregation of the French Oratory at Notre-Dame des Vertus, not far from Paris, rising to the office of superior of the community.

4. Both before and after the Restoration, Stephen Goffe served Henrietta Maria, the widow of Charles I and the mother of Charles II, as chaplain.

5. Colonel William Goffe.

6. Unidentified.

7. Henry Cromwell lost lands in England valued at £2,000 a year but retained his estate in Ireland. At this time he was living in obscurity in Cambridgeshire. C. H. Firth in *Dictionary of National Biography.*

8. John Hewson, the regicide, fled from England in May, 1660. He was excepted from the act of general pardon and oblivion as to pains and penalties on June 9 and as to life on July 9. He died at Amsterdam or Rouen in 1662. *Commons Journals,* VIII (n.p., n.d.), 61, 85; C. H. Firth in *Dictionary of National Biography.*

9. Queen Mary, 1553–1558.

10. John Hodson, Hodgson, Hodshon, or Hudson, a merchant at New Haven.

11. The acts passed by parliament May 8–July 30, 1661, were published as *Anno regni Caroli II. Regis ... decimo tertio. At the Parliament begun at Westminster, the Eighth day of May, Anno Dom. 1661. ... And there continued until Tuesday the 30th of July, 1661, etc.* (London, 1662). Although the title-page of the volume reads 1662, the first section was actually published in 1661.

12. For "W—W—to William Goffe, December 18, 1661," see Massachusetts Historical Society *Collections,* 4th series, VIII (Boston, 1868), 166–169.

Mr. John Davenport the 21: 4 Mo[nth] (62)[1]

B Y C[aptain] Woodgreene[2] wee heere, that 40 passengers are come, Major Bowrne,[3] and his family, and one younge Minister[4] A Bachelor, as a Messenger sent by Dr. Tho: Goodwin[5] (who had come over now if his wife had not opposed it) in the name and behalfe of sundry churches, and many men of considerable quallity and Estate, who have a desire to come into this Country if they may have any incouragem[en]t from hence. Capt. Pearce[6] is comeing with 2 or 300 passengers.

John Davenport *to* William Goffe[1]

T HERE was a Gen[era]ll Gouern[ou]r and a Majo[u]r Gen[era]ll chosen for this Countrie to seize upon the Melitia for the King: and a B[isho]p and a Suffracan, for Ecclesiasticall Goverm[en]t[2] but

1. Boston Public Library, Mather Papers, I, no. 23, p. 7 *verso;* printed in Massachusetts Historical Society *Collections,* 4th series, VIII (Boston, 1868), 189.

2. Captain Woodgreen was engaged in trans-Atlantic transportation. In 1661 he commanded the *Prudent Mary.* "The Diaries of John Hull," American Antiquarian Society *Transactions and Collections,* III (Boston, 1857), 202.

3. Major Nehemiah Bourne of Dorchester, Massachusetts, in 1635, Charlestown, Massachusetts, in 1638, and Boston, Massachusetts, in 1640, returned to England in the winter of 1644–1645 and entered the parliamentary army, serving as major in the regiment of Colonel Thomas Rainborow. Under date of April 28, 1662, he received a pass, permitting him to transport himself and family from Hamburg, Germany, to the plantations, and returned to New England. *Winthrop's Journal* (2 vols., New York, 1908), II, 253; Massachusetts Historical Society *Collections,* 4th series, VII (Boston, 1865), 297–306; *Calendar of State Papers, Colonial Series, 1661–1668* (London, 1880), nos. 291, 303.

4. James Allen arrived at Boston June 10, 1662. Uniting with the First Church, Boston, he was chosen teacher of the congregation and ordained December 9, 1668.

5. On May 18, 1660, the House of Lords restored John Oliver to his place as president of Magdalen College, Oxford, thus depriving Thomas Goodwin of that office. Otherwise Goodwin seems to have gone unmolested. Removing to London, he founded an independent congregation. *Lords Journals,* XI (n.p., n.d.), 33; A. Gordon in *Dictionary of National Biography.*

6. Captain John Pierce sailed from England for New England in April, 1662. He was expected at Boston by July 15, 1662, or sooner. Massachusetts Historical Society *Collections,* 4th series, VIII (Boston, 1868), 183, 189, 190.

1. Boston Public Library, Mather Papers, I, no. 24; printed in Massachusetts Historical Society *Collections,* 4th series, VIII (Boston, 1868), 198–199; A. B. Davenport, *Supplement* (Stamford, 1876), pp. 376–377.

2. At this time the council for foreign plantations had the government of New England under serious consideration. *Calendar of State Papers, Colonial Series, 1661–1668* (London, 1880), *passim.*

Mr. Norton,[3] writes, that theye are not yet out of hopes, to preuent it. The Govern[ou]rs Name, is S[i]r Rob[ert] Carr,[4] (a ranck Papist.). There are great thoughts of heart, (among the Godly) about vs, what Imposicions wilbe laid upon N[ew] E[ngland].

The Episcopal Goverm[en]t is by Act of Parliam[en]t proclaimed thoroughout England.[5]

Exceeding great Taxes laid upon the People.[6]

There is great talke of many Ministers with theire Congregacions, comeing ouer the next Yeare, if roome can be found for them.[7]

There is one Mr. Allyne[8] come ouer this yeare, of about 30. yeares of Age, a very able man, and 2. great March[an]ts[9] of London, with theire Familes, of £30000. estate, Godly men.

I saw in a Letter this Day, that Corne in England is at 14. 15. 16. 17. *s.* a Bushell,[10] the poore in great extremetie, and little care for theire releife.

The King is engaged to the utmost to promote Episcopacy.

3. With Simon Bradstreet, John Norton, teacher of the First Church, Boston, sailed for England, February 11, 1661/2, to secure confirmation of the charter of Massachusetts Bay. Without having accomplished their mission, the two men arrived back in Boston September 3, 1662.

4. Sir Robert Carr was one of four royal commissioners appointed April 23, 1664, to seize New Netherland and to inquire into the state of New England.

5. The act of uniformity (14 Charles II, c. 4) was passed May 19, 1662, and went into effect on St. Bartholomew's Day, August 24, 1662. See above, pp. 177–178n.

6. Up to this date the restoration parliament had voted the following taxes: An Act for a free and voluntary present to his Majesty (13 Charles II, Statute I, c. 4); An Act for granting unto the Kings Majestie £1260,000, to be collected £70,000 per month for eighteen months (13 Charles II, Statute II, c. 3); An Act for establishing an additional Revenue upon His Majestie, providing for a tax of 2 *s.* per year on every fire, hearth, and stove (14 Charles II, c. 10). Under date of February 13, 1661/2, one Brooks wrote to Davenport, "Taxes and burdens still continue, and like to be more and more increased, . . ." Massachusetts Historical Society *Collections*, 4th series, VIII (Boston, 1868), 181.

7. Under date of May 31, 1662, Samuel Pepys entered in his *Diary:* "The Act for Uniformity is lately printed, which, it is thought, will make mad work among the Presbyterian ministers." Richard Baxter says: "When *Bartholomew-day* came, about One thousand eight hundred or Two thousand Ministers were Silenced and Cast out." Richard Baxter, *Reliquiæ Baxterianæ* (London, 1696), Part II, p. 385.

8. James Allen.

9. Samuel Bache and Humphrey Davie. On August 11, 1662, Davenport asked the town of New Haven to make a grant of land to two merchants lately come to the Bay, and an offer was made and accepted. Samuel Bache and his sister Mary took up their residence at New Haven, purchasing the Malbon house that had once belonged to John Winthrop the Younger. Humphrey Davie remained in Massachusetts. *New Haven Town Records, 1662–1684* (New Haven, 1919), pp. 4, 16, 57, 74; Massachusetts Historical Society *Collections*, 4th series, VIII (Boston, 1868), 202–203.

10. See above, p. 195n.

The[re] is great likelehood of War, with France,[11] the french Ambassador,[12] is gone home in a rage. It is to be feared that there is a sad scourge at hand, for England.

There were 9. Ministers that went up to the B[isho]p to receiue theire Orders, and returning to the Country, to theire seue[ra]ll places, to put in execucion those Orders, 7. of the 9. were immediately struck dead, the 8th, struck blind, the 9th, mad, a very remarkable hand of God.[13]

The broad Seale, is bought and sould,[14] so that there is no hold of anything granted to any man.

There are aboundance more particulars. (I suppose that is ment in the Baye.) Thus much, as the sume of Intelligence, which Mr. Glover[15] brought in a Letter from the Baye, the 5t. Day last week to Springfield, and is since come hither.

Unto these I shall add 3. passages of Newes, which I heard from Mr. Jones and were reported to him by Mr. Hudson, from Mr. Auger as followeth.

1. The Charters of all the Cities and Corporacions, in England, are called in and nullefied, except London, and Bristol, or Yorke.[16]

2. That Masse, is tollerated thorough[ou]t England.[17]

3. That by the House of Commons, in Parliam[en]t it was voted, that the King should have the power of ordering, and disposing, mens person[a]ll Estates, but when it came to the House of Lords, it was opposed, for one of the L[or]ds stood up, and said that it was known

11. Although the *Calendar of State Papers, Domestic Series*, gives no indication of any breach between England and France, under date of February 13, 1661/2, one Brooks wrote Davenport that breaches with France, Holland, and Sweden were threatened. Massachusetts Historical Society *Collections*, 4th series, VIII (Boston, 1868), 181.

12. Godefroi, Comte d'Estrades.

13. Increase Mather sent Davenport a similar story June 2, 1662. Massachusetts Historical Society *Collections*, 4th series, VIII (Boston, 1868), 188.

14. For one attempt to buy the great seal, see *Calendar of State Papers, Domestic Series, 1661–1662* (London, 1861), p. 9.

15. Henry Glover of New Haven.

16. By An Act for the well Governing and Regulating of Corporations (13 Charles II, Statute II, c. 1), commissioners were authorized to investigate office-holders of cities, corporations, and boroughs. Existing office-holders were required to take the oaths of allegiance and supremacy and to repudiate the solemn league and covenant. Future office-holders were required to take the test within the year of their election. Officers of London seem to have been excepted from these requirements, but not those of Bristol and York.

17. Yet in 1662 the king in council forbade the English to flock to the chapels of the queen at St. James, the queen mother at Somerset House, and the foreign ambassadors! *Calendar of State Papers, Domestic Series, 1661–1662* (London, 1861), p. 451.

he had bene faithfull to the K[ing]s Interest, but could not consent to that, for he must be faithfull to his owne Interest, his Wife, and Children, who would thereby be undone, (or to that purpose).[18]

I heare, that the Synod, in the Baye, is broken up, without doeing any thing, and have adjurned the meeting, till Octo[ber] or Nov[ember] next.[19]

[Marginal note] Received the 3th. of 5 m: *1662*

Mr. JOHN DAVENPORT July 5th *1662*[1]

THIS day we rec[eive]d the inclosed (viz. these in sect[io]n 3)[2] from the Bay etc: one that came in the vessell informes that C: T:[3] wrote to Mr. Vsher etc: to secure the person and estate of Breeden.[4] Accordingly they procured a warrant, Arested him and seazed on his estate for giving ffalse information ag[ain]st N[ew] E[ngland]; he is at pr[e]sent vnder bayle; he asked for his accusers, they tould him in due time they would prove the charge, which he then denyed, saying far be it from him to doe any thing ag[ain]st his good ffreinds of N[ew] E[ngland]. He appeared in Boston in a strange habit with a 4 Cornerd Cap instead of a hat, and his Breeches hung with Ribbons from the wast downw[ard] a gr[ea]t depth, one row over another like shingles on a house: The Boyes when he came made an outcry, from one end of the

18. No account of this debate has been found.

19. On December 31, 1661, the general court of Massachusetts Bay called a synod of elders and brethren of the churches of the colony to meet at Boston on the second Tuesday of the following March to consider: 1. Who are the subjects of baptism? 2. Whether there ought to be a consociation of churches? The first session of this synod convened in March, 1662; the second, in June; and the third, on September 3.

1. Boston Public Library, Mather Papers, I, no. 23, p. 8 *recto;* printed in Massachusetts Historical Society *Collections,* 4th series, VIII (Boston, 1868), 192.

2. This section consists of letters from Benjamin Ling to Henry Rutherford of New Haven, from London, March 27, 1662, in which Ling states his intention of sailing for New Haven the latter end of April, 1662; Henry Rutherford to John Davenport, from Boston, July 1, 1662; and John Oxenbridge, a Puritan divine ousted by the act of uniformity, to John Davenport, April 5, 1662. It is printed in Massachusetts Historical Society *Collections,* 4th series, VIII (Boston, 1868), 189–192.

3. Colonel Thomas Temple.

4. Captain Thomas Breeden was a Boston merchant interested in Nova Scotia. In the course of a visit to England in 1660–1661, he appeared before the council for foreign plantations and gave information derogatory to Massachusetts Bay. In the spring of 1665 he entertained the royal commissioners at his house in Boston. *Calendar of State Papers, Colonial Series, 1661–1668* (London, 1880), no. 45; *New York Colonial Documents,* III (Albany, 1853), 39–41, 83, 85, 88–89, 94.

streete to the other calling him a Devill, which was so greate, that people woundering came out of there houses to see whatt the matter was: he went to visit the Governor,[5] who gave him thankes for the good words he had spoken for N[ew] E[ngland]. A Letter from Mr. Lang to Mr. Auger dated March: 4th. Informes that the Act for Conformity was then ffinished which (he saith) would cause many to remove:

John Davenport and others *to* the Commissioners of Connecticut[1]

To our much hono[u]r[e]d and Reverend ffrends The Comission[e]rs from the Gen[era]ll Court of Conecticutt to be Comunicated etc.

Much hono[u]r[e]d and Reverend

WEE have Rec[eiv]ed and pervsed your writing and heard the Coppy Read of his Maj[es]ties L[e]ttres Pattents to Connecticut

---

5. John Endecott was chosen governor of Massachusetts Bay May 7, 1662.

1. Connecticut State Library, Connecticut Archives, Miscellaneous Papers, I, no. 68; printed in *New Haven Colonial Records, 1653–1665* (Hartford, 1858), p. 469. The signers of this letter are six of the seven magistrates of the New Haven Colony and the elders of New Haven, Branford, and Milford.

The general court of the New Haven Colony of May 28, 1662, "not knowing what important affayres may happen respecting this colony, betweene the session of this and the next generall court, haue voted, and doe declare it to be their minds, that the govern[o]r being immediatly informed thereof, repayre to Newhauen, and there consult and advise with the magistrates and elders of that place and of Brandford what is fit and safe to be done in such an exigence, and to act and doe accordingly by the major vote of such magistrates, vpon such concurrent aduise of two or more of the elders, and to call in the aduise of the magistrate or magistrates of Milford or any other towne of this colony, provided that the gouern[o]r and such magistrates proceed not to treate or conclude any thing that may haue tendencie to change of the present governm[en]t, without a generall court be first called by advise of such counsell, wherein this court promiseth to stand by the s[ai]d govern[o]r and magistrates soe acting as afores[ai]d, and not otherwise." (*New Haven Colonial Records, 1653–1665*, Hartford, 1858, p. 453.)

The general assembly of Connecticut of October 9, 1662, appointed Mathew Allyn, Samuel Wyllys, Samuel Stone, and Samuel Hooker a committee to treat with the New Haven Colony regarding union. Accompanied by Joseph Fitch, these commissioners arrived in New Haven October 16 or 17, 1662.

Since John Davenport was a member of the various groups appointed by the New Haven Colony to negotiate with Connecticut, and since he more than any other seems to have inspired the opposition to the union of the two colonies, and composed at least some of the correspondence, the entire correspondence of the New Haven Colony with Connecticut from October 17, 1662, to January 5, 1664/5, has been included.

Colony² Wherein although Wee doe not find the Colony of Newhaven expressly included yet to shew our desire thatt matters may be yssued in the Conserving of peace and amity, with Righteousnes betweene them and vs, Wee shall Comunicat your writing and the Coppy of the Pattent to our ffreemen And afterwards with Convenient Speed Returne theire Answear.³ Only we desire that the yssueing of matters may be Respited till we may Receive fuller Informacion from the hono[u]r[e]d Mr. Winthropp, or Sattisfaccion otherwise And that in the meane tyme This Colony may Remaine Distinct intire and vninterupted as heeretofore Which we hope you will see Cause lovingly to Consent vnto, and Signify the Same to vs with Convenient Speed.

Newhaven 17th
of Octob[e]r 1662

WILL[IA]M LEETE.
MATHEW GILBERT
BENIAMIN FFENN
JASPER CRANE
ROBERT TREAT
W[ILLIA]M JONES
JOHN DAVENPORTE
NICHOLAS STREETE
ABRAH[AM] PIERSON
ROGER NEWTONNE

[Endorsed] October 17th :62 N[ew] Hauen Comittes return to ours[, and in another hand,] John Davenporte.

2. One copy of the charter of Charles II to Connecticut, dated April 23, 1662, arrived in New England September 3, 1662. After perusal by the commissioners of the United Colonies of New England in session at Boston, Massachusetts, from September 4 to September 16, 1662, it was forwarded to Connecticut. The Connecticut committee left a copy of the charter at New Haven.

3. After a day of extraordinary seeking of God by fasting and prayer for guidance regarding the proposed union of the New Haven Colony and Connecticut, October 29, 1662, the letter of the Connecticut committee and the copy of the charter were laid before a meeting of the freemen of the New Haven Colony at New Haven, November 4, 1662. The freemen voted to postpone consideration of union until after the return of John Winthrop the Younger to New England, and appointed the magistrates and elders of the colony and Richard Law of Stamford a committee to reply to Connecticut. On November 5, 1662, and May 27, 1663, and probably May 25, 1664—the records are incomplete—general courts of the New Haven Colony continued this committee. *New Haven Colonial Records, 1653-1665* (Hartford, 1858), pp. 465, 467-471, 472, 473-475, 488-489, 544.

Mr. JOHN DAVENPORT Writes as Followeth:[1]

ONE Mr. Foster[2] is arived at Boston, by letters and informations, the state of things is represented to be very bad with the peo[ple] of god in O[ld] E[ngland]: all good ministers put downe that would not Conforme.[3] There are not above 10: in or about London that have conformed: and in a letter *ex* Mr. Davie at Boston it is said sad newes *ex* England all good Minist[e]rs put out and the heighth of wickednes in church and state broken in. The tide soe turned that they say P[rince] Rupert[4] is L[or]d L[ieutenan]t of the Tower of London if not of England, allsoe Browne[5] (who was Lord Maior) Massey,[6] L[or]d Fairefax and many others either imprissoned or sought to be imprisoned: Monke Loosing his places, and Titles of honor apace.

The FREEMEN OF THE NEW HAVEN COLONY *to* THE GENERAL ASSEMBLY OF CONNECTICUT[1]

Hono[u]r[e]d Gent[lemen]:

WE haue heard both the Pattent and that writing read, which those Gent[lemen] (whoe s[ai]d they was sent from your Gene[ra]ll Assembly) left with our Committee, and haue Considered the Con-

1. Boston Public Library, Mather Papers, I, no. 32 *recto;* printed in Massachusetts Historical Society *Collections,* 4th series, VIII (Boston, 1868), 202.

2. Unidentified.

3. The act of uniformity of May 19, 1662. See above, pp. 177–178n.

4. Prince Rupert, Count Palatine of the Rhine, Duke of Bavaria, Earl of Holderness, was the third son of Elizabeth and Frederick V, Elector Palatine and King of Bohemia. Under date of October 21, 1662, Increase Mather wrote to Davenport, "P. Rupert is made Counstable of the Tower." Massachusetts Historical Society *Collections,* 4th series, VIII (Boston, 1868), 206.

5. Sir Richard Browne, woodmonger and citizen of London, was elected Lord Mayor October 3, 1660. For suppressing Venner's insurrection during his mayoralty, he was created a baronet.

6. Sir Edward Massey, a Presbyterian who joined the Royalists after Pride's Purge, and was knighted after the Restoration, was associated with a plot against Charles II in 1662, and seems to have been imprisoned in the Tower. Under date of October 21, 1662, Increase Mather wrote to Davenport, "One Letter saith that Fairefax, Booth, and Massey have withdrawne themselves, and that there is a proclamation out against them promising £1000. to whom soever shall bring any of them." *Calendar of State Papers, Domestic Series, 1661–1662* (London, 1861), p. 465; *1663–1664* (London, 1862), p. 579; Massachusetts Historical Society *Collections,* 4th series, VIII (Boston, 1868), 205–206.

1. Connecticut State Library, Manuscript New Haven Colonial Records, 1653–1664, fols. 335–336; printed in *New Haven Colonial Records, 1653–1665* (Hartford, 1858), pp. 473–475. This letter was probably dated November 4 or 5, 1662.

tents according to our capacities. By the one wee take notice of their
declared sence of the Pattent, and alsoe of your desire of our vniting
with your selues vpon that account: By the other we vnderstand, that
his Maj[es]tie hath been graciously pleased (at your earnest petition)
to grant liberty to the Colony of Connecticott, to acquire, haue, possess, and purchase etc. whateuer lands etc. you haue gained or shall
gaine by lawfull meanes within the pr[e]cincts or lines therein mentioned, and alsoe of his abundant grace to allow and establish you to
be one body Politique, for mannaging all your publique affaires and
gouernm[en]t in a religious and peaceable manner, to the intents and
purposes by his Maj[es]tie and the aduenturers therein professed, ouer
all persons, matters, and things, soe gained by purchase or conquest
at your owne proper Costs and charges, according as your selues informed you had already done, Now whateuer is soe yours; we haue
neither purpose nor desire to oppose, hurt, or hinder in the least; But
what our selues (by like lawfull meanes) haue attained, as to inheritances or jurisdicion as a distinct Colony, vpon our most solemne and
religious Couen[an]ts, soe well knowne to his Maj[es]tie and to all, We
must say that we doe not find in the Pattent any Command giuen to
you, nor prohibition to vs to disolue Couen[an]ts or alter the orderly
settlements of New England, nor any sufficient reason why we may
not soe remayne to be as formerly; Alsoe your beginning to procure
and proceeding to improoue the Pattent without vs doth confirme this
beleife, But rather it seemes that a way is left open to vs to petition
for the like fauo[u]r, and to enter our appeale from your declared sence
of the Pattent, and signify our greiuances. Yet if it shall appeare (after
a due and full information of our state) to haue beene his Maj[es]ties
pleasure soe to vnite vs as you vnderstand the Pattent, we must submitt according to god, But for the pr[e]sent we cannot answ[e]r otherwise then our Committee hath done, and likewise to make the same
request vnto you, that we may remaine distinct as formerly, and may
be succoured by you as Confederates; at least that none occasion be
giuen by your selues for any to disturb vs in our ancient settlem[en]ts,
vntill that either by the Hono[u]r[e]d Mr. Winthrop, by our other Confederates, or from his Maj[es]tie we may be resolued herein; All which
meanes are in our thoughts to vse except you pr[e]vent, for the gaine-
ing of a right vnderstanding, and to bring a peaceable issue, or recon-
cilem[en]t of this matter, and we wish you had better Considered then
to act soe suddenly to seclude vs from Pattent priuilidge at first, if we
are included as you say, and to haue soe proceeded since as may seeme
to giue advantage vnto dissaffected persons to slight or disregard

oathes, and couen[an]ts, and thereby to rend and make diuision, mannage Contention, and troubles in the towneships and societies of this
Colony, and that about religious worship, as the inclosed Complaint
may declare, which seemes to vs a great scandall to Religion before
the Natives and pr[e]judiciall to his Maj[es]ties pious intention, as
alsoe to hold forth a series of meanes very opposite to the end pr[e]-
tended, and very much obscured from the beauty of such a religious
and peaceable walking amongst english brethren, as may either invite
the Natives to the Christian faith, or vnite our spirits in this juncture,
and this occasion giuen before any conviction tendered or publication
of the Pattent amongst vs, or soe much as a treatie with vs in a Christian neighbo[u]rly way. Noe pr[e]tence for our disolution of gouer[n]-
m[en]t till then could rationally be imagined; such carriage may seeme
to be against the advise and mind of his Maj[es]tie in the Pattent, as
alsoe of your hono[u]r[e]d Govern[ou]r, and to cast reflect vpon him
when we compare these things with his L[ett]res to some here, for the
avoyding whereof, we earnestly request that the whole of what he hath
written to your selues soe far as it may respect vs in this busines, may
be fully Communicated to our veiw in a true Coppy or transcript of
the same. We must professe our selues greiued hereat, and must desire
and expect your efectuall endeavo[u]rs to repaire these breaches and
restore vs to our form[e]r Condition as Confederates, vntill that by all
or some of these wayes intimated we may attaine a cleare resolution
in this matter. Vnto what we haue herein propounded we shall adde
that we doe not in the least intend any dislike to his Maj[es]ties act,
but to shew our sence of your actings first and last soe much to our
detrim[en]t, and to manifest the Consequent efects to gods dishono[u]r,
as alsoe to giue you to know how we vnderstand the Pattent hopeing,
that you will both Candidly Construe, and freindly comply, with our
desires herein, and soe remoue the cause of our distraction and sad
afliction that you haue brought vpon this poore Colony, then shall we
forbeare to giue you further trouble, and shall pray to the god of spirits
to grant vs all humility, and to guide vs with his heauenly wisdome
to a happy issue of this affayre in loue and peace. Resting

> Gent[lemen]: Your very loueing ffreinds
> and neighbours the ffreemen of the
> Colony of Newhauen
>
> Per JAMES BISHOP *Secretary* in the name
> and by Order and Consent of the Committee and
> ffreemen of N[ew] Hauen Colony.

Postscript

We haue alsoe thought fit to send our reasons inclosed which are the ground of this answ[e]r we returne, and desire the whole may bee read and Communicated to the Gene[ra]ll Assembly intreating an answ[e]r with all Convenient speed, or from the Committee if soe impowered.

John Davenport *to* William Goffe[1]
1º *January. 1662*

ONE Mr. Wats,[2] a mariner, (who formerly lived at Plimouth, etc.) came lately from Virginia informed Br[other] Baldwin[3] as foll[ows].

That Capt. Higginson[4] (brother to Mr. Higg[inso]n of Salem) is come to Virginia, Commander of a new ship called the America, who came from Lond[o]n in the latter end of Oct[ober]. That the s[ai]d Capt. informed him that things were very sad in Eng[land] and soe like to be and that he wished him selfe in N[ew] E[ngland] and would make what hast he could hether after his returne into Eng[land]. Moreover he s[ai]d that he informed him in severall particular passages concerning affaires in England: (viz.) That Mounke is confined vnto his chamber, for not subscribing to the B[isho]ps and that its thought they will take away his life.

That the Q[ueen] M[other] is at Greenwich, and hath erected the High Altar, and that popery is Acted as much as ever.

That Prince R[upert] is out of the Land, and is in the straightes.

That the Speaker friggot met with 2 duch men of war, and commanded them to strike for the K[ing] of England, who answered they would strike for noe K[ing] vnder the sunn, and the Dutchmen made the ffriggot creep away, in danger of sinking and with losse of men. Moreover that the Dutch are well fitted with men and shipping for service.

That there are to the No. of 8 or 9000 protestant people, Banished out of some other country, who are come to Holland and there releeved.

That they had a plentifull Harvest in England last summer.

That there is a gen[era]ll discontent among the sea-men ag[ain]st the

1. Boston Public Library, Mather Papers, I, no. 31; printed in Massachusetts Historical Society *Collections*, 4th series, VIII (Boston, 1868), 199–201.
2. Unidentified.
3. Richard Baldwin of Milford.
4. Probably Samuel Higginson, who commanded a war vessel under the Protectorate.

K[ing]. And besides w[ha]tt this informer rec[eive]d from Capt. Hig-[ginso]n, he saith he spake with many other seamen, as well Bristol men as Londoners, who were formerly for the K[ing] but are now discontent with him, and wish for another Cromwell, he saith those that are come to Virginia, doe generally complaine of there greate Taxes, and say that Cromwell sought the good of the land etc.

That Trading is very low, and abundance doe leave there houses, and doe turne the key, and are gon its not knowne whether.

That theres very greate robbing in the Citty, a man can hardly walke in safety in the streetes, with a hat vpon his heade.

That there is a proclemation out that all that will not take the Oath to be subject to the K[ing] and B[isho]ps must departe the land by such a time, or ells shall be accounted Traitors, and therevpon abundance are pr[e]paring to come to N[ew] E[ngland] the next spring.

That the L[ord] fairfax is in England and keepes 6000 men vpon his owne Charge, and hath 60000 ready at Comand. That the K[ing] sent to him to come in, which he refused, and that that parte of the Country where he is is for him.

That the K[ing] and D[uke] of Yorke were at Woolledge with the seamen of the ffleete and did require of them to take an Oath to be subject to the K[ing] and B[isho]ps, who answered they were willing to serve him, but refused to subscribe to the B[isho]ps and did expect to be free from them for they had formerly fought against them. The D[uke] spake to the K[ing] to hang foure or 5 hundred of them and then the rest would conforme, wherevpon, they tould the K[ing] they and there relations, had cause to Curse the day in which they brought him and his relations into the land, or that they wished the curse of God vpon them selves for bringing them in, and soe continued in a Mutiny, and some men were killed. The K[ing] tould the D[uke] it was a very bad word that he had spoken enough to vndoe the land; and comanded him to be convaied away (and its thought if he had not got away the seamen would have killed him). The K[ing] endeavoured to pacefy the seamen. They demanded wages of him, or threatned to runn away with his ships, if they were not paide, its saide they had only dyet allowed and not wages. They allsoe desired there old officers, not willing to serve vnder pr[e]sent comanders: who were land Captaines not experienc[e]d at sea. Noe seamen are permitted to come out of the land but such as Navegat the ships. The K[ing] buyeth w[ha]tt shipping he can; he would have bought Capt. Higgesons. The seamen Generally complaine of the comanders of the K[ing's] ffleete: as Alsoe of there Ministers whose frequent practice they say is to goe among the seamen and say: God dam[n] you I am come to save you, come let vs goe to prayer, and many times, cause a company of Boyes to dance or whip one another naked before them, the seamen thinke they are not like to prosper on these accounts, they say how can they adventure there lives, having noe success in any of there designes with these men?

[Marginal note] Sect[io]n 3

The COMMITTEE OF THE NEW HAVEN COLONY *to* CONNECTICUT[1]

WHEREAS we discerne by the Order of the Generall Court of Connecticut Dated March the 11th $166\frac{2}{3}$[2] That the Gent[lemen] theire Comittee were Limitted to Conclude at this pr[e]sent meeting with vs, otherwise theire pow[e]r Ceased. Our answear in generall is, That we are not in a Capacity soe to doe.

1 ffirst because we are vnd[e]r an Apeale to the King[3] wherevnto we doe adheare And therefore Cannot act Contrarily without dishono[u]r to his Maj[es]tie and pr[e]judice to our owne Right vntill his Royall Determinacion be Knowne in the Question depending betweene vs.

2 Because we Cannot in Conscience Conclude to dissolve our distinct Colony by vniting with Connecticut without the express Consent

1. Connecticut State Library, Connecticut Archives, Miscellaneous Papers, I, no. 70; printed in *New Haven Colonial Records, 1653–1665* (Hartford, 1858), pp. 476–477.

2. The general assembly of Connecticut of March 11, 1662/3, appointed John Mason, deputy governor, Mathew Allyn, John Talcott, John Allyn, and, if the deputy governor were unable to serve, Samuel Wyllys a committee to visit New Haven to treat with the New Haven Colony regarding union or, if that were impossible, to settle terms of peace. The assembly ordered that if the committee failed to come to an agreement with the New Haven Colony, all proposals and instructions of the general assembly regarding union were to be voided. Under date of March 20, 1662/3, Mathew Allyn, Samuel Wyllys, and John Allyn presented proposals of union to the committee of the New Haven Colony. *Connecticut Colonial Records, 1636–1665* (Hartford, 1850), p. 396; *New Haven Colonial Records, 1653–1665* (Hartford, 1858), pp. 475–476.

3. On November 4, 1662, the freemen of the New Haven Colony had instructed the committee of the New Haven Colony to appeal to Charles II if satisfaction could not be obtained from Connecticut. Late in 1662 or early in 1663, John Scott sailed for England to appeal to John Winthrop the Younger or to Charles II. After Winthrop had stopped this appeal, a general court of the New Haven Colony of October 22, 1663, appointed the governor, magistrates, elders of New Haven, and Samuel Bache a committee to negotiate with the authorities in England. *New Haven Colonial Records, 1653–1665* (Hartford, 1858), pp. 471, 502.

of the oth[e]r Coloneyes declared from theire Generall Courts Respectively.

3 Because we are Limitted by our ffreemen not to Conclude any thing for altering our Distinct Colony-state and Governm[en]t without theire Consent.[4]

Yet shall we in order to an yssue betwixt vs with Love and peace, which we desire them by all Loving Cariages to promove (in the interim of our deliberacion) Consider of theire proposicions and Comunicat them to our ffreemen,[5] as we may have a Convenient oportunity.

But whereas we observe in theire proposicions, that Stamford is left out[6] as if it were noe member of vs, we must, and doe profess ourselvs vnsattisfied with that omission because we ap[p]r[e]hend ourselvs bound to seek and provide for their Liberties and Comforts as our owne.

Newhauen 20th of 1rst Mo: WILL[IA]M LEETE in the name
$\left(\frac{62}{63}\right)$ of our Comittee

JOHN DAVENPORT *to* JOHN COTTON the Younger[1]

Deare S[i]r

YOURS dated the 17th of the 11th m. I received the 9th day of the 12. m. and having so good an opportunity, by so safe an hand as Mr. Sam: Streete,[2] I returne such Answer as I can to your Letter, wherein I observe with thanckfullnes your kinde acceptance of my louing freenes in expressing my deepe sence of your sinfull miscarriages. I could not have approued my faithfulnes to God, to you, and to my owne Conscience if I had neglected such a season of so speaking

4. At the meeting of November 4, 1662, the freemen of the New Haven Colony had voted to "remaine in the same state as we are till" John Winthrop the Younger had returned to New England.

5. The proposals of Connecticut and this reply were laid before the general court of the New Haven Colony of May 6, 1663.

6. The general assembly of Connecticut of October 9, 1662, had received Stamford and Greenwich under its jurisdiction.

1. Boston Public Library, Mather Papers, I, no. 29; printed in Massachusetts Historical Society *Collections*, 4th series, VIII (Boston, 1868), 547–549; A. B. Davenport, *Supplement* (Stamford, 1876), pp. 372–374. The letter is in the handwriting of John Davenport, Jr.

2. Samuel Street, the son of Nicholas Street, teacher of the church at New Haven, was at this time a student at Harvard College.

to you, as I did, that being the first opportunity which was given me of treating with you, *ore tenus*, about such matters as were not fit to be committed to wrighting, which might fall into other hands, to the blemishing of your name, which I desired to preserve unspotted, by me, while I sincerely endeavoured the healing of your soul. How often have I fervently desired that, as you beare boath your fathers names, so you might hold forth the virtues of Christ, in your spirit and conversacion, which eminently shined in him! Thus you would be knowne to be his son, morally, by imitacion, as well as naturally, by generacion, which would have given you a double interest, in the hearts of Gods people, who knew, loued, and highly honoured your blessed Father, who being dead would thus have lived in you, as worthy Mr. Hooker,[3] doth in his good son,[4] at Farmington. Nor am I out of hope that yet it may be so, if the Lord conuince you powerfully of your former sins, and humble you effectually for them, to Justifie wisdomes counsels by your holding forth publickly your unfeined repentance, as, I told you Origen[5] did with many teares, that, scandal might be remoued, which, while it remaines, will be τὸ κατέχον,[6] to hinder the acceptance of your exercise of guifts in preaching, with men, and the blessing of it from God. You promised that you would send me a Copie of your publick acknowledgm[en]t, which is reported to be slight, and unsatisfying, and that you would propound some things in reference to your case, for further aduise. But you have done neither, whereby I am dissaduantaged from giving you that helpe, which otherwise I might have done, with Gods assistance. It is a temptacion from satan, to hinder you from propounding your case, upon a secret expectacion, to see more of God in it, hoping that God, who helped me before to speake as if I had knowne the inward frame of your heart, will againe direct me to speake some thing to the troubles of your heart, though I be not fully acquainted with them. For though if you had acquainted me with your troubles, and the grounds of them, and the effects, my bowells would have bene troubled with you, and for you, and from a true sympathy I should have endeavoured to asswage your greife, or to direct your apprehencions, or otherwise to speake suitably to your case; yet it is not Gods manner, nor may you expect it, to reveale to his serv[an]ts, by immediate inspiracion, the cases of others, which, by

3. Thomas Hooker, the first pastor of the church at Hartford, Connecticut.
4. Samuel Hooker, a graduate of Harvard College in 1653, was ordained as the successor of Roger Newton at Farmington in July, 1661.
5. Origen, *ca.* 185–*ca.* 254, a theologian of the ancient church.
6. the obstacle,

his ordinances they aught to expresse, themselues and seeke helpe in from others, that the communion of saints may be preserved and exercised among them mutually. Thus you see how satan tempteth you to tempt God. As for me, be you assured that, in any way of God, you shall finde me really ready, upon all occasions, to be helpfull to you as the case may require. Farewel, and account me, as I am

N[ew] H[aven] the 23: of the 1st. m.   Your true freind in the Lord
$\frac{1662.}{3.}$ JOHN DAVENPORTE

S[i]r

I thanck you for my letters to your Father, which you sent me, according to my desire and your promise. Some I rec[eive]d by Edm[und] Toolie, and some by Jacob molines,[7] with your letter. If any yet remain with you; you will further oblige me, if you send them to me. *iterum vale.*

The GENERAL COURT OF THE NEW HAVEN COLONY *to* THE GENERAL ASSEMBLY OF CONNECTICUT[1]

Gent[lemen]:

THE professed grounds and ends of your and our Commeing into these parts, are not vnknowne, Being plainely exprest in the prologue to that solemne Confederation, entred into by the 4 Colonies of New England printed and published to the world, Namely to advance the kingdome of our lord Jesus christ, and to enjoy the liberties of the gospell in purity with peace for which we left our deare natiue Country, and were willing to vndergoe the difficulties we haue since met with in this wildernes yet fresh in our remembrance: Being the onely ends we still pursue, haueing hitherto found by experience soe much of the pr[e]sence of god with vs, and of his goodnes and compassion towards vs in soe doeinge for these many yeares. Yet Considering how vnanswerable our returnes haue been to god, how vnfruitfull, vnthankefull and vnholy vnder soe much meanes of grace, and such liberties, we cannot but Lament the same, judge our selues, and justify

7. Jacob, the son of Cornelis Melyen or Moline, a Dutchman who had a seat in the church at New Haven as early as 1656 and bought Robert Seely's house at New Haven in 1659.

1. Connecticut State Library, Manuscript New Haven Colonial Records, 1653–1664, fols. 344–347; printed in *New Haven Colonial Records, 1653–1665* (Hartford, 1858), pp. 479–483.

god, should he now at last (after soe long patience towards vs) bring desolating Judgements vpon vs, And make vs drinke of the dregs of that cup of indignacion he hath put into the hands of his people in other parts of the world, or suffer such Contentions (in just displeasure) to arise among vs, as may hasten our Calamity and increase our Woe, which we pray the lord in mercy to pr[e]vent.—And whereas in the pursuance of the s[ai]d ends, and vpon other Religious and Ciuill Consideracions, as the security of the interest of each Colony within its selfe in wayes of Righteousnes and peace, And all and euery of the s[ai]d Colonies from the indians and other enemies, they did judge it to be their bounden duty for mutuall strength and helpfulnes for the future in all their s[ai]d Concernem[en]ts, to enter into a Consociacion among themselues, therevpon fully agreed, and concluded by and betweene the parties or jurisdiccions in diuers and sundry articles, and at last ratified as a perpetuall Confederation by their seuerall subscriptions.[2] Wherevnto we Conceiue ourselues bound to adheare, vntill with satisfaction to our Judgem[en]ts and Consciences, we see our duty with like vnanimous Consent of the Confederates orderly to Recede Leaueing the issue vnto the most wise and righteous god.

As for the Pattent, vpon your peticion, granted to you by his Maj[es]tie as Connecticott Colony, soe far, and in that sence we object not against it, much lesse ag[ain]st his Maj[es]ties act in soe doeing, the same being a Reall encouragem[en]t to other of his subjects to obtaine the like fauo[u]r vpon their humble peticion to his Royall Highnes, in the protection of their persons and purchased Rights, and Interests, Is alsoe a ground of hope to vs.—But if the Line of your Pattent doth Circumscribe this Colony by your Contriuem[en]t without our Cognizance or Consent, or regard to the s[ai]d Confœderacion on your parts, we haue, and must still testify against it, as not consistent (in our Judgm[en]t) with Brotherly loue Righteousnes, and peace. And that this Colony (for soe long time a Confœderate jurisdiccion, distinct from yours and the other Colonies) is taken in vnder the Adminestration of the s[ai]d Pattent in your hands, and soe its form[e]r being dissolued, and distinction Ceasing, there being noe one Line or Letter in the Pattent expressing his Maj[es]ties pleasure that way, although it is your sence of it, Yet wee Cannot soe apr[e]hend, of which we haueing already giuen our grounds at Large in writing, we shall not need to say much more, nor haue we met with any argumentatiue, or rationall Coniuctions from you, nor doe we yet see Cause to be of another mind.

2. The New England Confederation, entered upon in 1643.

As for your proceedings vpon pr[e]tence of the Pattent towards vs, or rather against vs, in taking in sundry inhabitants of this Colony vnder your protection and gouernm[en]t[3] whoe (as you say) offered them selues, from which a good Conscience, and the obligacion vnder which most of them stood to this Colony should haue restrayned them, without the Consent of the body of this Colony first had, and in Concurrence with them, vpon mature deliberation, and Conviction of duty yet wanting, We cannot but againe testify against as disorderly in them, and which admission on your parts we Conceiue your Christian prudence might haue easily suspended, for pr[e]vention of that great offence to the Consciences of your Confederat Brethren, and those sad Consequences which haue ffollowed disturbing the peace of our townes, destroying our Comforts, and hazard of our liues and liberties by their frequent threats and vnsufferable provokations, hath been, and is with vs matter of Complaint both to god and man, Especially when we Consider that thus you admitted them, and put power into their hands, before you had made any ouerture to vs, or had any treaty with vs about soe weighty a busines, as if you were in hast to make vs miserable, as indeed in these things wee are at this day.

And seeing vpon the answ[e]r returned to your propositions made by you afterwards of joineing with you in your gouernem[en]t, finding our selues soe already dismembred, and the weighty grounds and Reasons we then pr[e]sented to you, we could not pr[e]vaile soe far with you, as to procure a Respite of your further proceedings vntill Mr. Winthrops returne from England, or the graunt of any time that way, which was thought but reasonable by some of your selues, and the like seldome denied in Warr to very enemies, we saw it then high time, and necessary (feareing these beginnings) to appeale vnto his Maj[es]tie And soe we did, Concluding according to the Law of appeales in all Cases and among all nations, that the same (vpon your allegiance to his Maj[es]ty) would haue obliged you to forbeare all further processe in this busines, for our owne parts resoluing (notwithstanding all that we had formerly suffered) to sit downe patient vnder the same, waiting vpon god for the issue of our s[ai]d appeale.

But seeing that notwithstanding all that we had pr[e]sented to you by word and writing, notwithstanding our appeale to his Maj[es]tie, notwithstanding all that we haue suffered (by meanes of that power

3. The general assembly of Connecticut of October 9, 1662, received a majority of the inhabitants of Southold, several inhabitants of Guilford, and the plantations of Stamford and Greenwich under the jurisdiction of Connecticut. *Connecticut Colonial Records, 1636–1665* (Hartford, 1850), pp. 386–387, 388.

you had set vp vizt. a Constable at Stamford)[4] of which informations
haue beene giuen you yet you haue gone further to place a Constable
at Guilford[5] in like manner, ouer a partie there, to the further disturbance of of our peace and quiet, a narratiue whereof, and of the pro-
uokations and wrongs we haue met with at Stamford, we haue receiued attested to vs by diuers witnesses, honest men. We Cannot but
on behalfe of our appeale to his Maj[es]tie whose hono[u]r is highly
Concerned therein, and of our just Rights, But (as men exceedingly
aflicted and greiued) testify in the sight of god, angells, and men
against these things. Our end therein, being not to provoke or further
any offence, but rather as a discharge of duty on our parts as Brethren
and Christian Confœderates, to call vpon you to take some effectuall
Course to ease and right vs in a due redress of the greiuances you haue
caused by these proceedings, such, and that after you had complemented vs with Large offers of Pattent privilidges, with desire of a
treatie with vs for vnion of our Colonies, And you know as your good
words were kindly accepted soe your motion was fairely answered by
our Committee, That in regard we were vnder an Appeale to his Maj-
[es]tie, that being limited by our ffreemen not to Conclude any thing
for altering our distinct Colony state and Gouernm[en]t without their
Consent, And without the approbation of the other Confederate
Colonies, they were not in pr[e]sent Capacity soe to treate, But did
litle suspect such a designe on foote against vs, the efect whereof
quickly appeared at Guilford before mentioned. But we shall say noe
more at this time, onely to tell you whateuer we suffer by your meanes,
we pray the lord would help vs to choose it rather then to sin against
our Consciences hopeing the Righteous god will in due time looke
vpon our afliction, and incline his Maj[es]ties heart to fauo[u]r our
Righteous Cause.

New Hauen May. 6. *1663*   Subscribed in the name and by order
                             of the Gene[ra]ll Court of Newhauen
                             Colony Per JAMES BISHOP *Secretary*

4. The colonial records do not disclose exactly when Connecticut appointed the il-
literate Francis Brown constable for Stamford. He took the oath of office at the general
assembly of October 8, 1663. *Ibid.*, p. 413.

5. The records do not give the date of the original appointment of John Meggs as
constable for Guilford. The general assembly of May 14, 1663, continued him in office.
Ibid., p. 405.

JOHN DAVENPORT *to* JOHN WINTHROP the Younger[1]

To the R[igh]t Worship[fu]ll John Winthrope Esq. Governo[u]r of Connectacute these present at Hartford

Honour[e]d Sir)

THESE are to congratulate your safe arrival and returne to your familie, where you have bene ardently desired, and long expected. Blessed be our good God, in Jesus christ, who hath, at last, mercifully brought you off from Court-snares, and London-tumults, and European troubles, and from all perils at sea, and hath præserved your præcious life and health, and who hath carried your selfe, with your 2 sons[2] etc. as upon Eagles wings,[3] above the reach of all hurtful dangers, unto your habitation, and who hath kept your deare wife, and all your children alive, and made them joyfull by your safe and comfortable returne unto them! Together with them I also, and my wife, and son, and daughter,[4] rejoyce herein, as in a gracious answer of many praiers, and in persuasion that you are come with an olive branch in your mouth;[5] according to the encouragem[en]t and assurance which I have received in some letters to my selfe, from Captaine Scot,[6] and from Mr. Hatsel:[7] and from one sent to Mr. Leete,[8] which is, either the protograph, or a copie of your letter to Major Mason,[9]

1. Massachusetts Historical Society, Winthrop MSS., III, 147; printed in Massachusetts Historical Society *Collections*, 4th series, VII (Boston, 1865), 521–524. John Winthrop the Younger had just returned from his mission to England. Under date of July 10/20, 1663, Peter Stuyvesant, director general of New Netherland, sent him a similar letter of welcome. *Ibid.*, 5th series, I (Boston, 1871), 395–396.

2. Fitz John Winthrop and Wait Still Winthrop.

3. Exodus 19. 4.

4. John Davenport, Jr., and Abigail Pierson were married at Branford, November 27, 1662. Branford Records, I, 1645–1679, p. 173. A. B. Davenport erroneously gives November 27, 1663, as the date of the marriage.

5. Genesis 8. 11.

6. In an effort to settle the dispute between the New Haven Colony and Connecticut, Captain John Scott of Ashford or Setauket, Long Island, Nathaniel Whitfield, Robert Thompson, and William Hooke had met with John Winthrop the Younger, in London, March 2 or 3, 1662/3. Public Record Office, State Papers, Domestic, Charles II, LXIX, no. 5.

7. Henry Hatsell of Saltram, Plympton St. Mary, Devonshire, a member of parliament in 1654, 1656, and 1658, who had married Susanna, the widow of John Evance of New Haven and London, some time after May 2, 1661.

8. At this time William Leete of Guilford was governor of the New Haven Colony.

9. At this time John Mason was deputy governor of Connecticut. For Winthrop's letter to Major John Mason, deputy governor, the magistrates, and general court of Connecticut, March 3, 1662/3, see below, pp. 231–232. The manuscript is in Connecticut State Library, Robert C. Winthrop Collection of Connecticut Manuscripts, II, 250. It

which seemes to be written by your selfe, but the seale was broken open, before it came hither. Whether he hath that letter from Major Tomson,[10] which you mention, or not, I know not. But, I heare, he hath one from Mr. Whitfield,[11] the contents whereof I have not heard. Sir, give me leave to take notice of one passage in yours (that there is nothing but missunderstanding that could occasion such apprehensions of anie injurie done to N[ew] H[aven]; or theyre concernm[en]ts: and those freinds above mentioned were fully satisfied thereof, and wondered much that it was not better understood *by yours*.)[12] It was written, in the line, *them;* but being blotted out, it is interlined, *yours*, which makes the sense of the wholl verie darke to me. For if, by *yours*, be meant, our committee of magistrates, Elders, and deputies, entrusted by the Freemen of this Colonie to treate with our freinds of Connectacute; I shall wonder at theyre wondering. For, 1, that manifest injurie is done to this Colonie, is proved by instances, in the wrightings sent to Connectacute, and to England. 2. Nor did we missunderstand the patent, but saw and pleaded that N[ew] H[aven] Colonie is not mentioned therein, and that it was not the Kings purpose, nor yours, to destroy the distinction of Colonies, nor our Coloniestate: and, in that confidence, desired that all things might stand, *in statu quo prius*, til your returne, which when we could not obtaine, we were compelled to appeale to the King, yet, out of tender respect to your peace and Honour, advised, as you know, our freinds[13] to consult with you, before they prosecuted our appeale, or delivered my letter to my Lord Chamberlain.[14] Our freindes at Connectacute regarded not

is printed in *New Haven Colonial Records, 1653–1665* (Hartford, 1858), pp. 498–499, 522–523; Massachusetts Historical Society *Collections*, 5th series, VIII (Boston, 1882), 80–81. Connecticut claimed that the letter was never received in that colony. *New Haven Colonial Records, 1653–1665* (Hartford, 1858), p. 534.

10. Robert Thompson, a London merchant, was a friend of Edward Hopkins, a member of the society for the propagation of the gospel in New England, and recent purchaser of the Whitfield holdings in Guilford. A letter from Winthrop sent *via* Thompson and Scott reached Leete about June 25, 1663. Massachusetts Historical Society *Collections*, 4th series, VII (Boston, 1865), 551, 552.

11. Nathaniel Whitfield was the son of Henry Whitfield, the first pastor of the church at Guilford. In letters to Winthrop June 25, 1663, and July 20, 1663, Leete does not mention the receipt of this letter.

12. Although this quotation is inexact, Davenport seems to be referring to Winthrop's letter to John Mason, the magistrates, and general court of Connecticut of March 3, 1662/3.

13. John Scott, Nathaniel Whitfield, William Hooke, and Robert Thompson.

14. Edward Montagu, second Earl of Manchester, son-in-law of Robert Rich, Earl of Warwick, who was also the friend of John Winthrop the Younger.

our Argum[en]ts, which yet, I know, are pleadable and would beare due weight, in the chancery, and at the Council Table, and one of them yourselfe is pleased to establish, in your letter to Major Mason. 3. Nor is it to be wondered at, if we had missunderstood the things which we wanted meanes to understand from your selfe, who, neither in your letter to me, from London, dat[ed] May. 13. 1662[15] which I received by Mr. Ling: nor in your nexte, dated, March the 7th, this yeare,[16] signified to me any other thing, then that New Haven is stil a distinct Colonie, notwithstanding the Connectacute patent. I doe the more insist in this, because I am told that Mr. Stone, in a letter which he sent unto one in Fairefield[17] (*ni fallor*) saith that he had received a letter from Mr. Winthrope,[18] who wondereth that N[ew] H[aven] doe quæstion theyre being under Connectacute, or to that purpose; which is understood as concluding the dissolucion of this Colonie which I perceive, by what yourselfe and others have written, is a missunderstanding of your meaning, so that the missunderstanding is to be wondered at in them, not in us. As for what Mr. Leete wrote to your selfe;[19] it was his private doing, without the consent or knowledge of any of us, in this Colonie, it was not done by him, according to his publick trust, as Governour, but contrary to it. If they had treated with us, or should yet, as with a distinct Colonie; we should readily agree with them in any rational and æqual termes, for the settling of neighbourly peace, and brotherly amitie betweene them and us, mutually, who have alreadie, as you see, patiently suffered wrong, for peace sake, in hope of a just redresse, at your returne into these parts. I would not have mentioned these matters, in this letter (which I intended onely for a supplie of my want of bodily fitnes for a journey to Hartford, to give you a personal visit, in testimonie of my joy for your safe arrival and returne) but that the expression forenoted compelled me to speake some thing to it. I long to see your face, and am in hope

15. No copy of this letter has been found.
16. No copy of this letter has been found.
17. Possibly Nathan Gold, at this time a magistrate of Connecticut and a resident of Fairfield.
18. No copy of this letter has been found.
19. In a letter dated at Guilford, August 6, 1661, William Leete had written to Winthrop, "I wish that you and wee could procure one Pattent, to reach beyond Delawar, where we have expended a £1000 to procure Indian title, veiw, and begin to possesse." In his letters to Winthrop of June 25, 1663, and July 20, 1663, Leete refers to a letter that he had sent to Winthrop in England, asking Winthrop "to make your Pattent a covert, but no controule to our Jurisdiccion, vntill we accorded with mutuall satisfacion to become one, . . ." Massachusetts Historical Society *Collections*, 4th series, VII (Boston, 1865), 549, 552.

that shortly, after your first hurries are over, we shall injoy your much desired presence with us, in your chamber, at my house, which shall be as your owne, while it is myne. Then we may have opportunity, by the will of God, to confer placidly together, and to give and receive mutual satisfaction, through a right understanding of what is done in our concernm[en]ts. My selfe, my wife, my son and daughter, doe joyntly and severally, præsent our humble service to your Honoured selfe, and Mrs. Winthrope, with our respectful and affectionate saluta-cions to your 2 sons, and to all your daughters, praying that blessings from heaven may be multiplied upon you and them, through Jesus christ, in whom I rest

N[ew] H[aven] the 22th day of   Honoured Sir)
the 4th moneth called June 1663   Yours obliged to honour
                               and serve you in the Lord
                                  JOHN DAVENPORTE

Postscript.

The freshest newes here, and that which is *e re vestrâ*, is, that they have bene blowing, at the ironworke, and have runne from the last day to this 2d day, 5 sowes of iron, which are commended for very good, and this night, its thaught, they will run another, and begin to morrow to make pots. The worke is hopeful, but the workemen are thaught to be very chargeable, and froward.

[Endorsed] Mr. Davenport rec: Jun: 23 [by John Winthrop.]

The COMMITTEE OF THE NEW HAVEN COLONY *to* THE COMMITTEE OF CONNECTICUT[1]

To the hono[u]r[e]d Comittee from the Gen[era]ll Assembly of Connecticut Mr. Willis Mr. Clark and Mr. Allen.

Gent[lemen]:

I N Ord[e]r to a ffrendly treaty and amicable Composure of matters in difference between vs, we earnestly desire you wold restore vs to our Intire Colony state by disclaming that party at Gilford and Stam-

1. Connecticut State Library, Connecticut Archives, Miscellaneous Papers, I, no. 71; printed in *New Haven Colonial Records, 1653–1665* (Hartford, 1858), pp. 491–492. The general assembly of Connecticut of August 19, 1663, had appointed John Mason, deputy governor, Samuel Wyllys, Daniel Clarke, and John Allyn, or any three or two of them, a committee to treat with the towns of New Haven, Milford, Branford, and Guilford about union with Connecticut. *Connecticut Colonial Records, 1636–1665* (Hartford, 1850), p. 407.

ford, and soe doing: we offer the ffollowing Queries to your Consideracion: as matter for Such treaty vizt.

1 Wheth[e]r the fundamentall lawes for Governm[en]t especially that touching the Qualificacions of ffreemen shalbe the same with Boston or our (i. e.) members of some one or oth[e]r of our Churches.

2 Wheth[e]r our Church Ord[e]r and priviledges shall not be infringed, nor disturbed, and that both the Choice and Calling in of Ministers in each plantacion be established a Church right for euer.

3 Wheth[e]r all our pr[e]sent ffreemen shall be forthwith Admitted and Impowred to Act as your owne ffreemen to all intents and purposes.

4 Wheth[e]r any of our fformer Acscions in our distinct Co[lony] state shalbe liable to appeales, or be Called in Question.

5. Wheth[e]r we shalbe Imediatly established a Distinct County[2] and to have soe many Magistrats as necessary 4 at least with a Pr[e]sident Chosen y[ea]rly by our owne County Court togeth[e]r with oth[e]r inferio[u]r officers, to be nominated by ourselvs.

6. Wheth[e]r any Apeales shalbe at any tyme allowed from our County Court in ordinary Cases vnles to our owne Court of Assistance and that vpon waighty grounds and with good Caucion to pr[e]vent trouble, and Charge to the Country.

7 Wheth[e]r there shall not be a Court of Assistance at Newhaven yearly or oftner if need Require to try Capitall Causes, and heare such Apeales Consisting of our owne and such oth[e]r Magistrats as we shall desire by Ord[e]r from our pr[e]sident.

8 Wheth[e]r all our pr[e]sent Magistrats and officers shall Remaine in ffull pow[e]r to Govern the people as formerly vntill new be Orderly Chosen at the next Elleccion Court after this agreem[en]t.

9 Wheth[e]r all rates and publique Charges graunted or Levied or due in each Colony before this agreem[en]t be paid and discharged by the Inhabitants proporcionably, in a distinct way, and not oth[e]rwise.

10. Wheth[e]r at the next Elleccion there shalbe a Comittee Chosen and apointed Off your and our ablest Ministers and oth[e]r ffreemen to Consult and pr[e]pare a Body of Lawes out of your and our Lawes most Consonant to scripture.

11 Wheth[e]r vntill such a body of lawes be framed and agreed vpon

2. After the union of the New Haven Colony and Connecticut had been consummated, the general assembly of Connecticut of May 10, 1666, erected the territory between the eastern boundary of Guilford and the western boundary of Milford into the county of New Haven. *Connecticut Colonial Records, 1665–1677* (Hartford, 1852), p. 35.

a new, mutually, all matters in our townes and Court, shalbe yssued and don according to our owne lawes as formerly.

12. Wheth[e]r all our plantacions According to their Aunciently: Reputed and received bounds shall not soe Remaine vnalterably but receive Confirmacion by autority of the Pattent.

That such treaty shall not be binding to vs without Consent of our Confederats, and Gen[era]ll Court of ffreemen.

Wheth[e]r the ffreemen of each of our townes may not make ord[e]rs for the towne affaires.

Theise Imperfect Queries we at pr[e]sent offer to your Consideracion reserving Liberty to propound what ffurth[e]r we shall see needfull allowed by the Pattent.

WILL[IA]M LEETE in the name
and with Consent of the Comittee

[Endorsed] N[ew] Hauen Comite proposals August 26 1663

The COMMITTEE OF THE NEW HAVEN COLONY *to* CONNECTICUT[1]

Hono[u]r[e]d Gent[lemen]:

SEEING that it hath pleased the Almighty whoe is our defence (at this session of the Commission[e]rs, not to suffer any mine to spring for subverting that ancient wall of New Englands safety, which himselfe hath erected vpon the foundation of our soe solemne and Religious Confœderation, but further vnanimously to establish the same, Wee thought it might not be vnacceptable on our part, to pr[e]sent you with our request at this season of your Gen[era]ll Assemblyes meeting, that you would observe to doe according to their Conclusions, reminding to recall all and euery of your former acts of a Contrary tendency, and please to signify the same to vs before our Gen[era]ll Court held the 22th instant, whoe will then expect it before they returne answer to your Committees proposalls. Your Cordiall and ready attendance vnto this our request (we Conceiue) wilbe noe obstruction to an amicable Treaty for Complyance, but rather the Contrary, if the Lord shall please to owne and succeed such endeavo[u]rs as meanes for the better flourishing of Religion and Righteousnes with peace in

---

1. Connecticut State Library, Manuscript New Haven Colonial Records, 1653–1664, fol. 360; printed in *New Haven Colonial Records, 1653–1665* (Hartford, 1858), pp. 500–501.

this wildernes. And we cannot appr[e]hend that you need to feare any dammage to your Pattent hereby, from his Majesties takeing offence at soe honest a Carriage, there being noe express Interdiction of New-hauen Colony inserted therein, nor any intendm[en]t of your Agent to haue it soe injuriously carried against vs, And now alsoe haue you the encouragement of all your Confederates to Apollogise vpon that account in case any turbulent spirits should suggest a Complaint, whom the righteous god can Countermand and disapoint, to whose wisdome and grace we recommend you and all your weighty Con-cernem[en]ts, resting

New Hauen October: 6th: *1663*   Gentlemen:

> Your very loueing and
> expectant Confederates
> The Committee for N[ew] H[aven] Colony

> By JAMES BISHOP *Secretary*

The MAGISTRATES OF THE NEW HAVEN COLONY *to* THE COMMITTEE OF CONNECTICUT[1]

24th: 12: m: 1663.

Gentlemen

IN Order to treaty we propound as a necessary expedient, that you Redintigrate our Colony by Restoring our members at Stamford and Gilford, that the Confederacion may be repaired and pr[e]served.

Then we have pow[e]r from our Gen[era]ll Court to treat with you: And to settle agreem[en]ts according to God, between your Colony and ours for future peace betweene vs, for ourselvs, and our posterity mutually, which we shall readily attend vpon our Receipt of your positive Consent to the pr[e]mises, testified by your joint subscripcion therevnto, being made an authenticall act.

> WILL[IA]M LEETE
> MATHEW GILBERT
> W[ILLIA]M JONES
> JASPER CRANE
> ROBERT TREATT
> BENIAMIN FFENN

1. Connecticut State Library, Connecticut Archives, Miscellaneous Papers, I, no. 78; printed in *New Haven Colonial Records, 1653–1665* (Hartford, 1858), p. 516.

The MAGISTRATES OF THE NEW HAVEN COLONY *to* THE COMMITTEE OF CONNECTICUT[1]

Feb: 25: *1663*

Gentlemen.

As to your first artickle, in your paper sent vs, wee quærye; whyther it bee an authentick act as donne by you, or not tyll it bee confyrmed by your generall assembly: which if it bee, wee desyre that you doe signifye so much vnder your hands, as also that they are possitiuely restored to this iurysdiction, by vertue thereof:

> WILL[IA]M LEETE in the name
> of the rest of the Magistrates.

The COMMITTEE OF THE NEW HAVEN COLONY *to* THE COMMITTEE OF CONNECTICUT[1]

To the Hono[ured] Commitee ffor Connecticut Colony. 1663

ffeb: 25: 1663

Gentlemen

In returne to yours, if you please to perfect the first Artickle according to our Last Paper, that this Colony may bee satisfied that our members may be restored to this jurisdiccion, according to the Confederacion, and the Commission[e]rs Advice thereupon, and your Hono[u]r[e]d Governo[u]r Mr. Winthrops Letter, with his maj[es]ties gracious incouragem[en]t since, that being Clearely and fully done, our Committee have full power from our Gen[era]ll Court to treate with you about other expedients for Common peace, if you refuse thus to doe, we must Lay the hinderance of a further treaty, with all the Consequences thereof at your doore.

> Signed By the appointment of the Committee
> for New Haven Colonie

> Per JAMES BISHOP. Secretary

postscript

Nevertheless we purpose to acquaint our Generall Court with the whole matter.

1. Connecticut State Library, Connecticut Archives, Miscellaneous Papers, I, no. 79; printed in *New Haven Colonial Records, 1653–1665* (Hartford, 1858), pp. 516–517.

1. Printed in "The Wyllys Papers," Connecticut Historical Society *Collections*, XXI (Hartford, 1924), 149–150.

THE GENERAL COURT OF THE NEW HAVEN COLONY *to*
THE GENERAL ASSEMBLY OF CONNECTICUT[1]

*To the hono[u]r[e]d John Winthrop Esq[ui]r[e] Governo[u]r or
to the hono[u]r[e]d Majo[u]r Mason Deputy Governo[u]r of
Conecticut Colony to be Com[mu]nicated to the
hono[u]r[e]d The Generall Assembly
for the s[ai]d Colony*

Honoured and Beloved in the Lord

Newhavens Case Stated

WEE, the Generall Courte of Newhaven Colonie, being sensible of the wrongs which this Colonie hath lately suffred, by your vnjust pretences and Encroatchments vpon our just and proper Rights, haue vnanimously consented, though with greife of harte, being compelled therevnto, to declare vnto you, and vnto all whome the knowledge therof maye concerne, what yourselues doe or may knowe to bee true, as followeth, vizt.

1 That the first Beginners of these Plantations by the seaside, in these westerne parts of New England, being engaged to sundry freinds, in London, and in other places aboute London (who purposed to plant some with them, in the same Town, and others, as near to them as they might) to prouide for them, and themselues, some convenient places, by the seaside, arriued at Boston, in the Massachusetts (haueing a speciall right in theyr Pattent, two of them being joynt purchasers of it with others,[2] and one of them a patentee, and one of the Assistants chosen for the New England Company in London) where they aboade all the Winter followeing, but not findeing there a place suteable to their purpose were perswaided to view these parts, which those that viewed, approved and before theyr remoueall finding that no English were planted in any place, from the fortt (called Saye Brooke) to the Dutch, purposed to purchase of the Indians, the Naturall proprieto[u]rs of those lands, that whole Tract of Land by the seacoaste, for themselues and those that should come to them, which they also signified to theyr freinds at Hartforde, in Connecticott Colonie, and de-

1. Connecticut State Library, Connecticut Archives, Miscellaneous Papers, I, no. 80; printed in *New Haven Colonial Records, 1653–1665* (Hartford, 1858), pp. 517–530. A general court of the New Haven Colony of January 7, 1663/4, requested John Davenport and Nicholas Street "to draw up in writing all our grievances and then with the approbation of as many of the committee as could come together, to send it to Connecticutt, unto their gen[era]ll assembly." *Ibid.*, p. 514.
2. Theophilus Eaton and John Davenport.

sired that some fitt men from thence might be imployed in that buisness, at theyr proper cost and charges who wrote to them. Vnto which
letter haueinge receiued a satisfieing answer, they acquainted the
Courte of Magistrates of Massachusetts Colonie, with theyr purpose
to remoue,[3] and the Grounds of it: and with theyr consent begann a
Plantation, in a place situated by the sea, Caled by the Indians Quilli-
piack[4] which they did purchase of the Indians, the true proprieto[u]rs
thereof for themselues and theyr posterety, and haue quietly possessed
the same aboute six and twenty yeares, and haue buried greate Estates in Buildings, fensings, clearing the ground, and in all sorts of
husbandrye, without any healp from Connecticott, or Dependance
upon them. And by volluntary consent amoung themselues they
settled a Ciuill Courte, and Gouernm[en]t within themselues, upon
such foundamentalls as were Established in Massachusetts, by Allowance of theyr pattent, wherof the then Gouernor of the Bay, the
right worship[fu]ll Mr. Winthrop sent us a Coppie to improue for our
best advantage.[5] These foundamentalls, all the Inhabitants of the
s[ai]d Quillipyack approued, and bound themselues to submitt vnto,
and mantaine: and chose Theophilus Eaton Esq[ui]r[e], to be theyr
Gouerno[u]r with as good right as Connecticott settled theyre Governm[en]t amoung themselues and continued it aboue twenty yeares
without any pattent.

2 That when the healp of Mr. Eaton our Gouerno[u]r and some
others from Quillipyack was desired, for Ending of a Controuersie, at
Wethersfeild a Toune in Connecticott Colonie it being judged necessary for peace that one partie should remoue theyr dwellings vpon
æquall satisfieing tearmes proposed, the Gouerno[u]r, Magistrates,
Etc. of Connecticott offered for theyr part, that if the partie that
would remoue should finde a fitt place to plante in, upon the Riuer
Connecticott would graunte it to them, And the Gouerno[u]r of Quillipyack (now called Newhaven) and the rest there present ioyned with
him, and promised if they should finde a fitt place for themselues by
the seaside, Newhaven would graunte it to them, which accordingly
Newhaven performed, and so the Town of Standford[6] begann and became a Member of Newhaven Colonie, and so continueth unto this
daye. Thus in a publicke Assemblye in Connecticott, was the distinct

3. See above, pp. 66–68.
4. Quinnipiac, in 1640 renamed New Haven.
5. The laws and practices of Massachusetts, as they had been embodied in the Cotton
Code.
6. Stamford.

Right of Connecticott vpon the Riuer, and of Newhaven by the sea-side, declared, with consent of the Gouerno[u]r, Magistrats, Ministers and better sorte of the people of Connecticutt at that time.

3 That sundry other Townshipps by the seaside,[7] and South Hold[8] on Long Island (being settled in theyr Inheritances, by Right of pur-chase, of theyr Indyan propryeto[u]rs) did volutarily joyne themselues to Newhauen, to bee all vnder one jurisdiccion, by a firme Engag-m[en]t to the foundamentalls formerly settled in Newhaven; where-upon it was called Newhaven Colonie.[9] The Generall Courte being thus constituted, chose the s[ai]d Theophilus Eaton Esq[ui]r[e] a man of singular wisedome, godliness and Experience to be the Gouerno[u]r of Newhauen Colonie, and they chose a Competent number of Mag-istrates, and other officers for the seuerall Townes. Mr. Eaton so well managed that great trust, that he was chosen Gouerno[u]r euery Yeare while he liued, All this time Connecticutt neuer questioned what was done at Newhauen, nor pr[e]tended any right to it, or to any of the Townes belonging to this Colonie, nor objected against our being a distinct Colonie.

4 That when the Dutch claimed a right to Newhauen, and all a long the Coast by the seaside, it being reported that they would sett vp the prince of Oranges Armes, the Gouerno[u]r of Newhauen, to pr[e]-uent that, caused the King of Englands Armes to be fairly cutt in wood, and sett upon a post in the highway by the seaside to vindicate the Right of the English, without Consulting Connecticutt or seeking theyr Concurrance therein.

5 That in the Yeare 1643: vpon weighty considerations, an Vnion of four distinct Colonies, was agreed upon, by all New England (except Road Island) in theyr seuer[a]ll Generall Courts, and was Established by a most soliemne confederation, wherby they bound themselues mutually to pr[e]serue vnto each Collonie its intyre Jurrisdiction, within it self, respectiuely; and to a voide the putting of two into one, by any Act of theyr owne, without consent of the Commisson[e]rs from the four Vnited Colonies which were from that tyme and still are Called and Known by the title of the ffoure Vnited Colonies of New England; of these Colonies Newhauen was and is one, and in this sol-

---

7. Guilford and Milford.
8. Southold.
9. On October 23, 1643, Milford agreed to accept the form of government already established at New Haven. On October 26, 1643, a court of elections for the colony met. On October 27, 1643, the government of the colony was outlined. *New Haven Colonial Records, 1638–1649* (Hartford, 1857), pp. 110–116.

lemn confederation, Connecticutt joyned with the rest, and with vs.

6 That in the yeare 1644, the Generall Court for Newhauen Colonye then setting in the Town of Newhauen, agreed vnanimously to send to England for a Pattent,[10] and in the yeare 1645 committed the procureing of it to Mr. Gregson, one of our Magistrates who entred upon his voyage in January, that year from Newhauen, furnished with some Beauour in order therunto as we suppose, But by the prouidence of God, the shipp, and all the passengers and goods, were lost at sea, in theyr passage toward England, to our great loss and the frustration of the Designe for that time, after which the troubles in England put a stopp to our proceeding therin, This was done with the consent and desyre of Connecticutt to concurr with Newhaven therin, Wherby the difference of times, and of mens spiritts in them, may be disco--uered. For, then the Magistrates of Connecticutt, with consent of theyr Generall Courte, knoweing our purposes, desired to joyne with Newhauen in procureing that pattent for comon pr[i]uillidges to boath, in theyr distinct Jurisdictions, and left it to Mr. Eatons wisedome, to haue the pattent framed accordinly. But now, they seek to procure a pattent without the concurrance of Newhaven, and contrary to our mindes expresd before this pattent was sent for, and to theyr own promise, and to the tearmes of the confideration, and without sufficient warrant from theyr pattent, they haue enuaded our right, and seek to involue Newhaven, vnder Connecticutts jurisdiction.

7 That in the yeare 1646, when the Commission[e]rs first mett at Newhaven Keift the then Dutch Gouernour, by letters Expostulated, with the Commission[e]rs by what warrante they mett at Newhaven, without his consent, seeing it, and all by the sea Coast belonged to his princypalls in Holland, and to the Lords the Estates Gen[era]ll. The Answer to that letter was framed by Mr. Eaton, Gouerno[u]r of Newhauen, and then President of the Commission, approued by all the Commission[e]rs, and sent in theyr names, with theyr consent, to the then Dutch Gouerno[u]r who neuer replyed therunto.[11]

8 That this Colonye in the Raighne of the Late King Charles the first receiued a Letter from the Comittee of Lords and Comons, for

10. On November 11, 1644, a general court for the jurisdiction voted "to putt forth their best Endeuo[u]rs to procure a Pattent from the Parliament as Judging itt a fitt season now for thatt end." *New Haven Colonial Records, 1638–1649* (Hartford, 1857), pp. 149–150.

11. For the correspondence between William Kieft, director general of New Netherland, and Theophilus Eaton, governor of the New Haven Colony, and William Kieft and the commissioners of the United Colonies of New England in the summer and fall of 1646, see *Plymouth Colony Records*, IX (Boston, 1859), pp. 61–65, 76–79.

forayne Plantations, then setting at Westminster, which letter was deliuered to our Gouerno[u]r, Mr. Eaton, freeing the seuerall distinct Colonies of New England, from Molestations by the Appealing of troublesome spiritts vnto England, whereby they declared, that they had dismissed all causes depending before them from New England: and that they aduised all inhabitants to submitt to theyr respectiue Governm[en]ts there Estableished, and to acquiesce when theyr causes shall be there heard, and determined; as it is to be seen more largely Expressed in the originall which wee haue Subscribed.

Your assured freinds

PEMBROOKE	MANCHESTER	WARWICK
W. SAY and SEALE	FR. DA.	DENBIGH[12]

In this order they subscribed theyr Names, with theyr owne hands, which wee haue to shew and they Inscribed or Directed this Letter, To our Worthy freinds the Gouerno[u]r and Assistants of the Plantation of Newhauen in New England. Wherby you maye clearly see that the Right Honor[a]ble the Earle of Warwick, and the Lord Viscount Say and Seale (lately one of his Magistyes that now is, King Charles the Second his most honor[a]ble Priuye Counsell, as also the Right Honor-[a]ble Earle of Manchester still is) had noe purpose after Newhauen Colonie situated by the seaside was settled to be a distinct Gouernm[en]t that it should be putt vnder the Pattent for Connecticutt, wherof they had only framed a Coppie, before any House was Er-rected, by the seaside, from the Fortt to the Dutch, which Yett was not signed and sealed by the last King for a Pattent nor had you any Pattent, tyll your Agent Mr. Winthrop procured it aboute two Yeares since.

9 That in the yeare 1650, when the Commission[e]rs for the four Vnited Colonies of New England, mett at Hartford, the now Dutch Gouerno[u]r being then and there present, Mr. Eaton, the then Gouerno[u]r of Newhauen Colonie, complained of the Dutch Gouerno[u]rs Encroaching vpon our Colonie of Newhauen, by taking under his jurisdiction a Townshipp beyond Standford, Called Greenewich. All the Commission[e]rs (as well for Connecticutt, as for the other Colonies)

12. On November 2, 1643, the House of Lords appointed a commission of eighteen to control plantation affairs. Robert Rich, Earl of Warwick, headed the group. William Fiennes, Viscount Saye and Sele, Philip Herbert, Earl of Pembroke, and Edward Montagu, Earl of Manchester, were among the original members of the commission. Basil Fielding, Earl of Denbigh, and Francis Lennard, Lord Dacre, were apparently later appointees. *Lords Journals*, VI (n.p., n.d.), 291–292.

concluded that Greenwich and four Myles beyond it, belongs to New-haven jurisdiction, wherunto the Dutch Gouerno[u]r Yeelded, and restored it to Newhaven Colonie. Thus were our Bounds Westward settled by Consent of all.[13]

10 That when the Hono[u]r[e]d Governo[u]r of Connecticutt, John Winthrop Esq[ui]r[e] had consented to vndertake a voyage for Eng-land to procure a pattent for Connecticutt, in the yeer 1661, a freind[14] warned him by letter not to haue his hand in so vnrighteous an Act as so farr to Extend the line of theyr pattent, that the Colonie of New-haven should be involued within it, for Answer therunto, hee was pleased to certefie that friend, in two letters, which he wrote from two seuerall places, before his departure, that noe such thing was intended, but rather the contrarye: and that the Magistrates had agreed and Expressed in the pr[e]sence of some Ministers, that if theyr Lyne should Reach vs (which they knew nott the Coppie being in England)[15] yett Newhaven Colonie, should bee at full libertie, to joyne with them or nott. This Agreem[en]t so attested made vs secure who Elce could haue procured a pattent for ourselues, within our known Bounds, ac-cording to purchase without doeing any wrong to Connecticutt in theyr just Bounds and Lymitts.

11 That notwithstanding all the premisses in the year 1662, when you had receiued your Pattent vnder his Majesties hand and seale, contrarye to your promise and sollemne Confederation, and to comon Equitye; at your first Generall Assembly (which yett could not bee called Generall without vs, if we were vnder your Pattent, seeing none of vs were by you called therunto) you agreed amoung yourselues to

13. On the award arrived at by Peter Stuyvesant, director general of New Nether-land, and the commissioners of the United Colonies of New England at Hartford, Sep-tember 19, 1650, see *Plymouth Colony Records*, IX (Boston, 1859), 188–190.

14. Possibly John Davenport.

15. i.e., the copy of the grant of March 19, 1631/2, of Robert Rich, Earl of Warwick, to William, Viscount Saye and Sele, Robert, Lord Brook, Robert Rich, Charles Fiennes, Sir Nathaniel Rich, Sir Richard Saltonstall, Richard Knightly, John Pym, John Hamp-den, John Humphreys, Herbert Pelham, their heirs, assigns, and associates forever, of forty leagues of territory running west and southwest from Narragansett River in New England. By an agreement dated December 5, 1644, George Fenwick, representative of the patentees, conveyed to the colony of Connecticut the fort erected by the patentees at Saybrook, the lands on the Connecticut River, and agreed to transfer jurisdiction over the lands between the Narragansett River and Saybrook to Connecticut if it came within his power to do so. Although jurisdiction was never transferred to Connecticut, the Warwick grant is often referred to as the old patent of Connecticut. E. Hazard, *Historical Collections*, I (Philadelphia, 1792), 318–319; *Connecticut Colonial Records, 1636-1665* (Hartford, 1850), pp. 266–272, 573–574.

treat with Newhauen Colonie about Vnion, by your Commission[e]rs chosen for that End, within two or three dayes after that assembly was dissolued, but before the Ending of that session, you made an vn-righteous breach in our Colonie, by takeing vnder your Pattent, some of ours from Standford, and from Guilford, and from South Hould, contrarye to theyr Engagm[en]ts to New-Haven Colonie, and without our cosent or knowledge.[16] This being thus done, some sent from you to treat with vs, shewed some of ours your Pattent, which being read they declared to yours, that Newhauen Colonie is not at all mentioned in your Pattent, and gaue you some reasons why they beleiued that the King did not intend to putt this Colonie vnder Connecticutt with-out our desire or Knowledge: and they added that you took a præ-posterous course, in first dismembring this Colonie, and after that treating with it about vnion, which is as if one man, purposeing to treat with another man about vnion, first cutt of[f] from him an Arme and a Legg, and an Eare, then treate with him about vnion. Reuerend Mr. Stone also teacher of the Church at Hartford, was one of that Comittee who being asked what hee thought of this Action, answered, that he would not justefie it.[17]

12 After that conference our Comittee sent by order of the Generall Courte by two of our Magistrates and two of our Elders, a writeing containing sundry other Reasons for our not joyneing with you,[18] who also, findeing that you persisted in your own will, and waye, declared to you, our resolution, to Appeal to his Majestie, to Explaine his true intendm[en]t and meaning in your pattent; whither it was to subject this Colonie vnder it or not; being perswaided, as we still are, that it neither was, nor is his Royall will, and pleasure, to confound this Colonie with yours, which would distroy this so long continued and so strongly settled distinction of the four Vnited Colonies of New Eng-land, without our desire or knowledge.

13 That Accordingly, wee forthwith sent our appeal to be humblye pr[e]sented to his Majesty, by some freinds in London, yet out of our dear and tender respect to Mr. Winthorps peace and honour, some of vs aduised those freinds to communicate our papers first to Hon-o[u]r[e]d Mr. Winthrop himself, to the End that we might finde out some Effectuall Expedient, to putt a good End, to this uncomfortable difference, between you and vs:[19] Els to pr[e]sent our humble adress to

16. See above, p. 214n.
17. See above, p. 202n.
18. See above, pp. 204–207.
19. See above, p. 216n.

his majestie, Accordingly it was done; and Mr. Winthrop stopped, the proceeding of our Appeal, by undertakeing to our friends that matters should be issued to our satisfaction, and in order ther unto, hee was pleased to write a Letter to Majo[u]r Mason, your Deputye Gouerno[u]r and the rest of the Courte of Connecticutt Colonie; from London. Dated March: 3d. 1662 in these words. Gentlemen, I am enformed by some Gentlmen, who are Authorized to seeke remedy heer, that since you had the late Pattent there hath binn injury done to the Gouernm[en]t of Newhaven, and in particular at Guilford and Standforde in admitting seuer[a]ll of the Inhabitants there, vnto freedome with you, and appointing officers, which hath caused deuission in the s[ai]d Townes, which may proue of dang[e]rous consequence, if not timely pr[e]uented, though, I doe hope the rise of it is from missunderstanding, and not in Designe of pr[e]judice to that Colonie, for whom I gaue assurance to theyr freinds, that theyr Rights and Intrests, should not bee disquieted or pr[e]judiced by the pattent. But if both Governm[en]ts would with vnanimous agreem[en]t vnite in one, theyr freinds judged it would bee for Advantage to both, and farther, I must lett you knowe, that testimonie heer doth affirme, that I gaue assurance before Authoretye heer, that it was not intended to medle with any Towne or Plantation, that was settled vnder any other Gouernm[en]t. Had it binn any otherwise intended or declared, it had binn injurious in taking out the pattent, not to have enserted a proportionable number of theyr names in it, now vpon the whole haueing had serious conference, with theyr friends Authorized by them, and with others who are freinds to both, to pr[e]uent a tedious and Chargeable Tryall, and vncertaine Euent here, I promised them, to giue you speedily this representacion, how farr you are Engaged, if any injurye hath binn done, by admitting of freemen or appointing officers, or any other intermedling with Newhaven Colonie, in one kinde or other without approbacion of the Gouernm[en]te that it be forethwith recalled, and that for future there will bee noe imposeing upon them nor admitting of any members without mutuall consent, but that all things be acted as loueing Neighbouring Colonies, as before such pattent graunted. And vnto this I judg you are obliged, I haueing Engaged to theyr Agents here, that this wilbe by you performed and they haue therupon forboren to giue you, or mee, any further trouble. But they doe not doubt but upon future consideration there may be such a right vnderstanding between both Gouernm[en]ts that an vnion and friendly joyning may be established to the satisfaction of

al, which at my arriueall I shall endeauour (God willing) to promote
not haueing more at pr[e]sent in this case, I rest

Your humble s[e]rvante

JOHN WINTHROP.[20]

The Coppie of this letter was sent to Mr. Leete vnsealed; with Mr.
Winthrops consent, and was written by his owne hand, and the substance of this agreem[en]t between some of our friends, in London, is
fully attested by them, in theyre letters to some of vs. Say not that
Mr. Winthrops acting in this agreem[en]t is nothing to you; for he
Acted therin as your publick and Comon Agent and plenipotentiary,
and therfore his actings in that capacitie and relation are yours in
him.

14 That after Mr. Winthrops returne, when some from you treated,
againe with our comittee about vnion, it was answered, by our comittee, that we could not admitt any treaty with you about that matter,
tyll we might treate as an intire Colonie our members being restored
to vs, whome you haue vnrighteously withheld from vs, wherby also
those parties haue bine many wayes injuriouse to this Gouernm[en]t,
and disturbers of our peace; which is and will be a Barr, to any such
treatie, till it be remoued, for, tyll then we cannot joine with you in
one Gouernm[en]t without fellowship in your sin.

15 That after this, nothing being done by you for our just satisfaction; at the last meeting of the Commission[e]rs, from the four Vnited
Colonies of New England, at Boston on the [3rd] day of Septemb[e]r
1663,[21] the Commission[e]rs from Newhauen Colonie Exhibited, to the
other Commission[e]rs theyr confederates, a complainte of the greate
injuries done to this Colonie, by Connecticutt in the pr[e]sence of
your Commission[e]rs, who for answer therunto, shewed what
treaties, they haue had with Newhaven. But that plea was inconsiderable through your persisting in vnrighteously withholding our mem-
b[e]rs from vs, whearby our wounds remaine vnhealed, being keept
open and continually bleeding. The result of the Commission[e]rs
debates, about that complaint was in these words; The Commission[e]rs of Massachusetts and Plimouth haueing considerd the Complaints Exhibited by Newhaven, against Connecticutt, for infringeing
theyr power of jurisdiction, as in the complainte is more particularly

20. See above, pp. 216–217n.

21. The commissioners of the United Colonies of New England met at Boston, September 3–19, 1663. For the attitude of Massachusetts and Plymouth at that time, see
Plymouth Colony Records, X (Boston, 1859), 309–310.

expressed, togeither with the Answer returned therto by Connecticutt Commission[e]rs with some other Debates and conferences, that haue passed between them; doe judge meet to Declare that the s[ai]d Colonie of Newhauen, being owned, in the Articles of Confederation, as distinct from Connecticutt, and haueing bin soe owned, by the Colonies, in this pr[e]sent meeting in all theyr actings, may not by any act of viollence, haue their libertie of jurisdiction infringed by any other of the Vnited Colonies, without breach of the Articles of confœderation: and that where any Act of power hath bin Exerted, against their Authoritie, that the same ought to be recalled; and their power reserued to them intire: vntill such time as in an orderly waye, it shall be otherwise disposed And for particular greiuances, mentioned in theyr complainte, that they be reffered to the next meeting at Hartford, etc. Wee suppose that when they speak of disposeing it otherwise, in an orderly way, they mean with our free consent, there being noe other orderly way by any Act or power of the Vnited Colonies, for disposeing the Colonie of Newhauen, otherwise then as it is a distinct Colonie, haueing intire jurisdiction within it self; which our confederates are bound by theire solemne confederation to pr[e]serue, inviolate.

16 That before your Generall Assembly in Octob[e]r last 1663, our Comittee sent a letter vnto the s[ai]d Assembly,[22] wherby they did request, that our members, by you injustly rent from us, should be by you restored vnto vs, according to our former frequent desires, and according to Mr. Winthrops letter and, and, and promise to Authority in England: and according to justice: and according to the conclusion of the Commission[e]rs in theire last session at Boston, whereunto you returned a Reall negative answer contrary to all the pr[e]mises, by makeing one Brown[23] your Constable at Stamforde, who hath been sundrie wayes injurious to vs, and hath scandalously acted in the highest degree of contempt not onely against the Authority of this jurisdiction, but also of the King himself, pulling downe with contumelies, the declaration, which was sent thither, by the Courte of Magistrates for this Colonie, in the Kings name, and comanded to bee sett vp in a publick place, that it might bee read and obeyed by all his Majesties subjects inhabiting our Towne of Stamford.

17 That thereupon at a Generall Courte held at Newhaven for the jurisdiccion the 22th of Octob[e]r 1663, the Deputies for this Generall Courte signified, the minde of our freemen, as not at all satisfied with the proposall, of the comittee, from Conecticutt but thought there

22. See above, pp. 221–222.
23. See above, p. 215n.

should be noe more treatie with them vnless they first restore vs to our Right state againe. The matter was largely debated; and this Gener-[a]ll Courte considering how they of Conecticutt doe cast of[f] our motion, in the forementioned letter and giue vs noe Answer, but that contrary thereunto, as is reported they haue further encouraged those at Guilford and Stamford; therfore this Courte did then order, that noe treaty be made by this Colonie with Conecticutt, before such acts of power exerted vpon any of our Townes, be reuoked, and re-called according to Hono[u]r[e]d Mr. Winthrops letter ingageing the same, the Comission[e]rs advice, and our frequent desires.

18 That in this juncture of time wee receiued two letters from Eng-land, mentioned in the following Declaration, published by the Courte of Magistrates, vpon that occasion in these words: whereas this Colo-nie hath receiued one Letter under his Majesties Royall hand and seale (manuall in red wax) annexed, bearing date the 21th of June, 1663. from his Royall Courte at Whitehall, directed to his Trustie and well beloued subjects, The Governo[u]rs and assistants of the Massa-chusetts, Plimouth, Newhaven, and Conecticutt Colonies in New England,[24] And one other letter from the Lords of his Majesties most honourable priuie Counsell, from his Majesties Courte aforesaid, bear-ing date the 24th of June in the Yeare afores[ai]d, superscribed, for his Maj[es]ties speciall seruice and directed to our Very Loveing Friend, John Endeicott Esq[ui]r[e] Gouernour of his Maj[es]ties plantacions in New England, and to the Gouernour and consell of the Colonie of the Massachusetts, with the rest of the Gouerno[u]rs of the English Plantations in New England respectiuely: and by order of the Gener-[a]ll Courte at Boston, Recorded in that Courte it is particularly directed, to the Gouerno[u]r of the Colonie of Newhaven.[25] In which letters his Maj[es]ty hath Comanded this Colonie, many matters of weight, very much respecting his Maj[es]ties seruice and the good of this Cuntrye in Gener[a]ll, expecting vpon displeasure the strict ob-servance thereof, which this Courte (this Colonie being situated by the seaside and soe fitly accomodated to fullfill his Maj[es]ties Comandes)

24. For the letter of the king to the governors and assistants of Massachusetts, Plym-outh, New Haven, and Connecticut colonies, June 21, 1663, ordering them to protect the Narragansett proprietors, see *Calendar of State Papers, Colonial Series, 1661–1668* (London, 1880), nos. 494, 495, 496, 497; *New Haven Colonial Records, 1653–1665* (Hart-ford, 1858), pp. 499–500, 510–512.

25. For the letter of the privy council to the governors of the New England colonies, June 24, 1663, see *Calendar of State Papers, Colonial Series, 1661–1668* (London, 1880), nos. 500, 501, 539, 540, 541, 542; *New Haven Colonial Records, 1653–1665* (Hartford, 1858), pp. 510–512.

are resolued to theyr vtmost to obey and fulfill. But in theyr consultation thereaboute, they finde through the disloyall and seditious principles, and practises, of some men of inconsiderable Intrests some of
his Maj[es]ties good subjects in this Colonie haue binn seduced to
rent themselues from this Colonie, by which diuission his Maj[es]ties
affaires in these parts are like to suffer, the peace of this Countrey to be
indangered, and the Heathen amoung vs scandallized, in case some
speedie course be not taken for the pr[e]vention therof: the which if
wee should conive at, Espetially at this time, his Maj[es]ty haueing so
particularly directed his Royall comandes to this Colonie, as afore-
s[ai]d, we might justly encurr his displeasure against vs; this courte
therefore doth in his Maj[es]tys name require al the members and inhabitants of this Colonie heartily to close with the endeauo[u]rs of the
Governo[u]r and assistants therof, for fulfilling his Maj[es]ties
comandes in the s[ai]d Letters Expressed and in order there vnto to
returne to theire due obedience, and payeing theire Arrears of rates
for defraying the necessary charges of the Colonie, and other dues,
within six dayes after the publication hereof vnto such person or
persons, as are or shall be appointed to collect the same, in attendance
to the lawes and orders of this Colonie, All which being done, this
courte shall foreuer pass by, all former disobedience to this Govern-
m[en]t. But if any shall pr[e]sume to stand out against his Maj[es]ties
pleasure soe declared as afores[ai]d, concerneing this Colonie, at theire
perill be it: This Court shall not faile to call the s[ai]d persons to a
strict Account, and proceed against them as disloyall to his Maj[es]ty,
and disturbers of the peace of this Colonie, according to Lawe.

19 This Declaration being grounded in generall upon his Maj[es]ties
Comands expressed in those letters, and in speciall in order to the
pr[e]seruation of his Maj[es]ties Customes in that case prouided for by
Act of this pr[e]sent Parliament,[26] which Act was sent inclosed with
the letter to our Governo[u]r requireing his strict obseruance of the
same vnder the penalty of displaceing and a thousand pounds fine, and
therfore in case any differince should arrise to his Maj[es]ty vpon
these Accounts, we must be inforced, to laye the cause of it at your
doore, because when it was sent to the seuerall Townes of this Colonie,

---

26. The so-called First Navigation Act was passed by the Convention Parliament in
1660 and confirmed in 1661. An explanatory act was passed in 1662. The Second Navigation Act was passed in 1663. It was probably the first of these acts that was sent to
New England in the letter of June 24, 1663. 12 Charles II, c. 18; 14 Charles II, c. 11; 15
Charles II, c. 7; The Statutes of the Realm (9 vols., London, 1810–22), V, 246–250; 394–
395; 449–452.

and sett vp in publick places, to be seen and read of all, that all might obey it, it was at Stamford, violently plucked downe, by Browne your Constable, and with reproachfull speeches rejected, though sent in his Maj[es]ties name, and by the Authority of our Court of Magistrates. And after it was published at Guilford, Bray Rosseter,[27] and his sone, hastened to Conecticutt to require your Aid against this Gouernm[en]t, which accordingly, you to hastily performed, for on the 30th of Decemb[e]r 1663, two of your Magistrates with sundry young men,

27. The absorption of the New Haven Colony by Connecticut gave rise to a long-standing difference between William Leete, the last governor of the New Haven Colony, and Bray or Bryan Rossiter, an inhabitant of Guilford. As soon as Connecticut received a copy of the charter of 1662, it laid claim to the territory of the New Haven Colony and New Netherland. Before the New Haven Colony had submitted to the rule of Connecticut, sundry inhabitants of Guilford, of whom Rossiter was probably one, journeyed to Hartford and submitted to that colony. A general court of Connecticut of October 9, 1662, received these secessionists and promised them protection. An effort on the part of the New Haven Colony to collect arrears in rates from the secessionists in December, 1663, resulted in the complaint of Bryan Rossiter and other inhabitants of Guilford to Connecticut. On December 28, 1663, the council of Connecticut sent Samuel Wyllys and John Allyn, magistrates, and Wait Still Winthrop to Guilford to treat with Governor Leete. Apparently in expectation of a brawl, the delegates were accompanied by James Richards and other young men from Connecticut. Upon the arrival of the Connecticut men at Guilford at ten o'clock at night, December 30, 1663, a riot occurred. Governor Leete, himself a resident of Guilford, sent to New Haven and Branford for troops to quell the disorder, and Rossiter fled from Guilford. Although Leete acted in an official capacity, and upon the submission of the New Haven Colony to Connecticut was protected by an act of oblivion, Rossiter brought suit for damages to the amount of £300 against him in the general court of Connecticut of May 11, 1665. On July 13, 1665, Governor Winthrop called a meeting of the particular court at Hartford to deal with the case of Bryan Rossiter against William Leete and William Seward. At this time the jury disagreed. On October 12, 1665, William Leete appealed to the general court at Hartford for a hearing and determination of the case between Rossiter and himself. This court decided that Leete was protected by the act of oblivion. The general court of Connecticut of May 10, 1666, reversed this decision, however, and awarded Rossiter £100 damages, to be paid out of the levy of the following spring, £60 of which was to come from the towns of New Haven, Guilford, Branford, and Milford. Although the general court of May 9, 1667, remitted the £60 to be levied upon the towns of the *quondam* New Haven Colony, and decided that the whole £100 should be drawn from the treasury of Connecticut, animosity between Rossiter and his neighbors remained long unabated. *New Haven Colonial Records, 1653–1665* (Hartford, 1858), *passim; Connecticut Colonial Records, 1636–1665; 1665–1677* (Hartford, 1850, 1852), *passim; New Haven Town Records, 1662–1684* (New Haven, 1919), *passim;* Connecticut State Library, Connecticut Archives, Miscellaneous Papers, I, nos. 74, 75; Office of the Secretary of State, Hartford, Probate Records, III, 31, 38, 39; Massachusetts Historical Society *Collections*, 3d series, X (Boston, 1849), 73–76; 4th series, VII (Boston, 1865), 546–548, 564–565; B. C. Steiner, *A History of the Plantation of Menunkatuck and of the Original Town of Guilford, Connecticut* (Baltimore, 1897), pp. 99–108.

and your Marshall came speedily to Guilford, accompanieing Rosseter and his sone, and countinanceing them and theyr partie, against the Authority of this Gener[a]ll Court, though you knowe how obnoxious they were formerly to this jurisdiction, for contempt of Authority, and seditious practises, and that they haue been the Ring Leaders of this Rent, and that Bray Rosseter the father, hath been long, and still is a man of a turbulent, Restless, factous spiritt, and whose designe you haue cause to suspect, to be, to cause a Warre between these two Colonies, or to ruine Newhaven Colonie. Yet him you accompanied in oppossition to this Colonie, without sending, or writeing before to our Governo[u]r to be informed concerning the trueth in this matter. Sundry Horses (as we are informed) accompanied them, to Guilford; whither they came at vnseasonable houre, about tenn a Clock in the Night these short dayes, when you might rationally thinke that all the people were gone to bed, and by shooting of sundry Gunns, some of yours or of theyr partie in Guilford allarmed the Towne: which when the Gouerno[u]r took notice of, and of the unsatisfieing Answer giuen to such as inquired the reason of that disturbance, he suspected, and that not without cause, that hostile attempts were intended, by theyr company, whereupon he sent a letter to Newhaven, to informe the Magistrates there, concerning matters at Guilford, that many were affrighted, and he desired that the Magistrates of Newhauen would pr[e]sently come to theyr succour, and as many of the Troopers as could be gott, alleadging for a Reason, his apprihension of theyr desperate Resolutions. The Gouerno[u]rs messenger also excited to haste, as apprehending danger and reporting to them that Brandford went up in Armes, hastening to theyr releife at Guilford, which the Gouerno[u]r required with speed. Hereupon Newhauen was also allarmed that Night, by Beating the Drume, etc. to warne the Towne Militia to be readie, etc. This feare was not causeless, for what elce could bee gathered from the pr[e]perations of pistolls, bulletts, swords, etc. which they brought with them, and by the threatning speeches, giuen out by some of them; as is attested by the dopositions, of some and subscriptions of others, which we haue by vs to shew when need require, and your two Magistrates themselues who ought to haue kept the Kings peace amoung theyr owne partie, and in theire owne speeches threatned our Governo[u]r that if anything was done against those men, vizt. Rosseter and his partie; Conecticutt would take it as done against themselues, for they was bound to protect them, and they rose high in threatnings. Yet they joyned therwith theyr desire of another conference, with Newhaven, prætending theyr purpose of graunting to vs, what wee should desire, soe farr as they could, if wee would vnite with them. But still they held our members from vs, and vpheld them in theyr animosities against vs. Is this the Way to vnion? and what cann you graunte vs, which we haue not in our owne Right, within our selues without you? Yea it is the birthright of our posterity which we may not Barter a waye from them by treaties, with you. It is our purchased inheritances, which noe wise man would part with upon a Treatie to receiue in lieu therof a lease of the same, upon your Tearmes, who haue noe right thereunto. And why is our vnion with you by our comeing vnder your pattent vrged now as necessary for peace? seeing wee haue enjoyed peace Mutually, while wee haue bin distinct Colonies, for a boue twenty years past. And why doe you seperate the things which god hath joyned togeither, Vizt. Righteousness and peace? seeing you persist in your vnrighteous dealing with vs, and perswade vs to peace. It is true wee all came to New England for the same ends, and that we all agree in some maine things; but it doth not followe from thence wee ought therfore to vnite with you in the same jurisdiccion; for the same may be saide of all the Vnited Colonies, which neuertheless are distinct Collonies.

20 That vpon a more dilligent search of your pattent, we finde that Newhaven Colonie is not included within the line of your pattent for we suppose that your Bounds according to the Expression of your pattent, may be in a just Gramaticall construction, so cleared, as that this Colonie in Euery parte of it, may be Mathematically demonstrated to be Exempted from it.

21 That, the pr[e]mises being duely weighed, it will be your wisdome and way to desist wholy and foreuer from Endeauouring to draw vs unto an vnion vnder your Pattent by any Treatje for the future, and to applye your selues to your duety towards God, the King, and vs, 1th. Toward God, that you feare him, and therfore repent of your vnrighteous dealing with vs, and reforme what you haue done amiss, by restoreing our Members without delaye vnto vs againe, that you may escape the wrath of God which is reuealed from heaven against all vnrighteousness, and against all that dishonour his holy name, especially amoung the heathen: which you haue done therby. 2. Toward the King that you hono[u]r him by lookeing at vs as a distinct Colonie, within our selues, as you see by the præmises, his Maj[es]ty doth, and by restoring vs to our former intire state, and our members to vs in obedience to his Maj[es]ty, who hath comanded vs as a distinct Colonie, to serue him in weighty affaires, and wherein if you hinder vs (as you will if you still withhould our members from vs, as much as in

you lieth) you will incurr his Maj[es]ties just and high displeasure, who hath not giuen you in your Pattent the least appearance of a just ground for your Layeing any claime to vs. 3. Toward vs, your Neigh-bours, your Bretheren, your Confœderates, by vertue wherof it is your dutye to pr[e]serue vnto vs our Colonie state, power, and priui-lidges, against all others that would oppose vs there in, or incroach vpon vs. Is Rosseter, and his partie of such vallue with you that what this jurisdiccion doth against them, your Colonie will take it as done to them selues[?] But if it be said as one of your Comittee is reported to Express it, that you must performe your promise to them, as Joshua, and Eld[e]rs of Israell, did to the Gibeonites;[28] doe you not see the sundry disparities between that vow and yours? or doe you indeed make conscience of your vow to Gibeonites, if you tearm them soe and without regard to your consciences break your promise, and most sol-lemne confœderation to Israelites? Doubtless it will not be safe for this Colonie, to joyne in one Gouernm[en]t with persons of such prin-ciples and practises, noe treatye will be able to bring vs to it. Wee beleiue that our Righteous God, to whom wee haue sollemnly and publickly commended and committed our righteous cause, will pro-tect vs against all that shall any way wrong and oppress vs, Neither will wee at all doubt the justice of his Maj[es]tie our King, as well as yours, and of his most Hono[u]r[a]bl[e] Counsell, but that upon hear-ing the buisness opened before them, they will effectually releiue vs, against your unjust encroachm[en]ts, as the matter shall require. Wee desire peace and loue between vs, and that we may for the future liue in love and peace togeither, as distinct Neighbour Colonies as wee did above twenty years togeither, before you receiued and missunder-stood, and soe abused your pattent, and in hope that our uncomfort-able and afflictiue Excersises, by your Encroachments upon our Rights would issue herein, we haue soe long borne what wee haue suffred for peace sake, now it is high time that we bring these unbrotherly con-tests wherewith you have troubled vs to a peaceable issue. In order thereunto we doe offer you this choise; either to returne our members unto vs uolluntarily, which wilbe your hono[u]r, and a confirmation of our mutuall love, or to remoue them to some other plantation within your owne bounds, and free vs wholy from them; for we may not beare it that such fœdifrayeus disorderly persons shall continue within the Townes, belonging to this Colonie, to disturb our peace, dispise our Gouernm[en]t and disquiett our members, and disable us to obey the Kings comands: But if they stay where they now are, wee shall

28. Joshua 9. 15, 18–21, 26.

take our time to proceed, according to justice, Especially with Browne for his contempt of the Declaration, and therin of the Kings comands, and of the Authority of this jurisdiccion, and with Bray Rosseter and his sonne for all theyr seditious practices.

Lastly for pr[e]vencion of any misap[p]r[e]hencion, we Crave leave to explaine our meaning in any passages in this writing, which may seeme to Reflect Censure of vnrighteous dealing with vs, vpon your Colony, or Generall Assembly that we meane only such as have bin active instrum[en]ts therein:

New Haven
March 9th. 16$\frac{63}{64}$ ffrom the Committee By order of the Gen[era]ll Court of Newhaven Colony. JAMES BISHOP *Secretary*

[Endorsed] New Hauens Case Stated March 9th $\frac{63}{4.}$

JOHN DAVENPORT *to* JOHN WINTHROP the Younger[1]
To the Right Worsh[i]p[fu]ll John Winthrope Esq. Governo[u]r of Connectacute these present

Honoured Sir)

MY love to your person constraineth me, upon this occasion, to wright a few lines to you, if by any good meanes any inconvenience to yourselfe may be prevented. The acting of your general Assembly[2] will seeme very strange, if not irrational, to unbyassed

1. Massachusetts Historical Society, Winthrop MSS., III, 148; printed in Massachusetts Historical Society *Collections*, 4th series, VII (Boston, 1865), 525–526. Under the same date, both the magistrates of the New Haven Colony and John Scott wrote Winthrop on the same subject. "The Wyllys Papers," Connecticut Historical Society *Collections*, XXI (Hartford, 1924), 152–154.

2. An inhabitant of Setauket or Ashford, Long Island, early in 1663 John Scott was in England as the agent of the New Haven Colony. After his return to New England, he accepted a commission as magistrate on Long Island from Connecticut, but soon joined in a movement to take Long Island for James, Duke of York. On March 3, 1663/4, a court at Hartford ordered its secretary to authorize Richard Woodhull of Setauket to issue a warrant for the arrest of Scott if some one would undertake to prosecute him. On March 10, 1663/4, a general court at Hartford ordered the seizure of Scott as a traitor to the colony. On March 21, 1663/4, the day before the writing of this protest, Jonathan Gilbert, marshal of Connecticut, and five or six others attempted to take Scott at New Haven but failed. On March 26, 1664, Nathan Gold of Fairfield, a magistrate of Connecticut, sent Nathaniel Seely and fifteen or sixteen others to Setauket to arrest Scott on a special warrant. Scott was seized and carried first to Stratford and later to Hartford, where he was placed in "hold and chains." At this point the governor and

observers or hearers thereof, 1, that they take accusacions against such a man, as Capt. Scot, from such witnesses as his Accusers will be found to be, against whom he hath declared his exceptions before our Magistrates[3] and your Marshal and which will be allowed as sufficient to dissable theyre testimonie, in any Court in England. 2. That your Marshal[4] was sent to Newhaven Milford, Stratford etc. to apprehend C. S. as if these townes were alike under Connectecute jurisdiction.[5] And this, he saith, is done by order from your General Court. 3. That his Commission, as he saith, is to accuse any that doe not obeie it, as Abettors and Concealers of a notorious Malefactour, which he did twise most absurdly, 1st against our Deputie-Governo[u]r[6] before he had given any Answer. The 2d time, to boath our Magistrates[7] and those of the Committie then present, who onely required to have a copie of his Commission and charges ag[ain]st C. S. promising that when they had considered it, they would give theyre Answer in wrighting: and in the meane time, Mr. Jones, reading that Article of the Confœderacion, which concernes that case,[8] he promised to performe it punctually yet, after these passages, he so protested, whereupon he

magistrates of the New Haven Colony appealed to the assistants of Massachusetts to support Scott. On May 12, 1664, Connecticut sequestered Scott's estate. On May 18, 1664, William Pitkin, attorney of Connecticut, undertook to prosecute Scott for usurping the authority of the king and defaming the king's majesty before the particular court at Hartford. On May 24 Scott was found guilty, fined £250, and imprisoned. In July he escaped from his gaoler, and in August the general court of Connecticut ordered his seizure as a traitor. *Connecticut Colonial Records, 1636–1665* (Hartford, 1850), pp. 418, 420–422; *New Haven Colonial Records, 1653–1665* (Hartford, 1858), pp. 541–542.

3. At this time William Leete was governor; Mathew Gilbert, deputy governor; and William Jones, Benjamin Fenn, Robert Treat, and Jasper Crane, magistrates of the New Haven Colony.

4. Jonathan Gilbert.

5. Stratford lay within the limits of Connecticut, but New Haven and Milford were within the limits of the New Haven Colony.

6. Mathew Gilbert.

7. Probably Mathew Gilbert and William Jones, the two magistrates residing in New Haven.

8. "... And that vpon the escape of any prisoner whatsoeuer or fugitiue for any criminall cause, whether breaking prison or getting from the officer or otherwise escapeing vpon the certificate of two Magestrats of the Jurisdiccion out of which the escape is made, that he was a prisoner or such an offender at the tyme of the escape, The Ma[gis]-trates or some of them of that Jurisdiccion where for the pr[e]sent the said prisoner or fugitiue abideth shall forthwith graunt such a warrant as the case will beare for the appr[e]hending of any such person, and the deliuery of him into the hands of the officer, or other person who pursues him And if there be help required for the safe returneing of any such offendor, then it shalbe graunted to him that craues they same he payinge the charges thereof." *Plymouth Colony Records,* IX (Boston, 1859), 7.

was told that he was a rash man and that your General Assembly would not justifie him therein. Yet he stood to it, that it was according to his order. 4 Nor doth the law of England allow that any man shall be proclaimed a malefactor etc. til convicted. Many things I might add, but am called off. For yourselfe, Honour[e]d Sir) I feare you will not doe your selfe right, unles you protest against these irregular, illegal, I had almost said, unchristian actings, and enter it upon record. You now see, I suppose, that we have abundant cause to refuse union with that Colonie, which multiplies injuries against us, without ceasing. The Lord Jesus be with your spirit and familie! In whom I rest

N[ew] H[aven] the 22d of March. $166\frac{3}{4}$ Sir

Yours obliged assured

JOHN DAVENPORTE

[Endorsed] Mr. Davenport Senior [by John Winthrop, and] March 22d. *1663/4* [in a modern hand.]

Agreement Between JOHN DAVENPORT and WILLIAM GOODWIN Regarding the Disposal of the Legacy of EDWARD HOPKINS[1]

WHEREAS, the Wor[shi]p[fu]ll Edward Hopkins Esq[ui]r[e] a faithfull servant of the Lord, and our worthily honoured ffrend, hath in his last Will, and testament (proved according to law, in England, and Demonstracion thereof made to the Generall Court att Hartford in New England) Given, and bequeathed all his estate in New England (his debts there, and Legacies being first paid out of the same) Vnto Theophilus Eaton Esq[ui]r[e] John Davenport Pastor to the Church of Christ att Newhaven; Capt. John Cullick, and William Goodwin, sometyme of Hartford, since of Boston, and Had[ley] in the Colony of the Massachusets, Confideing in theire faithfullnes for the Improvem[en]t of the Same for the Educacion of Youth in good Litterature to fit them for the Service of Christ in theise fforraign parts, Wee therefore the said John Davenport, and W[illia]m Goodwin, the the only Survivo[u]rs of the s[ai]d Trustees, that we may answ[e]r the s[ai]d trust Reposed in vs, Doe Order and dispose of the s[ai]d Estate, as

1. New Haven, Hopkins Grammar School Records, I, 9–10; printed in L. W. Bacon, *An Historical Discourse, on the Two Hundredth Anniversary of the Founding of the Hopkins Grammar School, New Haven, Connecticut* (New Haven, 1860), pp. 51–52.

ffolloweth, Vizt. To the towne of Hartford we doe give the Summ of ffower hundred pounds, of which Hills ffarme[2] shall be a part att the Same price att which it was sold by vs, and the pay Ready to be delivered, if there had bin noe Interuption the Rest of the £400: in such debts, and goods as we, or our Agents shall see mett, provided that this part be Improved according to the ends of the Donor, vizt. for the erecting, and maintaining of a schoole at Hartford. Provided alsoe that the Gen[era]ll Court att Hartford doe graunt and give unto vs a writing legally Confirmed, engaging that neither themselvs will, nor any by from or vnd[e]r them shall disturbe, or hinder vs, in our Dispose, or Executing our dispose of the Rest of the estate, Which don this guift is in all Respects Valid. We doe also desire, and Request that the schoolehouse may be set vpon the houselot which was lately in the occupacion of Jeremy Adams,[3] where our Worthy ffrend did much desire, and endevo[u]r that a schoolehouse might be set. ffurther our desire is that the managem[en]t of the s[ai]d estate att Hartford may be in the hands of Deacon Edward Stebbing, and Leivt: Thomas Bull, and their Assignes. Wee doe further Order and appoint the Rest of the estate of the said Edward Hopkins Esq[ui]r[e] (the Debts being paid) to be all of it equally devided betweene the townes of Newhaven,[4] and Hadley,[5] to be in both these townes managed, and Improved for the erecting and maintaining of a schoole, in each of the s[ai]d townes, And the managem[en]t thereof to be in the hands of our Assignes, which are the towne Court of Newhaven Consisting of the Magistrats, and Deputyes together with the officers of the Church there in the behalfe of the said Mr. John Davenport, and John Russell Jun[io]r Levt: Samuell Smith[6] Andrew Bacon, and Peeter Tilton[7] of Hadley in

2. Four tracts at Hockanum, comprising fifty-six acres, originally known as the Hopkins farm, later in the improvement of William Hills. On January 18, 1665/6, it was recorded to the town for the "maintenance of the Latin School." W. D. Love, *The Colonial History of Hartford* (Hartford, 1935), pp. 251–275.

3. This was the original homelot of Samuel Greenhill, whose widow married Jeremy Adams. It was located on the west side of the present Main Street, between the Little River and Buckingham Street. The school was not settled there, however, but upon the original homelot of Andrew Warner.

4. On the early history of the Hopkins Grammar School at New Haven, see I. M. Calder, *The New Haven Colony* (New Haven, 1934), p. 143.

5. From Hopkins' estate in New England, the town of Hadley, Massachusetts, received £308. On the Hopkins Grammar School at Hadley, see S. Judd, *History of Hadley* (Northampton, 1863), pp. 56–70.

6. Lieutenant Samuel Smith had removed from Wethersfield, Connecticut, to Hadley, Massachusetts.

7. Peter Tilton had removed from Windsor, Connecticut, to Hadley, Massachusetts, in 1659.

the Behalfe of Mr. W[illia]m Goodwin, Only provided that one hundred pounds out of that halfe of the Estate which Hadley hath, shall be given, and paid to Harvard Colledge[8] soe soone, as we the said John Davenport, and W[illia]m Goodwin see meet, and to be ordered as we, or our assignes shall Judge most Conduceing to the end of the Donor.

Heerevnto as to our last order, dispose, and Determinacion touching the said estate we have set our hands, and Seales, in Severall Instrum[en]ts before Wittnesses, the far Distance of our habitacions, and our Vnfitnes for such a Jorney, denying vs oportunity of a Joint acting otherwise then by writeing. Therefore with mutuall Consent we thus Declare our agreem[en]t: I the s[ai]d W[illia]m Goodwin, doe Signe, and seale this Instrum[en]t as my true Agreem[en]t for Mr. John Davenport of Newhaven.

The words (of Hadley) betweene the 26 and 27 line were Interlined before the Subscribing and Sealing.   Seale

The 13th day of the 4th Moneth 1664.   W[ILLIA]M GOODWIN   *

Signed and Sealed in the pr[e]sence
of vs
    HENRY CLARKE[9]
    W[ILLIA]M WESTWOOD.[10]

The aboue and before Recorded Agreem[en]t is a true entry of the Originall made by
               me W[ILLIA]M JONES No[ta]ry publiq[u]e.

---

8. The £100 was paid to Harvard College in corn and meat some time after December, 1663. "Harvard College Records, I," Colonial Society of Massachusetts *Publications*, XV (Boston, 1925), 215.

9. Henry Clarke had removed from Windsor, Connecticut, to Hadley, Massachusetts.

10. William Westwood had removed from Hartford, Connecticut, to Hadley, Massachusetts.

A COMMITTEE OF THE NEW HAVEN COLONY *to* CONNECTICUT[1]

Hono[u]r[e]d Gent[lemen]:

WEE haveing been silent hithertoo, as to the makeing of any grievance knowne unto the kings Commission[e]rs, notwithstanding
what may be with us of such nature, from the severall transactions
that have been amongst us, are desirous soe to Continue the mannaging
of these Affayres in wayes Consistent with the Ancient Confœderation
of the united Colonies, Chuseing rather to suffer, then to begin any
motion hazardfull to N[ew]-England settlem[en]ts: In pursuance
whereof, (according to our promise to your Gent[lemen] sent lately to
demand our submission, though in a divided, if not deviding way,
within our townes severally, seeking to bring us under the government
by your selves already settled, wherein we have had noe hand to settle
the same, and before you had Cleared to our Conviction the Certaine
Limits of your Charter, which may justly increase the scruple of too
much hast in that and former actings upon us) the generality of our
undevided people, have orderly mett the 13th of 10th mo[nth] (64),
and by the vote inclosed have pr[e]pared for this answer (to be given)
of our submission, which being done by us, then for the accommodating
of matters betwixt us in amicable wise, by a Committee impowered to
issue with you on their behalfe, and in the behalfe of all Concerned,
according to instructions given to the s[ai]d Committee: Wee never
did, nor ever doe intend to damnify your Morall Rights, or just privi-
lidge, consistent with our like honest enjoym[en]ts, And we would hope
that you have noe further scope towards us, not to violate our Cove-
n[an]t interest, but to accomodate us with that we shall desire, and
the Pattent beare, as hath been often s[ai]d you would doe, And surely
you have the more reason to be full with us herein, seeing that your
success for Pattent Bounds with those Gent[lemen] now obtained,
seemes to be debto[u]r unto our silence before them, when as you thus
by single aplication and audience issued that matter; You thus per-
formeing to satisfaction, we may still rest silent, and according to pro-

1. Connecticut State Library, Manuscript New Haven Colonial Records, 1653–1664,
fols. 386–387; printed in *New Haven Colonial Records, 1653–1665* (Hartford, 1858),
pp. 552–553. A general court of the New Haven Colony, freemen of New Haven, Guilford, Branford, and part of Milford, and inhabitants met at New Haven December 13,
1664, and appointed the members of the general court, the elders, John Nash and James
Bishop of New Haven, Francis Bell of Stamford, and Robert Treat and Richard Baldwin of Milford, with John Fowler of Guilford as alternate, a committee to consummate
the union of the New Haven Colony and Connecticut.

fession by a studious and Cordiall endeavo[u]r with us to advance the interest of christ in this wildernes, and by the Lords blessing thereupon, love and union betweene us may be greatly Confirmed, and all our Comforts inlarged, which is the earnest prayer of

New Haven December 14th:

1664   Gent[lemen]: your Loveing ffriends
                     and neighbo[u]rs, The Committee ap-
                     pointed by the ffreemen and inhabitants
                     of N[ew]-Haven Colony now Assembled

                                   Per JAMES BISHOP *Secretary*

A COMMITTEE OF THE NEW HAVEN COLONY *to* CONNECTICUT[1]

                                   Newhaven Jan[ua]ry. 5th. *1664:*

Hono[u]r[e]d Gent[leme]n

WHEREAS by yours dat[e]d Decemb[e]r 21th. *1664:* you please to say, that you did the same as we, in not makeing any grievance knowne to the Com[missione]rs etc. unto that may be returned, that you had not the same cause soe to doe, from any pr[e]tence of injury by our intermedling with your Colony or Coven[an]t interest, unto which we referre that passage; for our expressing desires to mannage all our matters in consistencie with the Confœderation, we hope you will not blame us, how dissonant or consonant your actings with us have been, we leave to the confœderates to judge as their records may show; that article which allowes two colonies to joine doth alsoe with others assert the justnes of each colonyes distinct right untill joined to mutuall satisfaction, and the provision made in such case the last session we gainesay not, when the union is soe compleated, and a new settlem[en]t of the Confœderation by the respective gen[era]ll courts accomplished. Their patheticall advice and counsell for an amicable union we wish may be soe attended, In order whereunto we gave you notice of a Committee pr[e]pared to treate with you for such an accomodation unto which you give us noe answer, but in stead thereof send forth your edict from authoritie upon us before our conviction for submission was declared to you; the argum[en]t from our intermixt

1. Connecticut State Library, Manuscript New Haven Colonial Records, 1653–1664, fols. 389–390; printed in *New Haven Colonial Records, 1653–1665* (Hartford, 1858), pp. 555–557.

scituation is the same now as it was before our confœderating, and ever since, and affords noe more ground now to dissanull the coven[an]t then before; we might marveile at your Strange why we should thinke your successe should be debto[u]r to our silence, and that because the newes of our noncomplyance was with the Com[missione]rs, as if the meere newes of such a thing contained the strength of all we had to say or plead; Gent[leme]n we intreate you to consider that there is more in it then soe, yea that still we have to alledge things of weight, and know where and how, if wee chose not rather to abate and suffer, then by striveing to hazard the hurting yourselves or the common cause; we scope not at reflections but conviction and conscience satis-faction, that soe brethren in the fellowship of the gospell might come to a cordiall and regular closure, and soe to walke together in love and peace to advance christ his interest among them which is all our de-signe; But how those high and holy ends are like soe to be promoved betweene us without a treaty for accomodation, wee have cause to doubt, Yet that wee may not faile in the least to performe whatever wee have said, we now signify, That haveing seene the Coppye of his Maj[es]ties Commission[e]rs determination (deciding the bounds be-twixt his Highnes the Duke of Yorke and Connecticutts Charter) wee doe declare submission thereunto according to the true intent of our Vote, unto which we referre you. As to that part of yours concerneing our Magistrates and officers acceptance: Their answer is, that they haveing been chosen by the people here to such trust, and sworne there-unto for the yeare ensueing, and untill new be orderly chosen, And being againe desired to continue that trust, they shall goe on in due observance thereof according to the declaration left with us by Mr. John Allyn and Mr. Sam[ue]ll Shearman beareing date Novemb[e]r 19th. *1664:* in hopes to find that in a loveing treaty for accomodating matters to the ends professed by you; unto which our Committee stands ready to attend upon notice from you; that soe truth and peace may be maintained. Soe shall wee not give you further trouble but remaine.

> Gent[leme]n your very Loveing friends
> and neighbo[u]rs the Committee appointed by
> the ffreemen and inhabitants of N[ew]-haven
> Colony Signed Per their order

> Per me JAMES BISHOP *Secret[a]ry.*

JOHN DAVENPORT *to* JOHN LEVERETT[1]

Honorable Sir,

LET my first salutation be my congratulation for this addition of a further expression of Gods peoples affection and confidence in your courage, wisdom and faithfulnes for the interest of our Lord Jesus and the good and wellfare of church and commonwealth, in that they have unanimously called you to be one of the assistants for governing the civill affaires in the court, as well as to be their major generall in the campe. The good Lord assist and governe you by his spirit of wisdom, of courage, and of the feare of the Lord in both.

Sir, I received yours dated 27. 3d. 65.[2] for which I returne humble and hearty thanks, and for the inclosed narrative,[3] whereby I perceive that the powers of darknes which have prevailed in other parts of the world are at worke here also, to subvert the kingdom of Christ in these ends of the earth. But God hath not yet said that this is theire hour in reference to N. E. though our unthankfulnes for the gospel, unfruitfulness under it, dissobedience to it, declensions from the simplicity that is in Christ, and sinful compliances, etc. have deserved that our hedge should be broken down. That admonition which Christ sent unto the church at Ephesus[4] should sound in our hearts continually, Repent and doe thy first workes. For even David had his first and his latter wayes. Therefore it is noticed concerning Jehosaphat, in 2 Chron. 17. 3. that the Lord was with him, because he walked in the first waies of his father David. If N. E. would returne to the first waies of reformation here begun, according to gospel rules and patternes (from which the compas of the last synods[5] conclusions seemes to be varied by some degrees towards the antartique, or is newly discovered to be other than I formerly apprehended to have been the way of these churches) I would hope that the same onely wise God who dissappointed the councel of that archprelate[6] in the raigne of the last king (whereby

1. The manuscript copy of this letter has not been found. It is printed in Thomas Hutchinson, *A Collection of Original Papers relative to the History of the Colony of Massachusets-Bay* (Boston, 1769), pp. 392–396; A. B. Davenport, *A History and Genealogy of the Davenport Family* (New York, 1851), pp. 338–343; *Hutchinson Papers* (2 vols., Albany, 1865), II, 117–121. John Leverett was chosen major general of the forces of Massachusetts Bay in 1663 and an assistant of the colony in 1665.

2. No copy of this letter has been found.

3. Apparently a narrative concerning the activities of the commissioners of Charles II.

4. Revelation 2. 5.

5. The synod at Boston in 1662 had decided to admit to baptism the children of those who had been baptized but who had not entered into full covenant with the church.

6. William Laud.

your pattent[7] was once and againe demanded by the said king, and as often refused by your generall court, to be returned to England) would also still appeare, in this juncture, by frustrating the present designe and making it an abortion, or a mere tryall of the country, whether they will stand to their church rights and priviledges or permit them to be invaded and violated by such attempts, which when they are tried and found unsuccessful, will cease for the future. For the Lord is and will be with his people while they are with him; and if yee seeke him he will be found of you.[8] An experiment hereof you had in the quiet proceeding of your elections,[9] as a gracious answer to prayers. Their claiming power to sit authoritatively as a court for appeales,[10] and that to be managed in an arbitrary way, was a manifest laying of a ground worke to undermine your whole government established by your charter. If you had consented thereunto, you had plucked downe with your owne hands that house which wisdom had built for you and your posterity. For all your courts would then have signified nothing; the sentences of them being liable to be dissannulled, upon complaints to the commissioners made by delinquents, as appeareth in the case of Mr. Tho. Deane,[11] etc. and the execution of the

7. In 1634 the privy council ordered the Massachusetts Bay Company to send over its patent. Upon the refusal of the company to do so, the Council for New England appointed Thomas Morton to prosecute a suit for repealing the patent of the Massachusetts Bay Company. Proceedings in the court of king's bench, from Trinity term, 1635, to Easter term, 1637, resulted in a judgment to seize the franchises of the corporation, and on May 3, 1637, the privy council ordered Sir John Banks, attorney general, to call in the patent. *Winthrop's Journal* (2 vols., New York, 1908), I, 129; *Calendar of State Papers, Colonial Series, 1574–1660* (London, 1860), pp. 206, 251; *Acts of the Privy Council, Colonial, 1613–1680* (Hereford, 1908), no. 366.

8. 1 Chronicles 28. 9.

9. Early in 1665 George Cartwright, Samuel Maverick, and Sir Robert Carr, three of the four commissioners appointed by Charles II to inquire into the state of New England, met at Boston. In an effort to control the membership of the next general assembly, they asked John Endecott, governor, and the council to summon all inhabitants to the court of elections, May 3, 1665. When the governor and council refused, the commissioners themselves summoned the non-freemen to the election. Despite the presence of the above-mentioned commissioners, Colonel Richard Nicolls, the fourth commissioner, and the non-freemen, the election seems to have gone off without disorder. *Massachusetts Colony Records*, IV, Part II (Boston, 1854), 141–142, 173–174, 177–178; *New York Colonial Documents*, III (Albany, 1853), 87–89, 93–94, 96–97.

10. In the cases of John Porter, Jr., and Thomas Deane, the royal commissioners were claiming this right.

11. In July or August, 1661, Jacquis Pepin, merchant, arrived at Boston in the *Charles of Oléron*. Denied permission to trade at Boston under the navigation act of 1660, he departed. Some weeks later a small Boston vessel, Richard Patteshall, master, brought a cargo of European merchandise from Mohegan to Boston, consigned to

justest censure might be hindred and the course of justice obstructed, as you have alreadie found in the case of John Potter.[12] Nor can I see that your preserving that authority and jurisdiction which the last king, by his roial charter, gave you, can rationally be accounted an opposing the soveraignety which this king hath over you, seeing *id possunt reges quod jure possunt.*[13] There is indeed a verbal profession of preserving your liberties. But if the commission of these gentlemen[14]

Joshua Scottow and his wife. The merchandise had probably been transferred from the *Charles of Oléron*, and Thomas Deane, Thomas Kirke, and Thomas Kellond seized it, upon the grounds that the navigation act of 1660 was being violated. The goods were secured and the case finally came before the general court of November 27, 1661. At this time some of the complainants and witnesses were absent and the case was postponed to the next general court. At that time it was dropped. Deane and his associates complained to the authorities in England and the royal commissioners were instructed to inquire into this and other violations of the navigation and trade laws. On May 11, 1665, the general court of Massachusetts denied failure to enforce the acts. Nevertheless, the royal commissioners summoned the governor and company of Massachusetts and Joshua Scottow to appear before them at Thomas Breeden's house, May 24, 1665, at 9:00 A.M., to answer for failure to render justice to Thomas Deane and his associates. Massachusetts refused to accept the jurisdiction of the royal commissioners, and at this point issued the declaration of May 23, 1665, published on the following day. On May 26, 1665, the general court summoned Thomas Deane and Thomas Kellond to appear before it on the following day to explain their complaints to the authorities in England. *Massachusetts Colony Records*, IV, Part II (Boston, 1854), 35–36, 194, 202, 208–210, 214–215, 218–219; *New York Colonial Documents*, III (Albany, 1853), 95–96.

12. For rebelling against his parents, John Porter, Jr., of Salem, Massachusetts, had been tried by the county court at Salem, committed to the house of correction at Ipswich, and finally freed. When his conduct showed no improvement, his father again complained to the county court at Salem, November 24, 1663, and the son was committed to prison at Boston for trial before the court of assistants, March 4, 1663/4. The court of assistants sentenced the youth to stand upon the ladder at the gallows for one hour with a rope about his neck, to be severely whipped, to be imprisoned in the house of correction at Boston for an indefinite period, and to be fined £200. The general court of October 19, 1664, released him from prison on condition that he leave the colony and stand bound to the amount of £200 never to return. Porter made his way to Warwick, Rhode Island, and appealed to George Cartwright, Samuel Maverick, and Sir Robert Carr. By a warrant under their hands of April 8, 1665, the royal commissioners granted him their protection against all authority, officers, and people, and set May 8, 1665, as the date for a hearing of his case before themselves. *Massachusetts Colony Records*, IV, Part II (Boston, 1854), 137, 177, 216–218; *New York Colonial Documents*, III (Albany, 1853), 95.

13. Rulers may do that which they have a legal right to do.

14. For the commission of April 23, 1664, see *Calendar of State Papers, Colonial Series, 1661–1668* (London, 1880), nos. 708, 709, 710; *New York Colonial Documents*, III (Albany, 1853), 64–65, where the document is misdated April 25, 1664. For instructions regarding Massachusetts, also dated April 23, 1664, see *Calendar of State Papers, Colonial Series, 1661–1668* (London, 1880), nos. 711, 712, 713, 714; *New York Colonial Documents*, III (Albany, 1853), 51–54.

be of such a latitude as they say, it is a real destruction of that which they promise to preserve. *Quid verba audiam, cum facta videam?*[15] Therefore, to me, the matter of your answer[16] seemes to be rational, just and necessary. As for the solemnity of publishing it,[17] in three places, by sounding a trumpet, I believe you did it upon good advise, and therefore, suspending my own thoughts, I shall wait to see how it is resented at the court in England. Yet, upon serious second and third thoughts, I see not but that it was your prudent way so to do, considering that, 1. It was the answer of the generall court. 2. Published in the kings name. 3. For the cognisance of the whole country concerned in it. 4. For declaring the courage and resolution of the whole countrey to defend theire charter liberties and priviledges, and not to yeeld up theire right voluntarily, so long as they can hold it, in dependance upon God in Christ, whose interest is in it, for his protection and blessing, who will be with you while you are with him. If my advise were worthy any thing, I would say, let a collection of your grievances occasioned by the coming over of these commissioners, and by their actings, in one place and another, and of the 3 commissioners in prejudicing the Indians against the English,[18] whereby the good worke for theire conversion is in danger to be hindered and the safety and peace of the English to be hazzarded, for the future; let, I say, all instances of theire illegal and injurious proceedings, throughout the countrey, be fully collected and clearly proved, and speedily transmitted and represented to the king, the lord chancellor,[19] etc. by your next addres,[20] and therein let them fully and plainly understand that

15. Why should I listen to their words, when I see their deeds?

16. For "A Declaracion of the Gen[era]ll Court of His Ma[jes]ties Colony in the Massachusets in New England, held in Boston the 23d of May 1665," dated May 23, 1665, see *New York Colonial Documents*, III (Albany, 1853), 95–96.

17. The declaration was published, May 24, 1665, by Oliver Purchase, "one of the Deputies of the Court, (being by them thereunto commanded) with sound of trumpet in the Market place in Boston below the Court House, and at the Dock head, and at the cross-way by Capt. Breedons." *Calendar of State Papers, Colonial Series, 1661–1668* (London, 1880), no. 996; *New York Colonial Documents*, III (Albany, 1853), 96, 99.

18. The royal commissioners were instructed to inquire into the state of the neighboring Indian princes. When visiting the Narragansett country early in 1665, they accepted the allegiance of an Indian sachem who had previously submitted to Charles I and received him into the king's protection, presented the Indian chieftains with coats, and renamed the country the King's Province. Upon their return to Massachusetts, they informed the general court of the great complaints of the Narragansett Indians. *New York Colonial Documents*, III (Albany, 1853), 97; *Massachusetts Colony Records*, IV, Part II (Boston, 1854), 175, 190, 198.

19. Edward Hyde, Earl of Clarendon.

20. For the petition of Massachusetts Bay to the king, August 1, 1665, see *Massachusetts Colony Records*, IV, Part II (Boston, 1854), 274–275.

the whole countrey (for the generality of them) are much aggrieved at these doings and humbly desire to be resettled in theire former state, according to theire charter, and that they may be freed from those new encroachments; wherein the petition to the generall court presented in the names of so many non-freemen,[21] declaring theire full satisfaction in the settled government, as it is, with theire earnest desire that it may be still continued without alteration, may be signified to the higher powers, to good purpose. Sir, You see whether my zeale for preserving Christs interest in your parts (though in N.H.C. it is miserably lost)[22] and my unfeigned love to your colonie and my fervent desire of the wellfare of the churches and commonwealth (so far as they may be promoted and perpetuated by your circumspection) hath carried me, through my confidence in your wisdom and faithfulnes, that you will make no other use of this my scribbling then such as shall be safe both to you and me. To the honorable governor[23] you may communicate it, if you please, presenting also to him my humble and affectionate service.

Sir, I return your copie of the articles that concerne Commameene,[24] having received them formerly from your selfe, and lately from Mr. Bishop,[25] with many thanks to you for the sight and loan of them from us both. But I am and shall be discouraged from regarding such agreement made by a subject, though honourably, til I see your charter, sealed by the late King, and obliging his heirs and successors, really as well as verbally confirmed and performed, towards the purchasing whereof I paid £50.[26] and Mr. Eaton £100.[27] and sundry

21. Inhabitants of Billerica, Boston, Cambridge, Chelmsford, Concord, Dedham, Dorchester, Medfield, Reading, Roxbury, and Woburn presented petitions expressing their satisfaction with the existing government of Massachusetts to the general court of October 19, 1664. *Massachusetts Colony Records*, IV, Part II (Boston, 1854), 136–137.

22. A general court of the New Haven Colony and freemen of New Haven, Guilford, Branford, and part of Milford met at New Haven, December 13, 1664, and voted to submit to the jurisdiction of Connecticut. The town of New Haven accepted the decision January 7, 1664/5. *New Haven Colonial Records, 1653–1665* (Hartford, 1858), pp. 550–551; *New Haven Town Records, 1662–1684* (New Haven, 1919), p. 125.

23. Richard Bellingham.

24. Unidentified.

25. James Bishop was at this time a representative of the town of New Haven in the general assembly of Connecticut at Hartford.

26. Some years later Davenport said: "I shall conclude with a brief reminding you of the first beginning of this Colony of the *Massachusets*, which I have the better advantage, and more special engagement to do; being one of them, by whom the Patent, which you enjoy, was procured; and to whom it was committed, by King *Charles* the first, and His Majesties most Honourable Privy Council. My Name was not mentioned in the Patent, because I desired it might be left out, lest the then Bishop of *London*, who was

other merchants the same sums respectively, we being members of the London corporation for N. E. which doth ingage me to desire and endeavour, what I can and may, that the intended effects thereof may remaine, for the service of Christ and for the good of all his people, both at present and for the future. I heare well of your last address to the king.[28] I should take it for a favour if I might peruse it and the king's answer.[29] I shall now cease from giving you any further trouble, but not from praying for a good issue of your and our present afflictive exercises, and not ours only but of the distressed churches of Christ, in whom I rest,

N. H. the 24 of the 4. 65.   Sir,

Your obliged assured,
JOHN DAVENPORT.

JOHN DAVENPORT *to* JOHN WINTHROP the Younger[1]
To the Honor[a]ble John Winthrope Esq. Governo[u]r of Connectecute Colonie, these præsent in Hartford

Honor[a]ble Sir)

IT seemes that the difference betweene Mr. Leete and Mr. Rossetter[2] is brought upon the stage againe to be tryed and issued in a special Courte, and a new Jurie is impannaled, not of his compeeres, but of

of the Privy Council, should have an ill eye upon me for my appearing so far in that work, whereunto he was opposit: but in expences for any Helps to promove the Work, in the first beginnings of it, I bore my part, meerly for the service of Christ, and for the help of his People, I not knowing that ever I should remove unto these parts, by vertue of that Patent." John Davenport, *A Sermon Preach'd at The Election of the Governour, at Boston in New-England, May 19th 1669* (n.p., 1670), p. 15; reprinted in Colonial Society of Massachusetts *Publications*, X (Boston, 1907), 6.

27. Appointed an assistant by the charter of the governor and company of the Massachusetts Bay in New England, March 4, 1628/9, Theophilus Eaton was reëlected to that office May 13, 1629, and October 20, 1629. He gave up the office March 18, 1629/30, after the decision to transfer the company to New England.

28. For the address of the general court of Massachusetts to Charles II, October 19, 1664, see *Calendar of State Papers, Colonial Series, 1661–1668* (London, 1880), no. 832; *Massachusetts Colony Records*, IV, Part II (Boston, 1854), 129–133, 168–173.

29. For the letter of Sir William Morrice, secretary of state, to Massachusetts, February 25, 1664/5, see *Calendar of State Papers, Colonial Series, 1661–1668* (London, 1880), no. 945; *New York Colonial Documents*, III (Albany, 1853), 90–91.

1. Massachusetts Historical Society, Winthrop MSS., III, 148; printed in Massachusetts Historical Society *Collections*, 4th series, VII (Boston, 1865), 526–529. Winthrop replied to this letter, July 17, 1665. Winthrop MSS., V, 51.

2. See above, p. 236n.

others, which is the occasion of my putting pen to paper, at this time. Your selfe well know who said, *Judicis officium est, ut res, ita tempora rerum quærere* (and he addes, for him selfe) *quæsito tempore, tutus ero. Tutum,*[3] is the end of all lawes and Governm[en]ts, as well in reference to particular persons, as to Republicks. If the time when the subject of this dispute (viz. the assembling of sundrie at Gilford, upon Mr. Leete, our then Governors, letter to the Townes about Gillford) be duely considered; 3 things will conduce to his safety.

1. That it was when this Colonie was a distinct jurisdiction within itselfe, and aught to have bene conserved in its distinct liberties and priviledges intyre by the other Colonies, by virtue of the solemne confœderacion[4] betweene the 4 united Colonies, of which Connectecute is one, which Confœderacion is evidently violated, if Connectecute now bring things under theire judicature, which were then done in this Colonie. So that this case is *lis pendens coram non-judice.*[5]

2. That what was done therein was done in their necessary Defense, threatning words having bene given out by Mr. Rossetter, at Gillford, and actions suitable thereunto having bene done by him and his companie to the terrifying of the inhabitants there, before Mr. Leete sent abroad to call in helpe. Now selfe-defense against injuries and violence acted, or threatned, though it be provided for by armed men, cannot be accounted a riot, in the case of a particular person, either by law or reason, much less in the case of a Towneship. But they compassed about the plaintiffes house? Be it so. Yet if it was onely to secure him from coming forth to do mischeife, whom they looked at as the Author of their causeles trouble and danger; the peace was not broken, but præserved thereby. But they stood with their guns charged etc? Yet, if they did no hurt to any; that served onely to shew that they were in readynes to defend the place and the Inhabitants, for whose helpe and safety they were sent. But Mr. Leete sent his warrant[6] to call Mr.

---

3. *Judicis officium est, ut res, ita tempora rerum*
    Quærere. Quæsito tempore tutus eris.
    Ovid, *Tristium,* I, 1, 37–38.

As it is the duty of a judge to consider facts, so ought he to take into consideration the circumstances. In your case, when the circumstances are inquired into, you will be safe.
        H. T. Riley, *The Fasti, Tristia, Pontic Epistles, Ibis, and Halieuticon of Ovid, literally translated into English prose* (London, 1851), p. 249.

The addition to the quotation reads: "the circumstances having been investigated, I shall be secure. Security . . ."

4. The New England Confederation, entered upon in 1643.

5. a lawsuit pending before one who is not a judge.

6. Of this warrant no record has been found.

Rossetter before him? Mr. Leet being Governor made a warrant, onely to know of him what the cause was of such Disturbance and Affrightm[en]ts of the people. And yet, at the intreaty of some of your Magistrates, then præsent, it was stopped and the serving of it was prevented. But Mr. Rossetter was forced to flie from his house at midnight? That was without just cause no hurt being intended to his person, if the common safety might be otherwise secured. And it is most probable that Mr. Rossetter did so flie, in a malicious Designe, to possess others with the greater præjudice against Mr. Leete, as seeking his destruction, which was farr from his intendm[en]t. But the Court at Hartford had before promised Mr. Rossetter and his party protection? But not in their irregular and injurious actings against their neighbours. Nor was theire accepting them into theire Colonie, when they rent themselves from this, before matters in debate were issued betweene these 2 Colonies, justifiable before God or men, and must be answered for before the righteous judge, in that day. Therefore their promise of protecting them from this Colonie, to the Governm[en]t whereof they were bound to be subject by an oath of fidelity, was sinful, and much more, if they performe it, by protecting them in doing evil, and in giving just offenses to this jurisdiction.

3. That his complaining to the court at Connectecute for this cause is after he had bound himselfe by his solemne Agreem[en]t under his hand, that he would never trouble Mr. Leete etc.[7] for the future without the advise or consent of old Mr. Allin[8] Mr. Willis,[9] Mr. Street[10] and my selfe: which he hath not had nor saught, at this time. It will concerne your selfe and the courte, to be well advised, that nothing be done in this matter, to the dishonour of God, and to the justifying of the guilty and to the condemning of the Innocent. For, I beleive that, in a faire and impartial proceeding, Mr. Leet would be justified, as a præserver, and Mr. Rossetter condemned as a Disturber, of the common peace. Be carefull that parties be not judges: and let the judges minde theire charge, in 2. Chron. 19. 6. 7. The people here, as I am told, looke at themselves as censured or Acquitted, in Mr. Leetes censure or Acquittance, so farr as it is not for his personal miscarriages, but for his Regular actings, in his publick capacitie, according to his publick Trust. Sir, these things I make bold to suggest unto your selfe,

7. Such an agreement was later included in the settlement of May 19, 1666. *Connecticut Colonial Records, 1665–1677* (Hartford, 1852), p. 41.
8. Mathew Allyn was at this time an assistant of Connecticut.
9. Samuel Wyllys was at this time an assistant of Connecticut.
10. Nicholas Street, teacher of the church at New Haven.

out of my wonted faithfulnes, with which, I hope, you will excuse my boldnes and well accept my love. My selfe, my wife, my son, and daughter returne our thancks to you for our last injoym[en]t of your presence and helpefullnes, and we all present our humble service to Mrs. Winthrope, and our respectfull salutations to your sons and daughter. I rest in Jesus Christ

N[ew] H[aven] the 11th d. of the 5th m. 1665   Yours obliged assured

JOHN DAVENPORTE

[Endorsed] Mr. Davenport Sen. Rec. July. 13. 1665 [by John Winthrop.]

JOHN DAVENPORT *to* WILLIAM GOODWIN[1]
Davenport to Mr. Goodwin: 2 9 mo[nth] 1665

Most of the intelligence rec[eive]d by Mr. Russell was with vs before but that miracle of the Dumbe Boy I never heard till by his report. Did ever god speake soe loud, and shew soe cleerely, by multiplied signes, in heaven, earth, and sea, and in the Bodyes of men, giving speech to the Dumbe, and hearing to the Deafe, noe man knowes how? and causing an Infant 18 weekes old, yea, an Oxe to speake, and foretell callamities approching, as he hath done to England since the late change of goverment?[2] Noe history hath recorded the like, in soe few yeares. And the next age will wonder at the Dedolency, and stupidity of this age, wherein soe few discerne the signes of the times. If that of the Jewes be true wee may easily see what god is bringing about in the world even the greatest changes that have beene since the 1st coming of Christ. The witnesses that are now killed,[3] shall arise shortly. Rome shall be ere long ruined. Christ will take vnto himselfe his kingdome, which hath beene vsurped by Brutish men the vilenes of whose spirits hath appeared in scattering the churches gathered vnto Christ in sylencing the faithfull Ministers, in imprisoning and banishing the inocent in corrupting Religion with Antechristian superstitions; in killing sundry that deserved better vsage, for theire zeale for god, and ffaithfullnes to the publicke good, and in adding to all these, manifest contempt of god, and of the Covenant for

1. Boston Public Library, Mather Papers, I, no. 35½ *recto;* printed in Massachusetts Historical Society *Collections,* 4th series, VIII (Boston, 1868), 126–127.
2. The restoration of Charles II to the throne of England.
3. Possibly a reference to Revelation 11.

the quarrell whereof god hath brought a double sword vpon them the sword of the Angell in the noysome pestilence,[4] which hath slaine above 100000. persons throughout that land in 3 or 4 mounthes, and the sword of war.[5] By these god is making way for his anger, and his hand is stretched out still. N[ew] England allsoe hath cause to tremble, whose day is coming, if speedy repentance, and reformation prevent not, for our backesliding, and changing our waies,[6] from the ancient pathes to comply with Old England, in theire corruptions; But ah alas for the distressed ministers, that want food, and raiment, for whom sister Hooke hath written to me that a collection might be made, and releefe speeded to them wherein I believe you and sundry with you will not be wanting.

It would exeedingly refresh me, if I could speake freely and fully with those three worthyes[7] your neighbours But I had allmost forgot that I am wrighting a letter. The Lord lengthen your dayes, to see better dayes for the people of god.

JOHN DAVENPORT *to* JOHN WINTHROP the Younger[1]
To his Honor[a]ble freind John Winthrope Esq. Governo[u]r of Connectecute these present in Hartford

Honor[a]ble Sir)

To your motion concerning my preaching the election sermon, at Hartford, the 10th of the next moneth,[2] though my unfitnes for such a journey, is of itselfe a sufficient plea for excuse of my Negative Answer; yet I have sundry other weighty Reasons, whereby I am strongly and necessarily hindred from that service, which may more conveniently be given by word of mouth to your Honoured selfe, then expressed by wrighting. Be pleased to favour me with your acceptance of my Negative Answer, upon so cogent reasons, which I hasten, with all possible speed, that some other, whom you may please to call unto that worke, may have convenient time for præparacion. Also I make bold to pressent unto your view the inclosed paper not knowing that

4. The plague of 1665, which caused many deaths in London, and from there spread over England.

5. The second Anglo-Dutch War, 1664–1667.

6. The conclusions of the synod of 1662.

7. Edward Whalley, William Goffe, and John Russell, Jr.

1. Massachusetts Historical Society, Winthrop MSS., XII, 95; printed in Massachusetts Historical Society *Collections*, 3d series, X (Boston, 1849), 58–59.

2. Of this invitation there is no record.

you have seene it, onely be pleased, after you have made your use of it, to returne it unto mee, that I may send an answer to Boston, by Brother Alsup, who purposeth a voiage thither, toward the latter end of the next weeke, or the beginning of the following weeke. And, with him, our Teacher[3] intendeth to goe, which will be an impedim[en]t of my accepting and complying with your præmised motion, through our churches want of his helpe at home. I returne many thancks for my sight of the scheme of 3 suns and 4 rainbowes, seene at New Yorke, and drawne by General Nicols[4] his procurem[en]t. My son will be careful to returne it unto you by the 1st opportunity, which he hath wanted hitherto. No more, at present, but my service and my wifes to yourselfe and Mrs. Winthrope, together with our affectionate respects to yours, being presented, I rest in Jesus christ

Newh[aven] the 10th day of the 2d m. 1666. in which day I received yours dated the 6th d of the same moneth.

Sir)

Your worships obliged, assured

JOHN DAVENPORTE

Postscript.

The reason, which it pleased you to give, why I was not formerly desired to preach at the Election, holdeth as strong against my being invited thereunto now. For we are not yet fully joyned, by the Courts refusal of our Freemen to vote, in the last Election,[5] when they came thither, to that end, in obedience to theire absolute summons, and about 20 of ours were sent home, as repudiated, after they had suffered the difficulties and hazzards of an uncomfortable and unsafe journey, in that wett season. I shall crave leave to add my experience of my weakenes since the date of my letter. The 11th day was somewhat hot here and accordingly I found my spirits very faint, and listles unto action. This day, being the 12th, is a litle more moderate, and I finde my spirits a litle more revived, but stil feeble, and my stomack weake,

---

3. Nicholas Street. On May 15, 1666, Street wrote to Samuel Bache at Boston that his visit to the Bay was postponed because of Davenport's illness. Boston Public Library, Mather Papers, I, no. 34.

4. Richard Nicolls was one of the four commissioners of Charles II sent to inquire into conditions in New England, and first deputy governor of the province of New York.

5. Probably because Connecticut had not yet formally received the freemen of all towns of the *quondam* New Haven Colony, the river colony did not permit the freemen of the New Haven Colony to vote in 1665, but authorized Samuel Sherman and John Allyn to go to New Haven, Branford, Guilford, and Milford to administer the freeman's oath. *Connecticut Colonial Records, 1665–1677* (Hartford, 1852), p. 18.

whence I infer that in hotter weather I shall be unfit for such a journey and for that worke. Therefore, I pray, desist from that motion to mee, and urge it upon some fitter minister, and dwelling nearer to the place of the Election-Courte.

[Endorsed] Mr. Davenport Pastor [by John Winthrop, and] Dated April 10th. *1666.* [in a modern hand.]

JOHN DAVENPORT *to* JOHN WINTHROP the Younger[1]

Honor[a]ble Sir)

By the inclosed[2] you will see how it was with my son, when that was dated. Since that, yesterday, he was pretty well, all day, and slept well, that night. But an houre afore day, this morning, he complained much of a great paine on his left side, and it remained with him, all the morning, but not in that extremity as before, til afternoone. And about 3 a clock, he found himselfe chillish, and his paine in his left side was extreme, and in his thighes leggs and loines. After he received a glyster, he complained that the winde ran about his body, yet stil continueth in his left side. In his best day, which was yesterday, he was very faint and weake, and hath litle stomach, and is thirsty, especially, this day. My wife also is not well, but defers speaking of it now, hoping to see you here, upon this occasion, which we boath earnestly desire as that which will be much to our satisfaction, and we shall account it a special favour. But, if not; we desire you to send what directions you thinck best for him, and for his dyet. They give him possit drinck, which he takes willingly: but he desires small beare, which they accordingly give him with a toast. He makes litle urine. He is now in a hot fit, and very weake and faint with his paine. The Lord guide you to præscribe, and bless your præscriptions, and directions and what you send, for the good of my son! and the Lord do good to you and yours, through Jesus christ! in whom I rest

N[ew] H[aven] the 20th d. of the   Sir)
2d m. 1666
                              Yours assured obliged
                              JOHN DAVENPORTE Senior

[Endorsed] Mr. Davenport rec: Apr: 21: 66 [by John Winthrop.]

1. Massachusetts Historical Society, Winthrop MSS., XII, 96.
2. This enclosure has not been found.

JOHN DAVENPORT *to* JOHN WINTHROP the Younger[1]

To the Honor[a]ble John Winthrope Esq. Governo[u]r of
Connectecute these present in Hartford

Honor[a]ble Sir)

AFTER many hearty thancks for your helpe, and readynes thereunto, being præmised and præsented, as an acknowledgem[en]t of my great debt unto you; having this opportunity, by Capt: Clarke, I make bold to give you an Account how it hath bene with your patient, my son, since your departure. It seemes that your selfe was informed of a paine in his bellye by winde about his navil. After your departure, it increased unto great extremity, and was diffused about his bodie in his thighes, shoulders etc. that, he thought, it stirred, like a live-thing. That night was very painfull to him, and restles, save that he slept about an houre, as his wife thincks, on the Lords day. He tooke a glyster about 9 in the morning which wraught twice then. Yet his paine continued, with a litle abatement, at noone, and he had fre-quent returnes of paine, and when he yawned, he was sensible of such paine as made him skreame out. But betweene 8 and 9 at night, after he had a stoole (which may be from the further working of the glyster) he found more ease, and hath slept quietly the last night, with inter-missions, not constantly, but an houre at a time, or thereabouts, and when he awaked he found some paine but more moderate. His fitt is come 2 howres sooner then the last, the cold fit is now over, and his hot fit is begun, he is thyrsty, according to his wont. He now com-plaines of a shooting in his back. Capt. Clark, being now come, I am forced to breake off, and to leave the præmises to your serious con-sideracion, praying God to guide you and to bless your directions for the good of my son. I rest in Jesus Christ

N[ew] H[aven] the 26th d. of the   Yours obliged assured
2d m. 1666   JOHN DAVENPORTE

[Endorsed] Mr. Davenport rec: Apr: 30: 66. [by John Winthrop.]

1. Massachusetts Historical Society, Winthrop MSS., XII, 96.

John Davenport *to* John Winthrop the Younger[1]

To the Honor[a]ble John Winthrope Esq. Governo[u]r of Connectecute these present in Hartford

Honor[a]ble Sir)

To what I wrote, by Capt: Clarke, I shall now add, that my sons paine in his thighes and leggs (upon further intelligence, I understand that his paine is most in the side of his belly and upon his belly) stil continues, and workes up into his stomach, and ill affects that, so as he is sick at his stomack with it. All yesterday, and the last night, he hath bene afflicted with it, and stil is. It much hindered his sleepe, the last night, and causeth him to groane frequently. He saith, it weakeneth him more then his fits of the ague, whether cold or hot, have done. He saith he is hot and drie, and faint and pained, so that the interstitium betweene his fits, which was formerly a space of recovering some strength for the next fit, is, by this distemper of winde, a time of more weakening him. If it should thus continue; I feare, it will prostrate his spirits. The good Lord pitty him, and rebuke the distemper, in mercy, and send forth his word and heale him: and guide you what course to præscribe for his helpe, and bless the same for his good, through Jesus christ! in whom I rest

N[ew] H[aven] the 1st d. of the 2d [*sic*]   Honorable Sir)
m. called May, 1666.

Yours obliged

John Davenporte Senior

Postscr[ipt].

He is so feeble and faint that he cannot goe but betweene 2, and this morning he could not life up to himselfe to the stoole without great paine. And if he yawnes, he skreames out, as not able to beare it. My wife would know whether she may give him of Mrs. Bach[2] her water made of the spirits of minte and sack and saunders distilled, a litle bagg of amber greece hangd in it. She required that I should take 3 or 4 spoonefulls at a time, when I had a paine in my belly. Mrs. Fairechild[3] occasionally speaking formerly with my wife about sicknesses in London, she spake of a painful disease which was called the plague in the gutts. The remedie used was broath made of sheepes gutts which

---

1. Massachusetts Historical Society, Winthrop MSS., XII, 96. On May 10 and May 23, 1666, William Jones of New Haven wrote to Winthrop regarding the illness of John Davenport and his wife and son. Winthrop MSS., XIV, 73.

2. Mary Bache, the sister of Samuel Bache.

3. Catherine Cragg, a widow of London, contracted to marry Thomas Fairchild of Stratford, Connecticut, December 22, 1662. J. Savage, *A Genealogical Dictionary of the First Settlers of New England* (4 vols., Boston, 1860–1862).

they dranck, some dranck the fat and all, and she said it did some good. His paine is sometimes more extreme, some times more moderate, through Gods mercy, yet it is constantly upon him, though a cataplasme hath bene applied to him. My wife desires your judgem[en]t about that of Mrs. Bache and Mrs. Fairechild, and your speedy and full advise in the wholl case, for he is for the most parte in extremity, and she knowes not what to do for him. My wife and son, if it might not be thought too bold a request, would express theire earnest desire of your presence at this time of so greate need, as it is apprehended by them, wherein I also concurr with them.

Mr. Augur being now come to see my son, telles my wife, he is faint enough and much spent. He thincks that this distemper increaseth as his ague decreaseth. He præscribeth 4 or 5 and twenty graines of the powder of sinckfield[4] in 5 or 6 spoonefuls of white wine: and an handful of sinckfield boyled in spring water and given in his hot fitt. We desire to know your judgm[en]t about it speedily.

[Endorsed] Mr. Davenport rec: May 2: 1666 [by John Winthrop.]

JOHN DAVENPORT *to* JOHN WINTHROP the Younger[1]

To the Honor[a]ble John Winthrope Esq. Governour of Connectecute Colonie, these present, at Hartford

Honour[a]ble Sir)

MANY hearty thancks being præmised, to God, and you; to God, as to the principal efficient, who stirred up your heart, and guided your minde to pitch upon such meanes as his blessing made effectuall; and to yourselfe, as to a blessed Instrum[en]t in Gods hand, for our Recovery, my sons especially, from that weakenes, and those greate paines, wherewith he was lately and long afflicted, unto this measure of strength, whereby he was enabled to come into the publick Assembly, the last Lords day, to bless God the Authour of all blessings upon your endeavours: which, I pray, may be stil continued, for the good of many!

Yet, in the midst of our familie-comforts, I feele at my heart no

---

4. An obsolete form of cinquefoil. *A New English Dictionary.*

1. Massachusetts Historical Society, Winthrop MSS., XII, 96; printed in Massachusetts Historical Society *Collections,* 3d series, X (Boston, 1849), 59–62; A. B. Davenport, *A History and Genealogy of the Davenport Family* (New York, 1851), pp. 360–364.

small sorrow for the publick divisions and distractions at Hartford.[2] Were Mr. Hooker now *in vivis;* it would be as a sword in his bones, that the Church, which he had planted there, should be thus disturbed, by innovacions, brought in, and urged so vehemently, by his yong successour[3] in office, not in his spirit: who was so farr from these laxe waies, that he opposed the baptizing of grandchildren, by theire grand-fathers right: much more would he have decryed the baptising of Adopted children, by theire Adoptants right: most of all, the baptising of servants borne in the house, or bought with monie, *quâ tales,* unles they had a spiritual right, by being regularly joyned to the church, by theire owne personal faith, held forth to the satisfaction of the church, according to Gospel-rules. But he is at rest: and the people there are woefully divided, and the better sorte are exceedingly greived, while the looser and worser party insult, hoping that it will be as they would have it, viz., that the plantacions shall be brought into a parish-way, against which Mr. Hooker hath openly borne a strong Testimonie in print.[4] The most of the churches, in this jurisdiction, are professedly against this new way, both in judgem[en]t and practise, upon Gospel grounds, n, Newhaven, Milford, Stratford, Branford, Gillford, Nor-walke, Stamford, and those nearer to Hartford, n, Farmington, and the sounder parte of Windsor, together with theire Reverend pastor, Mr. Warham,[5] and, I thinck, Mr. Fitch,[6] and his church also. Nor may it be thaught that we all are mere spectatours, or that we shall be allwaies silent, as persons not concerned. It is the Cause of Christ, for which we must pleade: it is no slighte matter, as *de lanâ caprinâ,*[7] that

2. On the divisions in the church at Hartford at this time, see G. L. Walker, *History of the First Church in Hartford, 1633–1883* (Hartford, 1884), pp. 182–211.

3. In 1660 John Whiting, Harvard College 1653, was settled as the colleague of Samuel Stone. After the death of Stone, July 20, 1663, Joseph Haynes, the son of John Haynes, at one time governor of Connecticut, was settled as the colleague of Whiting. At this time Haynes was trying to introduce innovations in the practice of baptism.

4. Thomas Hooker, *A Survey of the Summe of Church-Discipline* (London, 1648). In Part 3, Chapter 2, pp. 11–28, Hooker considers: "Whether the Infants of Non-Confederates, who refuse to be Members of the Church, should be partakers of Baptisme, which is one of the speciall priviledges of the Church?"

5. John Warham, first pastor of the church at Windsor, was at this time an old man.

6. About 1660 James Fitch led a group from Saybrook to Norwich, where he subsequently served as pastor.

7. *Alter rixatur de lana saepe caprina,*
   Propugnat nugis armatus: . . .
   Horace, *Epistles,* I, 18, 15–16.

   Another in dispute engages,
   With nonsense arm'd for nothing rages,
      Horatius Flaccus Quintus, *Satires and Epistles in Latin and English, The English Version by Philip Francis* (London and New York, 1902).

is now agitated, but that which concernes the preserving of Christian Churches in peace, and Gospel-ordinances in purity: it is the faith and order of the churches of Christ, which we are called to contend for, that they may be preserved intyre and uncorrupted. When the Bay-Synod published theire booke;[8] I saw where theire Temptacion lay, and printed my Answer to it:[9] whereunto, when a seeming Reply was made,[10] I declared and proved the insufficiency of it, and sent my MSS to the Baye,[11] where it lyeth, in freinds hands unprinted, til further occasion shall obstetricate it. *Sed quorsum hæc?*[12] I shall breifly suggest unto you what I have heard, viz. that before the last lecture day, when it was yong Mr. Heynes his turne to preach, he sent 3 of his partie to tell Mr. Whiting, that, the nexte lecture day, he would preach about his way of baptizing, and would begin the practising of it, on that day. Accordingly he preached, and water was prepared for Baptisme, (which, I suppose, was never administred, in a weeke day, in that church before) But Mr. Whiting, as his place and duety required, testifyed against it, and refused to consent to it. Much was spoken, to litle purpose, by some of Mr. Heynes his partie. But, when Mr. Warham began to speake, one of the church rudely hindred him, saying, to this purpose, What hath Mr. Warham to do to speake in our church matters? This check stopped Mr. Warhams proceeding, at that time. The objectour considered not that this matter was not *res propria*[13] to that church alone, but *res communis*,[14] it being of common concernm[en]t to all the Churches in these parts, and to the Teaching Officers of them, and to Mr. Warham more especially; for *tum sua res agitur paries cum proximus ardet;*[15] which he might have answered.

8. *Propositions concerning the Subject of Baptism and Consociation of Churches* (Cambridge, 1662).

9. John Davenport, *Another Essay For Investigation of the Truth* (Cambridge, 1663).

10. Richard Mather and Jonathan Mitchell, *A Defence of the Answer and Arguments of the Synod Met at Boston in the Year 1662* (Cambridge, 1664).

11. American Antiquarian Society, John Davenport, A Vindication of the Treatise entituled Another Essay for Investigation of the Truth; The third Essay containing a Reply to the Answer unto the other Essay printed in Defense of the Synods Booke. The American Antiquarian Society possesses a copy of the first manuscript and the original of the second.

12. But what is the purpose of this?

13. a private matter

14. the common affair

15. *Nam tua res agitur, paries cum proximus ardet,*
     Horace, *Epistles*, I, 18, 84.

    When flames your neighbour's dwelling seize,
    Your own with instant rage shall blaze;
        Horatius Flaccus Quintus, *Satires and Epistles in Latin and English, The English Version by Philip Francis* (London and New York, 1902).

But we live in times and places, where the faces of the Elders are not duely honoured; and therefore its justly to be feared that God will soone take away the most Godly and judicious leaders from so unthanckfull and unworthy people, and leave them to be mislead by superficial verbalists. Your selfe prudently concluded that, that day was not a fit season to begin theire purposed practise, seing it was not consented to, but opposed. And so it ceased, for that time. But Mr. Heynes urged for a dispute about it with Mr. Whiting, the next lecture day, which will be the 20th day of this moneth:[16] which also, they say, is agreed upon. But *cui bono?*[17] No good issue can rationally be expected of a verbal dispute, at that time, and in that place, where so many are likely to disturbe the buisenes with interruptions and clamours; and to prepare a sufficient number to overvote the better party, for establishm[en]t of the worser way. So Trueth shall be dethroned, and errour set up in the throne. What then is to be done, in this case? Let Mr. Heynes give in wrighting to Mr. Whyting, his position, and his Argum[en]ts to prove it: and let Mr. Whyting have a convenient time to returne his Answer in wrighting. This is the most suitable way for a peaceable issuing of the dispute, with solid judgem[en]t, and with due moderation and satisfaction: and let all practise of Mr. Heynes his opinion be forborne, til the trueth be cleared. But, if Mr. Heynes refuseth this way; I shall suspect that he more confides in the clamours of his party, then in the goodnes of his cause, or in the strength of his Argum[en]ts, or in his ability for disputacion. These things I make bold to present to your serious consideracion, that, by your wisdom and care of the publick good and common peace, according to the duety of your place, the fire alreadie kindled may be speedily quenched, and the banckes may be seasonably strengthened, to prevent the irruption of waters, that may cause an inundacion, not to be stopped afterward.

Our service to yourselfe and Mrs. Winthrope, with our affectionate Salutacions to all yours, being præsented, I rest, in Jesus christ,

N[ew] H[aven] the 14th d. of   Yours obliged, assured,
the 4th m. 1666.   JOHN DAVENPORTE Senior

Postscr[ipt].

My Rev[eren]d brother, Mr. Street, being with me, and hearing this letter read, earnestly desired me, once and againe, to declare unto you his full consent to the contents thereof: so that you may take it

16. No record of this debate has been found.
17. Who benefits by it?

as from us boath. He also thincks that a synod of the Elders and Messengers of the churches, on this side of the countrey, i. e., of this jurisdiction,[18] might be a suitable expedient *motos componere fluctus.*[19] But that I leave to further consideracion. In the meane time, it will be *opera precium*[20] that you interpose your Authority and wisdom to stop all further proceedings and actings in this irregular and tumultuous way.

[Endorsed] Mr. Davenport Sen[io]r receiv[e]d Jun. 19: 1666 [by John Winthrop.]

18. A general assembly of Connecticut of October 11, 1666, called a synod or as sembly of the preaching and teaching elders of Connecticut and Jonathan Mitchell and three others of Massachusetts to meet at Hartford on the third Wednesday in May, 1667, to debate seventeen questions proposed by the general assembly. The assembly met, adjourned till autumn, and never reconvened. On the recommendation of the commissioners of the United Colonies of New England and the ministers of Connecticut, the general assembly of Connecticut of October 10, 1667, called a meeting of the clergy of New England to consider the questions propounded by the general assembly of October, 1666. Meanwhile, on May 16, 1668, the general assembly of Connecticut ordered James Fitch, Gershom Bulkley, Joseph Eliot, and Samuel Wakeman to meet at either Saybrook or Norwich, June 8 or 9, 1668, "to consider of some expedient for our peace." This group apparently advised the withdrawal of the dissatisfied minority in the church at Hartford. The petition of John Whiting and his supporters for a separation from the church at Hartford was before the general assembly of October 14, 1669, and early in the following year Whiting and thirty-two others entered into covenant and formed the Second Church of Hartford. *Connecticut Colonial Records, 1665–1677* (Hartford, 1852), pp. 53–55, 67, 69–70, 84, 107, 109, 120, 516–517; "The Wyllys Papers," Connecticut Historical Society *Collections,* XXI (Hartford, 1924), pp. 168–170.

19. . . . *sed motos praestat componere fluctus:*
    Virgil, *Aeneid,* I, 135.

    . . . but first 't is fit the billows to restrain;
    J. Dryden, *Vergil's Æneid,* I, 193.

20. works of prayers

JOHN DAVENPORT *to* JOHN WINTHROP the Younger[1]

To the Honor[a]ble John Winthrop Esq. Governo[u]r of
Connectecute these present with speed at his house
in Hartford. With the packet

Honor[a]ble Sir)

THESE few lines, in the midst of sundry distracting buisenesses
upon me, at present, tend onely to returne many thancks for your
kinde letter, and to usher the packet of intelligencies which I received
from London,[2] by Capt. Martin, which, I thinck, you will willingly
peruse, if you have not seene them alreadie. I thaught to have proposed a motion for your wrighting to the Governo[u]r of Mattachu-
sets,[3] that a day might be agreed upon, wherein all N[ew] E[ngland]
might, with one accord, bewaile the burning and devastacion of that
greate Citie: but, even now, an order is come to us from the Court[4] for
a fast to be kept publickly in these churches, on the 1st Wednesday in
April, which will be the next 4th day. The warning is too short for so
sollemne and extraordinary a duetie. Yet we purpose to obeie it, as it
may please God to inable. I also thaught to have added something
concerning the Synod,[5] whereunto I suspect that we are not regularly
and orderly called, by the Courts order, for many Reasons which are
of weight with me, who desire to see a due order attended in all things,
nedum[6] in so weighty affaires. But I shall suppresse that, for the present,
and also our just greivance for the ill usage of the messengers sent
from these churches to enquire of the causes of that scandalous division in the church at Hartford, to the end that we might consider fit
expedients for the quenching of that fire, and for the settling of trueth
and peace among them, as we are bound to endeavour by the commun-

1. Massachusetts Historical Society, Winthrop MSS., III, 149; printed in Massachusetts Historical Society *Collections*, 4th series, VII (Boston, 1865), 529–531; A. B.
Davenport, *Supplement* (Stamford, 1876), pp. 392–393.

2. Davenport is probably referring to *The London Gazette*, the issue of which for the
week of September 3–10, 1666, gave a detailed account of the great fire which broke out
in Pudding Lane, London, early in the morning of Sunday, September 2, 1666, and
continued for five days, destroying a region of four hundred and fifty acres. News of the
fire had reached Boston before February 24, 1666/7, and John Winthrop the Younger
at Hartford, *via* Barbados, before March 6, 1666/7. Massachusetts Historical Society
Collections, 5th series, VIII (Boston, 1882), 115–116.

3. Richard Bellingham.

4. This was probably an order of the governor and council. No general assembly met
between October 11, 1666, and May 9, 1667.

5. See above, p. 266n.

6. much more

ion of churches. This some of the magistrates laboured to hinder, by sending the marshal to convent them before them, and by reproving them before many witnesses. The cheife Actors herein were the 2 Allins[7] and Mr. Talkot.[8] I might add also a wrong done to this and the neighbour Townes, by an unrighteous order (as the Assistants and deputies from these Towneships declared it to be in the Court at Hartford) for a rate to be paid by them to Mr. Rossetor.[9] But I am loath to trouble you with complaints of things done in your absence, and without your consent. To the most high we commend our cause and case. For yourselfe, Honor[a]ble Sir; I am desirous to assure you that I am as heartily yours as ever, alwaies mindful of your love, and of my strong engagem[en]ts for the same, together with the effects thereof toward me and myne, who do joyntly and severally, present our service to your selfe and Mrs. Winthrop, with our affectionate and respectful salutacions to all yours, praying that all blessings may be accumulated upon you and them, through Jesus christ, in whom I rest

N[ew] H[aven] the 27th d. of the 1st   Sir, yours exceedingly obliged
m. 1667.   JOHN DAVENPORT, Senior

[Endorsed] Mr. Davenport rec: Mar: 29: 1667. [by John Winthrop.]

JOHN DAVENPORT *to* JOHN WINTHROP the Younger[1]
To the Honorable John Winthrop, Esq[ui]r[e] Governour of Connectecute, these present in Hartford.

HONORABLE Sir,—I made bold to send inclosed, in my last letter to your selfe, a letter præpared for General Nichols,[2] if you approved it; else my desire was that you would be pleased to returne it to me, with your advise. But I have not heard whether you received it, or

7. Mathew and John Allyn, at this time both assistants of Connecticut.
8. John Talcott, a son of one of the first settlers of Hartford, was at this time an assistant and treasurer of Connecticut.
9. See above, p. 236n.
1. The manuscript copy of this letter has not been found. It is printed in Massachusetts Historical Society *Collections*, 4th series, VII (Boston, 1865), 531–532.
2. Apparently complaints of Davenport's preaching had reached Richard Nicolls, deputy governor of New York, and Nicolls had written to Winthrop, asking him to speak to Davenport. In response to this letter, Winthrop visited New Haven, and from there wrote to Nicolls, July 15, 1667, assuring him that Davenport's statements had been misunderstood or misreported, and intimating that Davenport would himself write to Nicolls. Winthrop MSS., V, 68.

not, which makes me sollicitous about it. Having this occasion (by my deare wifes weakenes, and some discouraging apprehensions in her mind thereby,) of sending againe unto you, I thinck it my duety to second her desire of your making a journey to us, if it may consist with your health, in this hot season, and with your liberty in other respects. Our motion argueth our confidence in your love, whereof we have plentiful experience, unto our great ingagement for the same. My wife tooke but halfe of one of the papers, but could not beare the tast of it, and is discouraged from taking any more. I perceive that some speech with your selfe would best satisfie her; but if Gods providence puttes a barr in the way, we are called to submit thereunto. I shall cease to divert your minde from other necessary affaires, at present, and commend your selfe and all yours to his grace (our service to Mrs. Winthrop, together with your selfe, being præsented) in whom I rest

N[ew] H[aven] the 10th of the 5th, 67.   Honorable Sir,

Yours obliged, assured,

John Davenporte, Senior

[Endorsed] Mr. Davenport, senr. rec. July 10, 1667. [by John Winthrop.]

John Davenport *to* The First Church, Boston[1]

Hono[u]r[a]ble Rev[eren]d and dearly beloued in our Lord Jesus

THE hast of your Hon[o]r[ed] Messengers[2] to returne vnto you, compelleth me to be more briefe than other wise I should haue bin, Let it please you to accept many harty thankes for this reall expression of your loue in your invitation of me to such a service, as I accont the Minnistration of the Gospel in your Ch[urch] to be, both in respect of those emminent lights,[3] which haue formerly shined in that Golden Candlestick, and in reference to the Generall Influences from

1. Yale University Library, Stiles Folio Letters, I, Third Church Narrative, p. 5; printed in H. A. Hill, *History of the Old South Church (Third Church) Boston 1669-1884* (2 vols., Boston, 1890), I, 18-19. This letter was dated October 8, 1667.

2. The messengers sent by the First Church, Boston, to Davenport and the church at New Haven were Edward Tyng, James Oliver, and Richard Cooke.

3. John Wilson was teacher of the First Church, Boston, from 1630 to 1631, and pastor from 1632 to 1667; John Cotton was teacher from 1633 until his death in 1652; and John Norton was teacher from 1656 to 1663. At this time the church was without either pastor or teacher.

thence through out the Country, Inwhich respects I am apte to be discouraged from such an vndertaking, being conscious to my selfe of my nothingness in my selfe, yett when I consider the clearnes and strength of the call of Christ, by you vnto worthless me to come and helpe you in such a time of your streights, I finde my selfe incouraged to beleive that his power will be glorified in my weaknes; and his grace in my vnworthynes where vpon I wholy cast my selfe, and rely through the helpe of his spirit, waiting vpon God in Christ to manifest his will, and my way soe clearly to my selfe and to his people, that we might be brought into a full acquiescence therein and obedience there vnto, In order here vnto this Chu[rch] being assembled on the 7th day of this mo: I read your letters one directed to them[4] and the other sent to me, and hauing spoken some thing touching two things to be considered in a call of God, viz: that it be from such a place, 2ly. to such a place; And cleared my call from them by some arguments which were of force with me (and it appeares) that one of them was confessed by the ablest among them selves to be vnanswerable: And for clearing my call to you, the letter read before them were in my apprehensions sufficient; The conclusion was that the matter vnder debate was looked vpon, and that Justly soe weighty, as that a day for extraordinary humbling of our selves to seek the face of God and guidance by his Spirit, before the question be Issued: should be set a part the weeke following, and on the day after they would Consult and conclude with Gods helpe, After that you will receive from them their full answer, In meane time you may be pleased to take notice and to be assured of my strong inclynation to obey this call, which seemeth to me to be a call of Jes[us] Ch[rist] the Lord, your Lord and our, And accordingly I hope to be with you this winter with the consent of this Church if God permit, by the first opportunity after the fast is over in reference to all the pr[e]mises, I humbly and earnestly begg the helpe of your fervent prayers and rest in Jesus Christ

yours engaged to serve you in my worke
where vnto Jesus christ shall call me

Jo: DAVENPORT: Sen:

4. For the letter of the First Church, Boston, to the church at New Haven, September 28, 1667, see Massachusetts Historical Society, Boston, Letters and Papers, 1631–1783, II, 1; printed in H. A. Hill, *History of the Old South Church (Third Church) Boston 1669–1884* (2 vols., Boston, 1890), 1, 14–15.

JOHN DAVENPORT *to* THE FIRST CHURCH, BOSTON[1]

Reve[ren]d Sir

IN my last sent by your Hono[u]r[e]d Messengers (which I heare was publiquely read before the mixt assemblje) where my humble desire is that this may be read also, I declared my acceptance of the call tendred to me by the Ch[urch] of Boston, in hope that this Ch[urch] of N[ew]haven would haue consented there vnto, wherein I was strengthned [by] your approuing my reason for warranting my remoue from hence, grounded vpon 1 Timoth: 5: 8: I looke at your call as the act of the ch[urch] it being consented there to by the major by fare, for other wise nothing Shall pass as a Ch[urch] act if the Minor part dissent, which is contrary to the Scripture and to Reason, and constant[ly] aproved practices of all publique Societyes, hence I looke at your calling of me as cleare and full on your part, And accordingly signifyd my hope and purpose of coming to you, with the consent of this Ch[urch] after we had Sought God in an extraordinary Manner, for the guidance of his holy Spirit in this weighty afayer, this being done the B[rethre]n result, about an Answer vnto you, The result where of you will receive from them selves[2] where by you will finde they decline giving a possitiue answer, but leave that to me, (where as it is my judgm[en]t) that I should be puerly passive in a matter of this Importance concerning my selfe, that I might more clearly discerne the holy will and hand of God appearing in the whole busines, But soe farr as they doe answer it is a refusall of Consent which was a matter of no small Exercise to me, and that was increased partly by the greife of the whole Ch[urch] and Towne, and of many godly people in sundry townes aboute vs, vpon their feare of my departure hence, and partly by constant reports, of, not only the dissent, but of the strong oposition of aboue 40 Brethren of your Ch[urch] against my coming to you, some of them saying if I should come thither, it would be breaking of that Ch[urch], and some here fearing that it would be the breaking of this Ch[urch] If I should remoue hence, yet at our last meeting I

1. Yale University Library, Stiles Folio Letters, I, Third Church Narrative, pp. 7–8; printed in H. A. Hill, *History of the Old South Church (Third Church) Boston 1669–1884* (2 vols., Boston, 1890), I, 21–22. With the letter of the church at New Haven to the First Church, Boston, also dated October 28, 1667, this letter was carried to Boston by Captain Thomas Clarke.

2. For the answer of the church at New Haven to the First Church, Boston, October 28, 1667, see Yale University Library, Stiles Folio Letters, I, Third Church Narrative, p. 6; printed in H. A. Hill, *History of the Old South Church (Third Church) Boston 1669–1884* (2 vols., Boston, 1890), I, 19–20.

pr[e]sented my desire of making a journy to Boston for this winter, and part of the spring for a further triall for to finde out the minde of God, to my full satisfaction, promising for to returne to them againe, in case of my dissatisfaction, And if satisfied yett not to ingage my selfe for office vntill I had given them account of the Event (and shall receive theire answer) (Against this they Exprest them selves vnanimosly) I haueing Thus farr proceeded, considered the dificultie and hazard of winter voyage and journy, and in hope for to see the Ch[urch] better settled by that time, I consent to stay with them this winter, Yett telling them I must make a journy to Boston by the will of God, before the hott monthes of the next summer, for the reason before noted from the 1 Timoth: 5: 8: and all were satisfied.

What remaines Hon[o]r[e]d and Beloved in the Lord but that we conclude if this Counsill be of God it shall stand if not the will of the Lord be done.

My fanndamentall Reason from the Ch[urch] agrement with me in our first begining for my being at liberty to follow the call of God, either in any other place or to continue here is of the same force with me now, as it was two years since when I pleaded with them against my goeing to Dellaware,[3] Though while I stay here I am their Pastour, and doe accordingly officiate, with them passed with out oposition. It is onely the will of God that I looke at, and wait for to be clearly manifested to mee in this weighty buysines, being desirous for to be appr[o]v[e]d of him in all my waies, and to act in all things to his honnour. I shall humbly crave leave to add a word or two for your peace, the Prophet saith love the truth and peace,[4] truth and peace are sisters, and will not be separated, let the truth be first regarded and minded and your hearts be vnited to the truth of the gospell and . . .[5] yourselves for the truthes sake, It is recorded concerning Jehoshaphat that the L[ord] was with him because he walked in the first waies of his ffather david 2 Chr: 17: 3: soe will the L[ord] be with you Hon[o]r[e]d and beloved in the L[ord], if you walk in the first waies where in you walked according to his Rule vnd[e]r that faithfull and blessed servant

3. Following the absorption of the New Haven Colony by Connecticut, disgruntled inhabitants of the former New Haven Colony revived a claim to territory on the Delaware River and received the permission of Philip Carteret, representative of the proprietors of New Jersey, to settle there. In the following year, for a reason which is not clear, they abandoned their claim to territory on the Delaware River and began the settlement of Newark, New Jersey. I. M. Calder, *The New Haven Colony* (New Haven, 1934), pp. 253–256.

4. Zechariah 8. 19.

5. This blank is in the manuscript.

of Christ Mr. John Cotton; But if you fall into divissions amongst your selves, by different principles, some striveing for one way, some for another: I feare I feare and forwarne, that the Isshue will be a rent amongst you, vnto Gods great dishonour, to the corrupting of the Ch[urch] from the symplicity that is in Ch[rist] Jesus, which God in mercy avert; and I doe humbly Beseech you in the name of our Lord Jesus: The Bretheren that haue declared themselves oposite to my coming to you, let nothing be done through strife and vaine glory; And that theire be noe scisme amongst you for my sake, but that you be perfectly joyned together in the same minde, and in the same judgem[en]t, striveing together for the faith of the Gospel, and for the holy ord[e]r where in Christ hath appointed his Chu[rch] for to walke, Then will be given teaching officers according to his owne heart, which shall feed you with knowledge and vnderstanding, and god will Bless theire Administration for the spirituall Good of your selves and your posterity. The God of patience and consolation graunt you for to be like minded one towards another according to Jesus Christ, that you may with one minde and one mouth glorify God, even the father of our Lord Jesus Ch[rist].

28 October *1667*   J: D.

JOHN DAVENPORT *to* THE TOWN OF NEW HAVEN[1]

To all Christian people to whom these pr[e]sents shall come, I John Davenport sen[io]r Pasto[u]r of the Church of christ at New Haven in New england send greeting: Wheras Edward Hopkins Esq[ui]r[e] sometime of Hartford in the Colony of Connecticutt in New England afores[ai]d Governo[u]r, and since in old England deceased, by his last will and testam[en]t in writeing beareing date the 7th of March *1657* did give and bequeath to his father in law Theophilus Eaton Esq[ui]r[e] then Governo[u]r of New Haven Colony, the s[ai]d John Davenport, Mr. John Cullick and Mr. W[illia]m Goodwin sometime of Hartford afores[ai]d, all the residue and remaynder of his Estate in New England (his due debts being first payd and legacies discharged) and alsoe the summe of £500: out of his Estate in old England within 6 moneths after the decease of his wife Mrs. Anne Hopkins, by the Advice of Mr. Robert Thompson and Mr. ffrancis Willoughby,[2] to be

1. Manuscript New Haven Town Records, 1662–1684, pp. 121–123; New Haven, Hopkins Grammar School Records, I, 4–8; printed in *New Haven Town Records, 1662–1684* (New Haven, 1919), pp. 230–235.
2. Francis Willoughby, commissioner of the navy.

made over and conveyed into the hands of the s[ai]d Trustees in New England, In full assurance of their trust and faithfulnes in dispose of the s[ai]d Remainder of his Estate in new England, and of the s[ai]d £500: in old England, according to the true intent and purpose of him the said Edward Hopkins declared in his s[ai]d will, vizt: for the in-couragem[en]t, and breeding up of hopefull youths both at the Gram-mer schoole and Colledge, for the publique service of the Countrey in these forraigne plantations, as in and by the s[ai]d Will doth, and may, more fully and at large appeare.

And whereas the s[ai]d Mr. W[illia]m Goodwin, and I the s[ai]d John Davenport the onely surviveing Trustees of the above named Edward Hopkins, by an instrum[en]t or writeing under our hands and seales beareing date the 27th of Aprill. 1664.[3] have agreed upon an equitable division, settlem[en]t and dispose of the s[ai]d Remainder of Estate above mencioned, received, or secured by us severally, or our Attornies, and of the s[ai]d £500: to the use or uses afores[ai]d; Where-by the summe of £412, part of the s[ai]d remainder besides the full moiety, or halfe part of the s[ai]d £500, when it shall become due and received, as afores[ai]d, is by me the s[ai]d John Davenport to be dis-posed of according to the true intent and meaneing of the s[ai]d Tes-tato[u]r as in the s[ai]d instrum[en]t or writeing agreed upon, know ye therefore that I the s[ai]d John Davenport in pursuance of the s[ai]d trust in me reposed, And that the Grammer Schoole or Colledge at New Haven already founded and begun, may be provided for, main-tained, and Continued, for the encouragem[en]t, and bringing up of hopefull youths in the languages, and other good litterature, for the publique use and service of the Countrey, according to the sincere and true intent of the donor as above mencioned, and to noe other use, intent, or purpose whatsoeever, Doe Give, Graunt, enffeoffe and Con-firme, and have by these pr[e]sents Given, graunted, enffeoffed and Confirmed, unto Mr. William Jones Assistant of the Colony of Con-necticutt, the Reverend Mr. Nicholas Streete teacher of the Church of christ at New Haven, Mr. Mathew Gilbert, Mr. John Davenport jun[io]r and James Bishop Commissio[ned] Magistrates, deacon W[illia]m Pecke and Roger Alling,[4] and to their successo[u]rs to be nominated, appointed and Chosen, as hereafter in these pr[e]sents is

3. See above, pp. 242–244. The various drafts of the agreement of William Goodwin of Hadley, Massachusetts, and John Davenport of New Haven seem to have borne differ-ent dates. Davenport brought the matter to the attention of the town of New Haven on April 28, 1664. *New Haven Town Records, 1662–1684* (New Haven, 1919), pp. 83–86.

4. Roger Alling of New Haven.

ordered and directed, the s[ai]d summe of £412 and the s[ai]d moiety or
halfe part of the s[ai]d £500:[5] and all and every other summe, or
summes of money or other Estate, which is or may be due by vertue of
the afores[ai]d Graunt or agreem[en]t for Ever, under the name or title
of the Committee of Trustees for the s[ai]d Trust, Invested hereby with
full power and authority to improve, and dispose of the s[ai]d summs or
Estate as before expressed, And to oversee, Regulat, order and direct
the s[ai]d Grammer and Collegiat Schoole according to their best
skill, understanding, and ability, in pursuance of the s[ai]d Trust and
ends, In full assurance that they the s[ai]d Committee and their successo[u]rs Regularly Chosen, and appointed, shall soe mannage and dispose of the s[ai]d summs or other Estate herein mencioned, to the true
ends, purposes, and intents of the s[ai]d Donor, in his last Will and
Testam[en]t declared and expressed, and to the true meaneing and
intent of mee the s[ai]d John Davenport in theise pr[e]sents before
declared and directed, or to be hereby further declared and directed
and not otherwise, that is to say for the purchasing a farme, or ffarmes,
for a yearely revenue for the schoolemaster, or building such dwelling
house for the s[ai]d Schoolemaster as the s[ai]d Committee, their successo[u]rs, or the majo[u]r part of them shall judge necessary and Convenient; And the s[ai]d house, and pr[e]sent schoole house, (being
graunted and Confirmed by the s[ai]d Towne of New Haven for the
use of the s[ai]d schoole) to uphold, maintaine, and keepe in good and
sufficient repaire from time to time, out of the Rents, yssues, and
proffitts of the s[ai]d money or Estate soe given and graunted as afore-
s[ai]d. And the s[ai]d Committee, or the majo[u]r part of them, or of
their successo[u]rs, meeting together from time, to time, in some Convenient place, and agreeing, are hereby fully impowered and Author-
ised, to Consult, determine and Conclude, act and doe in the pr[e]m-
isses, as is above ordayned, appointed, and directed, And to Conclude,
act and doe all other thing, or things, thereabouts, in pursuance of the
s[ai]d Trust, and the true meaneing and intent of the fores[ai]d Donor,
as fully and amply, as I the s[ai]d John Davenport by vertue of the
trust to mee Committed in and by the s[ai]d Will, or by any other way
or meanes whatsoever might lawfully doe, in the dispose of the s[ai]d

5. Contrary to the agreement of William Goodwin and John Davenport in June, 1664,
and the expressed desire of John Davenport in 1668, a decree of the court of chancery in
England, March 19, 1712/3, awarded the £500 from the English estate of Edward
Hopkins, with interest since the death of Anne (Yale) Hopkins, to Harvard College and
the grammar school at Cambridge, Massachusetts. C. P. Bowditch, *An Account of the
Trust Administered by the Trustees of the Charity of Edward Hopkins* (n.p., 1889).

Estate, all, or any part of it to the ends afores[ai]d, And doe further Invest them the s[ai]d Committee and their successo[u]rs, and the majo[u]r part of them, with full power authority and trust, to order, Regulate and direct the s[ai]d Colledgiat schoole, by such lawes and Rules, as are by me provided, or shalbe further as Addicionalls by them, or the major part of them judged necessary and expedient for the better ordering, Regulating, and directing of the s[ai]d schoole, for the advancem[en]t of learneing and good governem[en]t therein; And to make Choice of such schoolemaster (and usher if need bee) as they shall approve of to be sufficiently quallifyed, to undertake such a Charge, and able to instruct and teach the 3 Learned Languages, Lattine, Greeke and Hebrew, soe farre as shall be necessary to pr[e]pare and fitt youth for the Colledge, And to state and Allow out of the s[ai]d Rents and profitts, such yearely stipend, and Sallary toward his, or their encouragem[en]t and maintenance, as they the s[ai]d Committee, or the majo[u]r part of them, or of their successo[u]rs, shall judge meet and Convenient. And alsoe, upon just grounds, either insufficiency, wilfull neglect of trust, scandall, or the like Causes, to exclude, or remove him or them, upon due proofe and Conviction of such offences, And to proceed, to nominate, and Chuse some other fit person, or persons, in his or their roome and place, And that there may be a Certaine and orderly succession, of able and fitt persons, to mannage the severall trusts, herein before mencioned, in the roome and place of any of the s[ai]d Committee, or trustees before named, that shall dye, or remove his, or their dwelling from New Haven afores[ai]d, The s[ai]d Committee, or the majo[u]r part of them surviveing, shall immediatly, or at furthest within 3 moneths after, Choose such other person, or persons of knowne integrity, and faithfulnes, to succeed in the roome and place of any such person, or persons soe dyeing or removeing as afores[ai]d, that the worke may be Carryed on (in the said Grammer or Colledgiat schoole) hereby Committed to them, that soe learneing may be duely incouraged, and furthered therein, in the trayneing up of such hopefull youth as in time by the blessing of god, upon good endeavo[u]rs may be fitted for publique service in Church, and Commonwealth, for the upholding and promoteing of the Kingdome of our Lord Jesus christ, in theise parts of the earth, according to the true, and sincere desires, and ends of the afores[ai]d Worthy Donor in his s[ai]d last Will and Testam[en]t mencioned and expressed. And because I stand under an ingagement to attend the will of the s[ai]d donor deceased, that his ends may be attained, in the dispose of his s[ai]d Legacy, if the s[ai]d Committee, or their successo[u]rs shall find the s[ai]d ends by this Graunt not attained at New Haven, and that the s[ai]d Grammar, or Collegiat schoole, hereby endowed, and provided for should be dissolved, and wholly Cease, I doe obtest them by the will of the dead, which noe man may alter, And by the trust Committed to mee and them whereof we must give our account to that great judge of all, that this gift of the s[ai]d Edward Hopkins Esq[ui]r[e] deceased, be by them the s[ai]d Committee wholly translated and disposed of elsewhere, where the s[ai]d ends may be attained, But if the true ends of the Testato[u]r, and of this settlem[en]t be attained at New Haven, I stand firme to the place in this my Graunt, Reserveing nevertheless to my selfe in all Cases, matters, and things respecting the laying out, or improvem[en]t of the s[ai]d Estate as fores[ai]d, for the s[ai]d schoole, full power of a negative voice, whilest it shall please god to Continue my liveing, and abideing in this Countrey, or any part of it, to hinder and pr[e]vent any act, or acts, thing, or things, to be acted or done in or about the pr[e]misses, to the detrim[en]t of the s[ai]d Estate, or Contrary to the s[ai]d trust to me Committed, and hereby transferred to the s[ai]d Committee, and their successo[u]rs afores[ai]d, upon this further Condicion, that the Rent, profitt and improvem[en]t of the oyster-shell field Contayneing by Estimacion 40 acres, more or less, formerly separated, and reserved for the use and Benefitt of a Colledge at New Haven; And alsoe one other field Commonly Called Mrs. Eldreds Lott, Contayneing by Estimacion 3 acres more or less, be to the use of the s[ai]d schoole at New Haven for ever settled, ratifyed and Confirmed by the s[ai]d Towne accordingly. And to pr[e]vent any further reinterruption which this Settlem[en]t by me made, may meete with by reason of a former Graunt of the aboves[ai]d summ or summs of money, and Estate for encouragem[en]t of a Colony schoole at Newhaven, made by a Memorandum in writeing under my hand, Contayneing sundry particulars to that purpose, and beareing date the 4th day of the 4th moneth 1660,[6] the same being Registred in the Records of the then Gen[era]ll Court, and by the s[ai]d Court at that time approved and accepted, as by the s[ai]d Records, page 260, doth appeare: I therefore the s[ai]d John Davenport, in regard that the s[ai]d Court by their Act beareing date the 5th of Novemb[e]r. 1662.[7] for sundry reasons therein alleadged, did lay downe and discharge the s[ai]d schoole, and withdraw the yearely exhibition by them

6. See above, pp. 161–166.

7. A general court of the New Haven Colony, November 5, 1662, voted to give up the attempt to maintain a grammar school for the colony. *New Haven Colonial Records, 1653–1665* (Hartford, 1858), p. 471.

formerly allowed; whereby (the s[ai]d schoole being soe dissolved) the s[ai]d Graunt by me made, became Null and Voyd: I do therefore hereby declare the same to be null and voyd accordingly, any thing in the s[ai]d writeing or memorandum to the Contrary notwithstanding; And the Graunt herein made of the pr[e]misses to be good against the same, and against all, or any other pr[e]tences whatsoever, according to my true intent, and meaneing herein before declared and expressed. In Witnes whereof I have hereunto sett my hand and seale the 18th day of the second moneth Commonly Called Aprill, one Thousand six hundred sixty and Eight.

JOHN DAVENPORT senior　　　seale

Signed, Sealed and delivered by the
Reverend Mr. John Davenport sen[io]r as his
Act and deed In pr[e]sence of

> Benjamin Linge
> John Hodshon

> This is a true Record of the originall, Examined,

Per me JAMES BISHOP. *Recorder:*

JOHN DAVENPORT *to* THE FIRST CHURCH, BOSTON[1]

AN outward call could not satisfy mee, if I had not an inward call, it hath bin the greatest exercise of my soule, next to the clearing of my good estate towards God in my effectuall calling, this call from N[ew]haven, and I have desired the Lord to shew mee his way, and not leave mee to any temptacion, but lead mee in a plaine path because of my observers, and in this way I have waited for a long time, for sundry months at N[ew]haven, and sundry months here, and soe continued vntill I received my dismission from N[ew]haven, and joyned in membership here, and Soe to office here: Now I look vpon it as a call from the Ch[urch]: an authorative call, I being a member with them. The former I looked on it as an Invitacion, and still kept mine ey on Ch[ris]t to cleare his will vnto mee, which I confesse he hath now done to the

1. Yale University Library, Stiles Folio Letters, I, Third Church Narrative, pp. 21–22. Another manuscript copy of this speech, made by Davenport to the First Church, Boston, on the occasion of his ordination as pastor, December 9, 1668, is in the possession of Mr. H. E. Tuttle, Master of Davenport College, Yale University. The phraseology of the two copies varies slightly. The speech is printed in H. A. Hill, *History of the Old South (Third Church) Boston 1669–1884* (2 vols., Boston, 1890), I, 41.

full satisfaction of my conscience, I am soe fully satisfyed in it, that I can plead it to god in Ch[ris]t in prayer, in the time of any difficulty or danger what euer difficulty I may be in, Thou Lord knowest I did not make hast to be a Past[o]r over this people, but waited on thee to know thy mind, and I can plead this allso to all the world, and am ready to publish to the world the grounds wherevpon I see my selfe called by Ch[ris]t to this service, I speak it the rather because of some vncomfortable speeches I have heard, that put mee vpon a necessity to declare thus much etc.

Elders of The First Church, Boston, *to* A Council of the Neighboring Churches[1]

WEE agree to propound the desire of the Rev[eren]d Eld[e]rs to the Ch[urch]: that when they come to a conclusion a bout our dissenting B[rethre]n, they would be willing to give them the reasons of their proceeding, which we for our owne parts judge to be most agreeable to the congregationall way, if they haue any Suspicion of any mall administration, till which time we can not give them a meeting without offence to the ch[urch]: which we humbly desire the Rev[eren]d Eld[e]rs candidly to Interpret.

1. Yale University Library, Stiles Folio Letters, I, Third Church Narrative, p. 33; printed in H. A. Hill, *History of the Old South Church (Third Church) Boston 1669–1884* (2 vols., Boston, 1890), I, 59. At this time John Davenport, James Allen, and James Penn were the elders of the First Church. At the request of the dissenting brethren of the First Church, Boston, a council of elders and messengers of the neighboring churches met at Boston, April 13, 1669, to endeavor to settle the dispute among the members of the First Church. This letter was dated April 13, 1669. It was without signatures.

JOHN DAVENPORT and JAMES PENN *to*
A COUNCIL of the Neighboring Churches[1]

Rev[e]r[en]d B[rethre]n,

THE answer[2] was not to the writing[3] which you were pleased to send by Rev[e]r[en]d Mr. Whiting[4] etc. But to a mocion made by him or some of them pr[e]sent, nor did I purpose to give you a meeting or Acco[unt] of the offences given by the dissenting B[rethre]n, when the Ch[urch] should come to a conclusion, for I doe not see that you are an orderly Councill, but my true meaning is that when the Ch[urch] had done their duty to their dissenting B[rethre]n, the Elders would move the Ch[urch] to send in convenient time, copies of their light held forth for conviction of the dissent[e]rs vnto your Ch[urche]s, wee cannot meet and act with you in matters that concerne this Ch[urch] ag[ains]t the expr[e]ssed mind of this Ch[urch].

13: (2) *69*   JOHN DAVENPORT Sen[io]r
                            JAMES PENN

JOHN DAVENPORT, JAMES ALLEN, and JAMES PENN *to*
THE ELDERS and MESSENGERS of the CHURCHES
Assembled at CHARLESTOWN for the Gather-
ing of THE THIRD CHURCH, BOSTON[1]

Sup[e]rscribed for the Hono[u]r[e]d and Rev[eren]d the Eld[e]rs
and Messeng[e]rs of the churches assembled at Charlstowne

Hono[u]r[e]d Rev[eren]d and Beloved in the Lord

WE being acquainted the Eleuenth day of this month By two of our dissenting B[rethre]n that on the 12th day of the same which is the 4th day of this weeke Itt was the purpose and intention of them

---

1. Yale University Library, Stiles Folio Letters, I, Third Church Narrative, p. 33; printed in H. A. Hill, *History of the Old South Church (Third Church) Boston 1669–1884* (2 vols., Boston, 1890), I, 59–60.

2. The preceding letter.

3. For the letter of a council of the neighboring churches to the First Church, Boston, April 13, 1669, see H. A. Hill, *History of the Old South (Third Church) Boston 1669–1884* (2 vols., Boston, 1890), I, 58–59.

4. Samuel Whiting, pastor of the church at Lynn, Massachusetts, one of the members of the council.

1. Yale University Library, Stiles Folio Letters, I, Third Church Narrative, p. 48; printed in H. A. Hill, *History of the Old South Church (Third Church) Boston 1669–1884* (2 vols., Boston, 1890), I, 80.

selves with the rest of them to gather into a Ch[urch] at Charlstowne
that we might not be wanting in our duty to God, our selves or them,
we thought [it] now seasonable to declare our appr[e]hensions therein,
How farr it may pr[e]uent sin in our B[rethre]n we know not, That it
might is our desire and hope, how euer we are p[e]rswaded we shall
hereby deliv[e]r our owne soules from the guilt or fruite [of] any Euill
in it, by renouncing participation or fellowship in that action. [We]
doe therefore declare these B[rethre]n who intend an imbodying by
them selves to be memb[ers] with vs by covenant, a bond as yet not
loosed that we know of, according to God, And [that] they are vnder
offences to this ch[urch] which they haue not indeavored regularly to
rem[ove] and therefore are not capable of such a Coalition among them
selves.

Boston: 11 (3) 69   JOHN DAVENPORT
                                                     JAMES ALLENE
                                                     JAMES PENN
                              With the consent of the B[rethre]n

JOHN DAVENPORT, JAMES ALLEN, and JAMES PENN *to* THE CHURCH AT ROXBURY[1]

REVEREND and Beloued in the Lord Grace Mercy and Peace bee
multiplied from God the ffather and our Lord Jesus Christ.

As we desire and earnestly endeauour according to the measure of
Grace wee haue receiued to haue Consciences vojd of Offence to God
and all Men soe it is our Solicitous care that our Practises may be without Just Blame to Jew or Gentill especially that they may be without
suspition of Evill to any of the Churches of Christ Wee are therefore
constrained thus farr att present to speake for our selues vnto you our
Deare Bretheren that you would bee sober and distrustfull about any
reports that may be bruited concerning our selues to the Prejudice of
any concerne of Christ labouring with vs or of our selues in the heartes
and affections of such who are Deare to Christ and Justly Valued by
vs Wee hope it will appeare in due time that it is not for our owne but

1. American Antiquarian Society, Curwin Papers, III, 103. At this time Samuel Dan-
forth and John Eliot were pastor and teacher of the church at Roxbury, Massachusetts.
Although the letter is undated, it was probably written shortly before May 16, 1669,
when a similar letter was read to the church at Salem in public assembly on the Sabbath.
H. A. Hill, *History of the Old South Church (Third Church) Boston 1669-1884* (2 vols.,
Boston, 1890), I, 92.

a labouring interest of the Kingdome of Jesus Christ wee are striueing and contending, his Authority in a particular Church, a concerne of as great moment as euer was in hazzard in these Churches which other Churches will quickly find themselues engaged about (if there be any of the first loue remaining to it) and as much afflicted for as our selues. If we may intreat that there be an open Eare to what we are ready and willing (vpon your desire to know the Reasons of our proceedings thus far) to communicate we shall acknowledge it as your Christian Tendernes to vs Nor is it more than equall, for it is a Ruled Case in Cannon law[2] that the action of both parties should fully be vnderstood and as the wise man hath lajd it downe, Hee that is first in his owne case is just, then cometh his Neighbour and searcheth him out[3] And againe hee that answereth a Matter before hee heareth it, it shall be folly and shame to him.[4] Wee doubt not If it shall bee desired and wee may be Candidly heard, that wee shall Evince our Carriage to the first Counsell[5] and your advice[6] as alsoe that vnto the last Messengers from seaverall Churches[7] To be noe other then what our loue and loyalty to Christ as Sole King and law-giuer to his Church did obleige us to doe That noething might bee admitted by vs that hee hath not appoynted or will approue. Wee doe owne Councills rightly called and regularly proceeding to be an ordinance of God And that the Churches may desire to vnderstand the reasons of our Publicke actions and wee are bound by virtue of our communion with you to giue a Brotherly account which wee for our parts are most willing and ready to doe. Nor haue the contrary by our wordes or actions been manifest as may more Evidently by our answer when desired appeare. In the meane time lett not your heartes be alienated from your Brethren some of which are not among the least who haue jeoparded their liues with you and for you when the common interest [of God] among vs was in hazard ... our Enemies hope for and our friends ... vs we may be led

2. Davenport probably means according to the practice in ecclesiastical courts.

3. Proverbs 18. 17. In 1636 Davenport had placed this verse on the title-page of his *An Apologeticall Reply To a booke Called An Answer to the unjust complaint of W. B.* (Rotterdam, 1636).

4. Proverbs 18. 13.

5. The first council of elders and messengers from the neighboring churches to deal with the trouble in the First Church, Boston, met at Boston from August 6 to August 8, 1668. H. A. Hill, *History of the Old South Church (Third Church) Boston 1669–1884* (2 vols., Boston, 1890), I, 25–27.

6. The Roxbury church gave its advice November 23, 1668. It was unrepresented at the second council. *Ibid.*, I, 37, 67–68 n.

7. A second council met at Boston from April 13 to April 16, 1669. *Ibid.*, I, 57–68.

into all truth . . . that Brotherly loue may continue and be increased among vs.

Wee are your loueing Bretheren in the ffellowshipp of the Gospell

JOHN DAVENPORT Senior
JAMES ALLEN
JAMES PENN

[Endorsed] Roxbury Papers. (Original) Letter from the Rev. John Davenport of Newhaven [sic] To the Rev. Pastors (Eliott) and Bretheren of the Ch[urc]h in Roxbury. probably about 1664. [sic].

JOHN DAVENPORT to THE FIRST CHURCH, BOSTON[1]

WHEN my dismi[ssi]on[2] from the Ch[urch] of N[ew]haven was sent to the Ch[urch] of Boston inclosed in my l[ett]re from my B[rothe]r Street sealed vp to the Ruling Eld[er][3] I did not open it, but when the Eld[er] came to mee with B[rothe]r Allen I deliverd it before him to the ruling Eld[e]r sealed as it was, he opened it and read it in my hearing, whereby both they and I perceived that the pr[e]face to the dismi[ssi]on was altogether superfluous, yet such as might cause difference, they took the l[ett]re away with them to consider further of it, accordingly when the substance of the dismi[ssi]on was extracted out of the origi- nal they brought it vnto mee the last day of the week when my thoughts were otherwise exercised, my B[rothe]r Allen read what was written, and what he wrote seemed to vs to be the true dismi[ssi]on, agreing with the originall signed by Mr. Street in the name and with the con- sent of the Ch[urch] of N[ew]haven, it was allso s[ai]d that no wrong would be done to that Ch[urch] nor vnto this, if the extract were read publiquely, the superfluities in the originall being left out, but that some dishonour to the Ch[urch] of N[ew]haven and disturbance to this Ch[urch] would thereby be pr[e]vented, I looked not at my self fit to give advice In this Case it being my owne Concernm[en]t but left it to them both to satisfy their Judgem[en]t, for I was at that time

1. Yale University Library, Stiles Folio Letters, I, Third Church Narrative, pp. 52–53; printed in H. A. Hill, *History of the Old South Church (Third Church) Boston 1669–1884* (2 vols., Boston, 1890), I, 83–84. This justification was read to the First Church, Boston, June 29, 1669.

2. Davenport's dismissal from the church at New Haven was dated October 12, 1668. See H. A. Hill, *History of the Old South Church (Third Church) Boston 1669–1884* (2 vols., Boston, 1890), I, 33–36.

3. James Penn.

neither member nor Eld[e]r of this Ch[urch][4] whereof B[rothe]r Allen
was member but no Eld[e]r, B[rothe]r Pen was the onely ruling Eld[e]r
nor did I add nor diminish or alter any thing that was written in the
Extract, nor came it to my thoughts what was best to be done, whence
I neither disswaded from reading the extract nor persswaded to the
reading of the Originall script in publique, leaving ev[en]ts to God,
nor had I any hand in contriving framing or penning the Extract as
both our rever[en]d Eld[e]rs have already testifyed to the Ch[urch]:
and whereas some would prove that I had a further hand in it, because
my son wrote the extract which was read to the Ch[urch]: this is not a
Cogent or sufficient prof thereof, for it was at their mocion and desire,
that my son wrote not the originall but Mr. Allens extract, which
when my son had done, it was still in their power and liberty to make
what vse of it, they pleased or to have made no vse of it, if their mindes
had bin altered.

My hope is that as God hath made hereby discouerie of the spirits
of many, soe that he will issue the whole in giving repentance, vnto
some for their harsh and wrong censures and reproches, and in vindicacion of his owne honour, and the name of his serv[an]ts who did
what is done to g[oo]d ends, and in true simplicity and f[aith]fullnes
according to their p[rese]nt light in the sight of god.

4. Davenport was propounded for membership in the First Church, Boston, October
25, 1668; the revised letter of dismissal was read to the church November 1, 1668, and
Davenport was admitted to membership; he was called to the vacant pastorate November 9, 1668; and ordained December 9, 1668. H. A. Hill, *History of the Old South Church
(Third Church) Boston 1669–1884* (2 vols., Boston, 1890), I, 32–41.

JOHN DAVENPORT, JAMES ALLEN, and JAMES PENN *to*
THE THIRD CHURCH, BOSTON[1]

Beloued in the lord:

THE letter[2] sent to be Communicated to us, deliuered to our Rulinge Elder, the 12th of this Instant, acquaintinge us with your purpose, to ordaine officers,[3] and desiringe our Concurrance therein hath giuen us a fitt occasion to manifest our sence of that spirit appeares in your letter, And the proceedinge mentioned therein. Wee Cannot but wonder and that with griefe of hearte, to behold that Confidence mentioned in yours: in Callinge your Combination, a regular Church Constitution; which agrees, neither with the lawes of Christ, nor (as wee Concieue) of this Collonie,[4] And that you dare, entitle the favor of god, to that, which is onely the fruit of your owne wills, and manifestly Crosse to the will of god revealed in his word. The wisdome of god permittinge, and gouerninge Such motions, wee readily acknowledge; but not graciously, Conductinge them. Wee

1. The original letter can be found in Massachusetts Historical Society, Boston, Letters and Papers, 1631–1783, V, 2. Manuscript copies of the letter can be found *ibid.*, IV, 1–3; Yale University Library, Stiles Folio Letters, I, Third Church Narrative, pp. 68–70; and in the possession of Mr. H. E. Tuttle, Master of Davenport College, Yale University. The letter is printed in H. A. Hill, *History of the Old South Church (Third Church) Boston 1669–1884* (2 vols., Boston, 1890), I, 156–159.

With the approval of the ministers of the neighboring churches and a majority of the magistrates of Massachusetts Bay, a group of secessionists from the First Church, Boston, met at Charlestown, May 12, 1669, and gathered the Third or Old South Church of Boston. At this time the First Church, Boston, did not recognize the new congregation as a church.

2. The letter of the Third Church, Boston, to the First Church, Boston, February 9, 1669/70, can be found in Massachusetts Historical Society, Boston, Letters and Papers, 1631–1783, IV, 1; Yale University Library, Stiles Folio Letters, I, Third Church Narrative, pp. 67–68. It is printed in H. A. Hill, *History of the Old South Church (Third Church) Boston 1669–1884* (2 vols., Boston, 1890), I, 155–156.

3. On February 16, 1669/70, the Third or Old South Church, Boston, ordained Thomas Thatcher, Sr., as pastor; Edward Rainsford as ruling elder; and Jacob Eliot and Peter Brackett as deacons. Thatcher had been dismissed by the First Church, Boston, to the church at Charlestown, November 29, 1669; and by the church at Charlestown to the recently gathered Third Church, Boston, December 13, 1669. He was received by the Third Church, Boston, December 19, 1669, and called to the pastorate January 12, 1669/70. *Ibid.*, I, 123–125, 151–153.

4. For *The Book of the General Lawes and Libertyes concerning the Inhabitants of the Massachusets, Collected out of the Records of the General Court, for the Several Years Wherin They Were Made and Established* (Cambridge, 1660), see W. H. Whitmore, ed., *The Colonial Laws of Massachusetts. Reprinted from the Edition of 1660, with the Supplements to 1672* (Boston, 1889).

gladly would Joyne with you, to double our Cryes, for grace, from the lord, for your repentance, and pardon that his displeasure may not break forth in your layinge the topstone of this provocation.

Most willingly wee would haue Concurred with your desires, had the way bene such, that without offence to our owne Consciences, wee might haue approved: but being as it is, wee must declare our dissattisfaction, in your proceedinge, to ordaine officers, either Elders, or Deacons, among you, The reasons whereof are,

1. Because the persons mentioned to be Called to those offices are not without blame, as such ought to bee, 1 Tim: 3: 2: 7: Tit: 1: 10: Mr. Thatcher though hee saw not light to Joyne with you, when you irregularly withdrew your selues from us, yet since Dismissed from us first hath Joyned, and so made himselfe pertaker of your sinnes, Contrary to: 1 Tim: 5. 22: the 3 others, haue bene Constant actors with you, from first to last.

2: all of them, haue accepted a Call to office among you, who are not Capable to Choose or receiue any such officers, accordinge to the rule of Christ or the lawes of this Jurisdiction (as wee understand them), ffor:

1 when wee were accordinge to rule laboringe to Conuince you of your offences, giuen to us, you did Contrary to that rule. Math: 18. 15: withdraw from us, not acknowledginge the authority of Christ Jesus in his Church, and soe not regardinge your Couenant engagement to subjection to it.

2. After which you appointed a time to gather into a pretended Church Society, by your selues, though not regularly free from your Couenant to this Church, Contrary to that law of Christ, 1 Cor: 12: 25: and the law of this Jurisdiction Tit: ecle sect: 1: (as wee Concieue).[5]

3 And notwithstandinge wittnesse bearinge by this Church,[6] against that proceedinge by messengers sent on purpose with a writeinge of the Churches testimonie againste it, as also 6 of our honnored mag-

---

5. All the People of God, within this Juricdiction who are not in a Church way, and by [sic] orthodox in judgment, and not scandalous in life shall have full Liberty to gather themselues into a Church estate, provided they doe it in a christian way, with the observation of the Rules of Christ revealed in his word.

Provided also that the Generall Court doth not, nor will hereafter approve of any such companies of men, as shall joyne in any pretended way of Church-fellowship, unless they shall acquaint the Magistrates, and the Elders of the neighbour churches, where they intend to joyne, and have their approbation therein.

6. See above, pp. 280–281.

istrates[7] of whom our honnored gouernor was one who did by A write-inge declare Theire desire of your desistinge at the present, yet you proceeded, neither regardinge offence to a Church of Christ, Contrary to 1 Cor. 10: 32: Nor hauinge due respect to the persons, or the authority of magistrates, Contrary to Tit: 3: 1: and that law of this Collonie tit: Eccl: sect. 3:[8] as wee thincke. Since which you haue erected a meetinge howse[9] in a place forbidden by the authority of this towne not Consented unto by the prudentials of the same offensiue to the Churches in it, and to many godly Christians in other places, neither suitinge the ends and Conueniency of this place, who by former agreement, appointed a lott for such a buildinge, onely grattifyinge your owne selfe ends and wills, Contrary: to 1: Cor: 10: 31:

Those things and many the like Considered, wee Judge it our duty to declare our dissattisfaction, in your proceedinge, to ordaine officers as an act highly displeasinge to god, and Dangerous to the wellfare of Ciuill and Church goverment as settled among us; And therefore wee being obliged in loue to Christ, Math: 10: 32: to Confesse his name not onely by acknowledginge any truth of his, wherein his Crowne and Dignity is Concerned, but also preuentinge soe farr as wee may the doinge any thinge destructiue thereunto, as also in loue and Duty to this gouerment, which the lord hath graciously set over us, they by that law Concerninge ordination, not onely giuinge leaue to organnick Churches, to declare against any disorderly proceedinge but, inviting them thereunto, that they by them may know how to prevent dammadge to the goverment as now Constituted, and in loue, and duty, to preserue the peace and purity of those Churches, which are soe

7. For the letter of Richard Bellingham, governor, Samuel Symonds, William Hauthorne, Eliezer Lusher, John Leverett, and Edward Tyng to the magistrates, elders, brethren, and messengers assembled at Charlestown for the gathering of the Third Church, Boston, May 12, 1669, see H. A. Hill, *History of the Old South Church (Third Church) Boston 1669–1884* (2 vols., Boston, 1890), I, 79.

8. Every church hath free libertie to exercise all the Ordinances of God, according to the rule of the Scripture.

9. Rejecting a site "nigh the windmill" offered by the town of Boston, the Third Church accepted a gift of land on the "high streete leading from Roxbury to Boston" from Mary Norton, widow of John Norton, teacher of the First Church, Boston, April 1, 1669. The digging of a trench for the foundation of the church was begun July 6, 1669. Richard Bellingham, governor, and John Leverett and Edward Tyng, magistrates living in Boston and members of the First Church, tried to halt the work, but on September 17, 1669, the council advised them to desist. Friends in neighboring towns brought timber September 13 and 27 and the building was raised October 1, 1669. The Third Church met for the first time in the new edifice December 19, 1669. H. A. Hill, *History of the Old South Church (Third Church) Boston 1669–1884* (2 vols., Boston, 1890), I, 122–129, 133–135, 140, 144–146, 153.

manifestly endangered, as wee are prest, in ps: 122: 6: and urged to doe by the use of all lawfull meanes, of which this is one, and in loue to our brethren, accordinge to the great rule of loue, in such Cases lev: 19: 17: doe bare this Testimony against it.

It is our hearty desire the lord would open your eyes to see, what you haue done amisse, you may bewaile and reforme it, and that he would blesse this our faithfull endeauor to that end, howeuer wee haue hereby giuen you warninge from the lord, and soe deliuered our owne soules, and shall leaue the issue to the wise and Soveraigne disposer of the hearts and wayes of men, to deliuer yours, in his good tyme for which wee pray,

The Messengers sent by the church with this lett[e]r vnto your Assembly are Capt. Thomas Clark Capt. Hutchisson[10] Leiftenant Cook: James Everill[11] and to declare the churches mind as they see cause.

Boston. Dat: 15:   JOHN DAVENPORT Senior
12: mo[nth]: 1669   JAMES ALLEN
                      JAMES PENN

              with the Consent of the Brethren

10. A member of the First Church, Boston.
11. A member of the First Church, Boston.

INDEX

At the Printing-Office of the Yale University Press,
in New Haven, Connecticut.